HANDBOOK OF
BIBLICAL CHRONOLOGY

HANDBOOK OF
BIBLICAL
CHRONOLOGY

PRINCIPLES OF TIME RECKONING
IN THE ANCIENT WORLD
AND PROBLEMS OF CHRONOLOGY
IN THE BIBLE

By JACK FINEGAN

PRINCETON, NEW JERSEY
PRINCETON UNIVERSITY PRESS
1964

PREFACE

i. In Gal 4:4 Paul refers to Jesus and says that God sent forth his Son "when the fulness of the time (τὸ πλήρωμα τοῦ χρόνου) was come." In various other passages Paul uses another Greek word for time, καιρός, *kairos*, which means a definite or fixed time, and hence can signify an opportune time as in Gal 6:10 or even the eschatological end time as in I Cor 4:5. In view of this meaning of *kairos* one might have expected that Paul would use it in speaking of what was assuredly the particular and proper time when God sent forth his Son. But instead in Gal 4:4 he chooses to use for "time" the Greek word χρόνος, *chronos*. Over against *kairos* which is a particular and appropriate time, *chronos* is time which is seen in its extent or duration. As *chronos*, time flows ceaselessly past us, a stream which cannot be stopped but which can be measured. It was in the fulness of this stream of *chronos* that the event of Jesus Christ took place. Therefore in Christian faith and in biblical study we are directed to the long sweep of time in which God has been working out his purpose, to time as *chronos*, and accordingly to the measurement of time which is *chronometry*, the writing about and recording of time which is *chronography*, and the science or doctrine of time which is *chronology*.

ii. The chronological references in the biblical records are numerous but not always easy to understand correctly. Bible time extends through thousands of years and Bible history touches many different lands of the Near Eastern and Mediterranean world. In the periods and places involved many different systems of time reckoning were employed, at least some of which may be presupposed in the biblical references. The work of early chronographers and commentators who occupied themselves with the biblical data is also important, and this extends the range of necessary inquiry even further. In this extremely complex and almost esoteric field much is, of course, not yet even known; what is known to the specialists in the areas involved is often quite inaccessible to the ordinary student and, if accessible, incomprehensible. A major part of our undertaking, therefore, is to give a clear description of the various matters involved and to provide, within the compass of one handbook, the necessary lists and tables with which to work, as well as to indicate sources and further literature.

[v]

iii. Then, on the basis of the best understanding we can obtain of the ancient methods of time reckoning—many of which, it may be added, are of a surprising degree of accuracy and sophistication —a further large part of the task is to try to work out against that background the correct significance of the biblical data themselves. Here it is not the attempt of the present handbook to deal with all the data or solve all the problems, but rather to indicate ways of taking up the problems in selected and representative areas. It may be hoped that some of the problems have been solved correctly. It may also be hoped that with the background materials of the first part of this handbook, and the sample engagements with particular problems in the second part, others may go on with those unfinished tasks in these areas, which will doubtless long continue to challenge students of ancient history and biblical record.

iv. My own involvement with such matters has come about in connection with the endeavor to write in the area of an archeological approach to biblical history. In revising my *Light from the Ancient Past* there has been a tendency to introduce, particularly in footnotes and appendix, an increasing amount of chronological material. Since the archeological materials increase steadily too, limits are reached. Also notes and appendix may be obscure places in which to have to search. Therefore, with the permission of Princeton University Press, some of the chronological sections have been taken out of that book and incorporated in the present handbook, where they are set in a wider context of specifically chronological considerations and made more readily available for those interested.

v. Here then is a Handbook prepared with the hope that it will be useful to those who concern themselves with that framework in time in which the events of Bible history are set. In his famous *Chronicle* Eusebius, who occupied himself with many of the same problems as we, quoted the saying that "it is not for you to know times or seasons (χρόνους ἢ καιρούς)" (Ac 1:7) as applying not only to the determination of the time of the end of the world but also to the attempted solution of other chronological problems. By the quotation he inculcates a proper humility in the approach to chronological questions; at the same time by his own example in the vast labor of writing the *Chronicle* he encourages us to believe that concern with the chronological data is one of the indispensable and unavoidable tasks in the study of the Bible. The materials in the present Handbook are intended to assist such study.

JACK FINEGAN

CONTENTS

CONTENTS

CONTENTS

CONTENTS

LIST OF TABLES

[xi]

ANCIENT SOURCES

LITERATURE: SWDCB; LSGEL pp. xvi-xli; M. Cary and others, eds., *The Oxford Classical Dictionary*. 1949; Johannes Quasten, *Patrology*. 3 vols. 1950-60; AGGEL pp. xxx-xxxiii; Berthold Altaner, *Patrology*. 1960.

Africanus, Sextus Julius. Christian writer. A.D. c.170-c.240.

Aristotle. Greek philosopher. 384-322 B.C.

Avadyah. Jewish rabbi. b. A.D. c.1325.

Barnabas, Epistle of. A.D. c.100.

Biruni, al-. Muslim author. A.D. 973-1048.

Cassiodorus Senator. Flavius Magnus Aurelius. Roman monk and historian. A.D. c.490-c.585.

Censorinus. Roman writer. Third century of the Christian era.

Chrysostom, John. Greek church father and preacher. A.D. c.345-407.

Clement of Alexandria, Titus Flavius Clemens. Christian scholar. d. before A.D. 215.

Clement of Rome. Bishop of Rome. A.D. c.92-c.101.

Cyril of Alexandria. Christian theologian. d. A.D. 444.

Dio Cassius, Cassius Dio Cocceianus. Greek historian. b. between A.D. 155-164, d. A.D. c.235.

Diodorus of Sicily, Diodorus Siculus. Greek historian. First century B.C.

Dionysius Exiguus. Roman monk. fl. A.D. c.525.

Dionysius of Halicarnassus, Dionysius Halicarnassensis. Greek historian. c.54-c.7 B.C.

Epiphanius. Bishop of Constantia (Salamis) on Cyprus. A.D. c.315-403.

Eratosthenes of Alexandria. Greek astronomer. c.276-c.194 B.C.

Eusebius of Caesarea, Eusebius Caesariensis, Eusebius Pamphili. Church historian. A.D. 263-339.

Gamaliel I the Elder. Jewish rabbi, grandson of Hillel. Second third of the first century of the Christian era.

Gamaliel II, Gamaliel of Jabneh (Jamnia). Jewish rabbi, grandson of Gamaliel I. fl. A.D. c.80-116.

Gellius, Aulus. Latin writer. A.D. c.123-c.169.

Hanina. Jewish rabbi. Third century of the Christian era.

Herodotus. Greek historian. c.484-425 B.C.

Hillel. Jewish teacher. c.60 B.C.-A.D. c.10.

Hipparchus. Greek astronomer. fl. c.146-c.126 B.C.

Hippolytus of Rome. Presbyter and writer. A.D. c.170-236.

Hippolytus of Thebes. Possibly identical with the foregoing.

Irenaeus. Greek bishop of Lyons. A.D. c.130-c.202.

Jerome. Latin church scholar. b. A.D. c.347, d. A.D. 419 or 420.

John Malalas. Byzantine monk and chronicler. A.D. c.491-c.578.

Jose ben Halafta. Jewish rabbi. d. A.D. c.160.

Josephus. Jewish historian. A.D. c.37-after 100.

Justin. Roman historian. Second century of the Christian era.

Justin Martyr. Christian apologist from Palestine. A.D. c.114-165.

Lactantius Firmianus. Latin church father in Africa. fl. A.D. c.310.

Livy. Roman historian. 59 B.C.-A.D. 17.

Macarius Magnes. Bishop of Magnesia. fl. A.D. c.400.

Maimonides. Jewish philosopher. A.D. 1135-1204.

Ma Tuan-Lin. Chinese historian. fl. A.D. 1240-1280.

Memnon of Heraclea Pontica. Hellenistic chronicler. First century of the Christian era.

Menander of Ephesus. Author of Greek history of the Phoenician kings. Cited by Josephus.

Origen. Christian scholar and theologian in Alexandria and Caesarea. A.D. c.185-c.253.

Orosius. Spanish historian and theologian. fl. A.D. c.415.

Pan Chao. Chinese historian. b. A.D. 45-51, d. 114-120.

Pan Ku. Chinese historian. A.D. 32-92.

Pan Piao. Chinese historian. A.D. 3-54.

Photius. Patriarch of Constantinople. A.D. c.820-891.

Pliny the elder. Roman naturalist. A.D. 23-79.

Plutarch, Plutarchus. Greek biographer. A.D. c.46-c.120.

Pompeius Trogus. Latin writer on history and natural science. Of the time of Augustus (44 B.C.-A.D. 14).

Porphyry of Tyre. Neoplatonist philosopher. A.D. 233-c.304.

Ptolemy, Claudius Ptolemaeus. Greco-Egyptian geographer. Second century of the Christian era.

Simeon II ben Gamaliel I. Jewish rabbi, son of Gamaliel I. fl. A.D. c.50-70.

Socrates. Church historian. b. A.D. c.380, d. after A.D. 439.

Ssu-ma Ch'ien. Chinese historian. c.140-c.80 B.C.

Strabo. Greek geographer. c.63 B.C.-after A.D. 21.

Suetonius. Roman historian. fl. A.D. c.100.

Tacitus. Roman historian. A.D. c.55-c.117.

Tatian. Syrian Christian apologist. fl. A.D. c.172.

Tertullian. Latin Christian writer at Carthage. b. A.D. c.160, d. after A.D. 220.

Theodoret. Bishop of Cyprus. A.D. c.393-453.

Theon. Alexandrian astronomer. Fourth century of the Christian era.

Thucydides. Athenian historian. c.471-c.400 B.C.

Tibullus. Latin poet. c.54-19 B.C.
Timaeus of Sicily. Greek historian. c.352-c.256 B.C.
Varro. Roman historian. 116-27 B.C.
Virgil, Vergil. Roman poet. 70-19 B.C.
Warraq, al-, Abu 'Isa. Muslim author. Ninth century of the Christian era.

LISTS OF ABBREVIATIONS

1. BOOKS AND PERIODICALS

AGGEL   *A Greek-English Lexicon of the New Testament and Other Early Christian Literature*, A translation and adaptation of Walter Bauer's *Griechisch-Deutsches Wörterbuch zu den Schriften des Neuen Testaments und der übrigen urchristlichen Literatur*, 4th ed. 1952, by William F. Arndt and F. Wilbur Gingrich. 1957.

AJP   *The American Journal of Philology.*

AJSL   *The American Journal of Semitic Languages and Literatures.*

AKGWG   *Abhandlungen der königlichen Gesellschaft der Wissenschaften zu Göttingen.*

ANEA   James B. Pritchard, *The Ancient Near East: An Anthology of Texts and Pictures.* 1958.

ANET   James B. Pritchard, ed., *Ancient Near Eastern Texts Relating to the Old Testament.* 2d ed. 1955.

ANF   Alexander Roberts and James Donaldson, eds., rev. by A. Cleveland Coxe, *The Ante-Nicene Fathers, Translations of the Writings of the Fathers down to A.D. 325.* 10 vols. 1885-87.

ARAB   Daniel D. Luckenbill, *Ancient Records of Assyria and Babylonia.* 2 vols. 1926-27.

ARE   James H. Breasted, *Ancient Records of Egypt.* 5 vols. 1906-7.

AS   *Assyriological Studies.* Oriental Institute.

BA   *The Biblical Archaeologist.*

BASOR   *Bulletin of the American Schools of Oriental Research.*

BDBHEL   Francis Brown, S. R. Driver, and Charles A. Briggs, *A Hebrew and English Lexicon of the Old Testament.* 1957.

BDSM   William H. Brownlee, *The Dead Sea Manual of Discipline.* BASOR Supplementary Studies 10-12. 1951.

BDSS   Millar Burrows, *The Dead Sea Scrolls.* 1955.

CAH   J. B. Bury, S. A. Cook, F. E. Adcock, M. P. Charlesworth, and N. H. Baynes, eds., *The Cambridge Ancient History.* 12 vols. and 5 vols. of plates, 1923-39.

CAP   R. H. Charles, ed., *The Apocrypha and Pseudepigrapha of the Old Testament in English with Introductions and Critical and Explanatory Notes to the Several Books.* 2 vols. 1913.

DACL   *Dictionnaire d'archéologie chrétienne et de liturgie.* 1924ff.

DJD   *Discoveries in the Judaean Desert.* I, *Qumran Cave I,* by D. Barthélemy and J. T. Milik. 1955.

DM   *The Mishnah Translated from the Hebrew with Introduction and Brief Explanatory Notes,* by Herbert Danby. 1933.

EB   *The Encyclopaedia Britannica.* 14th ed. 24 vols. 1929.

FLP   Jack Finegan, *Light from the Ancient Past, The Archeological Background of Judaism and Christianity.* 2d ed. 1959.

GBT   Lazarus Goldschmidt, *Der babylonische Talmud.* 9 vols. 1899-1935.

GCS   *Die griechischen christlichen Schriftsteller der ersten Jahrhunderte.*

GDSS   Theodor H. Gaster, *The Dead Sea Scriptures in English Translation.* 1956.

HDB   James Hastings, ed., *A Dictionary of the Bible.* 4 vols. 1898-1902.

HERE   James Hastings, ed., *Encyclopaedia of Religion and Ethics.* 12 vols. 1910-22.

HUCA   *Hebrew Union College Annual.*

HZNT   *Handbuch zum Neuen Testament.*

IEJ   *Israel Exploration Journal.*

JBL   *Journal of Biblical Literature.*

JCS   *Journal of Cuneiform Studies.*

JE   Isidore Singer, ed., *The Jewish Encyclopedia.* 12 vols. 1901-5.

JEA   *The Journal of Egyptian Archaeology.*

JNES   *Journal of Near Eastern Studies.*

JQR   *The Jewish Quarterly Review.*

JSS   *Journal of Semitic Studies.*

JTS   *The Journal of Theological Studies.*

KLT   *Kleine Texte für theologische und philologische Vorlesungen und Übungen,* ed. Hans Lietzmann.

KRAC   Theodor Klauser, ed., *Reallexikon für Antike und Christentum, Sachwörterbuch zur Auseinandersetzung des Christentums mit der antiken Welt.* 1950ff.

LCL   *The Loeb Classical Library.*

LSGEL   *A Greek-English Lexicon* compiled by Henry G. Liddell and Robert Scott, rev. by Henry S. Jones. 1940.

LXX   The Septuagint. Henry B. Swete, ed., *The Old Testament in Greek according to the Septuagint.* I, 4th ed. 1909; II, 3d ed. 1907; III, 3d ed. 1905. Alfred Rahlfs, ed., *Septuaginta, id est Vetus Testamentum Graece iuxta LXX inter-*

pretes. 2 vols. 1935. *Septuaginta, Vetus Testamentum Graecum auctoritate Societatis Litterarum Gottingensis editum.* 1931ff.

MPG   Jacques Paul Migne, *Patrologiae cursus completus. Series graeca.*

MPL   Jacques Paul Migne, *Patrologiae cursus completus. Series latina.*

MVAG   *Mitteilungen der Vorderasiatisch-Aegyptischen Gesellschaft.*

NPNFSS   Philip Schaff and Henry Wace, eds., *A Select Library of Nicene and Post-Nicene Fathers of the Christian Church.* Second Series. 14 vols. 1890-1900.

NSH   Samuel M. Jackson, ed., *The New Schaff-Herzog Encyclopedia of Religious Knowledge.* 12 vols. 1908-12.

NTS   *New Testament Studies.*

OP   *The Oxyrhynchus Papyri.*

PCAE   Richard A. Parker, *The Calendars of Ancient Egypt.* SAOC 26, 1950.

PDBC   Richard A. Parker and Waldo H. Dubberstein, *Babylonian Chronology 626 B.C.-A.D. 75.* 3d ed. 1956.

PEQ   *Palestine Exploration Quarterly.*

PWRE   Pauly-Wissowa, *Real-Encyclopädie der classischen Altertumswissenschaft.*

RA   *Reallexikon der Assyriologie.* 1928ff.

RB   *Revue Biblique.*

RHR   *Revue de l'histoire des religions.*

RQ   *Revue de Qumran.*

SAOC   *Studies in Ancient Oriental Civilization.* Oriental Institute.

SBT   I. Epstein, ed., *The Babylonian Talmud* (Soncino Press). 1935ff.

SHJP   Emil Schürer, *A History of the Jewish People in the Time of Jesus Christ.* 5 vols. 1896.

SWDCB   William Smith and Henry Wace, *A Dictionary of Christian Biography.* 4 vols. 1877-87.

TMN   Edwin R. Thiele, *The Mysterious Numbers of the Hebrew Kings.* 1951.

VT   *Vetus Testamentum.*

WCCK   D. J. Wiseman, *Chronicles of Chaldaean Kings (626-556 B.C.) in the British Museum.* 1956.

ZA   *Zeitschrift für Assyriologie.*

ZAW   *Zeitschrift für die alttestamentliche Wissenschaft.*

ZDPV   *Zeitschrift des Deutschen Palästina-Vereins.*

ZNW   *Zeitschrift für die neutestamentliche Wissenschaft und die Kunde der älteren Kirche.*

2. BIBLICAL BOOKS AND RELATED LITERATURE

(1) OLD TESTAMENT

Gen	Genesis	Ec	Ecclesiastes
Ex	Exodus	SS	Song of Solomon
Lev	Leviticus	Is	Isaiah
Num	Numbers	Jer	Jeremiah
Dt	Deuteronomy	Lam	Lamentations
Jos	Joshua	Ezk	Ezekiel
Jg	Judges	Dan	Daniel
Ru	Ruth	Hos	Hosea
I S	I Samuel	Jl	Joel
II S	II Samuel	Am	Amos
I K	I Kings	Ob	Obadiah
II K	II Kings	Jon	Jonah
I Ch	I Chronicles	Mic	Micah
II Ch	II Chronicles	Nah	Nahum
Ezr	Ezra	Hab	Habakkuk
Neh	Nehemiah	Zph	Zephaniah
Est	Esther	Hag	Haggai
Jb	Job	Zec	Zechariah
Ps	Psalms	Mal	Malachi
Pr	Proverbs		

(2) NEW TESTAMENT

Mt	Matthew	I Tim	I Timothy
Mk	Mark	II Tim	II Timothy
Lk	Luke	Tit	Titus
Jn	John	Phm	Philemon
Ac	Acts	Heb	Hebrews
Rom	Romans	Jas	James
I Cor	I Corinthians	I Pet	I Peter
II Cor	II Corinthians	II Pet	II Peter
Gal	Galatians	I Jn	I John
Eph	Ephesians	II Jn	II John
Phl	Philippians	III Jn	III John
Col	Colossians	Jd	Jude
I Th	I Thessalonians	Rev	Revelation
II Th	II Thessalonians		

(3) APOCRYPHA

I Esd	I Esdras	Jth	Judith
II Esd	II Esdras	Ad Est	Additions to Esther
Tob	Tobit	Wisd	Wisdom of Solomon

Sir, or	Sirach, or	Sus	Susanna
Ecclus	Ecclesiasticus	Bel	Bel and the Dragon
Bar	Baruch	Pr Man	Prayer of Manasses
Ep Jer	Epistle of Jeremy	I Macc	I Maccabees
Thr Ch	Song of the Three Children	II Macc	II Maccabees

(4) PSEUDEPIGRAPHA

Apc Bar	Apocalypse of Baruch	Jub	Jubilees
Asc Is	Ascension of Isaiah	Ps Sol	Psalms of Solomon
Asm M	Assumption of Moses	Sib Or	Sibylline Oracles
En	Enoch	XII P	Testaments of the Twelve Patriarchs

(5) THE DEAD SEA SCROLLS AND RELATED LITERATURE

1QpHab	Habakkuk Commentary, i.e., the *pesher* or commentary on Habakkuk from Cave 1 at Qumran
1QJub	Jubilees fragments from Cave 1 at Qumran
1QS	Manual of Discipline, i.e., the *serek* or "order" of the community from Cave 1 at Qumran
1Q 17 and 18	Numbered fragments from Cave 1 at Qumran
CD	Zadokite Document, or Cairo Document of the Damascus Covenanters

3. ERAS

A. Abr.	*Anno Abraham*	In the year of Abraham
A. A. C.	*Anno ante Christum*	In the year before Christ
A. Ad.	*Anno Adam*	In the year of Adam
A. C.	*Ante Christum*	Before Christ
A. D.	*Anno Domini*	In the year of the Lord
A. Diocl.	*Anno Diocletiani*	In the year of Diocletian
A. M.	*Anno Mundi*	In the year of the world
A. O. C.	*Anno orbis conditi*	In the year of the foundation of the world
A. S.	*Anno Seleucidarum*	In the year of the Seleucids
A. U. C.	*Anno urbis conditae*	In the year of the foundation of the city
	Ab urbe condita	From the foundation of the city
B. C.		Before Christ
B. C. E.		Before the Christian era
Ol.		Olympiad

4. DAYS

Sun   Sunday
Mon   Monday
Tue   Tuesday
Wed   Wednesday
Thu   Thursday
Fri   Friday
Sat   Saturday

5. MONTHS

1.	Jan	January	7.	Jul	July
2.	Feb	February	8.	Aug	August
3.	Mar	March	9.	Sep	September
4.	Apr	April	10.	Oct	October
5.	May	May	11.	Nov	November
6.	Jun	June	12.	Dec	December

In some tabulations, in order to save space, the months are designated by number, for example: 7/1 755 = Month 7 Day 1 Year 755 = July 1, 755.

6. MISCELLANEOUS

a.m.	*ante meridiem*	before noon
b.		born
c.	*circa*	about, around
cf.	*conferre*	compare
d.		died
f., ff.		following
fl.	*floruit*	he flourished
n.		note
p.		page
p.m.	*post meridiem*	after noon
pp.		pages

7. ARBITRARY SIGNS

=	equals
—	minus
+	plus
¶	paragraph
. . . .	omission of a passage of time

PART ONE

PRINCIPLES OF CHRONOLOGY
IN THE ANCIENT WORLD

I. NUMERALS

¶ 1. A number is an amount or quantity of units. It is also a character or symbol, such as a figure or word, which expresses such a magnitude. In the latter sense a number is synonymous with a numeral. The statement of a number or numeral in the form of a word or words is a usage found regularly in the Bible. Examples are: in the Hebrew text of Gen 5:3, "thirty and a hundred years" (שלשים ומאת שנה), i.e., "one hundred and thirty years"; in the Greek text of Mt 4:2, "forty days and forty nights" (ἡμέρας τεσσεράκοντα καὶ τεσσεράκοντα νύκτας); and in the Latin text of Lk 3:1, "in the fifteenth year" (*anno quinto decimo*).

¶ 2. A number or numeral may also be expressed by a figure or symbol. In the development of such figures or symbols, several principles are recognizable. In an "acrophonic" system the initial letter of the word by which a number is called is used to represent the number itself. In an "alphabetic" system the sequential characters of the alphabet serve as numbers. In a system of what we may call "arbitrary" signs, accepted or conventional symbols are employed as figures. From very early times, as on the Palermo Stone (¶148) for example, use was made simply of a straight mark or a succession of straight marks for at least the smaller numbers. Where individual symbols do not extend far enough to encompass all desired magnitudes, it is possible to make combinations of them to gain the desired result. In the combination the placement of the individual symbols may indicate the addition, or in some cases the subtraction, of the respective components.

¶ 3. In manuscripts and inscriptions where a numerical symbol, particularly an alphabetic character, might be relatively difficult to recognize as having this meaning, attention may be called to it as a numeral by leaving space around it or adding some mark of punctuation. In modern transcriptions it is often customary to use a mark above the line and following the letter like an acute accent, or also below the line and preceding the letter, to indicate numerals.

1. HEBREW NUMERALS

LITERATURE: Caspar Levias, "Numbers and Numerals," in JE IX, pp.348-350.

¶ 4. The letters of the Hebrew alphabet are used for numerals as shown in Table 1.

[3]

TABLE 1. HEBREW NUMERALS

א	Aleph	1	י	Yodh	10	ק	Qoph	100
ב	Beth	2	כ	Kaph	20	ר	Resh	200
ג	Gimel	3	ל	Lamedh	30	שׁ	S(h)in	300
ד	Daleth	4	מ	Mem	40	ת	Taw	400
ה	He	5	נ	Nun	50			
ו	Waw	6	ס	Samekh	60			
ז	Zayin	7	ע	Ayin	70			
ח	Heth	8	פ	Pe	80			
ט	Teth	9	צ	Tsadhe	90			

To distinguish a character as a numeral an accent may be placed after it. Numbers which exceed the limits of the sequence of letters are formed by addition of characters. These composite groups are written thus, for example: ת״ק = 500, תת״ק = 900.

2. GREEK NUMERALS

LITERATURE: Leonard Whibley, ed., *A Companion to Greek Studies*. 4th ed. 1931, pp.698-699; A. G. Woodhead, *The Study of Greek Inscriptions*. 1959, pp.107-111.

¶ 5.   In early Greek, simple straight vertical marks were used for the numbers one to four. Beyond that point the initial letters of the names of the numerals were employed. Thus, for example, Γ (now written Π) = πέντε = 5, Δ = δέκα = 10, ΔΙ = 11, etc. This acrophonic system is attested from the fifth century to around 100 B.C.

¶ 6.   From the first century B.C. to the end of the Roman empire and on into the Byzantine period, the less cumbersome alphabetic system was mainly used. The complete Ionic alphabet was employed including three signs now obsolete:

ς or ϝ   Vau or Digamma
Ϙ or ϙ   Koppa
ϡ or ϡ   Sampi

The numerical values of the letters of the alphabet are shown in Table 2.

3. ROMAN NUMERALS

LITERATURE: David E. Smith, "Roman Numerals," in EB 16, pp.612-613.

¶ 7.   As in Greek where in one system simple upright strokes were used for numbers one to four, so also in Latin the numerical sys-

TABLE 2. GREEK NUMERALS

α	Alpha	1	ι	Iota	10	ρ	Rho	100
β	Beta	2	κ	Kappa	20	σ	Sigma	200
γ	Gamma	3	λ	Lambda	30	τ	Tau	300
δ	Delta	4	μ	Mu	40	υ	Upsilon	400
ε	Epsilon	5	ν	Nu	50	φ	Phi	500
ϛ	Vau	6	ξ	Xi	60	χ	Chi	600
ζ	Zeta	7	ο	Omicron	70	ψ	Psi	700
η	Eta	8	π	Pi	80	ω	Omega	800
θ	Theta	9	ϙ	Koppa	90	ϡ	Sampi	900

To indicate the numerical employment of the letters a mark like an acute accent is placed after the character or characters up through 999; a similar mark is used below the line and preceding the letter for 1000 and above. Thus, for example, φνε′ = 555, ͵εφνε′ = 5555, etc. In the inscriptions and the papyri dates are given with the word ἔτος, "year," or ἔτους, "years," and this is often abbreviated to Ⳑ.

tem begins with I, II, III, IIII, and then goes on with other characters, V, X, L, C, and M, the derivation of which is at least in some cases recognizable as following the acrophonic principle, e.g., C = *centum* = 100, M = *mille* = 1000. Similarly, too, addition and also subtraction of characters gives composite numbers, e.g., MC = 1100, CM = 900, etc. The elements of the system are shown in Table 3.

TABLE 3. ROMAN NUMERALS

I	1	XI	11	XXX	30
II	2	XII	12	XL	40
III	3	XIII	13	L	50
IIII or IV	4	XIIII or XIV	14	C	100
V	5	XV	15	M	1000
VI	6	XVI	16		
VII	7	XVII	17		
VIII	8	XVIII	18		
VIIII or IX	9	XVIIII or XIX	19		
X	10	XX	20		

II. THE RECKONING
OF TIME IN
THE ANCIENT WORLD

A. UNITS OF TIME

LITERATURE: Cyrus Adler, "Calendar, History of," in JE III, pp.498-501; Michael Friedländer, "Calendar," in JE III, pp.501-508; F. H. Colson, *The Week*. 1926; Henry N. Russell, Raymond S. Dugan, and John Q. Stewart, *Astronomy, A Revision of Young's Manual of Astronomy*, I, *The Solar System*. rev. ed. 1945; *The American Ephemeris and Nautical Almanac;* A. Hermann, F. Schmidtke, and L. Koep in KRAC III, cols. 30-60.

¶8.   The chief units in the reckoning of time for calendrical purposes are the day, week, month, and year, while the year is also divided into seasons and the day into hours or other parts. Rev 9:15 mentions the units, hour, day, month, and year; and Gal 4:10 speaks of days, months, seasons, and years. There are some indications, to be noted in what follows, which suggest that recognition of the day, week, month, and year was based first upon climatic and agricultural factors; later these units of time were associated with the celestial bodies.

1. THE DAY

LITERATURE: Solomon Zeitlin, "The Beginning of the Jewish Day during the Second Commonwealth," in JQR 36 (1945-46), pp.403-414.

¶9.   In the Sumerian and Akkadian languages the word for "day" also means "wind." Likewise in SS 2:17 and 4:6 it is said that "the day breathes" or literally that it blows. It has been suggested, therefore, that it was first of all the daily land and sea breezes of the Mesopotamian and Palestinian coastlands which called attention to this time unit long before there was systematic observation of the sun.[1]

¶10.   The rising and setting of the sun and the alternation of light and darkness were also very obvious facts of nature, however, and these too must have been recognized very early as marking out the day. In Hebrew the word for day is יוֹם (*yom*). This is used to desig-

[1] Lewy in HUCA 17 (1942-43), pp.5f.

nate the day in the sense of daytime as distinct from nighttime as, for example, in Gen 1:5 where "God called the light Day." It is also used for day in the sense of the complete cycle which includes both the daytime and the nighttime as, for example, in Gen 1:5: "And there was evening and there was morning, one day." In Greek the corresponding word ἡμέρα is used for the daytime as, for example, in Mt 4:2 where Jesus fasted for "forty days and forty nights." For the complete cycle of light and darkness there is a word, νυχθήμερον, which combines "night" (νύξ) and "day" (ἡμέρα) in one term. This is used in II Cor 11:25 where it is translated "a night and a day." Usually, however, the "day" which includes the nighttime and the daytime is simply designated with the word ἡμέρα and the context makes plain what is meant as, for example, in Jn 2:12 or Ac 9:19 where the several "days" are certainly several successive periods each comprising daytime and nighttime.

⟨ 11.   A "day" in the sense of a complete period of light and darkness might be reckoned as beginning with the coming of the light or with the coming of the darkness, as well as of course theoretically at any other point in the daily cycle, midnight now being used as that point. In ancient Egypt the day probably began at dawn,[2] in ancient Mesopotamia it began in the evening.[3] Among the Greeks the day was reckoned from sunset to sunset, while the Romans already began the day in the "modern" fashion at midnight.[4] Summing up the different reckonings among different people in his time Pliny wrote:

> "The Babylonians count the period between two sunrises, the Athenians that between two sunsets, the Umbrians from midday to midday, the common people everywhere from dawn to dark, the Roman priests and the authorities who fixed the official day, and also the Egyptians and Hipparchus, the period from midnight to midnight."[5]

⟨ 12.   In the Old Testament the earlier practice seems to have been to consider that the day began in the morning. In Gen 19:34, for example, the "morrow" (ASV) or "next day" (RSV) clearly begins with the morning after the preceding night. The later practice was to count the day as beginning in the evening. In Lev 23:27 it

---

[2] PCAE p.10.   [3] PDBC p.26.

[4] James Gow, *A Companion to School Classics.* 3d ed. 1891, pp.78,147; and in Leonard Whibley, ed., *A Companion to Greek Studies.* 3d ed. 1916, p.589.

[5] *Natural History.* II, lxxix, 188.

is stated that the Day of Atonement is to be observed on the tenth day of the seventh month; in verse 32 it is said that the observance is to be "on the ninth day of the month beginning at evening, from evening to evening." These last words can hardly be intended to change the actual date of the fast; rather they appear to be an addition which simply defines what the tenth day of the month was at a time when the day had come to be reckoned as beginning in the evening: the tenth day of the month is the day which begins on the evening of the ninth and continues until the following evening. In making the shift from a morning reckoning to an evening reckoning, the "day" was therefore in fact moved back so that it began a half day earlier than had been the case previously.[6]

⟨ 13.   In the New Testament in the Synoptic Gospels and Acts the day seems usually to be considered as beginning in the morning. Mk 11:11 states that Jesus entered Jerusalem, went into the temple, and when he had looked at everything, since it was "now eventide" (ASV) or "already late" (RSV), went out to Bethany with the twelve; verse 12 continues the narrative and tells that on the "morrow" (ASV) or the "following day" (RSV) they came back to the city. It is evident that the new day has begun with the morning following the preceding evening. Likewise Mt 28:1, Mk 16:1f., and Lk 23:56-24:1 all picture the first day of the week beginning with the dawn following the preceding sabbath. And Ac 4:3, for an example in that book, tells how Peter and John were put in custody "until the morrow, for it was already evening," thus clearly indicating that the new day would begin the next morning. It has been suggested that this counting of the day as beginning with the morning is a continuation of the earlier Old Testament practice already described (¶12), and that this usage was maintained in parts of Galilee and was followed by Jesus and the early disciples, which would account for its appearing so frequently in the Synoptic Gospels and Acts.[7] On the other hand even though the common reckoning in the Synoptic Gospels is from the morning, in Mk 1:32 = Lk 4:40, the later Old Testament (¶12) and Jewish usage of counting the one day as ending and the next as beginning at sunset is plainly reflected in the fact that the people of Capernaum were

[6] Julian Morgenstern in HUCA 10 (1935), pp.15-28; 20 (1947), pp.34-38.
[7] Julian Morgenstern in *Crozer Quarterly.* 26 (1949), pp.232-240.

free to bring the sick to Jesus at sunset when the sabbath came to an end. As for the Fourth Gospel, in Jn 20:1 Mary Magdalene comes to the tomb while it is still dark, yet it is already "on the first day of the week." This can be explained by supposing that the late Old Testament and Jewish usage is in view, according to which the new day had begun at the preceding sunset, or it can be explained equally well by supposing that John is giving the description in terms of the official Roman day which, as Pliny told us (¶11), began at midnight. In either case, the new day had begun already before the sunrise.

⟦ 14.   The coming of light and the coming of darkness are of course gradual events, and it is therefore to periods of transition which are not necessarily sharply defined that the terms "morning" and "evening," as also dawn" (e.g. Jg 19:25f.) and "twilight" (e.g. I S 30:17), refer. For a more precise line of demarcation between one day and the next the time of sunrise or of sunset could be taken, and we have seen probable examples of such usage in Mk 16:2 and Mk 1:32 respectively. Or the determination could be made in terms of the intensity of the light or the completeness of the darkness. For example, it was held by the Jewish rabbis that Dt 6:4-7 required the recitation of the Shema in the evening and in the morning, and in the Talmud there is found an extended discussion of exactly what times are thereby intended. The recital could begin in the morning, it was declared, as soon as one could distinguish between blue and white (or between blue and green, as another rabbi taught), and it must be finished before sunrise.[8] As for the evening Neh 4:21 was cited, where work went on "till the stars came out," and from that analogy it was shown that the appearance of the stars was the sign that the day had ended and the recital could begin.[9] Thus in the morning it was either the dawning light or the following sunrise, and in the evening it was either the sunset or the ensuing nightfall when the stars became visible, that provided the line of demarcation.[10]

⟦ 15. Parts of the day were described at an early time in terms of the customary occupation then performed as, for example, the "time

[8] *Berakoth.* I, 2; DM p.2.   [9] *Berakoth.* 2b; SBT p.3.
[10] As the line between one day and the next, nightfall was later defined even more precisely as the moment when three stars of the second magnitude become visible. Friedländer in JE III, p.501.

for the animals to be gathered together" (Gen 29:7), or "the time
when women go out to draw water" (Gen 24:11). The nighttime
was divided into watches. Lam 2:19 speaks of "the beginning of
the watches," Jg 7:19 mentions "the middle watch," and Ex 14:24
and I S 11:11 refer to "the morning watch." The rabbis debated
whether there were three watches or four;[11] and Mk 13:35 names
four: evening, midnight, cockcrow, and morning. The daytime had
recognizable periods such as "the heat of the day" (Gen 18:1) and
"the cool of the day" (Gen 3:8), and was also divided broadly into
morning, noon, and evening (Ps 55:17). A division of the daytime
into three parts, and of the nighttime into three parts, is mentioned
in Jub 49:10, 12.[12]

¶ 16.   The word "hour" שׁעה, sha‘ah) occurs several times in Daniel
(3:6, etc.) in Aramaic, and is common in later Hebrew. In Daniel
it still denotes simply a short period of time and the phrase "the
same hour" (ASV) may properly be translated "immediately" (RSV).
In Greek the corresponding word is ὥρα, and it too is used for an
inexactly defined period of time, as for example in Jn 5:35 where
πρὸς ὥραν is translated "for a while."

¶ 17.   In Mesopotamia the entire day was divided into twelve periods of what we would call two hours each.[13] Herodotus[14] refers to
these "twelve divisions (μέρεα) of the day," and observes that the
Greeks learned of them from the Babylonians. Among the Greeks
themselves the day and the night were each divided into twelve
hours.[15] These hours naturally varied in length depending upon the
time of year and were known as ὧραι καιρικαί. For scientific purposes, an hour of standard length was used, the entire day (νυχθήμερον) being divided into twenty-four periods of equal length. The
astronomer Hipparchus (c.150 B.C.) speaks of these "equinoctial
hours" (ὧραι ἰσημεριναί),[16] as he calls them, and Ptolemy[17] also
distinguishes between ordinary and equinoctial hours. In order to
measure the hours there were available for the time when the sun
was shining the sunclock (πόλος) and the sundial (γνώμων), which

[11] *Berakoth.* 3a-b; SBT pp.5-8.   [12] CAP II, p.80.
[13] Georges Contenau, *Everyday Life in Babylon and Assyria.* 1954, p.11.
[14] II, 109.
[15] Gow, *A Companion to School Classics,* p.79.
[16] Hipparchus II, iv, 5. ed. C. Manitius, 1894, p.184.
[17] *Tetrabiblos.* 76. tr. F. E. Robbins, LCL (1948), pp.165-167.

are mentioned by Herodotus in the passage cited just above with the statement that they came from Babylonia. The same principle of measurement by the shadow of the sun was of course also known in Egypt, where the obelisks were evidently used for astronomical measurements.[18] For the measurement of time during the darkness as well as the light, there was the water clock (κλεψύδρα), which is mentioned by Aristotle[19] and others.

⟨ 18.   The division of the day into twelve hours appears in Jn 11:9 where it is asked, "Are there not twelve hours in the day?" Likewise in Mt 20:1-12 the householder goes to hire laborers early in the morning, and again at the third, sixth, ninth, and eleventh hours, and the last ones have only one hour to work before the end of the day. As we saw above (¶11), Pliny tells us that the common people everywhere reckoned the day from dawn to dark, so the twelve hours were presumably counted within that period. If an average daytime lasting from six a.m. to six p.m. was taken as the basis, then the third hour was what we would call nine o'clock in the morning, and so on. In the Talmud[20] there is a discussion in connection with the testimony of witnesses of the extent of reasonable error in a man's estimate of what the hour is, and it is noted that "in the sixth hour the sun stands in the meridian."

⟨ 19.   In the Fourth Gospel, on the other hand, we saw (¶13) that the day must have been reckoned from the preceding evening, according to later Jewish usage, or from the preceding midnight, according to what Pliny (¶11) tells us was official Roman usage. In this "modern" reckoning of the day from midnight, the first twelve hours would extend from midnight to midday, and another twelve hours would cover the time from midday to the next midnight. When various hourly notations are considered in the Gospel according to John it is found that they do in fact work out well in terms of the Roman reckoning. For example, in Jn 1:39 a reckoning from the morning would make the "tenth hour" four o'clock in the afternoon, but a reckoning from midnight would make it ten o'clock in the morning, the latter being more appropriate to the fact

---

[18] Russell, Dugan, and Stewart, *Astronomy*, I, *The Solar System*, p.78.
[19] *Athenian Constitution*. LXVII, 2. tr. H. Rackham, LCL (1952), p.187; cf. Sontheimer in PWRE Zweite Reihe, IV, ii, cols. 2017-2018.
[20] *Pesaḥim*. 11b-12b; SBT pp.51-56.

that the two disciples then stayed with Jesus "that day." In Jn 4:6 the "sixth hour" would be midday in the one case, but six o'clock in the evening in the other, and the latter would be a very likely time for the gathering at the well. In Jn 4:52 the "seventh hour" would be one p.m. or seven p.m., and the latter may be more likely for the arrival at Cana from Capernaum, a journey of twenty miles.[21]

⟨ 20.   Among the parts of the day the "evening" was of special importance. We have already seen (¶¶12, 14) how the regularly used day in later Jewish times began in the evening rather than in the morning, and how either the sunset or the appearing of the stars was taken as the exact time of its beginning. The evening was also important because of the sacrifices which were made at that time, and in this connection there was a discussion of exactly what period of time was meant. According to Num 28:4 the daily burnt offering called for the sacrifice of one lamb in the morning and of another "in the evening." According to Ex 12:6 the passover lambs were to be killed "in the evening" of the fourteenth day of the first month, and Lev 23:5 gives the same date for "the Lord's passover." In all three passages the Hebrew is literally "between the two evenings" (ASV margin), although in the first two cases the Septuagint translates simply πρὸς ἑσπέραν, "towards evening," and only in the Leviticus passage renders ἀνὰ μέσον τῶν ἑσπερινῶν, "between the evenings." The Mishnah[22] states that the daily evening burnt offering was slaughtered at eight and a half hours, that is two-thirty o'clock, and offered at nine and a half hours, that is three-thirty o'clock. If it was the eve of passover it was slaughtered at seven and a half hours, one-thirty o'clock, and offered at eight and a half hours, two-thirty o'clock, whether on a weekday or the sabbath; if it was the eve of passover and this fell on the eve of a sabbath, that is on a Friday, it was slaughtered at six and a half hours, twelve-thirty o'clock, and offered at seven and a half hours, one-thirty o'clock; and then the passover offering was slaughtered after that.

⟨ 21.   Explaining this procedure the accompanying Gemara[23] states that "between the evenings" means "from the time that the sun commences to decline in the west," and that the "two evenings" give

[21] Norman Walker in *Novum Testamentum*. 4 (1960), pp.69-73.
[22] *Pesaḥim*. v, 1; DM p.141.
[23] *Pesaḥim*. 58a; SBT pp.287f.

"two and a half hours before and two and a half hours after and one hour for preparation" of the sacrifice. This means that "evening" begins as soon as the sun passes its midday zenith, and that the "two evenings" are from twelve to two-thirty o'clock, and from three-thirty until six o'clock respectively. Thus the daily evening burnt offering is ordinarily sacrificed in the hour between these two evenings, but when the passover must also be sacrificed the same afternoon then the daily sacrifice is moved ahead. In another passage the Mishnah[24] deals with the requirement of Ex 34:25 that the passover sacrifice not be offered with leaven, and states that everything leavened must be burned at the beginning of the sixth hour, that is at twelve o'clock noon. As the accompanying discussion in the Gemara[25] shows, this indicates that the sacrificing could begin immediately after noon. According to Josephus[26] the passover sacrifices were conducted from the ninth to the eleventh hour, that is from three to five o'clock in the afternoon, and this was presumably the standard practice in the first century A.D.

【 22.　According to the foregoing passages, then, the "evening" was substantially equivalent to the entire afternoon. In Dt 16:6, however, it is said that the passover sacrifice is to be offered "in the evening at the going down of the sun." The Talmudic explanation of this was that the evening meant the afternoon and was the time when the passover was to be slaughtered, and that the sunset was the time when it was to be eaten.[27] The Sadducees and the Samaritans, however, held that the slaughtering of the lamb itself was to take place between sunset and darkness.[28] The Book of Jubilees seems to agree with this when it says about the passover lamb: "It is not permissible to slay it during any period of the light, but during the period bordering on the evening, and let them eat it at the time of the evening until the third part of the night" (49:12).[29] The Targum of Onkelos also rendered "between the two evenings" in Ex 12:6 as "between the two suns,"[30] and this was then explained

[24] *Pesaḥim*. I, 4; DM p.137.
[25] *Pesaḥim*. 5a; SBT p.17.
[26] *War*. VI, 423 (=VI, ix, 3).
[27] *Berakoth*. 9a; SBT pp.46f.
[28] Emil G. Hirsch in JE IX, p.553.
[29] CAP II, p.80.
[30] J. W. Etheridge, ed., *The Targums of Onkelos and Jonathan ben Uzziel on the Pentateuch; With the Fragments of the Jerusalem Targum from the Chaldee*. 2 vols. 1862-65, I, p.370.

as meaning the time between sunset and the coming out of the stars.[31]

〔23. In either case, however, whether it meant the afternoon time up until sunset, or the time from sunset until the stars became visible, the "evening" in the sense and in the regard just discussed evidently belonged to the closing part of the day, and it was only with the sunset or the appearing of the stars that the next day began.

2. THE WEEK

LITERATURE: Hildegard and Julius Lewy, "The Origin of the Week and the Oldest West Asiatic Calendar," in HUCA 17 (1942-43), pp.1-152c; Solomon Gandz, "The Origin of the Planetary Week or The Planetary Week in Hebrew Literature," in *Proceedings of the American Academy for Jewish Research.* 18 (1948-49), pp.213-254.

〔24. A sequence of seven days forms a week. Since the ancient Babylonians recognized seven winds, as may be seen in the Creation Epic where Marduk "sent forth the winds he had brought forth, the seven of them,"[1] it has been surmised that originally one day was dedicated to each of the winds and thus a week of seven days was formed.[2] As a period of seven days the week was called שבוע (shabua‘) in Hebrew (Gen 29:27, etc.), from sheba‘, "seven"; and in Greek it was σάββατον (Lk 18:12, etc.). In the Bible the days of the week are simply numbered and the seventh day is also named the sabbath (שבת, shabbat; σάββατον). In addition to this, the day before the sabbath was called the day of Preparation,[3] and by the Christians the first day of the week was called the Lord's day (Rev 1:10).

〔25. The custom of naming the seven days of the week after the seven planets is attested in the first century B.C. when Tibullus (d. 19 B.C.) mentions the day of Saturn, and in the first century A.D. when Greek and Latin wall inscriptions at Pompeii (A.D. 79) list "the days of the gods," namely of Saturn, the sun, the moon, Mars, Mercury, Jupiter, and Venus. This listing, with the later equivalents, is shown in Table 4.

[31] S. R. Driver, *The Book of Exodus* (The Cambridge Bible for Schools and Colleges). 1911, p.89 n.

[1] ANET p.66.   [2] Lewy in HUCA 17 (1942-43), pp.6-25.
[3] παρασκευή, Josephus, *Ant.* XVI, 163 (=XVI, vi, 2); Mt 27:62; Lk 23:54; Jn 19:31, 42; προσάββατον, Mk 15:42.

TABLE 4. THE PLANETARY NAMES OF THE DAYS OF THE WEEK

Θεων ημερας	(dies)	(the day of)	
Κρονου	Saturni	Saturn	Saturday
Ηλιου	Solis	the Sun	Sunday
Σεληνης	Lunae	the Moon	Monday
Αρεως	Martis	Mars	Tuesday (Tiw's day)
E[ρ]μου	(Mercurii)	Mercury	Wednesday (Woden's day)
Διος	Jovis	Jupiter	Thursday (Thor's day)
[Αφρο]δειτης	Veneris	Venus	Friday (Frigg's day)[4]

Dio Cassius[5] (d. A.D. c.235) says this custom of referring the days to the seven planets was instituted by the Egyptians and was in his own time found among all mankind. Dio's remarks in this connection, that the Jews dedicate to their God "the day called the day of Saturn," is of course correct as far as Jewish observance of Saturday or the sabbath is concerned, but they would hardly have designated the day by the name which the pagan writer uses. In an apocryphal rabbinic work, however, the *Pirqe de Rabbi Eliezer*, the final edition of which probably dates in the ninth century A.D., the planets which rule the week are named. For each day a pair is given, the first being the ruler of the nighttime and the second the regent of the following daytime: "The planets serve . . . as the regents of the seven days of the week, to wit: On the first day, Mercury and the Sun; on the second, Jupiter and the Moon; on the third, Venus and Mars; on the fourth, Saturn and Mercury; on the fifth, the Sun and Jupiter; on the sixth, the Moon and Venus; on the seventh, Mars and Saturn."[6]

3. THE MONTH

【 26.   If the day and the week were connected first of all with climatic conditions and only later with astronomical objects, it could be that something similar was true of the month. In fact, when the Israelite calendar is discussed below, it will be seen that

---

[4] Emil Schürer in zNW 6 (1905), pp.25, 27.

[5] *Roman History*. XXXVII, xvii-xix.

[6] VI, 13b. *Pirke de Rabbi Eliezer (The Chapters of Rabbi Eliezer the Great) according to the Text of the Manuscript belonging to Abraham Epstein of Vienna.* ed. Gerald Friedlander. 1916, p.32; Solomon Gandz in *Proceedings of the American Academy for Jewish Research.* 18 (1948-49), p.230.

the Gezer Calendar relates the months to the tasks to be performed in the successive phases of agricultural work, and that the old month names in the Old Testament describe their respective periods of time in terms of agricultural and climatic conditions.

⟨27. Etymologically, however, the word "month" shows the connection between this time unit and the moon. In Hebrew the word ירח (*yerah*) means both "moon" and "month," as may be seen for example in Dt 33:14 where the alternative translations are, "the precious things of the growth of the moons" (ASV), and "the rich yield of the months" (RSV). Likewise the term חדש (*hodesh*), which originally meant "the shining, glittering new moon," was later used as the designation of the festival of the day of the new moon, and also as the name of the entire month which is, as it were, the lifetime of the newly born moon. In Gen 29:14, for example, this word clearly means "month," in I S 20:5 and other passages it means the "new moon" day.[1] Likewise in Greek the word μήνη means "moon" and μήν means "month." In the Septuagint μήν is the translation of both ירח (Dt 33:14, etc.) and חדש (Gen 29:14). In the New Testament μήν regularly means "month" (Lk 1:24, etc.), but in one case (Gal 4:10) probably refers to the new moon festival.

⟨28. In so far as the month was related to the moon, the determination of its length depended upon observation of the phases of the moon. In Egypt, where the day probably began at dawn, it is thought that the month probably began with a lunar phenomenon which could be observed at that time of day. As the moon wanes, the old crescent is finally just visible in the eastern sky before sunrise one morning and on the next morning it is invisible. It may have been, therefore, on the morning when the old crescent could no longer be seen that the Egyptian lunar month began.[2] In Mesopotamia, on the other hand, the day began in the evening, and the month began when the crescent of the new moon was first visible in the western sky at sunset.[3]

⟨29. In modern astronomy the time from one new moon to the next, which is known as the synodic or ordinary month, is determined as 29.530588 days, or 29 days, 12 hours, 44 minutes, 2.8

---

[1] Solomon Gandz in JQR 39 (1948-49), pp.259f.
[2] PCAE pp.9-23. [3] PDBC p.1.

seconds.[4] This means that on the average the new moon will be seen approximately every twenty-nine and one-half days, and that the full moon will come approximately fourteen and three-quarter days after the appearing of the new moon, that is on the fifteenth day of the lunar month, with the day reckoned from evening to evening.[5] After the accumulation of data by observation, the month could have been calculated in advance. Likewise it could have been established as a standard unit, say of thirty days, rather than left variable as it must be to agree with the observed phases of the moon.

4. THE YEAR

¶ 30.   The ordinary Hebrew word for "year" is שנה (shanah). It is etymologically connected with the idea of "change" or "repeated action," and thus describes a "revolution of time." In the Septuagint it is translated both by ἐνιαυτός (Gen 1:14, etc.), properly a "cycle of time," and more frequently by ἔτος (Gen 5:3, etc.), and both Greek words are used for "year" in the New Testament (Jn 11:49, etc.; Lk 3:1, etc.).

¶ 31.   Climatic and agricultural factors doubtless first called attention to the cycle of time that is the year. In Egypt the annual inundation of the Nile was an unusually prominent reminder of the return of the cycle, and was regularly followed by the season of sowing. In Palestine the climate was marked by the "early rain" or "autumn rain" which came in Oct/Nov, and the "later rain" or "spring rain" which came in Mar/Apr (Dt 11:14; Jer 5:24),[1] as well as by the recurrence of summer and winter (Zec 14:8, etc.), and the agricultural seasons likewise returned regularly with the ripening of the olives in the fall (Sep/Oct-Oct/Nov), for example, and the shooting into ear of the barley in the spring (Mar/Apr).[2]

¶ 32.   The autumn and spring seasons, to which attention was thus particularly drawn by climatic and agricultural events, were also marked by the equality in length of day and night which occurs everywhere when the sun crosses the equator in each season. These

---

[4] *The American Ephemeris and Nautical Almanac for the Year 1958.* 1956, p.xvi.

[5] Julian Morgenstern in HUCA 10 (1935), p.25.

---

[1] E. Hull in HDB IV, p.195.

[2] W. F. Albright in BASOR 92 (Dec 1934), pp.22f. n.30 and n.37.

points are now called the equinoxes, and by our reckoning the autumnal equinox falls about September 23, the vernal equinox about March 21. Likewise the summer and winter were marked respectively by the times when the day was at its greatest length and at its shortest length, or the times when the sun seems to stand still in its northward movement and again in its southward movement. These points are called the summer solstice and the winter solstice, and come by our reckoning about June 21 and December 22. When these several points were recognized they provided definite markers in the course of the year, and it was no doubt possible to establish them with precision by observation of the length of day and night and by measurement of the shadow of the sun.[3]

⟨ 33.   When such a mark as the vernal equinox is established, the length of the year from that point through a "revolution of time" and back to the same point can be measured. In Egypt, as will be noted in discussing the Egyptian calendar below, the length of the year was probably recognized as early as the third millennium B.C. as being 365 days, and with more exact measurements it was later found to be about 365¼ days. Among the Jews, Mar Samuel (A.D. c.165-c.250), who directed a school at Nehardea in Babylonia and was said to be as familiar with the paths of heaven as with the streets of his own city,[4] reckoned the year at 365 days and 6 hours, while his contemporary, Rab Adda, made it 365 days, 5 hours, 55 minutes, 25 and a fraction seconds.[5] The Julian calendar (¶144) accepted the standard figure of 365¼ days with which we are familiar, but was therewith about eleven minutes longer than the astronomical year. In modern astronomy the length of the ordinary, tropical, or solar year, as it is called, is given as 365.24219879 days, or 365 days, 5 hours, 48 minutes, 45.975 seconds.[6]

⟨ 34.   When the four points of the vernal and autumnal equinoxes and the summer and winter solstices are taken, the year is readily divisible into four parts. Such a division of the solar year is found in the Talmud,[7] where the word תקופה (*tequfah*) is used as the name of each of the four periods. The word means "cycle" or "sea-

---

[3] Russell, Dugan, and Stewart, *Astronomy*, I, p.151.
[4] *Berakoth.* 58b; SBT p.365.
[5] JE III, p.500.
[6] *The American Ephemeris and Nautical Almanac for the Year 1958*, p.xvi.
[7] *Sanhedrin.* 11b; GBT VII, pp.36f.

son," and a related form is found as "circuit" in the Manual of Discipline (¶84).

⟪ 35.   In the course of the year the sun also seems to trace a path eastward against the background of the stars. This path is known as the zodiac. In a month the sun travels approximately one-twelfth of the way around this circle, and perhaps for this reason, the zodiac was divided into twelve sections.[8] Using the sexagesimal system of ancient Mesopotamia, the entire circle of the zodiac comprises 360 degrees, each of the twelve sections, 30 degrees. These divisions of the zodiac are designated according to the constellations of stars which they contain. Already in the Babylonian epic of creation we read of the work of Marduk:

> He constructed stations for the great gods,
> Fixing their astral likenesses as constellations.
> He determined the year by designating the zones:
> He set up three constellations for each of the
> twelve months.[9]

⟪ 36.   Later a single constellation was taken as the sign of each of the twelve parts of the zodiac. In the tractate Berakoth[10] of the Talmud, the "Sovereign of the Universe" says: "Twelve constellations have I created in the firmament, and for each constellation I have created thirty hosts, and for each host I have created thirty legions, and for each legion I have created thirty cohorts, and for each cohort I have created thirty maniples,[11] and for each maniple I have created thirty camps, and to each camp I have attached three hundred and sixty-five thousands of myriads of stars, corresponding to the days of the solar year." In the Sefer Yeṣirah, a Jewish work of unknown antiquity, the names of the constellations are given as follows:[12] Taleh, Shor, Te'omin, Sarṭan, Aryeh, Betulah, Moznayim, 'Aqrab, Qeshet, Gedi, Deli, and Dagim. The Greek names, as found in Hipparchus, were as follows, the Latin forms and the meanings also being given: (1) ὁ Κριός, Aries, the Ram; (2) ὁ Ταῦρος, Taurus, the Bull; (3) οἱ Δίδυμοι, Gemini, the Twins; (4) ὁ Καρκίνος, Cancer, the Crab; (5) ὁ Λέων, Leo, the Lion; (6) ἡ Παρθένος, Virgo, the Virgin; (7) αἱ Χηλαί, Libra, the Balance; (8)

[8] F. von Oefele in HERE XII, p.51.
[9] ANET p.67.   [10] 32b; SBT p.201.
[11] Like the other terms, a subdivision of the Roman military organization.
[12] JE XII, p.688.

ὁ Σκορπίος, Scorpio, the Scorpion; (9) ὁ Τοξότης, Sagittarius, the Archer; (10) ὁ Ἀιγόκερως, Capricornus, the Goat; (11) ὁ Ὑδροχόος, Aquarius, the Water Carrier; (12) οἱ Ἰχθύες, Pisces, the Fishes. Since most of these were animals, from the word ζῴδιον, "a little animal," the entire zone was called ὁ ζῳδιακὸς κύκλος,[13] the zodiacal circle, or zodiac.

B. CALENDARS

1. THE EGYPTIAN CALENDAR

LITERATURE: Eduard Meyer, *Aegyptische Chronologie.* Abhandlungen der königlich preussischen Akademie der Wissenschaften. 1904, Philosophisch-historische Classe, pp.1-212; *Nachträge zur ägyptischen Chronologie, ibid.* 1907, pp.1-46; Ed. Mahler, *Études sur le calendrier Égyptien.* Annales du Musée Guimet, Bibliothèque d'Études, 24. 1907, pp.1-135; Ludwig Borchardt, *Die Annalen und die zeitliche Festlegung des Alten Reiches der ägyptischen Geschichte.* 1917; Ludwig Borchardt, *Die altägyptische Zeitmessung.* 1920; O. Neugebauer, "The Origin of the Egyptian Calendar," in JNES 1 (1942), pp.396-403; Richard A. Parker, *The Calendars of Ancient Egypt.* SAOC 26, 1950 (=PCAE).

([37.   In ancient Egypt the year was divided into three seasons. The first was called Akhet or "Inundation" and was the time when the Nile rose and overflowed the fields. The second was Peroyet or "Coming-Forth" when the fields emerged again from the flood waters and seeding, tilling, growth, and harvest took place. The third was Shomu or "Deficiency" and was the season of low water which came after the harvest and before the next inundation.[1] The recognition of these seasons, based upon climatic and agricultural factors, was undoubtedly very old.

([38.   Astronomical factors were also soon recognized, and it was noticed that each of the agricultural seasons comprised approximately four lunar months. At an early time the year probably started with the lunar month which began after the river began to rise. The rise of the river normally began at Aswan in late May or early June, and was about ten days later at Memphis. Coming thus in the summer, the period of the great inundation included the time of the

[13] Hipparchus I, vi, 4. ed. Manitius, p.56.

[1] Henri Frankfort, *Kingship and the Gods.* An Oriental Institute Essay. 1948, p.367 n.3; PCAE p.32.

summer solstice. At about the same time another celestial phenomenon took place which also attracted attention in Egypt at an early date. This was the annual heliacal rising or first reappearance at sunrise of the star Sirius. Sirius is the brightest star in the heavens, and was known as Sothis in the Greek spelling of its Egyptian name, and also as Canicula, the Dog Star. The length of the year from heliacal rising to heliacal rising of Sirius was very close to the length of the solar year which, as we have seen (¶33), is now calculated as 365.24219879 days. In Table 5 the length of the Sirius-year is shown at several intervals.

TABLE 5. The Length of the Sirius-Year

Sirius-year	Length in Days
4231 B.C.	365.2498352
3231	365.2500000
2231	365.2502291
1231	365.2505225
231	365.2508804
A.D. 770	365.2513026

Thus in 3231 B.C. the Sirius-year was 365¼ days in length, exactly the same as the value taken for the Julian year (¶144), and it became longer only very slowly. In terms of the Julian calendar, the reappearance of Sirius at dawn in the latitude of Memphis fell on Jul 19 from the fifth millennium to the second half of the first millennium B.C.—i.e., throughout the whole course of ancient Egyptian history—and then gradually moved to Jul 20. In the same period of four thousand years, from 4231 to 231 B.C., in which the heliacal rising of Sirius moved later by one day in comparison with the Julian year, the summer solstice on the other hand moved thirty-one days earlier in the Julian year, namely from Jul 28 in the year 4231 to Jun 27 in the year 231 B.C. In accordance with these changes, the summer solstice took place in Memphis in the forty-third century (4300-4201) B.C. nine days after the heliacal rising of Sirius; in the thirty-first century (3100-3001) B.C., on the same day, i.e., on Jul 19; and in each century thereafter fell back another eighteen and two-thirds hours.[2] Thus if the great summer inundation was originally taken as signaling the beginning of a new year

[2] Meyer, *Aegyptische Chronologie*, pp.14-15, 23.

in an agriculturally oriented reckoning, these two celestial events which fell within the same period, the summer solstice, and the heliacal rising of Sirius which was at one time exactly coincident therewith, were available to provide a more precise point of beginning in an astronomically oriented reckoning. Since the reappearance of Sirius at sunrise was the more readily observable event, it is probable that this was what was first utilized. In fact an inscription of the First Dynasty probably reads: "Sothis, the opener of the year; the inundation."[3] Since the event of the heliacal rising had the remarkable stability which we have noted, it provided a fixed point of reference for a very long time, as we shall see (¶¶41, 45-48).

(1) THE THREE CALENDARS

¶ 39. Since the year was composed of lunar months the calendar whose probable origins have just been described may be called a lunar calendar; since the beginning of the year was fixed by reference to a star, it may be described more specifically as a luni-stellar calendar. A year composed of twelve lunar months, ordinarily alternating between twenty-nine and thirty days in length, makes 354 days, which is approximately eleven days short of the solar year. To keep the calendar year beginning in the spring in general and at the time of the heliacal rising of Sothis in particular, it must have been necessary to insert an additional month every three years or so. It seems that when this occurred, the intercalary month was put at the head of the new lunar year. This, it is believed, was the original lunar calendar of Egypt, and it was probably still in use in the Proto-dynastic period.[1]

¶ 40. Whether it was by averaging a series of these lunar years or by counting the days between successive heliacal risings of Sothis, it was also established that the true length of the year to the nearest number of days was 365. The disadvantages of a year composed now of twelve and again of thirteen lunar months must have been evident, and with the recognition of the year's length as 365 days the possibility of a new system emerged. After the analogy of the lunar system the year was still divided into three seasons and twelve

[3] PCAE pp.32, 34, 74 n.22.

[1] PCAE pp.30-50, 53.

months, but for the sake of simplicity and regularity each month
was made thirty days in length. This left a shortage of only five
days and, after the example of the intercalated month at the beginning of the lunar year, five epagomenal days were inserted before the new year. Since the months were no longer kept in relationship to the real moon but were fixed units in the solar year instead, this may be recognized as essentially a solar calendar, and
since the units have an artificial regularity it may be called a
"schematic" calendar. This system was introduced, there is reason
to believe, between c.2937 and c.2821 B.C. and from then on served
as the standard civil calendar of Egypt.[2]

【 41.   The civil calendar of 365 days was still, however, not in
exact agreement with the solar year since the latter is actually closer
to 365¼ days in length. At the outset, it may be assumed, the first
day of the civil year coincided with the heliacal rising of Sothis.
After four years it would begin on the day before the rising of
Sothis, after eight years, two days before, and so on. Only after
1,460 years, therefore, would the beginning of the civil year have
moved all the way around the cycle to coincide once again with
the rising of Sothis. Since the original lunar calendar was periodically corrected to keep its beginning point in connection with the
heliacal rising of Sothis, the civil calendar gradually diverged more
and more from the lunar calendar. It is assumed that this divergence
would have become apparent by say 2500 B.C., and that around that
time a second lunar calendar was introduced which was thereafter
maintained in substantial harmony with the civil year. Thus from
that time on, Egypt actually had no less than three calendars and
three calendar years, and all of these continued in use throughout
the remainder of ancient Egyptian history.[3] From here on we are
chiefly concerned with the standard civil calendar.

(2) THE MONTHS

【 42.   From early times the designation of the months of the Egyptian year was by number as, e.g., on the Palermo Stone, "Fourth

[2] PCAE p.53. This Egyptian calendar consisting of twelve months of thirty days
each and five additional days at the end of each year has been called by O. Neugebauer (*The Exact Sciences in Antiquity*. 1952, p.81) "the only intelligent calendar
which ever existed in human history."
[3] PCAE pp.54, 56.

month, thirteenth day";[1] or by number within one of the three seasons as, e.g., on a stela of Thutmose III, "Second month of the second season, tenth day."[2]

❨ 43. The months were also given names, however, and in the Hellenistic and Roman periods these appear in Greek as shown in Table 6.

TABLE 6. THE GREEK NAMES OF THE EGYPTIAN MONTHS

1.	Θώθ	Thoth	7.	Φαμενώθ	Phamenoth
2.	Φαῶφι	Phaophi	8.	Φαρμοῦθι	Pharmuthi
3.	Ἀθύρ	Hathyr	9.	Παχών	Pachon
4.	Χοίακ	Choiak	10.	Παῦνι	Pauni (or Payni)
5.	Τῦβι	Tybi	11.	Ἐπείφ	Epeiph
6.	Μεχείρ	Mecheir	12.	Μεσορή	Mesore
				ἐπαγόμεναι ἥμεραι	Epagomenal days

❨ 44. The preceding tabulation represents the year as beginning with the month Thoth, with Thoth 1 as New Year's day, which was the usual reckoning. There was also a reckoning from Mecheir 1. The latter is encountered in the papyri where it is indicated as ὡς αἱ πρόσοδοι. ἡ πρόσοδος means "a going to" and is used, mostly in the plural αἱ πρόσοδοι, for "the public revenues." Hence ὡς αἱ πρόσοδοι means "according to the financial calendar." It was also possible to date from a given point in the king's reign and examples are found, varying from reign to reign, so the reference point probably represented the anniversary of the king's accession.[3] From here on we shall be chiefly concerned with the year beginning Thoth 1. The standard civil calendar beginning Thoth 1 is found, however, in two forms, the earlier form with a shifting year, the later form with a fixed year.

(3) THE STANDARD CIVIL CALENDAR
WITH A SHIFTING YEAR

❨ 45. In accordance with the nature of the standard civil calendar (¶40), the months listed above had each thirty days, and the five

[1] ARE I, §93.   [2] ANET p.234.
[3] Campbell C. Edgar, *Zenon Papyri in the University of Michigan Collection.* 1931, p.50.

days inserted before the beginning of the new year made a total year length of 365 days. Since the total was one-fourth day short of the solar year, in four years the calendar fell back one whole day (¶41). This means that in each four years Thoth 1 fell one day earlier. The equivalents in Table 7, for example, have been established in the Ptolemaic period:

TABLE 7. DATES OF THOTH 1 IN THE PTOLEMAIC PERIOD

Under Ptolemy I Soter

305-302 B.C.	Thoth 1 = Nov 7
301-298	Thoth 1 = Nov 6
297-294	Thoth 1 = Nov 5
etc.	

Under Ptolemy II Philadelphus

285-282	Thoth 1 = Nov 2
281-278	Thoth 1 = Nov 1
277-274	Thoth 1 = Oct 31
etc.	

Under Ptolemy III Euergetes

245-242	Thoth 1 = Oct 23
241-238	Thoth 1 = Oct 22
237-234	Thoth 1 = Oct 21
etc.[1]	

Likewise, as already noted (¶41), in 1460 years as measured by the heliacal risings of Sirius Thoth 1 would move back 365 days and, supposing it coincided in the first year of such a period with the annual heliacal rising of Sirius, it would only after those 1460 years again so coincide. This period, which we may call a Sothic cycle, would be measured, it is evident, in terms of Julian years as comprising 1460 years, but in terms of the shorter Egyptian year as comprising 1461 years.

〖 46.   The shifting or wandering year (*Wandeljahr*) just described and the long Sothic cycle through which it moved continued to be observed for a long time. A clear statement of how the Egyptian civil year (*annus civilis*) is not related to the moon, has 365 days,

[1] A. Bouché-Leclercq, *Histoire des Lagides* (4 vols. 1903-7), III, pp.384-407.

and moves to a fresh beginning in 1461 years, is given by Censorinus, who also says that this Sothic period is called a "great year" (*annus magnus*) or "year pertaining to the Dog Star" (*annus canicularis* or κυνικός).[2] Writing in A.D. 238 he says[3] that in that year the Egyptian Thoth 1 fell on VII Kal. Iul. = Jun 25 (for such dates see below ¶141), and that one hundred years before when Antoninus Pius was consul for the second time along with Bruttius Praesens, i.e., in A.D. 139 (for dating by consuls see below ¶¶172ff.), it fell on XII Kal. Aug = Jul 21, a reference probably to be corrected to XIII Kal. Aug = Jul 20 which would agree with the date of the heliacal rising of Sirius in that period (¶38). Thus the year beginning Thoth 1 = Jul 20, A.D. 139 was evidently the first year of a new Sothic cycle. Counting forward from 139/140 as the first year, the year 238/239 was in fact the one hundredth year, and in the one hundred years the beginning of the calendar year had moved twenty-five days from July 20 to June 25. Counting backward 1460 years from 139/140 A.D., the first year of the preceding Sothic cycle would have been the year from Jul 19, 1321, to Jul 18, 1320 B.C., and similar cyclic points prior to that would have been 2781/2780 and 4241/4240 B.C.[4]

¶47. The Sothic cycle whose first year was Jul 19, 1321, to Jul 18, 1320 B.C., is probably also attested by Theon who wrote in the fourth century A.D. Expressly using the Egyptian shifting year, Theon reckons 1605 years "from Menophres" (ἀπὸ Μενόφρεως) to the end of the era of Augustus. The era of Diocletian began on Aug 29, A.D. 284 and the last year of the Augustan era was accordingly 283/284. One thousand six hundred and five of the shorter shifting Egyptian years are equal to 1604 Julian years less thirty-six days; and 1604 years before A.D. 283/284 brings us back to 1321/1320 B.C. Thus the reckoning "from Menophres" is probably the same as the reckoning from the Sothic period which began in 1321/1320 B.C. As for the name Menophres (Μενόφρης), it may be possible to recognize in it the prenomen of Ramses I, read as *Mn-ph-rʿ*. If this is the correct identification, the date 1321/1320 should fall in the reign of Ramses I. The accession of the famous

[2] XVIII, 10. *Censorini de die natali liber*, ed. F. Hultsch. 1867, p.38.
[3] XXI, 10. ed. Hultsch, p.46.
[4] Meyer, *Aegyptische Chronologie*, pp.23-29.

Ramses II is now probably to be put in 1304 B.C.[5] In the reign of his predecessor, Seti I, regnal years up to nine in number are attested and he probably reigned longer than that. Prior to him, Ramses I probably reigned about two years. The first year of this Sothic cycle and the year from which Theon counted "from Menophres" could well fall within the reign of Ramses I.[6]

¶ 48.   There is also a reference to the Sothic cycle in Clement of Alexandria where he says that Moses went forth from Egypt three hundred and forty-five years before the Sothic period (πρὸ τῆς Σωθιακῆς περιόδου).[7] After this, dates are given out of Greek legendary history down to the first year of the first Olympiad, and if these figures were intact and complete it would again be possible to make a calculation relative to the Sothic date, but since they probably are not this need not be considered further.[8]

(4) THE STANDARD CIVIL CALENDAR WITH A FIXED YEAR

¶ 49.   In contrast to this "wandering" year which existed for so long in the standard civil calendar of Egypt, we turn to what is known as the fixed Alexandrian year, which finally prevailed. In 22 B.C. Augustus introduced the Julian calendar (¶¶143f.) into Egypt and reformed the Egyptian calendar to bring it into harmony therewith. Every fourth year, in the year preceding the leap year of the Julian calendar—i.e., in A.D. 3/4, 7/8, etc.—a sixth epagomenal day was added in the Egyptian calendar. With this stabilization, the first day of Thoth was kept permanently on Aug 29 (where it fell at the time of the reform), except in the intercalary year when the addition of the sixth epagomenal day put Thoth 1 on Aug 30 and put each succeeding day through Phamenoth 4 = Feb 29 one day later than in the common years. After the intercalary year the calendar returns to its normal relation, and always Phamenoth 5 = Mar 1.[1] Table 8 shows this fixed Egyptian calendar, with the number of

[5] Richard A. Parker in JNES 16 (1957), pp.39-43; M. B. Rowton in JCS 13 (1959), pp.8-9; JNES 19 (1960), pp.15-22.
[6] Jaroslav Černý in JEA 47 (1961), pp.150-152.
[7] Stromata. I, 21, 136.
[8] Meyer, Aegyptische Chronologie, p.30.

[1] George Milligan, Selections from the Greek Papyri. 1910, p.xviii; Bernard P. Grenfell and Arthur S. Hunt, OP XII, p.291; cf. T. C. Skeat in Mizraim. 6 (1937), p.21, who says wrongly, I think, that Phamenoth 6 always equals Mar 1.

days in the Egyptian months and the equivalent Julian dates for the months both in an Egyptian common year and in an Egyptian intercalary year. At the point of the transition from the portion of the calendar affected by the intercalary year to the part following, the presentation is amplified to show the details of the change.

TABLE 8. THE EGYPTIAN CIVIL CALENDAR WITH THE FIXED YEAR

MONTH	NUMBER OF DAYS		JULIAN DATES	
	Common Year	Intercalary Year	Common Year	Intercalary Year
1. Thoth	30	30	Aug 29-Sep 27	Aug 30-Sep 28
2. Phaophi	30	30	Sep 28-Oct 27	Sep 29-Oct 28
3. Hathyr	30	30	Oct 28-Nov 26	Oct 29-Nov 27
4. Choiak	30	30	Nov 27-Dec 26	Nov 28-Dec 27
5. Tybi	30	30	Dec 27-Jan 25	Dec 28-Jan 26
6. Mecheir	30	30	Jan 26-Feb 24	Jan 27-Feb 25
7. Phamenoth	30	30	Feb 25-Mar 26	Feb 26-Mar 26
		Phamenoth 1 = Feb 25	Feb 26	
		Phamenoth 4 = Feb 28	Feb 29	
		Phamenoth 5 = Mar 1	Mar 1	
		Phamenoth 30 = Mar 26	Mar 26	
8. Pharmuthi	30	30	Mar 27-Apr 25	Mar 27-Apr 25
9. Pachon	30	30	Apr 26-May 25	Apr 26-May 25
10. Pauni	30	30	May 26-Jun 24	May 26-Jun 24
11. Epeiph	30	30	Jun 25-Jul 24	Jun 25-Jul 24
12. Mesore	30	30	Jul 25-Aug 23	Jul 25-Aug 23
Epagomenal days	5	6	Aug 24-Aug 28	Aug 24-Aug 29

2. THE BABYLONIAN CALENDAR

LITERATURE: Richard A. Parker and Waldo H. Dubberstein, *Babylonian Chronology 626 B.C.-A.D. 75*. Brown University Studies XIX. 1956 (=PDBC).

⟪50. In Mesopotamia also there was a lunar, or more strictly a lunisolar calendar. The moon-god was very prominent in Mesopotamia,[1] and observation of the moon no doubt began very early.

[1] The moon-god was known as Nanna to the Sumerians (ANET p.38), and as Sin to the Akkadians (ANET p.88). Sin was the son of the air-god Enlil, the husband of the goddess Ningal, and they were the parents of the sun-god Shamash (ANET p.164 n.10; p.400 n.3). Sin was called "the lamp of heaven and earth" (ANET p.390), and he was worshiped specially at the temple of Egishnugal in Ur (ANET p.164). The crescent which is his symbol is familiar in Mesopotamian art (ANEP Nos.453, 518, etc.), and the god himself may be represented on the cylinder seal

As based upon the sighting of the new moon, the months were usually alternately twenty-nine and thirty days in length, although sometimes months of the same length in days would come in sequence, and occasionally there seems even to have been a month of twenty-eight days, which is explained on the supposition that two months of twenty-nine days had come together but bad visibility had prevented the seeing of the crescent and the first month had been erroneously assigned thirty days. Whether the months were eventually determined by calculation instead of visual observation is not known.[2]

〖 51.   Twelve lunar months constituted the year, and the year began in the spring. The list in Table 9 gives the months in order together with their approximate equivalents in our calendar:[3]

TABLE 9. THE BABYLONIAN CALENDAR

1. Nisanu	Mar/Apr	7. Tashritu	Sep/Oct
2. Aiaru	Apr/May	8. Arahsamnu	Oct/Nov
3. Simanu	May/Jun	9. Kislimu	Nov/Dec
4. Duzu	Jun/Jul	10. Tebetu	Dec/Jan
5. Abu	Jul/Aug	11. Shabatu	Jan/Feb
6. Ululu	Aug/Sep	12. Addaru	Feb/Mar

〖 52.   Twelve lunar months fell of course approximately eleven days short of the solar year. At first the rectification of this discrepancy may have been made by simply taking the month which began nearest the vernal equinox as the first month of the new year. Later the method of intercalating an additional month as necessary was employed. This system was developed by the Sumerians and Babylonians and was adopted by the Assyrians probably by the time of Tiglath-pileser I (c.1114-c.1076 B.C.).[4]

〖 53.   By the eighth century B.C. there is evidence that it was recognized in Babylonia that the insertion of seven additional lunar months within a nineteen-year period would closely approximate

of an official of King Ur-Nammu of Ur (Hugo Gressmann, *Altorientalische Bilder zum Alten Testament*. 2d ed. [1927], fig. 323).

  [2] PDBC p.3.   [3] PDBC p.26.

  [4] P. van der Meer, *The Ancient Chronology of Western Asia and Egypt*. 1947, pp.1f.

the additional time needed to stabilize the calendar. By the fourth century B.C. fixed points were established for these seven intercalations, and the nineteen-year cycle was fully standardized. The months added were a second Ululu, the sixth month, or a second Addaru, the twelfth month.[5]

❲54.   Since new-moon dates can be calculated astronomically for ancient Babylonia, and since the system of intercalation has been reconstructed on the basis of intercalary months actually mentioned in cuneiform texts, it is possible to construct tables which represent the Babylonian calendar with a high degree of probable accuracy.[6]

❲55.   The achievement of the ancient Babylonian astronomers in devising the nineteen year cycle with its seven intercalated months was indeed remarkable. It has been noted above that one solar year equals 365.24219879 days while one lunar month equals 29.530588 days. Nineteen solar years, therefore, equals 6939.601777 days. In 19 12-month years there are 228 months; adding 7 more months makes a total of 235 months. Two hundred thirty-five lunar months equals 6939.688180 days. Thus, the difference between 235 lunar months and 19 solar years is only .086403 day or 2 hours, 4 minutes, 25.22 seconds. This is how close the ancient Babylonian system came to solving the problem of the relationship between the lunar year and the solar year.[7]

❲56.   How the system worked in actual practice may be seen in the accompanying tabulation (Table 10). This shows the first nineteen years of the reign of Nebuchadrezzar II (604-562 B.C.). The years are numbered and their equivalents in terms of B.C. are given; leap years are indicated by italicizing the last figure of the year when first given. The month names are abbreviated; U II and A II mean a second Ululu and a second Addaru respectively where these are intercalated. From the source table,[8] which shows the first day of each month in terms of our Julian calendar, the number of days in each month is counted and it is this figure which is shown for each month. The total number of days for the nineteen years is

TABLE 10. THE FIRST NINETEEN YEARS OF REIGN OF NEBUCHADREZZAR II

Yr.	B.C.	Nis	Aia	Sim	Duz	Abu	Ulu	U II	Tas	Ara	Kis	B.C.	Teb	B.C.	Sha	Add	A II	Days in Ye
1	604	29	29	30	29	30	30		29	30	30		30	603	29	29		3
2	603	30	29	29	29	30	30	30	29	30	30	602	29		30	29		3
3	602	30	29	29	30	29	30		30	29	30	601	29		30	30		3
4	601	29	30	29	29	30	29		30	30	29		30	600	29	30		3
5	600	29	30	29	30	29	30	28	30	30	30	599	29		29	30		3
6	599	30	30	29	30	30	29		30	29	29		30	598	29	30		3
7	598	29	30	29	30	30	30	29	30	29	29	597	30		29	29		3
8	597	30	29	30	30	30	30		29	29	30	596	29		30	29		3
9	596	29	30	29	30	30	30	30	29	29	30	595	29		30	29		3
10	595	29	30	29	30	30	29		30	30	29	594	30		29	30		3
11	594	29	29	30	29	30	30		29	30	29	593	30		30	29	30	3
12	593	29	29	30	29	30	29		30	29	30	592	30		30	29		3
13	592	30	29	30	29	29	30		29	29	30	591	30		30	29		3
14	591	30	30	29	30	29	29		30	29	29		30	590	30	29	30	3
15	590	30	29	30	29	30	29		30	29	30	589	29		29	30		3
16	589	30	29	30	29	30	30		29	30	29	588	30		29	29		3
17	588	30	29	30	29	30	30		30	29	30		29	587	30	29	29	3
18	587	30	29	30	29	30	30		30	29	30	586	29		30	29		3
19	586	29	30	29	29	30	30		30	30	29	585	30		29	30		3
																Total		69

6940; this is the nearest full number to the exact figure already noted above of 6939.601777 days.

❰ 57. In Egypt we saw that the complexity of the original lunar calendar led to the introduction of a simplified civil calendar with twelve months of thirty days each plus five additional days prior to the new year. In Mesopotamia, too, there was a second calendar of exactly this same sort which was used alongside the real lunar calendar. Since its twelve months of thirty days each, running on in regular sequence regardless of the real moon, were really standardized divisions of the solar year, this was a solar calendar or a "schematic calendar." In Babylonian documents many dates have been found which are evidently given in this schematic calendar, and in some cases it is not possible to prove whether it is the schematic calendar or the real lunar calendar which is intended. But whereas the schematic calendar became the generally used civil calendar in Egypt, in Babylonia it seems to have been the lunar calendar which remained in most general usage, and Mesopotamia has properly been called "the classical country of the strictly lunar calendar."[9]

3. THE ISRAELITE CALENDAR

LITERATURE: Julian Morgenstern, "The Three Calendars of Ancient Israel," in HUCA 1 (1924), pp.13-78; Morgenstern, "Supplementary Studies in the Calendars of Ancient Israel," in HUCA 10 (1935), pp.1-148; Morgenstern, "The New Year for Kings," in *Occident and Orient, Gaster Anniversary Volume*, ed. Bruno Schindler, 1936, pp.439-456; Morgenstern, "The Chanukkah Festival and the Calendar of Ancient Israel," in HUCA 20 (1947), pp.1-136; 21 (1948), pp.365-496; J. B. Segal, "Intercalation and the Hebrew Calendar," in VT 7 (1957), pp.250-307.

〔58. The Gezer Calendar is a small limestone tablet, about four inches long and three inches wide, found at Tell Jezer in Palestine, the probable site of the Old Testament city of Gezer (Jg 1:29, etc.). On it is written, in good biblical Hebrew and perhaps simply as a schoolboy's exercise, a list of the months and the agricultural work done in them. The date of the text is probably around 925 B.C. It reads:

> His two months are (olive) harvest,
> His two months are planting (grain),
> His two months are late planting;
> His month is hoeing up of flax,
> His month is harvest of barley,
> His month is harvest and feasting.
> His two months are vine-tending,
> His month is summer fruit.[1]

The word used for "month" is ירח, and the months are obviously grouped and designated according to the type of agricultural work done in them. Since the agricultural seasons in Palestine are well known (¶31), including the ripening of the olive crop in Sep/Oct-Oct/Nov, the shooting into ear of the barley in Mar/Apr, and the subsequent barley harvest in Apr/May,[2] it is possible to tabulate the sequence of months in the Gezer Calendar together with their equivalents in the outline of the year in Table 11 on page 34.

---

[9] O. Neugebauer in JNES 1 (1942), pp.398-401.

[1] W. F. Albright in ANET p.320 (ANEA pp.209f.); cf. BASOR 92 (Dec 1943), pp.16-20; Sabatino Moscati, *L'epigrafia ebraica antica 1935-1950*. 1951, pp.8-26.
[2] The harvest of barley begins in the Jordan Valley about the middle of April and in the highlands up to a month later. J. W. Paterson in HDB I, p.49.

TABLE 11. THE MONTHS OF THE GEZER CALENDAR

1.	2 months	olive harvest	Sept/Oct
2.			Oct/Nov
3.	2 months	planting grain	Nov/Dec
4.			Dec/Jan
5.	2 months	late planting	Jan/Feb
6.			Feb/Mar
7.	1 month	hoeing flax	Mar/Apr
8.	1 month	harvest of barley	Apr/May
9.	1 month	harvest and festivity	May/Jun
10.	2 months	vine tending	Jun/Jul
11.			Jul/Aug
12.	1 month	summer fruit	Aug/Sep

We see, therefore, that at this time in Palestine the year was reckoned as beginning in the fall, and that it contained twelve months which were related to agriculture.

《 59.   Turning to the Old Testament we find first a group of month names which are connected with agriculture and climate. There are four of these as follows: (1) The month Abib.[3] This word means a "fresh ear" of grain, as in Lev 2:14, and is used of barley when it is "in the ear," as in Ex 9:31; hence used as a month name and with the article, "the Abib," it refers to the period when the barley shoots into ear. (2) The month Ziv.[4] This term signifies "splendor" and is used of the "beauty of flowers"; hence the month name refers to the time of flowers. (3) The month Ethanim.[5] Coming from a word which means "permanent," this term is used in the plural and with the article as a month name which refers to "the permanent streams." (4) The month Bul.[6] The word probably refers to a period of "rain." Of these words both Ethanim and Bul have also been found as month names in North Semitic inscriptions,[7]

[3] חדש האביב, Ex 13:4; 23:15; 34:18; Dt 16:1.
[4] חדש זו, I K 6:1; ירח זו, I K 6:37.
[5] ירח האתנים, I K 8:2.   [6] ירח בול, I K 6:38.
[7] Mark Lidzbarski, *Handbuch der nordsemitischen Epigraphik nebst ausgewählten Inschriften.* I (1898), pp.231, 236, 412. According to a very recent report, one more early month name has just been discovered. An ink inscription on a clay jar found at Arad, to be dated at the beginning of the sixth century B.C., mentions the third day of the month of Tsach (ṣaḥ). This makes it possible to recognize that this month name occurs in Is 18:4 where the phrase כחם צח, formerly translated "like clear heat" (RSV), may now be rendered, "like the heat of the month of Tsach." Since the word is evidently connected with heat, Tsach must be one of the summer months. PEQ Jan-Jun 1963, pp.3-4.

hence these names, and probably others like them for other months, were no doubt common property among various Semitic peoples in this part of the world. We may call them the Canaanite month names.

⟨ 60. Since Abib is, by the etymology of the name, the month when the barley shoots into the ear, we know that it must have been approximately equivalent to Mar/Apr (¶31), and it may therefore be equated with the seventh month in the list of the Gezer Calendar. According to Dt 16:1 Abib is the month of the passover, and according to Ex 12:2f. the passover is held in the first month. This manner of reference makes Abib the first month rather than the seventh, and must simply represent a time when the year was reckoned as beginning in the spring rather than the fall and when the months were numbered from the spring. Similarly Ziv, the month of flowers, must be a spring month, and in I K 6:1 its name is followed by the explanation, "which is the second month." Likewise Bul, the month of rain, must be the month of "early rain" or Oct/Nov (¶31), and it is called the eighth month in I K 6:38. Ethanim, too, is named as the seventh month in I K 8:2. Showing, then, the months numbered both from the fall and from the spring, the Canaanite month names fit into the calendar as shown in Table 12:

TABLE 12. THE CANAANITE MONTH NAMES

1	7	Ethanim	Sep/Oct
2	8	Bul	Oct/Nov
3	9		Nov/Dec
4	10		Dec/Jan
5	11		Jan/Feb
6	12		Feb/Mar
7	1	Abib	Mar/Apr
8	2	Ziv	Apr/May
9	3		May/Jun
10	4		Jun/Jul
11	5		Jul/Aug
12	6		Aug/Sep

⟨ 61. It is perhaps not without significance that it is precisely the first two months of the fall and the first two of the spring of which the names are preserved in the Old Testament. These are not only

[35]

times of special importance in Palestinian agriculture but also the times of the two equinoxes. It will also be remembered (¶11) that in the early period the day was probably reckoned from the morning. These facts suggest that the orientation of this calendar was primarily toward the sun: the rising of the sun began the day; the equinoxes were the turning points of the year. If this was the case then, in the lack of other evidence, the guess may be hazarded that the months were not tied closely to the phases of the moon but were units of the solar year, probably thirty days in length, as in the "schematic" calendars of Egypt and Mesopotamia, and that the resultant shortage of about five days was simply made up by the insertion of additional days at the end of the year.[8]

⟨ 62.   The supposition is, therefore, that the Israelite calendar was originally agricultural and that as it was harmonized more accurately with the movements of the celestial bodies it was primarily the relationship to the sun that was kept in view. In this period both Egyptian and Phoenician influences were strong in Israel, and both would be expected to have contributed to the solar emphasis. As far as Egypt is concerned, this was the great power which cast its shadow over Palestine until the defeat of Pharaoh Necho by Nebuchadrezzar in 605 B.C. In Egypt the sun was very prominent, as evidenced by the numerous sun deities in the pantheon, and a schematic solar calendar was the standard civil calendar (¶40).

⟨ 63.   As far as Phoenicia is concerned, we know that Solomon, who reigned shortly before the time ascribed to the Gezer Calendar, entered into close relationships with Hiram, King of Tyre, particularly for help in the building of the temple at Jerusalem (I K 5, etc.). According to Josephus,[9] Hiram built new temples to Astarte and Herakles, which suggests interest in the celestial bodies particularly including the sun, since Astarte was generally associated with the planet Venus or with the moon, and Herakles was connected with the sun especially in Phoenicia. According to Porphyry (A.D. 233-c.304) who was born in Phoenicia, probably at Tyre, the Phoenicians gave the name of Herakles to the sun and considered the

----

[8] In his study of intercalation and the Hebrew calendar (in vt 7 [1957], pp.250-307), J. B. Segal adduces evidence to show that intercalation was already practiced in Israel in the early days of the monarchy (ibid., p.259).

[9] Against Apion. I, 18; Ant VIII, 146 (=VIII, v, 3).

twelve labors of Herakles to represent the passage of the sun through the twelve signs of the zodiac.[10]

《 64. At Jerusalem the temple which Hiram helped Solomon to build may have been so constructed that the sun shone directly in through its eastern gate on the two equinoctial days of the year,[11] and we find that later Josiah "removed the horses that the kings of Judah had dedicated to the sun, at the entrance to the house of the Lord" and "burned the chariots of the sun with fire" (II K 23:11), and that again in Ezekiel's time men stood at the door of the temple, "with their backs to the temple of the Lord, and their faces toward the east, worshiping the sun toward the east" (Ezk 8:16). Therefore it seems entirely likely that at least from the time of Solomon and under the influence of Egypt and Phoenicia the calendar of Israel was a schematic solar calendar.[12]

4. THE BABYLONIAN CALENDAR IN PALESTINE

LITERATURE: Solomon Gandz, "Studies in the Hebrew Calendar," in *Proceedings of the American Academy for Jewish Research*. 17 (1947-48), pp.9-17; Gandz, "Studies in the Hebrew Calendar," in JQR 39 (1948-49), pp.259-280; 40 (1949-50), pp.157-172; 251-277; Gandz, "The Calendar of the *Seder Olam*," in JQR 43 (1952-53), pp.177-192; 249-270; Elias Auerbach, "Die babylonische Datierung im Pentateuch und das Alter des Priester-Kodex," in VT 2 (1952), pp.334-342.

《 65. In the foregoing discussion of the Israelite calendar it has been noted that the month names Abib, Ziv, Ethanim, and Bul appear in the Old Testament, that these are probably the old Canaanite designations, and that in some instances the occurrence of the names is followed by an explanatory statement indicating, for example, that Ziv is the second month, Ethanim the seventh month, and so on. These numerical equivalents look as if they were added to the records at a time when the old names were no longer so commonly employed and when a different system had come into use, namely a designation of the months by number alone. Such a system is actually found elsewhere in Kings (I 12:32, etc.), Jeremiah (1:3, etc.), Ezekiel (1:1, etc.), and many other books of the Old Testament,

---

[10] Quoted by Eusebius, *Praeparatio Evangelica*. III, xi, 25. ed. Karl Mras in GCS, Eusebius VIII, 1 (1954), pp.139f. Cf. Charles Anthon, *A Classical Dictionary*. 1843, p.599.

[11] Julian Morgenstern in HUCA 6 (1929), pp.16-19.

[12] Julian Morgenstern in VT 5 (1955), pp.67-69.

and all of the months from the first to the twelfth are so designated. Likewise in the majority of the apocryphal and pseudepigraphical writings the same system of indicating the months by number is followed.[1]

〖 66.   It has also been noted that in the earlier system the months were listed from the fall, but in the new system where the months are designated by number the numbering begins in the spring. In addition to evidence already cited, there is a plain example of the latter usage when Jer 36:9 mentions the ninth month and the following verse 22 indicates that it was in the winter: counting from the fall, the ninth month would be in the summer; counting from the spring, the ninth month would be in the winter.

〖 67.   The beginning of the year in the spring is in accordance with what we have seen was the usage in Mesopotamia, and it is therefore a reasonable surmise that the new calendrical system was derived from that source. The latest contemporary use of the old Canaanite names is probably in Dt 16:1.[2] The book of Deuteronomy is commonly supposed to have been edited in connection with the reformation of Josiah and found in the temple in 621 B.C. (II K 22:8).[3] The earliest citation in terms of the new system is probably that of the ninth month in the fifth year of Jehoiakim (604/603 B.C.) in Jer 36:9. According to this evidence, the new system was introduced in Judah between 621 and 604 B.C. In 605 B.C. Nebuchadrezzar defeated Necho (¶312), and Palestine passed from the sway of Egypt to the domination of Babylon. It may be concluded, accordingly, that it was at that time that the Babylonian way of reckoning was officially established in Palestine (¶315).[4]

〖 68.   That the new system of months numbered from a point of beginning in the spring was really the Babylonian system is shown by the fact that the Babylonian names for the months are also found later in the Old Testament. In a number of passages in Esther and Zechariah the month is cited first by number and then by name. The months which so appear are: "the first month, which is the month of Nisan" (Est 3:7); "the third month, which is the month

---

[1] Julian Morgenstern in HUCA 1 (1924), p.19.
[2] Morgenstern in HUCA 1 (1924), p.18.
[3] Robert H. Pfeiffer, *Introduction to the Old Testament*. 5th ed. 1941, p.181.
[4] Elias Auerbach in VT 2 (1952), p.336.

of Sivan" (Est 8:9); "the ninth month, which is Chislev" (Zec 7:1); "the tenth month, which is the month of Tebeth" (Est 2:16); "the eleventh month, which is the month of Shebat" (Zec 1:7); and "the twelfth month, which is the month of Adar" (Est 3:7, etc.). In Ezra and Nehemiah the month is sometimes referred to by number (Ezr 7:8, etc.; Neh 7:73, etc.), but in the following cases is cited by name alone: Nisan (Neh 2:1), Elul (Neh 6:15), Chislev (Neh 1:1); Adar (Ezr 6:15). The sources just cited are generally considered to be among the latest books in the Old Testament, and thus the use of these month names must have begun relatively late, perhaps from the fourth century B.C. on.[5] The first work in which only the Babylonian names are employed is probably Megillat Ta'anit, the "Scroll of Fasting." This is essentially a list, written probably just after the beginning of the first century A.D., of thirty-six Jewish festivals. The book is divided into twelve chapters, corresponding to the twelve months. The first chapter treats the memorial days of the first month, Nisan, and so on to the twelfth chapter which deals with those of the twelfth month, Adar.[6]

⟨ 69.   The fact that the numbering of the months according to the Babylonian system came into use among the Jews before the actual month names were adopted may indicate a complex evolution,[7] but would seem to be explicable most simply on the grounds that the numbers did not carry the associations of pagan religion which some of the names did. Thus the month Tammuz (Babylonian Duzu) bore the name of the famous dying god of Mesopotamia, wept by the women of Jerusalem to the distress of Ezekiel (8:14); and the month Elul may have meant "shouting for joy" in the celebration of the restoration to life of the same deity.[8]

⟨ 70.   As a result of the development just sketched, then, the list of months in use among the Jews at the end of the Old Testament period was as shown in Table 13 where the number, Babylonian name, Hebrew name, and approximate equivalent in our months are given:[9]

[5] Morgenstern in HUCA 1 (1924), p.20.
[6] Hans Lichtenstein in HUCA 8-9 (1931-32), pp.257-351; J. Z. Lauterbach in JE VIII, pp.427f.
[7] Morgenstern in HUCA 1 (1924), p.21.
[8] I. Abrahams in HDB IV, p.765.
[9] PDBC p.24.

TABLE 13. THE BABYLONIAN CALENDAR IN PALESTINE

Number	Babylonian Name	Hebrew Name		Approximate Equivalent
1.	Nisanu	ניסן	Nisan	Mar/Apr
2.	Aiaru	איר	Iyyar	Apr/May
3.	Simanu	סיון	Sivan	May/Jun
4.	Duzu	תמוז	Tammuz	Jun/Jul
5.	Abu	אב	Ab	Jul/Aug
6.	Ululu	אלול	Elul	Aug/Sep
7.	Tashritu	תשרי	Tishri	Sep/Oct
8.	Arahsamnu	מרחשון	Marheshvan, or Heshvan	Oct/Nov
9.	Kislimu	כסלו	Kislev	Nov/Dec
10.	Tebetu	טבת	Tebeth	Dec/Jan
11.	Shabatu	שבט	Shebat	Jan/Feb
12.	Addaru	אדר	Adar	Feb/Mar

⟨71.   The Babylonian calendar was, as we have seen, essentially lunisolar. The months began with the first appearing of the crescent of the new moon in the evening sky, and the intercalation of seven months in nineteen years kept the year of lunar months in close approximation to the solar year. The question which now arises is whether along with the Babylonian order and names of the months, the full Babylonian system of strictly lunar months and of the intercalation of months was also adopted? The sources which will next be cited show that in general this is what was done, but that there were some variations in Jewish practice from Babylonian.

⟨72.   In Palestine it was the responsibility of the Sanhedrin in Jerusalem to determine matters connected with the calendar, and in practice this was done by a council of three men.

⟨73.   As in Babylonia, the month began when the new moon was first seen in the evening, but since the new moon was visible at Jerusalem thirty-seven minutes before it was visible at Babylon, it was possible that upon occasion the new month would begin a day earlier than in Babylonia.[10] The determination that the new moon had actually appeared and the declaration that the new month had

---

[10] PDBC pp.23f.

thereby begun had to be made by the council just referred to, and
the rules according to which this was done are presented and discussed in the Talmud in the tractate Rosh Hashanah.[11] The testimony of at least two witnesses was required to establish that the
new moon had been seen. So important were the observations of
these witnesses that for the fixing of the new moons of Nisan and
Tishri, the pivotal points of the year in the spring and fall, they
might even exceed the travel limit of two thousand cubits on the
sabbath day to bring their report to Jerusalem.[12] In Jerusalem there
was a special courtyard where the witnesses were examined and
entertained. In earlier time if they came on the sabbath they could
not leave this place the whole day, because they had doubtless already used up their allowed travel distance, but Rabbi Gamaliel
the Elder ruled that they could go two thousand cubits from it.[13]
In the examination of the witnesses they were interrogated with
such questions as whether the moon had been seen to the north or
to the south of the sun. The point of this question lay in the fact that
the new moon always appears due west; hence in the summer when
the sun sets in the northwest the new moon is south of the sun, in
the winter it is north of the sun.[14] Rabbi Gamaliel II even had a
diagram of the phases of the moon on a tablet hung on the wall of
his upper chamber, and used this in questioning the witnesses.[15]

⟨ 74.   When it was determined that the new moon had been seen,
the beginning of the new month was proclaimed. On the scriptural
warrant of Lev 23:44 where "Moses declared . . . the appointed
feasts of the Lord," this was done by the solemn declaration of the
head of the Sanhedrin that the new moon was "sanctified."[16] Also
a trumpet was sounded,[17] as it is said in Ps 81:3, "Blow the trumpet
at the new moon." At one time flares were lighted also to signal the
new month, but when the Samaritans introduced confusion by light-
ing misleading flares, messengers were sent out instead.[18]

[11] I, 3-III, 1; 18a-25b; SBT pp.73-115; cf. *Sanhedrin.* I, 2; DM p.382.
[12] *Rosh Hashanah.* 19b; SBT p.81 n.4.
[13] *Rosh Hashanah.* II, 5; 23b; SBT p.101.
[14] *Rosh Hashanah.* II, 6; 23b-24a; SBT pp.102f.
[15] *Rosh Hashanah.* II, 8; 24a; SBT p.105.
[16] *Rosh Hashanah.* II, 7; 24a; SBT p.104.
[17] *Rosh Hashanah.* III, 3; 26a; SBT p.115.
[18] *Rosh Hashanah.* II, 2-4; 22b-23b; SBT pp.96-100.

⟨ 75. While it was considered "a religious duty to sanctify [the new moon] on the strength of actual observation,"[19] it was also recognized that conditions might be such that the actual visual sighting could not be made and in this case it was established that one month would have thirty days and the next twenty-nine. The month with twenty-nine days was considered "deficient" by half a day, the month with thirty days was "full," being half a day over the true lunar period. It was agreed that the year should not have less than five nor more than seven "full" months. At least in post-Talmudic times Nisan, Sivan, Ab, Tishri, Kislev, and Shebat had thirty days, and Iyyar, Tammuz, Elul, Heshvan, Tebeth, and Adar had twenty-nine. The science by which these determinations were made was known as the "fixing of the month" or as the "sanctification of the new moon."[20]

⟨ 76. In his work entitled *Sanctification of the New Moon,* Maimonides (A.D. 1135-1204) gives in Chapters I-V a description of the way in which the calendar was anciently regulated by the Sanhedrin, and in his description of the manner of determining the new moon he shows that calculation as well as observation was employed. Maimonides writes:[21]

> "Just as the astronomers who discern the positions and motions of the stars engage in calculation, so the Jewish court, too, used to study and investigate and perform mathematical operations, in order to find out whether or not it would be possible for the new crescent to be visible in its 'proper time,' which is the night of the 30th day. If the members of the court found that the new moon might be visible, they were obliged to be in attendance at the court house for the whole 30th day and be on the watch for the arrival of witnesses. If witnesses did arrive, they were duly examined and tested, and if their testimony appeared trustworthy, this day was sanctified as New Moon Day. If the new crescent did not appear and no witnesses arrived, this day was counted as the 30th day of the old month, which thus became an embolismic[22] month."

⟨ 77. It was also necessary for the same council of the Sanhedrin to determine when an intercalary month should be added to the year. There is a discussion of "the intercalating of the year" in the

[19] *Rosh Hashanah.* 20a; SBT p.81.
[20] JE III, pp.499f. (Cyrus Adler); 502f. (M. Friedländer).
[21] *The Code of Maimonides, Book Three, Treatise Eight, Sanctification of the New Moon,* tr. by Solomon Gandz, with introduction by Julian Obermann, and astronomical commentary by Otto Neugebauer (Yale Judaica Series, 11). 1956, pp.4f. (I, 6).
[22] That is, a month containing an added day.

tractate Sanhedrin.[23] Here in addition to mention of the council of three it is also stated that "A year cannot be intercalated unless the Nasi sanctions it."[24] The Nasi was the "prince" or chief of the Sanhedrin, and it would appear that he might or might not be a member of the council of three. An example is given where "Rabban Gamaliel was away obtaining permission from the Governor of Syria,[25] and, as his return was delayed, the year was intercalated subject to Rabban Gamaliel's later approval."[26]

(78.   The rabbis taught, it is stated, that "a year may be intercalated on three grounds: on account of the premature state of the corn crops; or that of the fruit trees; or on account of the lateness of the Tequfah. Any two of these reasons can justify intercalation, but not one alone."[27] The minute calculations involved are referred to, and an example is given where the rabbis did not finish their calculation until the last day of the month preceding the month to be intercalated.[28] In Babylonia, as we saw, either a second Ululu or a second Addaru might be inserted in the year, but here it is stated flatly that "only an Adar can be intercalated."[29] When the intercalation took place the added month was called the Second Adar.[30] The length of the added month was left to the judgment of the council, and it might be either twenty-nine or thirty days in length.[31]

(79.   In the same tractate letters are quoted which were sent out by Rabbi Simeon ben Gamaliel and Rabban Gamaliel II. Simeon, son of Gamaliel I and head of the Sanhedrin in the two decades before the destruction of the Temple, wrote as follows: "We beg to inform you that the doves are still tender and the lambs still young, and the grain has not yet ripened. I have considered the matter and thought it advisable to add thirty days to the year." The letter of Gamaliel II differs only in that he, more modestly as the

[23] I, 2; DM p.382; 10b-13b; SBT pp.42-61.
[24] 11a; SBT p.47.
[25] Probably to obtain confirmation of his appointment as Nasi rather than to secure permission for intercalating the year, since it seems unlikely that the latter would have been required.
[26] 11a; SBT p.47.   [27] 11b; SBT p.49.
[28] 12b; SBT p.57.   [29] 12b; SBT p.55.
[30] The book of Esther was specified to be read in the month Adar, and in Megillah I, 4 (DM p.202) it is discussed whether, if the book has already been read in the First Adar and the year is subsequently intercalated, it must be read again in the Second Adar.
[31] 11a; SBT p.48.

Talmud observes, associates his "colleagues" with himself in the decision of intercalation.[32]

¶ 80.   In agreement with the foregoing, Maimonides[33] also gives a lucid account of the process of intercalation as conducted under the Sanhedrin. Noting that the solar year exceeds the lunar year by approximately eleven days, he says that whenever this excess accumulates to about thirty days, or a little more or less, one month is added and the particular year is made to consist of thirteen months. The extra month is never anything other than an added Adar, and hence an intercalated year has a First Adar and a Second Adar. This added month may consist of either twenty-nine or thirty days. The decision is made by the Council of Intercalation, with a minimum membership of three; if the Nasi or chief of the supreme court was not one of them his assent was also necessary. Continuing with his own exposition of the mathematics involved, Maimonides states that each group of nineteen years contains seven intercalated years and twelve ordinary years.[34] Therefore, in spite of the fact that the Jewish system used only added Adars, the result was the same as in the Babylonian system and seven months were intercalated in each nineteen years.

¶ 81.   Both the tractate Sanhedrin and Maimonides[35] also show that the solar year was divided likewise into four seasons or *tequfoth* and into twelve signs of the zodiac (¶¶34-36). On the basis of a year of 365¼ days, one Tequfah was reckoned at 91 days, 7½ hours. The four Tequfoth were: the Tequfah of Nisan which began at the vernal equinox when the sun enters the constellation of Aries; the Tequfah of Tammuz at the summer solstice when the sun enters Cancer; the Tequfah of Tishri at the autumnal equinox when the sun enters Libra; and the Tequfah of Tebeth at the winter solstice when the sun enters Capricorn.

5. THE CALENDAR AT QUMRAN

LITERATURE: William H. Brownlee, *The Dead Sea Manual of Discipline*, BASOR Supplementary Studies 10-12, 1951 (=BDSM); S. Talmon, "Yom Hak-

[32] 11a-11b; SBT pp.47-49.
[33] *Sanctification of the New Moon*, I, 2; IV, 1-17. ed. Gandz, pp.4, 16-22.
[34] *Sanctification of the New Moon*, VI, 10. ed. Gandz, p.29.
[35] *Sanhedrin*. 11b; SBT p.49 and n.5; Maimonides, *Sanctification of the New Moon*, IX, 2-3. ed. Gandz, pp.36f.

kippurim in the Habakkuk Scroll," in *Biblica* 32 (1951), pp.549-563; H. H. Rowley, *The Zadokite Fragments and the Dead Sea Scrolls*. 1952; A. Jaubert, "Le calendrier des Jubilés et de la secte de Qumrân, ses origines bibliques," in VT 3 (1953), pp.250-264; *Discoveries in the Judaean Desert*, I, *Qumran Cave I*, by D. Barthélemy and J. T. Milik. 1955 (=DJD); Millar Burrows, *The Dead Sea Scrolls*. 1955 (=BDSS); Theodor H. Gaster, *The Dead Sea Scriptures in English Translation*. 1956 (=GDSS); Ernst E. Ettisch, "Die Gemeinderegel und der Qumrankalender," in RQ 9 (1961), pp.125-133.

⟨ 82.   In the Jewish community at Qumran, known through the now famous Dead Sea Scrolls and probably to be identified or connected with the Essenes described by Josephus,[1] Philo,[2] and Pliny,[3] there was a special interest in and emphasis upon times, seasons, and the calendar. The Manual of Discipline (1QS) describes the members of the covenant as desiring to walk before God "perfectly in all things that are revealed according to their appointed seasons" (I, 8-9; III, 10). They are also "not to advance their times, nor to lag behind any of their seasons" (I, 14-15). Likewise the duties of the council of fifteen include "the proper reckoning of the time" (VIII, 4),[4] while the wise man is admonished "to walk . . . according to the proper reckoning of every time," "to do God's will according to all that has been revealed for any time at that time, and to study all the wisdom found with reference to the times" (IX, 12-13).

⟨ 83.   Again in the latter part of our copy of the same Manual there is a long poem in which it is told how the devout worshiper blesses God at different times and seasons. The section with which we are concerned begins as follows (IX, 26-X, 1):

> With an offering of the lips he shall bless Him
> During the periods which Aleph ordained:
> At the beginning of the dominion of light with its circuit;
> And at its withdrawal to the habitation of its ordinance.

⟨ 84.   Aleph is the first letter of the Hebrew word for God (אלהים, *'Elohim*) and is probably used here as a somewhat mysterious abbreviation for God. The "beginning of the dominion of light" is evidently dawn. In this connection it may be noted that Josephus says it was the custom of the Essenes to offer certain traditional

---

[1] *Ant.* XVIII, 18-22 (=XVIII, i, 5); *War.* II, 119-161 (=II, viii, 2-13).

[2] *Every Good Man is Free.* 75-91.

[3] *Natural History.* V, XV.

[4] Another translation, however, is simply, "in conduct appropriate to every occasion" (GDSS p.55).

prayers "before the sun is up" and "as though entreating him to rise";[5] and in another passage reports them as regarding the rays of the sun as "the rays of the deity" (τὰς αὐγὰς τοῦ θεοῦ).[6] The word "circuit" (תקופתו, tequfato) is the same that is used in Ps 19:6[7] for the circuit of the sun. The "withdrawal" of the light is likewise the sunset, and the word (אסף, 'asaph) is the same that is also used in the Old Testament for the setting of moon (Is 60:20) and stars (Jl 2:10) Thus sunrise and sunset were taken account of by the community as times of worship.

¶ 85.   After this the poem mentions the time "when luminaries shine from the abode of holiness" (x, 2-3). The word "luminaries" (מאורות, me'orot) is the same as that translated "lights" in Gen 1:14, and the "abode of holiness" (זבול קודש, zebul qodesh) is the same as the "holy habitation" of God in Is 63:15. According to Gen 1:14 the "lights" serve "for signs and for seasons and for days and years," and the Qumran community undoubtedly looked to the heavenly bodies for the marking out of periods of time.

¶ 86.   Using the same word "seasons" (מועדים, mo'adim) as is in Gen 1:14, the poem next speaks of "the coming together of seasons to the days of a new moon" (x, 3). This probably means in effect, "whenever the days and nights add up to a month,"[8] and indicates concern with this unit of time.

¶ 87.   Following this the characters Mem and Nun are introduced into the poem (x, 4). As seemed probable in the case of the Aleph above (x, 1), there was doubtless also an esoteric meaning attaching to these letters. Mem, it may be noted, is the first letter of the word "luminaries" and also of the word "seasons." As it lends itself readily to doing, the letter Nun is written in the manuscript in a form which looks like a simple key, and the text reads, "the sign Nun is for the unlocking of His eternal mercies, at the beginnings of seasons in every period that will be" (x, 4-5). Together Aleph, Mem, and Nun form the word Amen, and it seems probable that this acrostic is intended. A possible allusion contained in it would be to Is 65:16 where it is said that "he who blesses himself in the

[5] *War.* II, 128 (=II, viii, 5).
[6] *War.* II, 148 (= II, viii, 9).
[7] Verse 7 in the Hebrew text.
[8] BDSM p.39 n.13.

land shall bless himself by the God of Amen,"[9] while the probable relationship to the calendar will be explained below (¶112).

⟨ 88. Having spoken of days and months the poem refers also to times "at the beginnings of years and at the completion of their terms" (x, 6). In this connection there is mention of how the seasons are joined to each other, namely "the season of reaping to the season of summer-fruit, the season of sowing to the season of green herbage" (x, 7), this manner of speech being reminiscent of the Gezer Calendar (¶58). Then the poem speaks of the adding together of "seasons of years to their weeks, and the beginning of their weeks to a season of release" (x, 7-8). The week of years must refer to the provision found in Lev 25:1-7 according to which the children of Israel are to sow their fields for six years but in the seventh year to allow the land "a sabbath of solemn rest"; and the season of release must be the "year of jubilee" of Lev 25:8-55 when, after seven "weeks" of seven years, in the fiftieth year they are to proclaim liberty throughout the land and each return to his property and to his family.

⟨ 89. The Zadokite Document (CD) reveals a similar interest in times and seasons and shows that the covenant community believed that it was faithful to the divine laws in these regards whereas all the rest of Israel had erred (III, 12-16 = 5:1-3): "But with them that held fast to the commandments of God who were left over of them, God established His covenant with Israel even until eternity, by revealing to them hidden things concerning which all Israel had gone astray. His holy sabbaths and His glorious appointed times, His righteous testimonies and His true ways and the requirements of His desire, which man shall do and live thereby, these He laid open before them; and they digged a well for much water, and he that despises it shall not live."

⟨ 90. Over against the failure of Israel otherwise, it was the undertaking of those who entered the covenant "to keep the sabbath day according to its exact rules and the appointed days and the fast-day according to the finding of the members of the new covenant in the land of Damascus" (VI, 18-19 = 8:15). The "appointed days" must be those of the various religious festivals of the year.

---

[9] See the margin of the ASV, and cf. II Cor 1:20; Rev 3:14. BDSM p.38 n.2.

The "fast-day" (יום התענית, *yom ha-ta'anit*), although only designated with the same general word for fasting which occurs in Ezr 9:5, is no doubt the most solemn fast of the year, the Day of Atonement (יום הכפרים, *yom ha-kippurim*), described in Lev 16 and 23:26-32, and in Ac 27:9 also called simply "the fast" (ἡ νηστεία).

❡ 91.   Again, even as the Manual of Discipline referred to the "season of release" which must be the year of jubilee, so the Zadokite Fragment says that "the exact statement of the epochs of Israel's blindness" can be learned "in the Book of the Divisions of Times into Their Jubilees and Weeks" (xvi, 2-4 = 20:1). This seems plainly enough to be a reference to the writing commonly called the Book of Jubilees, the prologue of which begins: "This is the history of the division of the days of the law and of the testimony, of the events of the years, of their (year) weeks, of their Jubilees throughout all the years of the world."[10] Since two fragments of the book of Jubilees were found in Cave 1 at Qumran (1QJub = 1Q17 and 18), it is evident that the work was used by this community.[11]

❡ 92.   In the Habakkuk Commentary (1QpHab) there is reference to the observance by the community of the day of atonement (*yom ha-kippurim*), and it is stated that "the wicked priest," an enemy for whom various identifications have been proposed, chose that very occasion to appear among them in order "to confound them and to make them stumble on the day of fasting, their Sabbath of rest" (xi, 6-8, commenting on Hab 2:15).[12] That the wicked priest could break in upon the community on this solemn occasion would suggest that they were celebrating the fast on a day other than that which he himself recognized, and thus again it is indicated that the Qumran group was separated from other Jews by its calendar of festivals and fasts.[13]

❡ 93.   The foregoing references suggest, then, that the Qumran community had its own religious calendar and that this was similar to the calendar of the book of Jubilees. This has been confirmed by the discovery, announced in 1956 by J. T. Milik, in Cave 4 at Qumran of an actual liturgical calendar. The fragments on which

[10] CAP II, p.11.   [11] DJD I, pp.82-84.
[12] BDSS p.370; cf. GDSS pp.255, 268f.
[13] See S. Talmon in *Biblica*. 32 (1951), pp.549-563.

this is contained appear to belong, paleographically, to the first part of the first century A.D. The calendar gives the dates of service in rotation of the priestly families and the dates of the religious festivals. These dates are always stated in terms of days of the week and sometimes in days of the month. The liturgical days fall regularly on Wednesday, Friday, and Sunday. The passover is celebrated on Tuesday evening. The offering of the sheaf of first fruits (Lev 23:11) falls on the twenty-sixth day of the first month, a Sunday. The New Year begins on the first day of the seventh month, a Wednesday. The day of atonement, the tenth day of the seventh month (Lev 16:29), comes on Friday. The feast of tabernacles, the fifteenth day of the seventh month (Lev 23:34), is on Wednesday. Occasionally in the case of historical rather than liturgical dates, these are expressed in terms of Babylonian month names. This suggests that a calendar derived from Babylonia was in common use for everyday purposes, but that the other calendar, which was presumably more ancient, was adhered to for liturgical purposes.

6. THE CALENDAR OF JUBILEES

LITERATURE: Julian Morgenstern, "The Calendar of the Book of Jubilees, Its Origin and Its Character," in VT 5 (1955), pp.34-76; A. Jaubert, "Le calendrier des Jubilés et les jours liturgiques de la semaine," in VT 7 (1957), pp.35-61; E. R. Leach, "A Possible Method of Intercalation for the Calendar of the Book of Jubilees," in VT 7 (1957), pp.392-397; Joseph M. Baumgarten, "The Beginning of the Day in the Calendar of Jubilees," in JBL 77 (1958), pp.355-360.

❨ 94. In the foregoing discussion it has been established that the Qumran community was zealous in its observance of what it held to be correct times and seasons, that these were different from what other Jews adhered to, that in this connection the community cited and possessed the book of Jubilees, and that in fragments of an actual calendar found in Cave 4 at Qumran historical dates are cited in Babylonian month names but liturgical dates are given in a system in which days of the week are fixed points as well as days of the month. The date of passover, for example, is fixed by Old Testament law (Ex 12:6) as the evening of the fourteenth day of the first month of the year. It is evident that this date can readily be ascertained in terms of the Babylonian calendar, but that in this calendar the date will fall on different days of the week in dif-

ferent years. The Qumran liturgical calendar, however, also identi-
fies the passover date as the evening of Tuesday, hence this was a
calendar in which the days of the week remained constant in relation to the days of the month. Since the clue is available that the
community referred to the book of Jubilees in the reckoning of
time, it is necessary to ascertain if the calendar of Jubilees satisfies
the condition just mentioned and to establish the nature of this
calendar.

⟨ 95.   The book of Jubilees was probably written in the original
Hebrew between 135 and 105 B.C., and is preserved in Ethiopic
manuscripts and Latin and Greek fragments as well as the two
Hebrew fragments which have now been found in Cave 1 at Qumran. Essentially a rewriting of the book of Genesis in the form of a
communication from "the angel of the presence" to Moses on Mount
Sinai, Jubilees places the biblical narrative within a chronological
framework of years, weeks of years, and jubilees, and lays much
emphasis upon the institution and proper observance of the festivals
of the religious year.[1]

⟨ 96.   The passage in this book which tells most about the calendar
is Jub 6:23-32.[2]

"And on the new moon of the first month, and on the new moon of
the fourth month, and on the new moon of the seventh month, and on the
new moon of the tenth month are the days of remembrance, and the days
of the seasons in the four divisions of the year. These are written and ordained as a testimony for ever. And Noah ordained them for himself as
feasts for the generations for ever, so that they have become thereby a
memorial unto him. And on the new moon of the first month he was bid-
den to make for himself an ark, and on that (day) the earth became dry
and he opened (the ark) and saw the earth. And on the new moon of the
fourth month the mouths of the depths of the abyss beneath were closed.
And on the new moon of the seventh month all the mouths of the abysses
of the earth were opened, and the waters began to descend into them. And
on the new moon of the tenth month the tops of the mountains were seen,
and Noah was glad. And on this account he ordained them for himself
as feasts for a memorial for ever, and thus are they ordained. And they
placed them on the heavenly tablets, each had thirteen weeks; from one
to another (passed) their memorial, from the first to the second, and
from the second to the third, and from the third to the fourth. And all the
days of the commandment will be two and fifty weeks of days, and (these

[1] CAP II, pp.1-10; A. C. Headlam in HDB II, p.791.
[2] CAP II, pp.22f.

will make) the entire year complete. Thus it is engraven and ordained on the heavenly tablets. And there is no neglecting (this commandment) for a single year or from year to year. And command thou the children of Israel that they observe the years according to this reckoning—three hundred and sixty-four days, and (these) will constitute a complete year, and they will not disturb its time from its days and from its feasts; for everything will fall out in them according to their testimony, and they will not leave out any day nor disturb any feasts."

⟪ 97. From this we learn that the year was divided into four periods or seasons. The beginning of each of the four successive periods was marked by the "new moon," which probably means simply the "first day," of the first month, the fourth month, the seventh month, and the tenth month, in other words each period comprised three months. Each period also contained thirteen weeks. Since this equals 91 days, there must have been two months of 30 days each and one month of 31 days in each group of three months. The complete year was composed, therefore, as it is also explicitly stated, of 52 weeks or of 364 days.

⟪ 98. The nature of the calendar just outlined will be discussed further in a moment but first it is necessary to indicate that what seems to be the same system of reckoning is found in the book of Enoch. The book of Enoch[3] is a large and composite work preserved in a number of Ethiopic manuscripts and Greek and Latin fragments. Of the 108 chapters into which it is customarily divided, chapters 72-82 are called the "Book of the Heavenly Luminaries" and constitute a treatise on the laws of the celestial bodies. This part, and at least much of the rest of the book, was probably written originally in Hebrew. This section must be referred to in Jubilees 4:17 where it is said that Enoch "wrote down the signs of heaven according to the order of their months in a book, that men might know the seasons of the years according to the order of their separate months." This citation indicates a date earlier than Jubilees for the "Book of the Heavenly Luminaries," say not later than 110 B.C., and also shows that the author of Jubilees held it in high regard, therefore presumably agreed with it as to calendar.

[3] Also known as I Enoch or the (Ethiopic) book of Enoch. On the book see CAP II, pp.163-187; R. H. Charles in HDB I, pp.705-708. For a date for all the principal sections of I Enoch in the reign or shortly after the death of Antiochus Epiphanes see H. H. Rowley, *Jewish Apocalyptic and the Dead Sea Scrolls.* 1957, pp.8f.

⟨99.   In the "Book of the Heavenly Luminaries" the motion of the sun is described (I En 72) in relation to twelve "portals" which must be the equivalent of the signs of the zodiac. Beginning at what must be the vernal equinox, the sun rises, it is said, in the fourth of the six eastern portals. It comes forth through that portal thirty mornings in succession, during which time the day grows daily longer and the night nightly shorter. Moving into the fifth portal, the sun rises for thirty mornings; moving on into the sixth portal, it rises for thirty-one mornings. The relative lengths of day and night continue to change, and by this time the day reaches its maximum duration and the night its minimum, in other words it is the summer solstice. Then "the sun mounts up to make the day shorter and the night longer" (v. 15), and after thirty, thirty, and thirty-one mornings the day and night are of equal length, in other words the autumnal equinox is reached. The corresponding sequence is followed on through the second half of the year until at last again day and night are of equal length and the cycle has been completed at the vernal equinox. So, it is concluded, "the year is exactly as to its days three hundred and sixty-four" (v. 32).

⟨100.   This certainly appears to be the same calendar as in Jubilees, and is of special importance because it answers a question on which specific information was not provided in Jubilees, namely which month in each series of three months has the added day to make it thirty-one days in length. Here we learn that in each group of three months their respective lengths are thirty days, thirty days, and thirty-one days.

⟨101.   We may, accordingly, outline a series of three months in the calendar of Jubilees and I Enoch as shown in Table 14:[4]

⟨102.   Since thirteen weeks are thus filled out exactly, it is evident that this same tabulation can represent not only the first three-month period of the year but also the second, third, and fourth groups of months as well. In other words, the first month is identical with the fourth, seventh, and tenth months; the second month is identical with the fifth, eighth, and eleventh months; and the third month is identical with the sixth, ninth, and twelfth months. Thus the one tabulation suffices to represent the entire year.

[4] A. Jaubert in VT 7 (1957), p.35.

TABLE 14. THE MONTHS IN THE CALENDAR OF JUBILEES

I.IV.VII.X.	II.V.VIII.XI.	III.VI.IX.XII.
1 8 15 22 29	6 13 20 27	4 11 18 25
2 9 16 23 30	7 14 21 28	5 12 19 26
3 10 17 24	1 8 15 22 29	6 13 20 27
4 11 18 25	2 9 16 23 30	7 14 21 28
5 12 19 26	3 10 17 24	1 8 15 22 29
6 13 20 27	4 11 18 25	2 9 16 23 30
7 14 21 28	5 12 19 26	3 10 17 24 31

⟨ 103.　From I Enoch we also learn that the calendar year must have been considered as beginning at the vernal equinox, since the description there starts at the point where the days are first beginning to grow longer than the nights.

⟨ 104.　It is also necessary to ask on what day of the week the calendar begins. A clue is found in *The Chronology of Ancient Nations* by the Muslim author al-Biruni (A.D. 973-1048). As a source concerning Jewish sects al-Biruni uses the Kitab al-Maqalat, a manual of the history of religions written by Abu 'Isa al-Warraq in the ninth century. In this work this author speaks, says al-Biruni, "of a Jewish sect called the Maghribis, who maintain that the feasts are not legal unless the moon rises in Palestine as a full moon in the night of Wednesday, which follows after the day of Tuesday, at the time of sunset. Such is their New Year's Day. From this point the days and months are counted, and here begins the rotation of the annual festivals. For God created the two great lights on a Wednesday. Likewise they do not allow Passover to fall on any other day except on Wednesday. And the obligations and rites prescribed for Passover they do not hold to be necessary, except for those who dwell in the country of the Israelites. All this stands in opposition to the custom of the majority of the Jews, and to the prescriptions of the Torah."[5]

⟨ 105.　The Maghribis were a "cave sect," and there is reason to believe that they may have been the Qumran group or others connected with them.[6] Since it is stated that Wednesday is their New

[5] *The Chronology of Ancient Nations*, ed. C. Edward Sachau. 1879, p.278.
[6] R. de Vaux in RB 57 (1950), pp.422f.; Rowley, *The Zadokite Fragments and the Dead Sea Scrolls*, pp.23f.; cf. Ernst Bammel in ZNW 49 (1958), pp.77-88.

Year's Day, the calendar should probably begin with that day, and the days of the week should fall as shown in the tabulation below. The theological reason given for this beginning point is that on a Wednesday God created the two great lights. This is an obvious reference to Gen 1:14-19 where God made the sun, moon, and stars on the "fourth day," and ordained that these "lights in the firmament" should be "for signs and for seasons and for days and years." It is evident that though the year begins with Wednesday, as far as numbering the days of the week is concerned Wednesday is still the fourth day, Saturday or the sabbath is the seventh, and so on. That the beginning of the year is also marked by the rise of the full moon can hardly be taken as anything other than an ideal statement, since even if in a given year Wednesday was full moon day it would not be so regularly.

TABLE 15. THE DAYS OF THE WEEK IN THE CALENDAR OF JUBILEES

MONTHS	DAYS						
	Sun	Mon	Tue	Wed	Thu	Fri	Sat
I. IV. VII. X.				1	2	3	4
	5	6	7	8	9	10	11
	12	13	14	15	16	17	18
	19	20	21	22	23	24	25
	26	27	28	29	30		
II. V. VIII. XI.						1	2
	3	4	5	6	7	8	9
	10	11	12	13	14	15	16
	17	18	19	20	21	22	23
	24	25	26	27	28	29	30
III.VI. IX. XII.	1	2	3	4	5	6	7
	8	9	10	11	12	13	14
	15	16	17	18	19	20	21
	22	23	24	25	26	27	28
	29	30	31				

([106.   While in the calendar that is arranged as we have just indicated, the days of the week and the days of the month cannot possibly remain in a fixed relationship to the phases of the moon, it is plain that the days of the week do remain in a fixed relation with the days of the month. Therefore it is possible to identify the position of festivals or other dates in terms of both the day of the month and the day of the week. Thus if the passover sacrifice is slain on the fourteenth day of the first month (Ex 12:6) and the fifteenth day is the first day of passover,[7] it is Tuesday which is the eve of passover and Wednesday which is the passover day, and this is the case in every year. This agrees with the date of passover as given in the calendar fragments from Qumran Cave 4, and the other festival dates as given there (¶93) are also in exact agreement with what may be ascertained in our present tabulation, falling regularly on Wednesday, Friday, and Sunday.

《 107.   The fixed relationship of the days of the month with the days of the week is of course precisely what is not found in a calendar of lunar months. As we have stated, in the Babylonian lunisolar calendar the fourteenth day of the first month falls upon different days of the week in different years. The point at issue here was evidently of much importance to those who used the calendar of Jubilees. By the observance of this calendar, it was said, as we have seen, "they will not disturb its time from its days and from its feasts . . . and they will not leave out any day nor disturb any feasts." Together with this positive affirmation concerning its own calendar, the book of Jubilees speaks strongly of the harm that is done by the use of a different calendar (6:36f.):

> "For there will be those who will assuredly make observations of the moon—how (it) disturbs the seasons and comes in from year to year ten days too soon. For this reason the years will come upon them when they will disturb (the order), and make an abominable (day) the day of testimony, and an unclean day a feast day, and they will confound all the days, the holy with the unclean, and the unclean day with the holy; for they will go wrong as to the months and sabbaths and feasts and jubilees."

《 108.   That the calendar to which Jubilees objects is a lunar calendar is shown by the statement that it is based upon "observations of the moon," and also that it makes the year come in annually "ten days too soon." According to Jubilees, "three hundred and sixty-four days . . . constitute a complete year"; in the Babylonian calendar, twelve lunar months of alternately twenty-nine and thirty days each make a year of three hundred and fifty-four days.

《 109.   If Jubilees objects to lunar reckoning, its own system is presumably essentially solar. That this is indeed its basis is made explicit

[7] JE III, p.505.

by the mention of "the rule of the sun" in Jub 4:21, and the fuller statement in Jub 2:9: "And God appointed the sun to be a great sign on the earth for days and for sabbaths and for months and for feasts and for years and for sabbaths of years and for jubilees and for all seasons of the years." As a solar calendar, then, it evidently began the year with the vernal equinox, and it divided the year into four solar periods, twelve solar months, fifty-two weeks, and three hundred and sixty-four days as has already been outlined.

¶ 110.   While the calendar is thus based upon the solar year and actually corresponds with it quite closely and subdivides it quite symmetrically, its total of three hundred and sixty-four days is still actually about one and one-quarter days short of the true solar year of about 365¼ days. With the passage of time this annual shortage would have accumulated into an obvious discrepancy with the seasons and would have required rectification. How the rectification was accomplished is not indicated in the sources with which we have just been dealing, but there is a possible clue in the Pirqe de Rabbi Eliezer where it is stated: "The great cycle of the sun is 28 years."[8] In twenty-eight years an annual shortage of one and one-quarter days would amount to thirty-five days. Thus if there were some system for intercalating five weeks in each 28-year cycle, the calendar would be kept in adjustment. Since a nineteen-year cycle of intercalation was derived from the Babylonian calendar, this 28-year cycle must have had some other origin and it would at any rate have fitted perfectly with the calendar of Jubilees.

¶ 111.   The calendar of Jubilees seems, therefore, to have been the calendar of the Qumran community. The community was willing to use the Babylonian calendar for matters of everyday life, but for dating the all-important festivals of the religious year it adhered to this other calendar which did "not leave out any day nor disturb any feasts." The Babylonian calendar was no doubt in general and official use at this time, but the community of the covenant evidently did not feel that it did justice to the requirements of the religious year. The calendar to which the community adhered was presumably, therefore, an older one which was believed to be con-

---

[8] vi; ed. Friedlander, p.34. This work, already cited above (¶25), treats of the creation and at this point has reached the fourth day (vi-viii), therefore discusses the course of the planets, the sun, and the moon.

nected with the proper arrangement of the festivals from some au-
thoritative antiquity. Since this was a solar calendar, in distinction
from the lunisolar Babylonian calendar, and since, as we have
seen reason to believe, the ancient Israelite calendar developed in
a solar form, it seems likely that the community believed itself to
be maintaining the traditions of an immemorial past.

⟨ 112.   In the poem on times and seasons in the Manual of Discipline, we found (¶¶84-87) the acrostic Aleph, Mem, Nun, form-
ing the word Amen. The numerical values of these letters of the
Hebrew alphabet are 1, 40, and 50, making a total of 91, exactly
the number of days in each of the four divisions of the calendar.
Thus, to the initiated ear, the liturgical response of the community
in its prayers was a solemn affirmation of the divine wisdom so
marvelously shown forth in the stately movement of the sun through
the four 91-day seasons of the solar year, a movement which set the
splendid pattern within which the divine Being was rightly to be
worshiped.

7. THE GREEK CALENDAR

LITERATURE: Bischoff, "Kalender (griechischer)," in PWRE X, ii, cols. 1568-
1602; James Gow, "The Calendar," in *A Companion to Greek Studies*, ed.
Leonard Whibley, 3d ed. 1916, pp. 589-591; H. J. Rose, "Calendar, Greek,"
in EB 4, pp.578-579; Benjamin D. Meritt, *The Athenian Year*. 1961.

⟨ 113.   The Greek calendar is not of major concern in relation to
biblical dates but will be considered briefly, principally because of
its relationship to the Macedonian calendar (¶¶117ff.) and to the
Greek era of the Olympiads (¶185). In Greece the month began
with the new moon. The lunar months varied between twenty-nine
and thirty days, and extra months or days were intercalated from
time to time. From the Greek ἐμβάλλω, "to throw in," an inserted
month was called μὴν ἐμβόλιμος, an "embolismic month," and this
designation was abbreviated in inscriptions as EM or EMB. The
names of the months were mostly based on the names of deities or
of festivals with which the month was particularly connected, and
the names differed from city to city. The year, too, began at different
points in different states.

⟨ 114.   At Athens, chief city of Attica, the year began at the first
new moon after the summer solstice. Between 432 and 263 B.C.,

it has been computed, the date of this event ranged from June 22 to August 9 but in the majority of cases fell in July.[1] For the purpose of the following table we may take Jul 1 as the approximate beginning point of the year, and list the months with approximate equivalents as shown in Table 16.

TABLE 16. THE CALENDAR AT ATHENS

1.	Ἑκατομβαιών	Hekatombaion	Jul
2.	Μεταγειτνιών	Metageitnion	Aug
3.	Βοηδρομιών	Boedromion	Sep
4.	Πυανοψιών	Pyanopsion	Oct
5.	Μαιμακτηριών	Maimakterion	Nov
6.	Ποσιδηϊών	Posideion	Dec
7.	Γαμηλιών	Gamelion	Jan
8.	Ἀνθεστηριών	Anthesterion	Feb
9.	Ἐλαφηβολιών	Elaphebolion	Mar
10.	Μουνυχιών	Mounychion	Apr
11.	Θαργηλιών	Thargelion	May
12.	Σκιροφοριών	Skirophorion	Jun

Here the intercalary month was usually a second sixth month, Posideion.

(115.   At Delphi, in Phocis, the year began at about the same time as at Athens and the months, listed from the beginning of the new year on approximately Jul 1, are shown in Table 17.

TABLE 17. THE CALENDAR AT DELPHI

1.	Ἀπελλαῖος	Apellaios	Jul
2.	Βουκάτιος	Boukatios	Aug
3.	Βοαθόος	Boathoos	Sep
4.	Ἡραῖος	Heraios	Oct
5.	Δαιδαφόριος	Daidaphorios	Nov
6.	Ποιτρόπιος	Poitropios	Dec
7.	Ἀμάλιος	Amalios	Jan
8.	Βύσιος	Bysios	Feb
9.	Θεοξένιος	Theoxenios	Mar
10.	Ἐνδυσποιτρόπιος	Endyspoitropios	Apr
11.	Ἡράκλειος	Herakleios	May
12.	Ἰλαῖος	Ilaios	Jun

Here the intercalary month was usually a second sixth month, Poitropios.

[1] R. D. Hicks in *A Companion to Greek Studies*, p.71.

⟮116. The days of the month in the Greek calendar were divided into three groups. The first ten days were days of the "rising" month and were referred to thus, for example: "on the sixth day of the rising month of Metageitnion (Μεταγειτνιῶνος ἕκτῃ ἱσταμένου)." The next ten days were indicated as "plus ten." "On the sixteenth day of Metageitnion," for example, was expressed as: "on the sixth day plus ten of Metageitnion (Μεταγειτνιῶνος ἕκτῃ ἐπὶ δέκα)." The last nine or ten days were days of the "waning" month, or days "after the twenties," and were counted backward from the end of the month. So for the twenty-sixth day of Metageitnion, for example, we have: "on the fifth day of the waning month of Metageitnion (Μεταγειτνιῶνος πέμπτῃ φθίνοντος)"; or: "on the fifth day after the twenties of Metageitnion (Μεταγειτνιῶνος πέμπτῃ μετ' εἰκάδας)." As already noted (¶11), the Greek day began at sundown.

8. THE MACEDONIAN CALENDAR

LITERATURE: "Hémérologue ou Calendrier de différentes villes, comparé avec celui de Rome," in *Histoire de l'Académie Royale des Inscriptions et Belles-Lettres*. Paris, 47 (1809), pp.66-84; Ludwig Ideler, *Handbuch der mathematischen und technischen Chronologie*. 2 vols. 1825-26; Campbell C. Edgar, *Zenon Papyri in the University of Michigan Collection*. 1931.

⟮117. Since the Macedonians were related to the Greeks in origin, language, and culture, it is to be expected that their calendar would be similar to the Greek calendar. Like the Greek calendar, the Macedonian was also made up of lunar months, but the year began in the fall. The beginning point was presumably at the new moon after the autumnal equinox, hence about the end of September, and in Table 18 for a rough preliminary equivalent we may show the first month of the year as approximately corresponding to October. More exact equivalents in different areas will be shown later.

⟮118. As lunar months, these most probably alternated between thirty and twenty-nine days in length. This is confirmed by Egyptian papyri which give Gorpiaios and Hyperberetaios together fifty-nine days, and Apellaios thirty days, and Audynaios twenty-nine days.[1]

⟮119. There must also have been some system of intercalation. In his *Life of Alexander*, Plutarch[2] states that the Macedonian kings

[1] Edgar, *Zenon Papyri*, p.51.   [2] *Alexander*. 16.

TABLE 18. THE MACEDONIAN MONTHS

1.	Δῖος	Dios	Oct
2.	Ἀπελλαῖος	Apellaios	Nov
3.	Αὐδυναῖος	Audynaios	Dec
4.	Περίτιος	Peritios	Jan
5.	Δύστρος	Dystros	Feb
6.	Ξανθικός, Ξανδικός	Xanthikos, or Xandikos	Mar
7.	Ἀρτεμίσιος	Artemisios	Apr
8.	Δαίσιος	Daisios	May
9.	Πάνεμος	Panemos	Jun
10.	Λῷος	Loos	Jul
11.	Γορπιαῖος	Gorpiaios	Aug
12.	Ὑπερβερεταῖος	Hyperberetaios	Sep

were not accustomed to go into battle in the month of Daisios, and relates that Alexander, accordingly, on the eve of the battle of Granicus ordered the month to be called a second Artemisios. Whether this was the regular intercalary month in Macedonia is not certain. In Egypt a papyrus of the late second century of the Christian era[3] gives a date in terms of a day of

$$μη[νος] \ Αρτεμι[σι$$
$$ον \ εμβο[λ]ιμου,$$

i.e., "of the intercalary month Artemisios," which supports the idea that, at least in that place and time this month was so treated. On the other hand there is evidence that under Ptolemy II Philadelphus the month Peritios was repeated every second year.[4]

〖 120.   With the conquests of Alexander the Great the Macedonian calendar became widely used throughout Asia. Interesting evidence of this dissemination is to be seen in the Ἡμερολόγιον μηνῶν διαφόρων πόλεων, a *Hemerologium* or Calendar of the months of different cities. This work, preserved in two manuscripts, one in Florence, one in Leiden, gives the Roman calendar beginning in January and, in comparison with it, the calendars of some sixteen other peoples and cities. In the manuscript at Florence are given the calendars of (1) the Alexandrians, (2) the Greeks (meaning the Syrian Greeks, especially the inhabitants of the chief city of the

[3] OP No.2082, Fragment 3, Lines 17-18.
[4] Edgar, *Zenon Papyri*, p.51; OP XVII (1927), p.93.

Seleucid empire and later of the Roman province of Syria, Antioch), and of the peoples of (3) Tyre, (4) Arabia, (5) Sidon, (6) Heliopolis (i.e., Baalbek), (7) Lycia, (8) Asia (i.e., the Roman province), (9) Crete, (10) Cyprus, (11) Ephesus, (12) Bithynia, and (13) Cappadocia. In the manuscript at Leiden, in place of Crete, Cyprus, and Ephesus are given the calendars of (14) Gaza, (15) Ascalon, and (16) Seleucia Pieria. In a tabulation of these calendars[5] one readily recognizes in the majority of them some or all of the Macedonian month names. For example, Xanthikos is found in the calendars of the Greeks and of Tyre, Arabia, Sidon, Lycia, Ephesus, Cappadocia, Gaza, Ascalon, and Seleucia Pieria; Artemisios is found in Asia; Hyperberetaios in Crete; Loos in Cyprus. The comparative tables show also the dates of the beginnings of the months and the number of days in them. Since the Hemerologium represents the Roman period it will be cited at a relatively late point in each area dealt with in what follows.

(1) IN SYRIA AND IN BABYLONIA

LITERATURE: *The Excavations at Dura-Europos, Second Season*, ed. by P. V. C. Baur and M. I. Rostovtzeff, 1931; Jotham Johnson, *Dura Studies*. University of Pennsylvania Thesis. 1932; Robert H. McDowell, *Coins from Seleucia on the Tigris*. University of Michigan Studies, Humanistic Series, 37. 1935; *The Excavations at Dura-Europos, Preliminary Report of the Seventh and Eighth Seasons of Work*, ed. by M. I. Rostovtzeff, F. E. Brown, and C. B. Welles. 1939.

⟨ 121.   In Syria as in Macedonia the year began in the fall and in connection with the Seleucid era we will note (¶193) how, when the Seleucid administration was centered in Syria, the Macedonian New Year (Dios 1) in the fall was made the beginning point of the era. In Syria many of the local month names were recognizably similar to the Babylonian and Jewish, and this will appear in column two of the following tabulation where variant spellings, approximating the Syrian pronunciation, are shown.[1] It will be noted that, at the beginning of the year, there were two months Tishri, a first and a second, and also two months Kanun, a first and a second. According to the *Chronicle* of John Malalas[2] it was Seleucus I

[5] *Histoire de l'Académie Royale des Inscriptions et Belles-Lettres.* 47 (1809), pp.66-84; Ideler, *Handbuch der mathematischen und technischen Chronologie*, I, pp.410ff.

[1] Ideler, *op.cit.*, p.430 n.1.
[2] *Chronicle of John Malalas*, tr. by Matthew Spinka. 1940, p.14.

Nicator (312-281 B.C.), founder of the Seleucid empire and builder of Antioch (in Syria), who commanded that the months of Syria be named according to the Macedonian names. The resultant equation of months was probably that shown in Table 19, a table which may be labeled (for reasons which will appear later) as giving the earlier correlation of the months.

TABLE 19. THE MACEDONIAN CALENDAR IN SYRIA (EARLIER CORRELATION)

	Macedonian Months	Syrian Months	Jewish Months
1.	Dios	The first Tishri or Teschrin	Tishri
2.	Apellaios	The second Tishri or Teschrin	Marheshvan
3.	Audynaios	The first Kanun or Conun	Kislev
4.	Peritios	The second Kanun or Conun	Tebeth
5.	Dystros	Shebat or Schvot	Shebat
6.	Xanthikos	Adar or Odor	Adar
7.	Artemisios	Nisan or Nison	Nisan
8.	Daisios	Iyar or Ior	Iyyar
9.	Panemos	Hasiran or Chsiron	Sivan
10.	Loos	Tamus or Tomus	Tammuz
11.	Gorpiaios	Ab or Ov	Ab
12.	Hyperberetaios	Elul or Ilul	Elul

◖ 122.   Evidence that the calendar was in fact arranged thus and continued in use in this order until in the first Christian century is found at Dura-Europos. This was a fortress on the Euphrates at the eastern edge of the Syrian desert founded under Seleucus I Nicator, and it remained an important caravan city under the Parthians. In the excavations at Dura, in the Temple of Zeus Kyrios a cult relief was found with an inscription in both Palmyrene and Greek and a date corresponding to A.D. 31.[3] The Palmyrene inscription mentions the month Tishri, the Greek inscription gives the month Apellaios. If it is the second month Tishri which is meant, this correspondence agrees with the tabulation just given and shows that the equation represented therein prevailed at least until this date.

◖ 123.   In Babylonia at this same time the Macedonian months were presumably equated with the Babylonian months according to the same scheme just observed but with the year beginning in the

[3] The Excavations at Dura-Europos, Preliminary Report of the Seventh and Eighth Seasons of Work, plate XXXVII and pp.307-309.

spring in accordance with Babylonian custom. This gives a calendar (Table 20), which again may be labeled as representing the earlier correlation.

TABLE 20. THE MACEDONIAN CALENDAR IN BABYLONIA
(EARLIER CORRELATION)

Macedonian Months	Babylonian Months	Jewish Months
1. Artemisios	Nisanu	Nisan
2. Daisios	Aiaru	Iyyar
3. Panemos	Simanu	Sivan
4. Loos	Duzu	Tammuz
5. Gorpiaios	Abu	Ab
6. Hyperberetaios	Ululu	Elul
7. Dios	Tashritu	Tishri
8. Apellaios	Arahsamnu	Marheshvan
9. Audynaios	Kislimu	Kislev
10. Peritios	Tebetu	Tebeth
11. Dystros	Shabatu	Shebat
12. Xanthikos	Addaru	Adar

⟨ 124. Interesting confirmation of this arrangement of the calendar is found at Seleucia on the Tigris, a site opposite the later Ctesiphon and below the present Baghdad. Seleucia was founded by Seleucus I Nicator, and was an important center both in the Seleucid empire and the succeeding Parthian empire. In the exploration of this site a large number of coins was found, the greater number probably minted right here. Those of the Seleucid period did not bear dates but in the Parthian period in the reign of Mithridates I, after 141 B.C., the coins begin to show dates and in later issues some coins show not only the year but also the month. One group (No. 136) giving both year and month is from the reign of Artabanus II (A.D. 11-30/31[?]). The year dates are ϚKT = 326, and ZKT = 327; assuming that the Seleucid era is intended they correspond to A.D. 15/16 and 16/17. The months mentioned are shown in Table 21A.

The first four bear one monogram or countermark, which is the sign of the controller of the mint; the last six bear another monogram. Arranged in the order just given, the months stand in a proper sequence according to the Babylonian calendar (with Arte-

TABLE 21A. The Macedonian Months at Seleucia
IN A.D. 15/16–16/17

A.S. 326	Gorpiaios
	Hyperberetaios
	Apellaios
	Audynaios
	Peritios
	Dystros
	Xandikos
A.S. 327	Artemisios
	Panemos
	Peritios

misios = Nisanu as the first month of the new year beginning in
the spring), and the change in monograms indicates one change in
mint administration during the period. This sequence will be more
evident if the months are listed again by their number in the calendar as in Table 21B.

TABLE 21B. The Macedonian Months at Seleucia
IN A.D. 15/16–16/17

A.S. 326	5.	Gorpiaios
	6.	Hyperberetaios
	8.	Apellaios
	9.	Audynaios
	10.	Peritios
	11.	Dystros
	12.	Xandikos
A.S. 327	1.	Artemisios
	3.	Panemos
	10.	Peritios

But if it were assumed that the Macedonian calendar, with Dios
as the first month, were used, then the order would have to be as
in Table 21C.
And, as the breaking up of the monogram groups indicates, it
would be necessary to suppose a very unlikely alternation of mint
controllers. A similarly unlikely breaking up of the simple sequence
of the monograms would result if the coins were arranged on the
supposition that another month than Artemisios, say Xandikos,

TABLE 21C. THE MACEDONIAN MONTHS AT SELEUCIA
IN A.D. 15/16–16/17

A.S. 326		
	2.	Apellaios
	3.	Audynaios
	4.	Peritios
	5.	Dystros
	6.	Xandikos
	11.	Gorpiaios
	12.	Hyperberetaios
A.S. 327	4.	Peritios
	7.	Artemisios
	9.	Panemos

were equated with Nisanu as the first month of the year. Therefore it may be taken as established that at Seleucia at this time the Macedonian months were used according to the Babylonian calendar, with Artemisios the equivalent of Nisanu as the first month of the year, as shown in Table 20 above.[4]

⟨ 125. But both in Syria and in Babylonia, i.e., at Dura-Europos and at Seleucia on the Tigris, there is evidence for a shift in the calendar which probably took place before the middle of the first Christian century. At this time, due perhaps to the insertion of an extra intercalary month in the Greek and Macedonian calendar, the sequence of the Macedonian months shifted one place in relation to the Babylonian and Jewish months.

⟨ 126. At Dura-Europos a horoscope was found scratched in the plaster of a room of a private house. It consists essentially of an ellipse, divided by two lines at right angles. One line connects the zenith with the nadir; one line connects the point in the heavens which was rising (the ὡροσκόπος proper) at the time indicated, with the point which was setting. Around the outside of the ellipse the signs of the zodiac are given by abbreviations of their names, ΤΟΞ for Τοξότης (Sagittarius), etc. Among these signs the positions of the sun, moon, and planets are shown at the time the horoscope was cast. For example, at ΔΙΔ = Δίδυμοι (Gemini) is marked ΦΑΙΝ, an abbreviations for Φαίνων, the Greek name for Saturn; and at ΛΕωΝ (Leo) are three abbreviations: ΠΥ = Πυρόεις, Mars; ΦωCΦ =

[4] McDowell, Coins from Seleucia on the Tigris, pp.103-104, 138-139, 147-153.

Φωσφόρος, Venus; CTIAB = Στίλβων, Mercury. At the top the date is given as: ZΠΤΠΑΝΘ. ZΠΤ equals 487; ΠΑΝ is an abbreviation for Πανήμου, "of the month Panemos"; and Θ equals nine. The date is therefore the ninth day of the month Panemos in the year 487, a year which it may be surmised is stated in terms of the Seleucid era.

⟨ 127.   Within the limits of the occupation of Dura from 300 B.C. to A.D. 275 the planets were in the positions indicated in this horoscope in July A.D. 176. This was in the year 487 of the Seleucid era and proves that it was in fact this era which was employed for the year date. The position of the moon is lost in gaps in the plaster but the possible places for it would be in Aquarius, Scorpio, or Cancer. For the year in question Cancer would be impossible because the relations of the other planets would not hold. If the moon was in Scorpio the date was Jul 3-5, A.D. 176; if the moon was in Aquarius the date was Jul 10-12, A.D. 176. Shortly prior to those dates the new moon became visible at Babylon on the evening of Jun 25. This appearance began the month Duzu (Jun/Jul) in the Babylonian calendar. In the earlier correlation between the Babylonian and Macedonian calendars (Table 20) Duzu was equated with Loos. In the present inscription, however, the month is named Panemos. Therefore the one month relative shift has taken place and the calendars are in what we may call their later correlation.[5]

⟨ 128.   At Seleucia on the Tigris another group of coins now comes into consideration.[6] This group (No. 92) is from the reign of Gotarzes II (A.D. c.44-51) and, like the group just treated (¶124), also gives dates with both year and month. The year date is ZNT = A.S. 357 = A.D. 46/47. The months mentioned can be listed satisfactorily from either Artemisios or Xandikos as the first month of the year. Since Dura provides the evidence of the shift just considered (¶127), since Josephus will shortly be found equating Xanthikos with Nisan (¶138), and since the evidence here at Seleucia fits equally well in this pattern, it is likely that at this time at Seleucia as well as at Dura the sequence of Macedonian months began with Xandikos as the equivalent of Nisanu. Therefore we may list the months from these coins in the order shown in Table 22.

[5] *The Excavations at Dura-Europos, Second Season*, pp.161-164; Johnson, *Dura Studies*, pp.1-15.
[6] McDowell, *Coins from Seleucia on the Tigris*, pp.73-74, 119.

TABLE 22. THE MACEDONIAN MONTHS
AT SELEUCIA IN A.D. 46/47

1. Xandikos	5. Loos
2. Artemisios	6. Gorpiaios
3. Daisios	7. Hyperberetaios
4. Panemos	

From the evidence here at Seleucia the change in the correlation of the months took place between A.D. 16/17 (¶124) and A.D. 46/47. From the Palmyrene-Greek inscription in the Temple of Zeus Kyrios at Dura-Europos (¶122) the change must have come after A.D. 31, therefore between A.D. 31 and 46/47.

❬ 129. As valid, then, for shortly before the middle of the first century A.D. onwards, we may show this later correlation of the calendar in Tables 23 and 24 representing the beginning of the year respectively in the spring as in Babylonia, and in the fall as in Macedonia and Syria.

TABLE 23. THE MACEDONIAN CALENDAR IN BABYLONIA
(LATER CORRELATION)

Macedonian Months	Babylonian Months	Julian Months
1. Xanthikos	Nisanu	Mar/Apr
2. Artemisios	Aiaru	Apr/May
3. Daisios	Simanu	May/Jun
4. Panemos	Duzu	Jun/Jul
5. Loos	Abu	Jul/Aug
6. Gorpiaios	Ululu	Aug/Sep
7. Hyperberetaios	Tashritu	Sep/Oct
8. Dios	Arahsamnu	Oct/Nov
9. Apellaios	Kislimu	Nov/Dec
10. Audynaios	Tebetu	Dec/Jan
11. Peritios	Shabatu	Jan/Feb
12. Dystros	Addaru	Feb/Mar

¶130. Returning now to the *Hemerologium* (¶120), it is precisely this calendar which we have just established as in use in Syria in the later period (Table 24) which is given in the *Hemerologium* as the "calendar of the Greeks," i.e., the calendar of the

TABLE 24. THE MACEDONIAN CALENDAR IN SYRIA
(LATER CORRELATION)

	Macedonian Months	Babylonian Months	Julian Months
1.	Hyperberetaios	Tashritu	Sep/Oct
2.	Dios	Arahsamnu	Oct/Nov
3.	Apellaios	Kislimu	Nov/Dec
4.	Audynaios	Tebetu	Dec/Jan
5.	Peritios	Shabatu	Jan/Feb
6.	Dystros	Addaru	Feb/Mar
7.	Xanthikos	Nisanu	Mar/Apr
8.	Artemisios	Aiaru	Apr/May
9.	Daisios	Simanu	May/Jun
10.	Panemos	Duzu	Jun/Jul
11.	Loos	Abu	Jul/Aug
12.	Gorpiaios	Ululu	Aug/Sep

Syrian Greeks, especially the inhabitants of Antioch. In the *Hemerologium* this calendar is presented in the form in which it was brought into a fixed relationship to the Julian calendar, and the dates of the beginnings of the months and the number of days in the months are given.[7] This is shown in Table 25 where the year is made to begin, according to Macedonian and Syrian custom, in the fall.

(2) IN ARABIA

¶ 131. Among the numerous other calendars presented in the *Hemerologium* (¶120) we will note that of Arabia only briefly and then turn to Egypt. The calendar of the province of Arabia also used the Macedonian month names but began in the spring and followed the Egyptian pattern in that it had twelve months of thirty days each and then five epagomenal days before the beginning of the new year. On the basis of the *Hemerologium* it may be shown in Table 26.[1]

---

[7] *Histoire de l'Académie Royale des Inscriptions et Belles-Lettres.* 47 (1809), p.81; Ideler, *Handbuch der mathematischen und technischen Chronologie*, I, p.430; PWRE X, ii, col. 1595.

[1] *Histoire de l'Académie Royale des Inscriptions et Belles-Lettres.* 47 (1809), p.81; Ideler, *Handbuch der mathematischen und technischen Chronologie*, I, p.437; PWRE X, ii, col. 1595.

TABLE 25. THE SYRO-MACEDONIAN CALENDAR
(LATER CORRELATION) IN RELATION TO THE JULIAN CALENDAR

Macedonian Months	Beginning On	Number of Days
1. Hyperberetaios	Oct 1	31
2. Dios	Nov 1	30
3. Apellaios	Dec 1	31
4. Audynaios	Jan 1	31
5. Peritios	Feb 1	28
6. Dystros	Mar 1	31
7. Xanthikos	Apr 1	30
8. Artemisios	May 1	31
9. Daisios	Jun 1	30
10. Panemos	Jul 1	31
11. Loos	Aug 1	31
12. Gorpiaios	Sep 1	30

TABLE 26. THE MACEDONIAN CALENDAR IN ARABIA

Macedonian Months	Beginning On	Number of Days
1. Xanthikos	Mar 22	30
2. Artemisios	Apr 21	30
3. Daisios	May 21	30
4. Panemos	Jun 20	30
5. Loos	Jul 20	30
6. Gorpiaios	Aug 19	30
7. Hyperberetaios	Sep 18	30
8. Dios	Oct 18	30
9. Apellaios	Nov 17	30
10. Audynaios	Dec 17	30
11. Peritios	Jan 16	30
12. Dystros	Feb 15	30
Epagomenae	Mar 17	5

(3) IN EGYPT

LITERATURE: *The Tebtunis Papyri*, I, ed. by Bernard P. Grenfell, Arthur S. Hunt, and J. Gilbart Smyly. 1902; *The Hibeh Papyri*, I, ed. by Bernard P. Grenfell and Arthur S. Hunt. 1906; A. Bouché-Leclercq, *Histoire des Lagides*. 4 vols. 1903-7; George Milligan, *Selections from the Greek Papyri*. 1910; T. C. Skeat, "The Reigns of the Ptolemies," in *Mizraim*. 6 (1937), pp. 7-40; and in *Münchener Beiträge zur Papyrusforschung und antiken Rechtsgeschichte*. Heft 39, 1954; Skeat, "Notes on Ptolemaic Chronology," in JEA 46 (1960), pp.91-94.

¶ 132.   In Egypt the Macedonian calendar at first existed alongside the Egyptian calendar without a fixed relationship. In the papyri the Macedonian month names are found many times as well as the Egyptian names. Where double dates are given there is material on which to base attempts at synchronization of the two, but in the absence of exact information about the method of intercalation in the Macedonian calendar this is difficult and the results remain uncertain at many points. Two examples of synchronisms follow.

¶ 133.   Alexander the Great died in the year 323 B.C. Plutarch,[1] citing Aristobulus, says he died on the thirtieth day of the month Daisios (τριακάδι Δαισίου). Again,[2] citing the ἐφημερίδες or royal journals, he places the death "on the twenty-eighth, towards evening (τῇ τρίτῃ φθίνοντος πρὸς δείλην)." With the Greek day beginning at sundown (¶116), the death could easily have been assigned to the twenty-ninth of Daisios. Also in a month of twenty-nine days it is probable that the twenty-ninth day was in effect omitted and the last day of the month was called instead of the twenty-ninth, the thirtieth (τριάκας). Hence there is probably no inconsistency and the day was actually Daisios 29. Codex A of Pseudo-Callisthenes gives the date as Pharmuthi 4. Thus a synchronism is established and may be continued: Daisios 29 = Pharmuthi 4; Panemos 1 = Pharmuthi 5, etc.[3]

¶ 134.   The Rosetta Stone contains a decree in honor of Ptolemy V Epiphanes (c.203-c.181 B.C.) dated in the ninth year (196 B.C.) of his reign. This synchronism is given: "on the fourth day of the month Xandikos, which corresponds to the eighteenth day of the Egyptian month of Mecheir (μηνὸς Ξανδικοῦ τετράδι Αἰγυπτίων δὲ Μεχεὶρ ὀκτωκαιδεκάτηι)."[4] Accordingly reckoning backward, we establish that Xanthikos 1 = Mecheir 15. From these and other attested synchronisms tables of at least approximate correspondences may be compiled, and from them it may be concluded that the general tendency of the Macedonian months was to lose in relation to the Egyptian months, i.e., to fall later in the Egyptian year, although

---

[1] *Alexander.* 75.
[2] *Alexander.* 76.
[3] Skeat in *Mizraim.* 6 (1937), pp.28-29; Grenfell and Hunt, *The Hibeh Papyri,* I, pp.334, 339.
[4] E. A. Wallis Budge, *The Rosetta Stone in the British Museum.* 1929, pp.53, 67.

sometimes, presumably due to the manner of intercalation, they moved ahead.[5]

〖135. But in the time of Ptolemy IX Euergetes II (Physkon) (145-116 B.C.), the Macedonian calendar was finally equated to the Egyptian. Among the papyri found at Tebtunis in the Fayum is a portion of a letter written by an official under Euergetes II.[6] Line seven contains this date: ἔτους νγ Ξαν ιζ Μεχεὶρ ιζ. The year date (νγ = 53) indicates the fifty-third year of Euergetes II. The future Euergetes II was first proclaimed king in Alexandria in 170 B.C.;[7] his fifty-third year is 117 B.C. Ξαν abbreviates Ξανδικοῦ, and the seventeenth day (ιζ = 17) of Xandikos is equated with the seventeenth day of Mecheir. This date—the seventeenth day of Xandikos and the seventeenth day of Mecheir in the fifty-third year of Euergetes II—shows an exact correspondence of the two calendars and also implies, as Table 27 will show, that at the beginning of the year Dios 1 was equated with Thoth 1. From this time on, the two calendars remained in this exact agreement.

〖136. Under the Roman empire the months in Egypt were also given names in honor of the Roman emperors, and a number of these names are known. We may call them the honorific imperial names. The several names of the months, and their equivalents in Julian dates (in exact agreement with the *Hemerologium* [¶120]) are shown in Table 27.[8]

(4) IN PALESTINE

LITERATURE: Ideler, *Handbuch der mathematischen und technischen Chronologie*, I, pp.400-402; F.-M. Abel, *Les livres des Maccabées*. 1949, pp.XLIX-LII; J. C. Dancy, *A Commentary on I Maccabees*. 1954, pp.49-50.

〖137. Evidence of the use of the Macedonian calendar in Palestine appears in II Maccabees and in Josephus. In its account of the Maccabean period the book of II Maccabees (considered to have been written in Greek in Alexandria in the middle of the first century B.C.) quotes a letter from King Antiochus to the Jewish senate and the rest of the Jews, and also a letter from the Romans to them

[5] Grenfell and Hunt, *The Hibeh Papyri*, I, pp.334, 336-337.
[6] Grenfell, Hunt, and Smyly, *The Tebtunis Papyri*, No.25, pp.102-103.
[7] Bouché-Leclercq, *Histoire des Lagides*, II, p.393.
[8] Bouché-Leclercq, *Histoire des Lagides*, IV, pp.287-289; Milligan, *Selections from the Greek Papyri*, p.xviii; Bischoff in PWRE X, ii, col. 1588.

TABLE 27. THE MACEDONIAN CALENDAR IN EGYPT

MONTH NAMES

Macedonian	Egyptian	Roman		Julian Dates In A Common Year
1. Dios	Thoth	Σεβαστός	Sebastos	Aug 29-Sep 27
2. Apellaios	Phaophi	Δομιτιανός	Domitianos	Sep 28-Oct 27
3. Audynaios	Hathyr	Νέος Σεβαστός	Neos Sebastos	Oct 28-Nov 26
4. Peritios	Choiak	Ἀδριανός	Hadrianos	Nov 27-Dec 26
5. Dystros	Tybi			Dec 27-Jan 25
6. Xanthikos	Mecheir			Jan 26-Feb 24
7. Artemisios	Phamenoth			Feb 25-Mar 26
8. Daisios	Pharmuthi	Νερώνειος	Neroneios	Mar 27-Apr 25
9. Panemos	Pachon	Γερμανίκειος	Germanikeios	Apr 26-May 25
10. Loos	Pauni	Σωτήριος	Soterios	May 26-Jun 24
11. Gorpiaios	Epeiph			Jun 25-Jul 24
12. Hyperberetaios	Mesore	Καισάρειος	Kaisareios	Jul 25-Aug 23
Epagomenal days				Aug 24-Aug 28

in which the dates of Xanthikos 15 and Xanthikos 30 are given (II Macc 11:30, 33, 38). Here we may suppose that the Syro-Macedonian calendar was in use in the earlier correlation (Table 19) which we have established as probably prevailing prior to sometime between A.D. 31 and 46/47 (¶128). In this correlation Xanthikos was equivalent to Adar, and this and the other equivalences would appear as in Table 28.

TABLE 28. THE MACEDONIAN CALENDAR IN PALESTINE
(EARLIER CORRELATION)

	Macedonian Months	Jewish Months	Julian Equivalents
1.	Artemisios	Nisan	Mar/Apr
2.	Daisios	Iyyar	Apr/May
3.	Panemos	Sivan	May/Jun
4.	Loos	Tammuz	Jun/Jul
5.	Gorpiaios	Ab	Jul/Aug
6.	Hyperberetaios	Elul	Aug/Sep
7.	Dios	Tishri	Sep/Oct
8.	Apellaios	Marheshvan	Oct/Nov
9.	Audynaios	Kislev	Nov/Dec
10.	Peritios	Tebeth	Dec/Jan
11.	Dystros	Shebat	Jan/Feb
12.	Xanthikos	Adar	Feb/Mar

¶ 138. In his *Jewish Antiquities* and *Jewish War* Josephus commonly uses Macedonian month names and from time to time adds
their Jewish equivalents. In *Ant.* I, 80-81 (= I, iii, 3) he states that
Dios and Marheshvan are the same and that this was the second
month. This means that in a year beginning in the fall Hyperberetaios = Tishri was the first month. He also says that Xanthikos and
Nisan are the same and are the first month of the year for divine
worship and for ordinary affairs. Again in *Ant.* III, 248 (= III, x, 5)
he equates Xanthikos and Nisan and states that this month begins
the year. Also in *Ant.* XI, 148 (= XI, v, 4); XII, 248 (= XII, v, 4);
and XII, 319 (= XII, vii, 6) he equates Apellaios and Kislev and
makes no difference between the twenty-fifth day in the one month
and in the other. As would be expected in the time at the end of
the first century A.D. when Josephus wrote, these correspondences
agree with the later correlation between the Macedonian and Babylonian months established above (Tables 23, 24). In Josephus,
therefore, the Macedonian months may be taken as fully and exactly
equivalent to the Jewish months as shown in Table 29.

TABLE 29. The Macedonian Calendar in Palestine
(Later Correlation)

	Macedonian Months	Jewish Months	Julian Equivalents
1.	Xanthikos	Nisan	Mar/Apr
2.	Artemisios	Iyyar	Apr/May
3.	Daisios	Sivan	May/Jun
4.	Panemos	Tammuz	Jun/Jul
5.	Loos	Ab	Jul/Aug
6.	Gorpiaios	Elul	Aug/Sep
7.	Hyperberetaios	Tishri	Sep/Oct
8.	Dios	Marheshvan	Oct/Nov
9.	Apellaios	Kislev	Nov/Dec
10.	Audynaios	Tebeth	Dec/Jan
11.	Peritios	Shebat	Jan/Feb
12.	Dystros	Adar	Feb/Mar

9. THE ROMAN CALENDAR

LITERATURE: Walter F. Wislicenus, *Der Kalender in gemeinverständlicher
Darstellung.* 1905; H. J. Rose, "Calendar, Roman," in EB 4, p.579.

⟨ 139.   From an early time the Roman calendar was made up of lunar months. The earliest year was supposed to have been introduced by Romulus, the legendary founder of Rome, and to have comprised only ten months. The introduction of a calendar of twelve lunar months was attributed to Numa Pompilius, second legendary king of Rome (715-672 B.C.). Livy (I, xix, 6-7) describes the work of Numa as follows:

> "And first of all he divided the year into twelve months, according to the revolutions of the moon. But since the moon does not give months of quite thirty days each, and eleven days are wanting to the full complement of a year as marked by the sun's revolution, he inserted intercalary months in such a way that in the twentieth year the days should fall in with the same position of the sun from which they had started, and the period of twenty years be rounded out. He also appointed days when public business might not be carried on, and others when it might, since it would sometimes be desirable that nothing should be brought before the people."

⟨ 140.   The twelve months were supposed to have begun in the spring and to have had the order and number of days shown in Table 30.

TABLE 30. THE EARLY ROMAN CALENDAR

Name of Month		Number of Days
1.	Martius	31
2.	Aprilis	29
3.	Maius	31
4.	Junius	29
5.	Quintilis	31
6.	Sextilis	29
7.	Septembris	29
8.	Octobris	31
9.	Novembris	29
10.	Decembris	29
11.	Januarius	29
12.	Februarius	27
		354

In Table 30 it is recognizable that the month names were derived in part from the Roman gods as in the case of the first month, sacred to Mars; and in part from place in the sequence as in the case of the fifth month, Quintilis, from *quinque*, "five." The length of the months—keeping to uneven numbers—may have been influenced by the wish to have a day exactly in the middle of each month. To bring this lunar year of 354 days at least approximately into harmony with the solar year an intercalary month was inserted each second year.

❡ 141.   In the division of the Roman month, the first day of each month was termed *kalendae*, that is Kalends or Calends. From Latin *calare* and Greek καλῶ, "to call," this meant "callings" and probably referred to an official calling out of the day. The full moon was called the Ides. In the long months—Martius, Maius, Quintilis, and Octobris—this was the fifteenth day; in the short months—the other eight—this was the thirteenth. The Nones were the ninth day, counted inclusively, before the Ides: therefore in the long months the seventh, in the short months the fifth day of the month. Other days were counted backward and inclusively from these fixed points. Thus, for example, *a d iii non Quint* abbreviates *ante diem iii nonas Quintiles*, means "the third day before the Nones of Quintilis," and equals July 5. There was also a week of eight days, but it was independent of the months and simply marked the time from one market day to the next; and the seven-day week was only gradually introduced from the East and through its use by the Christians. Of the cumbersome system of Kalends, Ides, and Nones, and related reckoning, Wislicenus remarks that it is fortunate nothing has survived in modern usage except the word "calendar" which comes from the Latin *kalendae*. As for what is now meant by "calendar," that was designated by the Romans as *Fasti* (from Greek φάσκω, φημί, "to say") meaning, first, a day on which it is allowed to speak; hence a day on which judgment may be pronounced, i.e., a court day; and, finally, an enumeration of all the days of the year with their festivals, etc., specially including the *Fasti consulares*, or lists of the magistrates according to their years of service.

❡ 142.   Although the Roman calendar just described (¶140) began in the spring with Martius 1, we are told by Cassiodorus Senator[1] that in A.U.C. 601 = 153 B.C. the consuls, elected for one year, began to take office on January 1. Under the influence of this cus-

[1] ed. Mommsen, *Chronica minora*, II, p.130.

tom the beginning of the year was put back to Januarius 1, and the year continued to be reckoned regularly from this point.

⟨ 143.   By the end of the Roman republic the calendar had come into a state of confusion, particularly due to difficulties and inaccuracies in the system and practice of intercalation. In the year A.U.C. 708 = 46 B.C. Julius Caesar undertook a major reform of the calendar. He intercalated and added days to bring the civil year into harmony with the solar year, and changed the length of months as shown in Table 31. Also the Senate changed the name of the month Quintilis to Julius in his honor, and later Sextilis was changed to Augustus in honor of that emperor. With these changes the calendar appeared as follows in a common year.

TABLE 31. The Julian Calendar

Name of Month		Number of Days
1.	Januarius	31
2.	Februarius	28
3.	Martius	31
4.	Aprilis	30
5.	Maius	31
6.	Junius	30
7.	Julius	31
8.	Augustus	31
9.	Septembris	30
10.	Octobris	31
11.	Novembris	30
12.	Decembris	31
		—
		365

⟨ 144.   The year as just outlined was still one-fourth day short of the solar year, and adjustment was also made for this fact in the scheme initiated by Julius Caesar. In the first year of the new calendar (i.e., 45 B.C.) Februarius was given twenty-nine days and the year had 366 days; in the three following years Februarius had twenty-eight days and the year 365 days; and this same pattern was repeated continuously with an added day in every fourth year. In the Roman calendar the added day followed the twenty-fourth day of Februarius which was the sixth day before the Kalends

$$\text{of March} \begin{cases} \text{Feb 24, [24], 25, 26, 27, 28, Mar 1} \\ \\ \ \ 6 \qquad [6] \quad \ 5 \quad \ 4 \quad \ 3 \quad \ 2 \qquad 1 \end{cases}$$

hence was counted as a second sixth day; hence the year in which this was done was called *annus bissextus*. At present the added day is at the end of the month—Feb 29—and the year is known as a leap year because in it any fixed date after February "leaps" over a day of the week and falls on the day following that on which it would normally fall. In the transition from B.C. to A.D. as far as leap years are concerned, 45 B.C. was a leap year and so too were 5 B.C. and 1 B.C.; then the leap years in the Christian era became A.D. 4, A.D. 8, and so on.

⟦ 145.   Known as the Julian calendar in honor of Julius Caesar, the calendar just described has continued in use in the western world until now, with only a small correction instituted by Pope Gregory XIII in 1582. Even with its leap year arrangement the Julian calendar was still about eleven minutes longer than the astronomical year (¶33). To correct the error accumulated by this time, ten days were dropped so that Oct 5, 1582, became Oct 15, 1582. To counteract further error a small refinement was made in the treatment of leap years. While leap years are those exactly divisible by 4, of the centesimal years such as 1600, 1700, etc., only those exactly divisible by 400 are leap years.

C. OFFICIAL AND REGNAL YEARS

⟦ 146.   The question naturally arises as to how a particular year is to be designated. In general this was done at first by reference to some important event in the year and later by reference to the year of a ruler or other official.

1. IN EGYPT

LITERATURE: Kurt Sethe, "Die Entwicklung der Jahresdatierung bei den alten Aegyptern," in *Untersuchungen zur Geschichte und Altertumskunde Aegyptens.* III (1905), pp.60-100; Alan H. Gardiner, "Regnal Years and Civil Calendar in Pharaonic Egypt," in JEA 31 (1945), pp.11-28.

⟦ 147.   The earliest stages known in the development of the Egyptian system may be seen on the famous Palermo Stone.[1] On the

[1] FLP Fig. 27.

front the first line gives the names in successive rectangles of pre-dynastic kings of Lower Egypt without indication of how long each reigned. Beginning with line two the right side of each rectangle is marked by a vertical line which curls over at the top. This is the hieroglyphic sign for a palm tree and the symbol for a year. Each rectangle is therefore a year-compartment. The stone is a fragment but as far as it is preserved, lines two and three record the First Dynasty; four and five the Second Dynasty; line six the Third Dynasty; the lost lines seven and eight on the front and the first line on the back the Fourth Dynasty; and the rest of the back the Fifth Dynasty. Within each year-compartment the hieroglyphs describe one or more outstanding occurrences of the year. In the record of the First Dynasty, for example, one year is designated as that of the "Smiting of the Troglodytes."[2]

【 148.   In the middle space above the long rows of year-compartments are written the names of kings. Thus the years are also years of their reigns. Several entries represent the transition from one reign to the next. One of these is found at the beginning of the first line on the back. Here the year-compartment is divided by a plain vertical line. To the right of this line the king's name has been lost but hieroglyphic signs are in part preserved and in part plainly to be restored in terms of the space that was available.[3] Four crescent moons indicate four months. A sun signifies days and is followed by two signs for ten (two vertical strokes joined by a curve at the top) and four vertical strokes for four units. Together the signs mean: "four months and twenty-four days." To the left of the plain vertical dividing line is to be read "seven months and eleven days," and in the middle space above and on to the left the name of King Shepseskaf, one of the last kings of the Fourth Dynasty. Four months and twenty-four days plus seven months and eleven days equals twelve months (of thirty days each) and five days, which is exactly the length of the standard civil year in Egypt (¶40). Therefore this year was divided by the amounts specified between the last part-year of the reign of the preceding king and the first part of a year of the reign of King Shepseskaf. Further hieroglyphs to the left also call this part-year the "rising," i.e., the accession of the

[2] ARE I, §104.
[3] Gardiner in JEA 31 (1945), p.12 and Fig. 1c.

new king, and the "union of the two lands," a name for a feast celebrating the accession. At this time, therefore, the years of a king simply coincided with the years of the civil calendar, plus such parts of years as were involved in the beginning and the ending of a given reign.

⟨ 149.   Furthermore, the Palermo Stone shows the first steps toward the numbering of regnal years. In the reign of a First Dynasty king is mentioned the "First occurrence of the Feast of Djet."[4] This can hardly have been the inauguration of this feast but only its first observance in the reign of this king. The numbered recording of events of regular occurrence in the several years of a king's reign is almost the same as the numbering of the regnal years themselves. That such numbering was continued is shown not only by a "Second occurrence of the Feast of Djet" in the reign of another First Dynasty king[5] but also by this formula found in every other year of kings of the Second Dynasty: "Fourth occurrence of the numbering"; "Fifth occurrence of the numbering"; "Sixth occurrence of the numbering"; and so on.[6] In some cases this is called a "numbering of gold and lands,"[7] and later it is a "numbering of large cattle."[8] Since the numbering took place only every second year there is also such a designation as the "year after the seventh numbering."[9] Here then in the first dynasties and in the Old Kingdom are all the elements of the system which continued in use throughout most of Egyptian history: the years of the king are the same as the years of the civil calendar; the years are identified by a consecutive numbering.

⟨ 150.   In the New Kingdom (Eighteenth to Twentieth Dynasties), however, a different manner of reckoning was introduced and for a time employed. Instead of equating a regnal year with a year of the standard civil calendar, each regnal year was reckoned from the actual accession day, whenever it was, to the anniversary of the same, and so on. This may be called a factual regnal year in distinction from a regnal year equated with a calendar year.

⟨ 151.   But again in the Saite period (Twenty-sixth Dynasty) and from then on, the old system was employed and the regnal years

[4] ARE I, §101.   [5] ARE I, §107.   [6] ARE I, §§120, 122, 124.
[7] ARE I, §135, etc.   [8] ARE I, §157.   [9] ARE I, §161.

were the same as the years of the civil calendar, i.e., each regnal year began with New Year's day, the first day of the first month of the first or Inundation season, the first day of the month Thoth.

¶ 152.   Given the system just described (¶¶149, 151) where the regnal year was counted as the calendar year, the question naturally arises as to how to treat portions of years. It must usually have been the case that a preceding ruler died with some portion of his last calendar year unfinished and a new ruler acceded to the throne at some point prior to the next New Year's day. At least from the time of the Ptolemies it is possible to see how the Egyptian scribes handled this problem. From his accession to the end of the then current calendar year was the new king's first regnal year. This fractional first regnal year and the unfinished part of the last regnal year of the preceding ruler occupied a single calendar year. In the texts such a year is referred to by some such phrase as "the last year which is also the first." Thus, for example, the year 52/51 B.C. in which Ptolemy XII Auletes was succeeded by his daughter Cleopatra VII is called ἔτος λ τὸ καὶ α, "the thirtieth year which is also the first."[10] Then the next calendar year, beginning Thoth 1, was the new king's second regnal year.

¶ 153.   In a consecutive tabulation this means that the last unfinished calendar year of a ruler, in which his successor begins to reign, is not credited to the expiring king but is counted to the new king. In the example just given (¶152), the transition from Ptolemy XII Auletes to Cleopatra VII would have to be tabulated as in Table 32. By such a manner of reckoning, in giving consecutive totals, Ptolemy XII Auletes would be credited with twenty-nine years of reign.

¶ 154.   Another interesting example of the manner of reckoning under discussion is found in Oxyrhynchus Papyrus No. 98.[11] This papyrus is an acknowledgement, written in the fifth year of Antoninus Pius, by a certain Chaeremon that he had received from Archias, a freedman, the sum of 168 drachmae, the balance due on a loan of 700 drachmae made four years earlier. This previous date of the original loan is stated thus in lines 12-15 of the papyrus:

[10] T. C. Skeat in *Mizraim* 6 (1937), p.8; and in JEA 46 (1960), p.91.
[11] OP I, pp.160-161.

TABLE 32. Egyptian Regnal Years at the Transition
from Ptolemy XII Auletes to Cleopatra VII

Regnal Year	New Year's Day, Thoth 1	Calendar Year	
		PTOLEMY XII AULETES	
29	Sep 5, 53 B.C.	53/52 B.C.	Last full regnal year = calendar year of Auletes' reign.
		CLEOPATRA VII	
1	Sep 5, 52 B.C.	52/51 B.C.	"The thirtieth year which is also the first," i.e., the thirtieth and uncounted year of Auletes in which this king died; the accession and first year of Cleopatra.
2	Sep 5, 51 B.C.	51/50 B.C.	Second year of Cleopatra.

τῷ ʿΑθὺρ μηνὶ [τοῦ
δευτέρου καὶ ἰκοστοῦ ἔτους θεοῦ ʿΑδρια[νοῦ,
ὃ ἔσ[τ]ι πρῶτον ἔτος ᾿Αντωνίνου Κ[αίσαρος
τοῦ κυρίου

in the month of Hathyr
in the twenty-second year of the deified Hadrian
which is the first year of our sovereign Antoninus Caesar

⟨ 155. This double date may be readily understood from the tabulation in Table 33 of the regnal years of Hadrian and the transition to the reign of Antoninus Pius in Egyptian reckoning. All years are shown as common years.

The papyrus also mentions the month Hathyr. Since Hathyr falls in Oct/Nov, the date was in Oct/Nov, A.D. 137.

⟨ 156. The way just illustrated is the way reigns are recorded in the *Canon* or list of rulers given by the Alexandrian astronomer Claudius Ptolemaeus in the second century of the Christian era. This means that in an extended sequence of this sort, kings who inaugurated and terminated their reigns within a single calendar year are not even counted in the list, because it was the next king who was newly on the throne as the year ended to whom the year was credited. This accounts for the omission in the Canon of Ptole-

TABLE 33. THE REGNAL YEARS OF HADRIAN IN EGYPTIAN RECKONING

Egyptian Regnal Year's	Calendar Years in the Christian Era	
1	Aug 29, 116-Aug 28, 117	On Aug 8 or 9, A.D. 117, Trajan died and Hadrian succeeded him. The balance of that year in the Egyptian calendar, i.e., through Epagomenae 5 = Aug 28, 117, constituted regnal year 1 of Hadrian.
2	Aug 29, 117-Aug 28, 118	Hadrian's regnal year 2 began with the beginning of the next calendar year on Thoth 1 = Aug 29, and so extended from Aug 29, 117, to Aug 28, 118. Succeeding regnal years were therefore:
3	Aug 29, 118-Aug 28, 119	
....	....	
20	Aug 29, 135-Aug 28, 136	
21	Aug 29, 136-Aug 28, 137	
22	Aug 29, 137-Aug 28, 138	In this calendar year Hadrian died on Jul 10, 138, and was succeeded by Antoninus Pius. This calendar year was therefore at the same time regnal year 22 of Hadrian and regnal year 1 of Antoninus.

my VII Neos Philopator, Berenice III, and Ptolemy XI Alexander II, as well as of Galba, Otho, and Vitellius.[12]

2. IN MESOPOTAMIA

LITERATURE: Julius Lewy, "Forschungen zur alten Geschichte Vorderasiens," in MVAG 29 (1924), 2; A. Ungnad, "Datenlisten," in RA II, pp.131-194; Arno Poebel, "The duration of the Reign of Smerdis, the Magian, and the Reigns of Nebuchadnezzar III and Nebuchadnezzar IV," in AJSL 56 (1939), pp.121-145; Poebel, "The Use of Mathematical Mean Values in Babylonian King List B," in *Miscellaneous Studies.* AS 14, 1947, pp.110-122; P. van der Meer, *The Ancient Chronology of Western Asia and Egypt.* 1947.

◖ 157.   In Mesopotamia as in Egypt the oldest known way to designate a year was by an outstanding occurrence in it. In the Old

[12] Skeat in *Mizraim* 6 (1937), pp.7-8.

Akkadian period (c.2360-c.2180 B.C.) and under King Naram-Sin year-designations such as these are found:[1]

> In the year that Naram-Sin laid the foundation of the temple of Enlil in Nippur and of Inanna in Zabalam.
> Year: Naram-Sin brought the mouth of the canal E-erina to Nippur.

In the later Third Dynasty of Ur there are such year-designations as these,[2] in the reign of Shulgi:

> To Shulgi was strength given.
> The high priest of Shulgi was installed and exalted.

And in the reign of Pur-Sin:

> King Pur-Sin destroyed Urbilum.

In the First Dynasty of Babylon under Hammurabi (now probably to be dated around 1728-1686 B.C.), year-designations include ones such as these:[3]

> Hammurabi (became) king.
> He established justice in the country.
> Uruk and Isin were conquered.
> The canal Hammurabi-hegal (was dug).

For the reign of Samsuiluna, immediate successor of Hammurabi, a tablet in the British Museum[4] begins:

> Year: Samsuiluna (became) king.
> Year: He established freedom (from taxation) for Sumer and Akkad.

It continues with successive years, including:

> Year: Canal "Samsuiluna is a source of prosperity (for the people)."
> Year: All the enemies.
> Year: The wall of Isin was demolished.
> Year: Upon the command of Enlil.
> Year following (the year): Upon the command of Enlil.
> Year: He redug the canal Durul and Taban.

After all have been given there is a summary statement that thirty-eight year-names have been listed, and a concluding note giving the date when the list was written:

> Thirty-eight year-(names) of king Samsuiluna.
> (Written) Aiaru 2 (of)
> the year: Ammisaduga (son of Samsuiluna, became) king.

[1] Ungnad in RA II, p.133.   [2] Ungnad in RA II, pp.140, 143.
[3] Ungnad in RA II, pp.178-179; ANET pp.270-271.
[4] Ungnad in RA II, p.182; ANET p.271.

《 158. As in the example just given, such lists of successive year-names can be totaled up to the number of years in the reign of a king, and then summaries of successive reigns can also be given. Another British Museum tablet gives this summary, for example, for the First Dynasty of Babylon:[5]

> Sumuabi, king, 15 years.
> Sumulail, 35 years.
> Sabu, his son, same (i.e., king), 14 years.
> Apil-Sin, his son, same, 18 years.
> Sinmuballit, his son, same, 30 years.
> Hammurabi, his son, same, 55 years.
> Samsuiluna, his son, same, 35 years.
> Ebishum, his son, same, 25 years.
> Ammiditana, same, 25 years.
> Ammisaduga, same, 22 years.
> Samsuditana, same, 31 years.
> Eleven kings, dynasty of Babylon.

In this case it is at once noticeable, however, that Samsuiluna is credited with thirty-five years whereas the list of year-names for his reign just previously considered (¶157) totaled thirty-eight. Presumably the total where the actual year-names are listed one after the other is correct, and there is reason to think that in the case of the summary tablet just quoted a later scribe no longer had access to all the original figures and used some mean values to fill in his list.[6] After the compilation of lists such as the above, it was a natural development to number the years of the king's reign, and reckoning according to regnal years designated by number is found from the Kassite period (c.1650-c.1175 B.C.) on.[7]

《 159. In Assyria, however, a system of dating according to eponyms was used, and long lists of these eponyms are found in the cuneiform sources.[8] While the first full year of a king's reign is named after himself, each of the following years is designated with the name of a high official. The choice of the official who was to give his name to the year was first by lot, but later was a matter of his rank in the hierarchy, regular turns being taken from the king on down. In the lists the name of the official is introduced with the word *limmu*, hence these are also called *limmu*-lists, but the mean-

---

[5] ANET p.271.
[6] Poebel, *Miscellaneous Studies*, pp.110-122.
[7] Ungnad in RA II, p.132.
[8] ARAB II, §§1194-1198.

ing is still eponym-year or eponymat. The extant sources make possible a reconstruction of the list beginning with Adad-nirari about
911 B.C. and continuing to the middle of the seventh century B.C.
In the tenth year of Ashur-dan III, the year designated by the name
of Bur-Sagale as eponym, a solar eclipse is mentioned. This has
been identified with an astronomically computed eclipse of Jun 15,
763 B.C., so that a fixed point is established in the list.[9]

《160.   Returning now to the reckoning of years by the numbered
years of kings' reigns, this was introduced according to present
evidence, as noted above (¶158), in the Kassite period (c.1650-
c.1175 B.C.), was used in Assyria alongside the eponym dating,
and continued in use in Babylonia until in the time of the Seleucid
era.[10] As we have already seen in discussing Egyptian records of
reigns, it is important to know how regnal years are related to
calendar years, and how the years are counted at the point of transition from one reign to another. Already on the Palermo Stone we
saw (¶148) how a calendar year was divided between the last portion of the last year of the preceding king and the first portion of the
first year of the new king. We noted also (¶152) that the prevailing
solution of the problem of how to count these part-years at such a
transition point was to reckon the part of a year from a new king's
accession to the next New Year's day—whether this part was long
or short—as his first regnal year, and to count the next full calendar
year as constituting already his second regnal year. In Mesopotamia
the problem was handled in a different way. The part-year at the
outset of a new reign was designated by a name of its own. Already the Sumerians called it *mu-sag-namlugal-a(k)*, meaning "year
(representing) the beginning of the kingship (of someone)," and
the corresponding term in Babylonian is *resh sharruti*. The latter
in turn is translated word for word in the Hebrew ראשית מלכות,
reshiyt malkut (¶302). In English the common and convenient ren-
dering is "accession year."[11]

《161.   Using this term, the system of reckoning which prevailed
in Babylonia, Assyria, and Persia, may be called the accession-year
system. This means that the balance of the calendar year in which

9 Ungnad in RA II, pp.412-457; ANET p.274.
10 Ungnad in RA II, pp.132, 412; ANET pp.278-279.
11 Lewy in MVAG 29, 2, p.25 n.3; Albright in JBL 51 (1932), p.102; Poebel in
AJSL 56 (1939), p.121 n.3.

a preceding king died or was removed and a new king came to the throne was counted as the accession year of the new king, and the first full year of his reign was reckoned as beginning with the next New Year's day, i.e., with the next Nisanu 1 in the Babylonian calendar. The calendar year in which the predecessor occupied the throne for only a part of the year and then died or was removed, could therefore still be counted as corresponding to his own last numbered regnal year. If we may most unambiguously designate the system just described, then, as the accession-year system, we may also use as the most unambiguous designation for the contrasting system discussed in relation to Egypt and summarized in the preceding paragraph (¶160) as the nonaccession-year system. To recapitulate: In the accession-year system the portion of a year from the accession of the king to the end of the then current calendar year is only his "accession year" (and for chronological purposes remains a part of the last numbered regnal year of his predecessor), and the new king's Year 1 begins only on the first day of the new calendar year after his accession. In the nonaccession-year system the portion of a calendar year, no matter how brief, remaining from the accession of the king to the end of the then current calendar year is treated not as an uncounted accession year but as already Year 1 of the new king; therewith the preceding king fails to be credited with that calendar year as a regnal year in which he does not live out a full year on the throne.

《 162.   The way in which the chronological data are presented in accordance with the accession-year system may be seen most clearly in the tables of Parker and Dubberstein, *Babylonian Chronology* (= PDBC) where, as we have noted (¶54), the data of the cuneiform sources and of astronomy are correlated. For a single example we may note the transition from the reign of Nabopolassar to that of Nebuchadrezzar II. From the annalistic references in the cuneiform document known as the Babylonian Chronicle (British Museum 21946) and from the astronomical reconstitution of the Babylonian calendar it can be established that Nabopolassar died on the eighth day of the month Abu in the twenty-first year of his reign, a date corresponding to Aug 15, 605 B.C.; and that Nebuchadrezzar II ascended the throne in Babylon soon thereafter on the first day of Ululu, a date corresponding to Sep 7, 605 B.C.[12] The transition may therefore be tabulated as in Table 34.

TABLE 34. BABYLONIAN REGNAL YEARS AT THE TRANSITION FROM NABOPOLASSAR TO NEBUCHADREZZAR II

Regnal Year	New Year's Day, Nisanu 1	Calendar Year	
		NABOPOLASSAR	
21	Apr 12, 605 B.C.	605/604 B.C.	Nabopolassar dies on Abu 8 = Aug 15 in his twenty-first regnal year. Nebuchadrezzar II ascends the throne on Ululu 1 = Sep 7, and the balance of this calendar year until the next New Year's day, i.e., the next Nisanu 1, is accounted his "accession year."
		NEBUCHADREZZAR II	
1	Apr 2, 604 B.C.	604/603 B.C.	This is now the first regnal year of Nebuchadrezzar, and successive years are counted consecutively onward in the same manner.
2	Mar 22, 603 B.C.	603/602 B.C.	

3. AMONG THE JEWS

LITERATURE: Julian Morgenstern, "The New Year for Kings," in *Occident and Orient, Gaster Anniversary Volume*, ed. Bruno Schindler, 1936, pp.439-456; Edgar Frank, *Talmudic and Rabbinical Chronology, The Systems of Counting Years in Jewish Literature*. 1956.

⟨ 163. In the foregoing discussion (¶¶146ff.) of materials reflecting practices in Egypt and in Mesopotamia in the reckoning of regnal years points have come into view, implicitly or explicitly, which must always be kept in mind in any consideration of the reckoning of such years in any land. In explication and recapitulation of such points, it is evident that at least the following items must be noticed in the attempt to understand any system of reckoning by regnal years.

(1) *Accession.* At what point is the reign considered to begin? This point most often coincides, no doubt, with the death of the

[12] PDBC p.12.

preceding ruler, yet there may be an interval before the new king is selected, installed, or confirmed in office. Other possibilities as to when his reign is considered actually to begin include the time when a coregency is established, when a capital is occupied, when a decisive victory is won, or when some remaining rival is eliminated.

(2) *Factual year or calendar year.* Is the regnal year counted from the actual accession to the annual anniversary of the same? If so, it may be called a factual year. Is the regnal year counted as equivalent to the calendar year? The latter is probably much more often the case, and therewith additional questions arise. (3) *Accession year or nonaccession year.* If the regnal year is equated with a calendar year, is the reckoning by the accession-year or the non-accession-year system? In the accession-year system the balance of the calendar year in which the point of the beginning of the reign falls is considered as an "accession year" and only the next full calendar year is considered as regnal Year 1. In the nonaccession-year system the calendar year in which the beginning point of the reign falls is itself counted as Year 1 of the reign. (4) *Calendar.* If the regnal year is equated with a calendar year, which calendar is in use? The following calendars have already been discussed in some detail (¶¶37ff.) and are simply listed here (Table 35) by their name and the date (in the order of the Julian year) of their New Year's day, which is the crucial point for reckoning by regnal year equated with calendar year.

⟦ 164.   Which of the methods just outlined (¶163) were those employed by the Jews is a question which must necessarily be raised in connection with many biblical dates. Some of the concrete problems in this regard will be taken up in Part Two of this book. In extra-biblical Jewish sources there is one passage in particular which, because of its relative antiquity and its relatively explicit statements as to how years are reckoned, must be considered in the present context. This passage is found in the Mishnah and gives concise definitions of four different New Year's days; in the accompanying Gemara these definitions are elucidated and discussed at length; and the whole is now contained in the Babylonian Talmud in the division Moed ("Feasts") and in the tractate Rosh Hashanah ("New Year").[1] The Mishnah reads as follows:

[1] Rosh Hashanah I, 1, DM p.188; 2a ff. SBT II, 7, pp.1ff.

TABLE 35. Calendars and New Year's Days

NAME	NEW YEAR'S DAY
Roman (Julian) (Table 31)	Jan 1
Babylonian (Table 9)	Nisanu (Mar/Apr) 1
Jewish (Table 36)	Nisan (Mar/Apr) 1
Macedonian in Babylonia (earlier correlation) (Table 20)	Artemisios = Nisanu (Mar/Apr) 1
Macedonian in Babylonia (later correlation) (Table 23)	Xanthikos = Nisanu (Mar/Apr) 1
Macedonian in Palestine (earlier correlation) (Table 28)	Artemisios = Nisan (Mar/Apr) 1
Macedonian in Palestine (later correlation) (Table 29)	Xanthikos = Nisan (Mar/Apr) 1
Macedonian in Arabia (Table 26)	Xanthikos 1 = Mar 22
Greek (Attic) (Table 16)	Hekatombaion (Jul) 1
Greek (Delphic) (Table 17)	Apellaios (Jul) 1
Egyptian (fixed standard civil calendar) (Table 8)	Thoth 1 = Aug 29
Macedonian in Egypt (fixed equation) (Table 27)	Dios 1 = Thoth 1 = Aug 29
Honorific Imperial in Egypt (Table 27)	Sebastos 1 = Thoth 1 = Aug 29
Israelite (Tables 12, 37)	Tishri (Sep/Oct) 1
Macedonian in Syria (earlier correlation) (Table 19)	Dios = First Tishri = Tishri (Sep/Oct) 1
Macedonian in Syria (later correlation) (Table 24)	Hyperberetaios = Tishri (Sep/Oct) 1
Syro-Macedonian in relation to the Julian (Table 25)	Hyperberetaios 1 = Oct 1

"There are four New Years. On the first of Nisan is New Year for kings and for festivals. On the first of Elul is New Year for the tithe of cattle. Rabbi Eleazar and Rabbi Simeon, however, place this on the first of Tishri. On the first of Tishri is New Year for years, for release and jubilee years, for plantation and for tithe of vegetables. On the first of Shebat is New Year for trees, according to the ruling of Beth Shammai; Beth Hillel, however, place it on the fifteenth of that month."

⟨ 165. We are here concerned with two of the New Years thus defined in the Talmud, and the first is that which begins with the month Nisan in the spring: "On the first of Nisan is New Year for kings and for festivals." According to this statement one would suppose that regnal years always coincided with calendar years beginning Nisan 1. In the ensuing rabbinic discussion of the Gemara it is further explained:

"If a king ascends the throne on the twenty-ninth of Adar, as soon as the first of Nisan arrives he is reckoned to have reigned a year. This teaches us that Nisan is the New Year for kings, and that one day in a year is reckoned as a year. But if he ascended the throne on the first of Nisan he is not reckoned to have reigned a year till the next first of Nisan comes round."[2]

According to this statement, not only do regnal years coincide with calendar years beginning Nisan 1 but they are also reckoned by what we have called the nonaccession-year method. Indeed we recognize here as a general or normal principle of Jewish reckoning that the part stands for the whole: a part of a month is considered a whole month and a part of a year is considered a whole year.[3] In reckoning the years of life of a person, however, this does not hold but it is completed years which are counted. Thus Rabbi Avadyah, elucidating another passage in the Mishnah (Para VIII, 9), says: "Like a man whose son is born on passover. He has fulfilled his first year on passover of the next year."[4]

❪ 166.   Returning to the passage in Rosh Hashanah, the fact that kings' reigns are always reckoned as commencing from Nisan 1 is substantiated in the rabbinic discussion by the citation of I K 6:1. Here the year is given as at the same time the four hundred and eightieth after the Israelites came out of Egypt and the fourth year of Solomon, and the month is given only once as Ziv, the second month. Ziv, using the old Canaanite month name (¶60), is clearly the same as Iyyar, the second month in the list of month names patterned after the Babylonian (¶70). Since Ziv = Iyyar was the second month both in the four hundred and eightieth year reckoned from the exodus and in the fourth year of the reign of Solomon, both series of years were stated in terms of years reckoned from Nisan 1.

❪ 167.   After that a considerable discussion ensues,[5] as to whether the rule that New Year for kings is Nisan 1 was meant to apply only to the kings of Israel, and it is strongly maintained at least by some that the years of non-Israelite kings are reckoned not from Nisan 1 but from Tishri 1. Here Neh 1:1 and 2:1 are cited. Neh 1:1 mentions the month of Kislev in the twentieth year; Neh 2:1 mentions

2 SBT p.2.
3 Cf. also Rosh Hashanah 10b, SBT p.38.
4 Quoted by Frank, *Talmudic and Rabbinical Chronology*, p.18 n.17.
5 Rosh Hashanah 3a f., SBT pp.7ff.

the month of Nisan in the twentieth year of King Artaxerxes. Supposing that it is the same "twentieth year" that is meant in both cases, in one and the same year Nisan would come later than Kislev only if the year began with Tishri. Other rabbis, however, denied that this argument was conclusive. In spite of this uncertainty, however, it was affirmed as certain that the numbering of the months always commences with Nisan. Using the formula customary for the introduction of a Baraitha, it was said: "Our Rabbis taught: On the first of Nisan is New Year for months,"[6] i.e., the order of the months always begins with Nisan.

《 168.   The second New Year mentioned in Rosh Hashanah with which we are here concerned is defined in the words: "On the first of Tishri is New Year for years." This statement is explained in the Gemara as meaning that this is the New Year which is used for reckoning cycles.[7] The cycles are the four *tequfoth* (¶34) which are the four dividing points of the year, and the four seasons which they introduce respectively: the Tequfah of Tishri (autumnal equinox); the Tequfah of Tebeth (winter solstice); the Tequfah of Nisan (vernal equinox); the Tequfah of Tammuz (summer solstice).

《 169.   In the same connection it is stated that the world was created in Tishri, a topic taken up again a little later in the discussion.[8] Among the rabbis who held this opinion, Rabbi Eleazar is quoted as saying:

> "In Tishri the world was created; in Tishri the patriarchs [Abraham and Jacob] were born; in Tishri the patriarchs died; on passover Isaac was born; on New Year [Tishri 1] Sarah, Rachel, and Hannah were visited [i.e., remembered on high]; on New Year Joseph went forth from prison; on New Year the bondage of our ancestors in Egypt ceased [six months before the redemption which was the exodus]; in Nisan they were redeemed and in Nisan they will be redeemed in the time to come."

This opinion that the world was created in Tishri was supported by Rabbi Eleazar by reference to Gen 1:11 where the putting forth of vegetation was held to imply the autumnal season of rainfall (¶31); another rabbi, however, cited the same verse to show that the time was Nisan. In the reckoning of years from the creation

---

6 Rosh Hashanah 7a, SBT p.23.
7 Rosh Hashanah 8a, SBT p.30.
8 Rosh Hashanah 10b-11a, SBT pp.38-39.

of the world (¶¶204ff.) it was generally considered that the start should be made from Tishri. Another argument in support of Tishri as the month in which the world was created was based upon the first word in Genesis, בראשית, "In the beginning." The letters of this word can be rearranged to make א' בתשרי, "the first day in the month Tishri."[9]

⟪ 170.   In summary we find ourselves concerned chiefly with two Jewish years, one beginning in the spring on Nisan 1, one beginning in the fall on Tishri 1. Regardless of which year is used, numbering of the months is normally in sequence from Nisan (¶167). The two Jewish years therefore appear as in Tables 36 and 37.

TABLE 36. THE JEWISH YEAR WITH NISAN 1 AS NEW YEAR'S DAY			TABLE 37. THE JEWISH YEAR WITH TISHRI 1 AS NEW YEAR'S DAY		
1.	Nisan	Mar/Apr	7.	Tishri	Sep/Oct
2.	Iyyar	Apr/May	8.	Marheshvan	Oct/Nov
3.	Sivan	May/Jun	9.	Kislev	Nov/Dec
4.	Tammuz	Jun/Jul	10.	Tebeth	Dec/Jan
5.	Ab	Jul/Aug	11.	Shebat	Jan/Feb
6.	Elul	Aug/Sep	12.	Adar	Feb/Mar
7.	Tishri	Sep/Oct	1.	Nisan	Mar/Apr
8.	Marheshvan	Oct/Nov	2.	Iyyar	Apr/May
9.	Kislev	Nov/Dec	3.	Sivan	May/Jun
10.	Tebeth	Dec/Jan	4.	Tammuz	Jun/Jul
11.	Shebat	Jan/Feb	5.	Ab	Jul/Aug
12.	Adar	Feb/Mar	6.	Elul	Aug/Sep

4. IN GREECE

LITERATURE: R. D. Hicks, "Chronology," in *A Companion to Greek Studies*, ed. Leonard Whibley. 3d ed. 1916, pp.69ff.

⟪ 171.   In regard to official and regnal years the Greek system again is not of major concern in our area of investigation, but may be mentioned briefly as we make the transition to the Roman system. Throughout the historical period the custom was to date events by a local official or local officials in office at the time. Those particularly singled out to serve in this way were the first archon at Athens, the first ephor at Sparta, and the priestess of Hera at Argos, the last named being chosen for life. Thus, for a single example, the

---

[9] Frank, *Talmudic and Rabbinical Chronology*, p.16 n.15.

Athenian historian Thucydides[1] gives a date equivalent to April
431 B.C. by naming the following officials:

"When Chrysis was in the forty-eighth year of her priesthood at Argos,
and Aenesias was ephor at Sparta, and Pythodorus had still four months
to serve as archon at Athens, in the sixteenth month after the battle of
Potidaea, at the opening of spring."

5. IN ROME

LITERATURE: T. Mommsen, *Chronica minora* 1-3. Monumenta Germaniae
Historica 9, 11, 13. 1892-98; Willy Liebenam, *Fasti Consulares Imperii Romani von 30 v. Chr. bis 565 n. Chr. mit Kaiserliste und Anhang.* KLT 41-43.
1909; J. S. Reid, "Chronology and Chronological Tables," in *A Companion
to Latin Studies*, ed. John E. Sandys, 3d ed. 1925, pp.90-148; A. Cappelli,
*Cronologia, cronografia e calendario perpetuo dal principio dell'êra cristiana
ai giorni nostri.* 2d ed. 1930; "Chronological Tables," in CAH X, 1934, at end;
Arthur E. Gordon, *Album of Dated Latin Inscriptions*, I, *Rome and the
Neighborhood, Augustus to Nerva*, Text and Plates, 1958.

(1) CONSULS

⟨172. In a method somewhat similar to that seen in the eponym
lists of Assyria (¶159) and the reference to various officials in
Greece (¶171), it was the custom in Rome to designate a year by
mention of two officials, the consuls, who were in office in that year.
When the ancient Roman monarchy fell the king was replaced by
two magistrates who, throughout the republic, were the heads of
administration at home and abroad. Under the later rule of the
Caesars the office continued and the emperor himself was often
elected to the position. Since the post was held for one year—from
153 B.C. on, a year beginning on Jan 1 (¶142)—a reference to the
two consuls then in office sufficed to define a year-date.

⟨173. The rise and use of this system are clearly shown by the
Roman historian Livy. He tells[1] how "the rule of the kings at Rome,
from its foundation to its liberation, lasted two hundred and forty-
four years," and how then two consuls were chosen in the assembly
of the people, those for the first year (A.U.C. 245 [for dating A.U.C.
see ¶¶188ff.] = 509 B.C.) being Lucius Junius Brutus and Lucius
Tarquinius Collatinus. Collatinus resigned before his year of office
ended, and was replaced by Publius Valerius.[2] For the following

[1] II, ii, 1.

[1] I, ix, 4.   [2] II, ii, 10-11.

year (A.U.C. 246 = 508 B.C.) Livy states:[3] "Next Publius Valerius (for the second time) and Titus Lucretius were made consuls." And so the framework of Roman history continues. Typical further references from Livy are:

> A.U.C. 249 = 505 B.C.
> *Consules M. Valerius P. Postumius. Eo anno bene pugnatum . . .*
> The consulship of Marcus Valerius and Publius Postumius. This year a successful war was waged. . .[4]

> A.U.C. 254 = 500 B.C.
> *Consules Ser. Sulpicius M'. Tullius; nihil dignum memoria actum.*
> In the consulship of Servius Sulpicius and Manius Tullius nothing worthy of note occurred.[5]

> A.U.C. 256 = 498 B.C.
> *Consules Q. Cloelius et T. Larcius, inde A. Sempronius et M. Minucius. His consulibus aedis Saturno dedicata.*
> The consuls Quintus Cloelius and Titus Larcius were followed by Aulus Sempronius and Marcus Minucius. In the latter year a temple to Saturn was dedicated.[6]

> A.U.C. 432 = 322 B.C.
> *Insequenti anno, Q. Fabio L. Fulvio consulibus. . . .*
> In the following year, when Quintus Fabius and Lucius Fulvius were consuls. . . .[7]

【 174. For an example of consular dates in inscriptions, a marble tablet may be cited which was found on the Via Latina in Rome. It appears to be the epitaph of Scirtus, who was a slave charioteer, and it contains a list of his races dated by consuls. These dates begin (line 3) with L. Munatius and C. Silius (= A.D. 13); they include (line 8) Tiberius Caesar III and Germanicus Caesar II (= A.D. 18); and (line 11) Tiberius Caesar IIII and Drusus Caesar II (= A.D. 21); and they extend to (line 15) Cossus Cornelius Lentulus and M. Asinius (= A.D. 25).[8]

【 175. Lists of the consuls were compiled at an early date but often contained discrepancies or gaps. Livy tells of certain consuls whose names he could find *neque in annalibus priscis neque in libris magistratuum*, "neither in the ancient annals nor in the lists of magistrates."[9] Among the sources of this sort were the *Annales Maximi*

---

[3] II, ix, 1.   [4] II, xvi, 1.
[5] II, xix, 1.   [6] II, xxi, 1.   [7] VIII, xxxviii, 1.
[8] Gordon, *Album of Dated Latin Inscriptions*, I, p.67 No.60.
[9] IV, vii, 10.

or annals of the Pontifical College published by Mucius Scaevola in 130 B.C.; and the *Fasti Capitolini* (for the *fasti* cf. ¶141), affixed to the wall of the *Regia* or official residence of the Pontifex Maximus and extant in fragments in the Museum on the Capitol.[10] The *Fasti Capitolini* in turn were a source ultimately drawn upon, with revision, by the "Chronographer of the Year 354."

¶176. *Chronographus Anni CCCLIIII* or "Chronographer of the Year 354" is the anonymous title under which there has come down in two late copies of older manuscripts a work which may have been edited in the year indicated by Furius Dionysius Filocalus, later the calligrapher of Pope Damasus (A.D. 366-384). This work, which is available in Mommsen's *Chronica minora* 1, contains: (1) a list of the consuls beginning with Brutus and Collatinus (¶173) and extending to A.D. 354 (Mommsen pp.50-61); (2) a list of the dates of Easter from 312 to 411 (Mommsen pp.62-64); (3) a list of the prefects of the city from 254 to 354 (Mommsen pp.65-69); (4) a list of the burial places of bishops (*depositio episcoporum*) and martyrs (*depositio martyrum*) and the days on which they were remembered (Mommsen pp.70-72); and (5) a list of the bishops of Rome from Peter to Liberius (*catalogus Liberianus*) (Mommsen pp.73ff.). The Depositio Martyrum became the basis of the vast Martyrologium Hieronymianum in the sixth century, and the Catalogus Liberianus developed into the Liber Pontificalis (¶493) of the seventh century.[11]

¶177. The Roman monk and historian Cassiodorus Senator (A.D. c.490-c.585) also compiled in his *Chronica* (published in A.D. 519) a list of the consuls.[12] It begins with Junius Brutus and Lucius Tarquinius (A.U.C. 245 = 509 B.C.), then Publius Valerius II and Titus Lucretius (A.U.C. 246 = 508 B.C.), and so on down to the time of Cassiodorus himself.

¶178. For the time with which we are chiefly concerned in relation to such dates, the list of consuls given by the Chronographus Anni CCCLIIII appears in Table 38. In each case one is to understand, *Caesare V et Antonino consulibus*, and so on, as in the example from Livy for A.U.C. 432 = 322 B.C. given above (¶173).

10 Reid in *A Companion to Latin Studies*, pp.103f.
11 Hans Lietzmann, *Die drei ältesten Martyrologien*. KLT 2, 1903, pp.3f.
12 ed. Mommsen, *Chronica minora* 2. 1894, pp.109-161.

TABLE 38. ROMAN CONSULS FROM 44 B.C. TO A.D. 135

A.U.C.	B.C.	Consuls	A.U.C.	A.D.	Consuls
710	44	Caesare V et Antonino	755	2	Vinicio et Varo
711	43	Pansa et Hirstio	756	3	Lamia et Servilio
		(C. Pansa and A. Hirti-	757	4	Catulo et Saturnino
		us were killed and Oc-	758	5	Voleso et Magno
		tavius [later to be Au-	759	6	Lepido et Arruntio
		gustus] was declared con-	760	7	Cretico et Nerva
		sul)	761	8	Camello et Quintiliano
712	42	Lepido et Planco	762	9	Camerino et Sabino
713	41	Petate et Isaurico	763	10	Dolabella et Silano
714	40	Calvino et Pollione	764	11	Lepido et Tauro
715	39	Censorino et Sabino	765	12	Caesare et Capitone
716	38	Pulchro et Flacco	766	13	Planco et Silano
717	37	Agrippa et Gallo	767	14	duobus Sextis
718	36	Publicula et Nerva	768	15	Druso Caesare et Flacco
719	35	Cornificio et Pompeio	769	16	Tauro et Libone
720	34	Libone et Atratino	770	17	Flacco et Rufo
721	33	Augusto II et Tullo	771	18	Tito Caesare III et Ger-
722	32	Henobulbo et Sossio			manico Caesare II
723	31	Augusto III et Messala	772	19	Silano et Balbo
724	30	Augusto IIII et Grasso	773	20	Messala et Cotta
725	29	Augusto V et Apuleio	774	21	Tito Caesare IIII et Dru-
726	28	Augusto VI et Agrippa II			so Caesare II
727	27	Augusto VII et Agrippa	775	22	Agrippa et Galba
		III	776	23	Pollione et Vetere
728	26	Augusto VIII et Tauro	777	24	Caethego et Varro
729	25	Augusto VIIII et Silano	778	25	Agrippa et Lentulo
730	24	Augusto X et Flacco	779	26	Getulico et Sabino
731	23	Augusto XI et Pisone	780	27	Grasso et Pisone
732	22	Marcello et Arrutio	781	28	Silano et Nerva
733	21	Lollio et Lepido	782	29	Gemino et Gemino
734	20	Apuleio et Nerva	783	30	Vinicio et Longino
735	19	Saturnino et Lucretio	784	31	Tiberio Caesare V solo
736	18	Lentulo et Lentulo	785	32	Arruntio et Ahenobarbo
737	17	Turnio et Silato	786	33	Galba et Sulla
738	16	Henobarbo et Scipione	787	34	Vitello et Persico
739	15	Libone et Pisone	788	35	Camerino et Noniano
740	14	Grasso et Augure	789	36	Allieno et Plautino
741	13	Nerone et Varo	790	37	Proculo et Nigrino
742	12	Messala et Quirino	791	38	Iuliano et Asprenate
743	11	Tuberone et Maximo	792	39	C. Caesare II et Caesiano
744	10	Africano et Maximo	793	40	C. Caesare III solo
745	9	Druso et Crispino	794	41	C. Caesare IIII et Sa-
746	8	Censorino et Gallo			turnino
747	7	Nerone et Pisone	795	42	Tito Claudio II et Longo
748	6	Balbo et Vetere	796	43	Tito Claudio III et Vi-
749	5	Augusto XII et Sulla			tellio
750	4	Sabino et Rufo	797	44	Crispo II et Tauro
751	3	Lentulo et Messalino	798	45	Vinicio et Corvino
752	2	Augusto XIII et Silvano	799	46	Asiatico II et Silano
753	1	Lentulo et Pisone	800	47	Tito Claudio IIII et Vi-
754	A.D. 1	Caesare et Paulo			tellio III

A.U.C.	A.D.	Consuls	A.U.C.	A.D.	Consuls
801	48	Vitellio et Publicula	843	90	Domitiano XV et Nerva
802	49	Verannio et Gallo	844	91	Clabrione et Traiano
803	50	Vetere et Nerviliano	845	92	Domitiano XVI et Saturnino
804	51	Tito Claudio V et Orfito			
805	52	Sulla et Othone	846	93	Collega et Priscino
806	53	Silano et Antonino	847	94	Asprenate et Laterano
807	54	Marcello et Aviola	848	95	Domitiano XVII et Clemente
808	55	Nerone Caesare et Vetere			
809	56	Saturnino et Scipione	849	96	Valeriano et Vetere
810	57	Nerone II et Pisone	850	97	Nerva II et Rufo III
811	58	Nerone III et Messala	851	98	Nerva III et Traiano II
812	59	Capitone et Aproniano	852	99	Palma et Senecione
813	60	Nerone IIII et Lentulo	853	100	Traiano III et Frontino
814	61	Turpillino et Peto	854	101	Traiano IIII et Peto
815	62	Mario et Gallo	855	102	Servillo II et Sura II
816	63	Regulo et Rufo	856	103	Traiano V et Maximo II
817	64	Grasso et Basso	857	104	Surano II et Marcello
818	65	Nerva et Vestino	858	105	Candido II et Quadrato
819	66	Telesino et Paulo	859	106	Commodo et Cereale
820	67	Capitone et Rufo	860	107	Sura et Senecione
821	68	Trachala et Italico	861	108	Gallo et Bradua
822	69	Galva II et Vinio	862	109	Palma II et Tullo
823	70	Vespasiano II et Tito	863	110	Priscina et Ortito
824	71	Vespasiano III et Nerva	864	111	Pisone et Bolano
825	72	Vespasiano IIII et Tito II	865	112	Traiano VI et Africano
826	73	Domitiano II et Messalino	866	113	Celso et Crispino
827	74	Vespasiano V et Tito III	867	114	Vopisco et Asta
828	75	Vespasiano VI et Tito IIII	868	115	Messala et Pedone
			869	116	Aeliano et Vetere
829	76	Vespasiano VII et Tito V	870	117	Nigro et Aproniano
830	77	Vespasiano VIII et Domitiano V	871	118	Adriano II et Salinatore
			872	119	Adriano II et Rustico
831	78	Commodo et Prisco	873	120	Severo II et Fulvo
832	79	Vespasiano VIIII et Tito VI	874	121	Vero II et Augure
			875	122	Aviola et Pansa
833	80	Tito VII et Domitiano VII	876	123	Petino et Aproniano
			877	124	Glabrione et Torquato
834	81	Silva et Pollione	878	125	Asiatico II et Aquilino
835	82	Domitiano VIII et Sabino	879	126	Vero III et Ambibulo
			880	127	Titiano et Gallicano
836	83	Domitiano VIIII et Rufo	881	128	Asprenate et Libone
837	84	Domitiano X et Sabino	882	129	Marcello II et Marcello II
838	85	Domitiano XI et Furvo			
839	86	Domitiano XII et Dolabella	883	130	Catulino et Apro
			884	131	Pontiano et Rutino
840	87	Domitiano XIII et Saturnino	885	132	Augurino et Sergiano
			886	133	Hibero et Sisenna
841	88	Domitiano XIIII et Rufo	887	134	Serviano et Varo
842	89	Fulvo et Atratino	888	135	Luperco et Attico

(2) HONORS

❲ 179.   Roman dating also made use of reference to various honors received by the emperor from the senate in the course of his reign. Of these honors three were the most important. One is the honor of being elected consul, and in the foregoing list of consuls (Table 38) we have seen many examples where the emperor appears and the number of times he holds the consulship is given. A second honor is that called *tribunicia potestate*, δημαρχικὴ ἐξουσία, or "tribunician power." The Roman magistrates known as "tribunes" enjoyed a certain sacrosanctity and a similar privilege was conferred upon the emperor when he was granted this honor. Dio explains the matter in these words:[1]

> "The tribunician power (ἡ ἐξουσία ἡ δημαρχική), as it is called, which used to be conferred only upon men of the greatest influence, gives them the right to nullify the effects of measures taken by any other official, in case they do not approve it, and makes them immune from scurrilous abuse; and if they appear to be wronged in even the slightest degree, not merely by deed, but even by word, they may destroy the guilty party, as one accursed, without a trial. The emperors, it should be explained, do not think it right to be tribunes, inasmuch as they belong altogether to the patrician class, but they assume the power of the tribunes to its full extent, as it was when it was greatest; and in numbering the years they have held the imperial office they use the tribunician power to mark the stages, the theory being that they received it year by year along with those who are regularly made tribunes."

In the case of Augustus there were occasional grants of the honor earlier, but from 23 B.C. on the tribunician power was renewed annually and was reckoned from July 1, 23 B.C. Thus in his own record of life and work, the Res Gestae, completed in A.D. 14, he states that he was "in the thirty-seventh year of his tribunician power."[2] From then on at each change of reign the new emperor was accorded the honor at the moment of his accession to the throne. For the successors of Augustus up to Trajan, therefore, the first tribunician year was the actual year which began on the accession day and extended through the day prior to the anniversary day one year hence, and the further tribunician years were reckoned in like manner.[3]

❲ 180.   The third honor to be mentioned was that of the "imperial acclamation" signified by the designation *imperator*, αὐτοκράτωρ.

---

[1] LIII, 17, 9-10.   [2] CAH X, p.139.
[3] L. Hennequin in *Dictionnaire de la Bible*, Supplément, II, col. 359.

Originally this was an honorary appellation by which the Roman soldiers saluted their general after a military victory. Subsequently the designation was conferred by the senate and received at frequent intervals by Augustus and his successors. According to a description by Dio,[4] the title was often conferred on account of achievements and sometimes also carried the sense of supreme power. Telling of the year when Augustus was consul for the fifth time (29 B.C.), Dio continues:

> "And he assumed the title of *imperator*. I do not here refer to the title which had occasionally been bestowed, in accordance with the ancient custom, upon generals in recognition of their victories—for he had received that many times before this and received it many times afterwards in honor merely of his achievements, so that he won the name of *imperator* twenty-one times—but rather the title in its other use, which signifies the possession of the supreme power, in which sense it had been voted to his father Caesar and to the children and descendants of Caesar."

As the sources also show, an emperor often received this imperial acclamation not only a number of times in the course of the years of his reign but also even several times within a single year.

⟨ 181. In listing the three honors just discussed, usual practice was to put them in the order, tribunician power, imperial acclamation, and consulship. In illustration of the importance attached to them, we may recall the report of Tacitus[5] of the comments that were made upon the death of Augustus concerning his numerous honors:

> "Much, too, was said of the number of his consulates (in which he had equaled the combined totals of Valerius Corvus and Caius Marius [i.e., 6 + 7 = 13]), his tribunician power unbroken for thirty-seven years, his title of imperator twenty-one times earned, and his other honors, multiplied or new."

(3) YEARS OF REIGN

⟨ 182. As in other lands, there was also of course reference in Roman custom to the years of reign of the emperors, and in the interpretation of references to regnal years the same kind of problems arise which have already been noted elsewhere (¶163). Such a reference to regnal years might also be combined with reference to consuls, to the consulship of the emperor, or to other of his honors. And in the provinces there might be added, too, some reference to

---

[4] LII, 41, 3.   [5] *Annals.* I, 9.

some system of dating prevailing in the area. Thirty-five large papyrus documents found in a cave at Nahal Hever in the State of Israel provide interesting illustration of the combined methods of dating. These manuscripts are written in Greek, Aramaic, and Nabatean, and evidently constitute the archive of a Jewish family living at the south end of the Dead Sea in what was the kingdom of Nabatea and what was made into Provincia Arabia by Trajan in A.D. 106. The manuscripts belong to the fifty-year period from near the end of the first century of the Christian era to just before the Bar Kokhba revolt, i.e., from A.D. 88 to 132. Most of them begin by stating the date according to the Roman consuls, the emperor (e.g., the ninth year of Hadrian = A.D. 125), and the local date of the province (e.g., the twenty-fifth year of the "New Arabian Province" = A.D. 130).[1]

(4) TABLES OF EMPERORS

❴ 183.   In Tables 39-43, therefore, we provide for ready reference outlines of events and honors in the lives and reigns of the emperors from Augustus to Nero. Events are chiefly such as need to be kept in mind in relation to the question of when the reign was considered to begin. Honors, when held simultaneously, are listed in the usual order: tribunicia potestate, imperator, consul. Ultimate sources are ancient literary records and inscriptions; a compilation is provided by Liebenam, *Fasti Consulares*.

TABLE 39. EVENTS AND HONORS IN THE LIFE AND REIGN
(Mar 15, 44 B.C.–Aug 19, A.D. 14) OF AUGUSTUS

B.C. MONTH AND DAY	CHRONOLOGY
63 Sep 23	Birth of C. Octavius
44 Mar 15	Assassination of Julius Caesar
43 Apr 15	Octavian Imperator I
Aug 19	Octavian Consul I
42	
41	
40 Dec	Imperator II
39	
38	Imperator III?
37	

[1] Yigael Yadin in BA 24 (1961), pp.94-95; and in IEJ 12 (1962), pp.235-257; H. J. Polotsky in IEJ 12 (1962), pp.258-262.

B.C. MONTH AND DAY	CHRONOLOGY
36	Imperator IV
35	
34 (or 33)	Imperator V
33	Consul II
32	
31	Consul III
Sep 2	Octavian defeated Antony at Actium
Sep 2	Imperator VI
30	Consul IIII
Aug	Death of Antony and Cleopatra
29	Imperator VII
	Consul V
28	Consul VI
27	Consul VII
Jan 16	Octavian received title Augustus
26	Consul VIII
25	Imperator VIII
	Consul VIIII
24	Consul X
23	Consul XI
Jul 1, 23-June 30, 22	Tribunicia potestate I
22	
Jul 1, 22-June 30, 21	Tribunicia potestate II
21	
Jul 1, 21-Jun 30, 20	Tribunicia potestate III
20	Imperator VIIII?
Jul 1, 20-Jun 30, 19	Tribunicia potestate IIII
19	
Jul 1, 19-Jun 30, 18	Tribunicia potestate V
18	
Jul 1, 18-Jun 30, 17	Tribunicia potestate VI
17	
Jul 1, 17-Jun 30, 16	Tribunicia potestate VII
16	
Jul 1, 16-Jun 30, 15	Tribunicia potestate VIII
15	Imperator X?
Jul 1, 15-Jun 30, 14	Tribunicia potestate VIIII
14	
Jul 1, 14-Jun 30, 13	Tribunicia potestate X
13	
Jul 1, 13-Jun 30, 12	Tribunicia potestate XI
12	Imperator XI
Jul 1, 12-Jun 30, 11	Tribunicia potestate XII

B.C. MONTH AND DAY	CHRONOLOGY
11	Imperator XII
Jul 1, 11-Jun 30, 10	Tribunicia potestate XIII
10	
Jul 1, 10-Jun 30, 9	Tribunicia potestate XIIII
9	Imperator XIII
Jul 1, 9-Jun 30, 8	Tribunicia potestate XV
8	Imperator XIIII
Jul 1, 8-Jun 30, 7	Tribunicia potestate XVI
7	
Jul 1, 7-Jun 30, 6	Tribunicia potestate XVII
6	
Jul 1, 6-Jun 30, 5	Tribunicia potestate XVIII
5	Consul XII
Jul 1, 5-Jun 30, 4	Tribunicia potestate XVIIII
4	
Jul 1, 4-Jun 30, 3	Tribunicia potestate XX
3	
Jul 1, 3-Jun 30, 2	Tribunicia potestate XXI
2	Consul XIII
Jul 1, 2-Jun 30, 1	Tribunicia potestate XXII
1 B.C.	
Jul 1, 1 B.C.-Jun 30, A.D. 1	Tribunicia potestate XXIII
A.D. 1	
Jul 1, 1-Jun 30, 2	Tribunicia potestate XXIIII
2	Imperator XV
Jul 1, 2-Jun 30, 3	Tribunicia potestate XXV
3	
Jul 1, 3-Jun 30, 4	Tribunicia potestate XXVI
4	Imperator XVI
Jul 1, 4-Jun 30, 5	Tribunicia potestate XXVII
5	
Jul 1, 5-Jun 30, 6	Tribunicia potestate XXVIII
6	Imperator XVII
Jul 1, 6-Jun 30, 7	Tribunicia potestate XXVIIII
7	
Jul 1, 7-Jun 30, 8	Tribunicia potestate XXX
8	Imperator XVIII?
Jul 1, 8-Jun 30, 9	Tribunicia potestate XXXI
9	Imperator XVIIII
Jul 1, 9-Jun 30, 10	Tribunicia potestate XXXII
10	
Jul 1, 10-Jun 30, 11	Tribunicia potestate XXXIII
11	Imperator XX
Jul 1, 11-Jun 30, 12	Tribunicia potestate XXXIIII

A.D. MONTH AND DAY	CHRONOLOGY
12	
Jul 1, 12-Jun 30, 13	Tribunicia potestate XXXV
13	
Jul 1, 13-Jun 30, 14	Tribunicia potestate XXXVI
14	Imperator XXI
Jul 1-Aug 19, 14	Tribunicia potestate XXXVII
Aug 19	Death of Augustus

TABLE 40. Events and Honors in the Life and Reign
(Aug 19, A.D. 14–Mar 16, A.D. 37) of Tiberius

B.C. MONTH AND DAY	CHRONOLOGY
42 Nov 16	Birth of Tiberius Claudius Nero
13	Tiberius Consul I
9	Tiberius Imperator I
8	Imperator II
7	Consul II
6	
Jul 1, 6-Jun 30, 5	Tribunicia potestate I
5	
Jul 1, 5-Jun 30, 4	Tribunicia potestate II
4	
Jul 1, 4-Jun 30, 3	Tribunicia potestate III
3	
Jul 1, 3-Jun 30, 2	Tribunicia potestate IIII
2	
Jul 1, 2-Jun 30, 1	Tribunicia potestate V
1	
A.D. 1	
2	
3	
4 Jun 26	Tiberius adopted by Augustus and designated as his successor; called Tiberius Julius Caesar
Jul 1, 4-Jun 30, 5	Tribunicia potestate VI
5	
Jul 1, 5-Jun 30, 6	Tribunicia potestate VII
6	Imperator III
Jul 1, 6-Jun 30, 7	Tribunicia potestate VIII
7	
Jul 1, 7-Jun 30, 8	Tribunicia potestate XXXIIII

A.D. MONTH AND DAY	CHRONOLOGY
8	
Jul 1, 8-Jun 30, 9	Tribunicia potestate X
9	Imperator IIII
Jul 1, 9-Jun 30, 10	Tribunicia potestate XI
10	
Jul 1, 10-Jun 30, 11	Tribunicia potestate XII
10/11	Imperator V

A.D. MONTH AND DAY	CHRONOLOGY
11	Imperator VI
Jul 1, 11-Jun 30, 12	Tribunicia potestate XIII
12	Tiberius governs the provinces jointly with Augustus
Jul 1, 12-Jun 30, 13	Tribunicia potestate XIIII
13	
Jul 1, 13-Jun 30, 14	Tribunicia potestate XV
14	Imperator VII
Aug 19	Death of Augustus
c. Sep 12	Funeral of Augustus
Sep 17	Tiberius voted new head of state; called Tiberius Caesar Augustus
Jul 1, 14-Jun 30, 15	Tribunicia potestate XVI
15	
Jul 1, 15-Jun 30, 16	Tribunicia potestate XVII

A.D. MONTH AND DAY	CHRONOLOGY
16	
Jul 1, 16-Jun 30, 17	Tribunicia potestate XVIII
17	
Jul 1, 17-Jun 30, 18	Tribunicia potestate XVIIII
18	Consul III
Jul 1, 18-Jun 30, 19	Tribunicia potestate XX
19	
Jul 1, 19-Jun 30, 20	Tribunicia potestate XXI
20	
Jul 1, 20-Jun 30, 21	Tribunicia potestate XXII

A.D. MONTH AND DAY	CHRONOLOGY
21	Imperator VIII
	Consul IIII
Jul 1, 21-Jun 30, 22	Tribunicia potestate XXIII
22	
July 1, 22-Jun 30, 23	Tribunicia potestate XXIIII
23	
Jul 1, 23-Jun 30, 24	Tribunicia potestate XXV
24	
Jul 1, 24-Jun 30, 25	Tribunicia potestate XXVI
25	
Jul 1, 25-Jun 30, 26	Tribunicia potestate XXVII

A.D. MONTH AND DAY	CHRONOLOGY
26	
Jul 1, 26-Jun 30, 27	Tribunicia potestate XXVIII
27	

A.D.	MONTH AND DAY	CHRONOLOGY
28	Jul 1, 27-Jun 30, 28	Tribunicia potestate XXVIIII
29	Jul 1, 28-Jun 30, 29	Tribunicia potestate XXX
30	Jul 1, 29-Jun 30, 30	Tribunicia potestate XXXI
	Jul 1, 30-Jun 30, 31	Tribunicia potestate XXXII
31		Consul V
32	Jul 1, 30-Jun 30, 32	Tribunicia potestate XXXIII
33	Jul 1, 32-Jun 30, 33	Tribunicia potestate XXXIIII
34	Jul 1, 33-Jun 30, 34	Tribunicia potestate XXXV
35	Jul 1, 34-Jun 30, 35	Tribunicia potestate XXXVI
36	Jul 1, 35-Jun 30, 36	Tribunicia potestate XXXVII
37	Jul 1, 36-Mar 16, 37	Tribunicia potestate XXXVIII
	Mar 16	Death of Tiberius

TABLE 41. EVENTS AND HONORS IN THE LIFE AND REIGN
(Mar 16, A.D. 37–Jan 24, A.D. 41) OF GAIUS (CALIGULA)

A.D.	MONTH AND DAY	CHRONOLOGY
12	Aug 31	Birth of Gaius (Caligula)
37		Gaius Consul I
	Mar 16	Death of Tiberius
	Mar 18	Gaius Imperator; as emperor called Gaius Caesar Augustus Germanicus
	Mar 18, 37-Mar 17, 38	Tribunicia potestate I
38		
39	Mar 17, 38-Mar 17, 39	Tribunicia potestate II
		Consul II
40	Mar 18, 39-Mar 17, 40	Tribunicia potestate III
		Consul III
41	Mar 18, 40-Jan 24, 41	Tribunicia potestate IIII
		Consul IIII
	Jan 24	Gaius killed

TABLE 42. EVENTS AND HONORS IN THE LIFE AND REIGN

(Jan 25, A.D. 41-Oct 12, A.D. 54) OF CLAUDIUS

B.C. MONTH AND DAY	CHRONOLOGY
10 Aug 1	Birth of Tiberius Claudius Drusus
A.D.	
37	Claudius Consul I
41 Jan 24	Death of Gaius (Caligula)
Jan 24	Claudius Imperator I; also II and III in 41?
Jan 25	Claudius made emperor; called Tiberius Claudius Caesar Augustus Germanicus
Jan 25, 41-Jan 24, 42	Tribunicia potestate I
42	Consul II
Jan 25, 42-Jan 24, 43	Tribunicia potestate II
43	Imperator IIII-VIII
	Consul III
Jan 25, 43-Jan 24, 44	Tribunicia potestate III
44	
Jan 25, 44-Jan 24, 45	Tribunicia potestate IIII
45	Imperator VIIII-XI
Jan 25, 45-Jan 24, 46	Tribunicia potestate V
46	Imperator XII
Jan 25, 46-Jan 24, 47	Tribunicia potestate VI
47	Imperator XIII-XV
	Consul IIII
Jan 25, 47-Jan 24, 48	Tribunicia potestate VII
48	Imperator XVI
Jan 25, 48-Jan 24, 49	Tribunicia potestate VIII
49	Imperator XVII, XVIII
Jan 25, 49-Jan 24, 50	Tribunicia potestate VIIII
50	Imperator XVIIII-XXI
Jan 25, 50-Jan 24, 51	Tribunicia potestate X
51	Imperator XXII-XXV
	Consul V
Jan 25, 51-Jan 24, 52	Tribunicia potestate XI
52	Imperator XXVI, XXVII
Jan 25, 52-Jan 24, 53	Tribunicia potestate XII
53	
Jan 25, 53-Jan 24, 54	Tribunicia potestate XIII
54	
Jan 25-Oct 12, 54	Tribunicia potestate XIIII
Oct 12	Claudius poisoned

TABLE 43. EVENTS AND HONORS IN THE LIFE AND REIGN
(Oct 13, A.D. 54-Jun 9, A.D. 68) OF NERO

A.D. MONTH AND DAY	CHRONOLOGY
37 Dec 15	Birth of Lucius Domitius Ahenobarbus
50 Mar 1	Claudius adopts Domitius; henceforth called Lucius Claudius Nero
54 Oct 12	Claudius poisoned
Oct 13	Nero made emperor; called Nero Claudius Caesar Augustus Germanicus
Dec 4	Tribunicia potestate granted to Nero, and reckoned from this date or from Oct 13, 54 until A.D. 59; then reordered so that the following figures finally prevail:
Oct 13-Dec 9, 54	Tribunicia potestate I
Dec 10, 54-Dec 9, 55	Tribunicia potestate II
54	Imperator I
55	Imperator II
	Consul I
Dec 10, 55-Dec 9, 56	Tribunicia potestate III
56	
Dec 10, 56-Dec 9, 57	Tribunicia potestate IIII
57	Imperator III
	Consul II
Dec 10, 57-Dec 9, 58	Tribunicia potestate V
58	Consul III
Summer	Imperator IIII, V
Dec 10, 58-Dec 9, 59	Tribunicia potestate VI
Dec 10, 59-Dec 9, 60	Imperator VI
59 Sep	Tribunicia potestate VII
60	Consul IIII
Summer 60 (or 59)	Imperator VII
Dec 10, 60-Dec 9, 61	Tribunicia potestate VIII
61	Imperator VIII, VIIII
Dec 10, 61-Dec 9, 62	Tribunicia potestate VIIII
62	
Dec 10, 61-Dec 9, 62	Tribunicia potestate X
63	
Dec 10, 63-Dec 9, 64	Tribunicia potestate XI
64	
Dec 10, 64-Dec 9, 65	Tribunicia potestate XII
Between 64 and 66	Imperator X
65	
Dec 10, 65-Dec 9, 66	Tribunicia potestate XIII
66	Imperator XI
Dec 10, 66-Dec 9, 67	Tribunicia potestate XIIII
67	Imperator XII
Dec 10, 67-Jun 9, 68	Tribunicia potestate XV
68	Consul V
Jun 9	Suicide of Nero

D. ERAS

LITERATURE: Kubitschek, "Aera," in PWRE I, cols. 606-666.

〖 184.   An era (Latin *aera*) is a sequence of years reckoned from a definite point of time which is called the epoch (Greek ἐποχή). There was at least some manner of idea of the use of an era in ancient Egypt for a stela found at Tanis attests a celebration at that place by a vizier named Seti (about 1330 B.C.) of a four-hundredth anniversary in the form of worship of the god Seth. The text reads in part: "Year 400, fourth month of the third season, day 4 . . . Seti . . . said: 'Hail to thee, O Seth. . . .' "[1] There is also an enigmatic reference to "the era of Ishtar" in connection with Sargon king of Agade in the Sargon Chronicle, a cuneiform tablet written in the New Babylonian period, now in the British Museum.[2]

1. THE ERA OF THE OLYMPIADS

LITERATURE: R. D. Hicks, "Chronology," in *A Companion to Greek Studies*, ed. Leonard Whibley. 3d ed. 1916, p. 70; Hans Lietzmann, *Zeitrechnung*. 1934, pp. 11f.

〖 185.   Except for points in biblical history employed as epochs in later Jewish and Christian systems of chronology, the earliest epoch in any widely used ancient era was the traditional point of the beginning of the Olympic games which was so employed in the Greek era of the Olympiads. The Olympic games (τὰ ᾽Ολύμπια) were held every four years, and the period of four years from one celebration to the next was known as an ᾽Ολυμπιάς, or "Olympiad" (abbreviated Ol.). The time when the games were started was supposed to have been at a point which would correspond to 776 B.C. For the purpose of this reckoning the year was the normal Greek calendar year and we saw (¶¶114-115) that this began at Athens with Hekatombaion 1, at Delphi with Apellaios 1, both of which may be taken as approximately equivalent to Jul 1. The first year of the first Olympiad was accordingly equivalent to approximately Jul 1, 776 to Jun 30, 775 B.C. In other lands it was presumably possible to maintain the dating by Olympiads but to state the years in terms of other calendars, for

[1] ANET pp.252-253; cf. Alan H. Gardiner in JEA 19 (1933), p.124; 31 (1945), p.28.
[2] ANET p.266.

example the Egyptian beginning on Thoth 1 = Aug 29, or the Syro-Macedonian beginning on Hyperberetaios (Sep/Oct) 1. But normally in the homeland and wherever else standard Greek practice was followed, we may assume a year extending approximately from Jul 1 to Jun 30.

❨186. Dating by the Olympiadic system is used already by the Sicilian historian, Timaeus (c.352-c.256 B.C.), and is found in many ancient sources. Oxyrhynchus Papyrus No. 12,[3] for example, which is a portion of a scroll written about A.D. 250, gives a list of events in Greek, Roman, and Oriental history covering the years 355-315 B.C., and the dating is by Olympiads and by the archons at Athens. A typical item (column 6, lines 1-5) reads:

"In the 115th Olympiad Damasias of Amphipolis won the foot race. The archons at Athens were Neaechmus, Apollodorus, Archippus, Demogenes."

❨187. In Table 44 the Olympiadic years are listed for selected periods of particular relevance to our investigation.

TABLE 44. OLYMPIADS

Ol.	B.C.				Ol.	B.C.			
	Month Day	Year	Month Day	Year		Month Day	Year	Month Day	Year
1, 1	7/1	776	6/30	775	3	7/1	758	6/30	757
2	7/1	775	6/30	774	4	7/1	757	6/30	756
3	7/1	774	6/30	773	6, 1	7/1	756	6/30	755
4	7/1	773	6/30	772	2	7/1	755	6/30	754
2, 1	7/1	772	6/30	771	3	7/1	754	6/30	753
2	7/1	771	6/30	770	4	7/1	753	6/30	752
3	7/1	770	6/30	769	7, 1	7/1	752	6/30	751
4	7/1	769	6/30	768	2	7/1	751	6/30	750
3, 1	7/1	768	6/30	767	3	7/1	750	6/30	749
2	7/1	767	6/30	766	4	7/1	749	6/30	748
3	7/1	766	6/30	765	8, 1	7/1	748	6/30	747
4	7/1	765	6/30	764	2	7/1	747	6/30	746
4, 1	7/1	764	6/30	763	3	7/1	746	6/30	745
2	7/1	763	6/30	762	4	7/1	745	6/30	744
3	7/1	762	6/30	761	9, 1	7/1	744	6/30	743
4	7/1	761	6/30	760	2	7/1	743	6/30	742
5, 1	7/1	760	6/30	759	3	7/1	742	6/30	741
2	7/1	759	6/30	758	4	7/1	741	6/30	740

[3] OP I, pp.25-36.

Ol.		B.C.				Ol.		B.C.			
		Month Day	Year	Month Day	Year			Month Day	Year	Month Day	Year
10,	1	7/1	740–	6/30	739	21,	1	7/1	696–	6/30	695
	2	7/1	739–	6/30	738		2	7/1	695–	6/30	694
	3	7/1	738–	6/30	737		3	7/1	694–	6/30	693
	4	7/1	737–	6/30	736		4	7/1	693–	6/30	692
11,	1	7/1	736–	6/30	735	22,	1	7/1	692–	6/30	691
	2	7/1	735–	6/30	734		2	7/1	691–	6/30	690
	3	7/1	734–	6/30	733		3	7/1	690–	6/30	689
	4	7/1	733–	6/30	732		4	7/1	689–	6/30	688
12,	1	7/1	732–	6/30	731	23,	1	7/1	688–	6/30	687
	2	7/1	731–	6/30	730		2	7/1	687–	6/30	686
	3	7/1	730–	6/30	729		3	7/1	686–	6/30	685
	4	7/1	729–	6/30	728		4	7/1	685–	6/30	684
13,	1	7/1	728–	6/30	727	24,	1	7/1	684–	6/30	683
	2	7/1	727–	6/30	726		2	7/1	683–	6/30	682
	3	7/1	726–	6/30	725		3	7/1	682–	6/30	681
	4	7/1	725–	6/30	724		4	7/1	681–	6/30	680
14,	1	7/1	724–	6/30	723	25,	1	7/1	680–	6/30	679
	2	7/1	723–	6/30	722		2	7/1	679–	6/30	678
	3	7/1	722–	6/30	721		3	7/1	678–	6/30	677
	4	7/1	721–	6/30	720		4	7/1	677–	6/30	676
15,	1	7/1	720–	6/30	719	26,	1	7/1	676–	6/30	675
	2	7/1	719–	6/30	718		2	7/1	675–	6/30	674
	3	7/1	718–	6/30	717		3	7/1	674–	6/30	673
	4	7/1	717–	6/30	716		4	7/1	673–	6/30	672
16,	1	7/1	716–	6/30	715	27,	1	7/1	672–	6/30	671
	2	7/1	715–	6/30	714		2	7/1	671–	6/30	670
	3	7/1	714–	6/30	713		3	7/1	670–	6/30	669
	4	7/1	713–	6/30	712		4	7/1	669–	6/30	668
17,	1	7/1	712–	6/30	711	28,	1	7/1	668–	6/30	667
	2	7/1	711–	6/30	710		2	7/1	667–	6/30	666
	3	7/1	710–	6/30	709		3	7/1	666–	6/30	665
	4	7/1	709–	6/30	708		4	7/1	665–	6/30	664
18,	1	7/1	708–	6/30	707	29,	1	7/1	664–	6/30	663
	2	7/1	707–	6/30	706		2	7/1	663–	6/30	662
	3	7/1	706–	6/30	705		3	7/1	662–	6/30	661
	4	7/1	705–	6/30	704		4	7/1	661–	6/30	660
19,	1	7/1	704–	6/30	703	30,	1	7/1	660–	6/30	659
	2	7/1	703–	6/30	702		2	7/1	659–	6/30	658
	3	7/1	702–	6/30	701		3	7/1	658–	6/30	657
	4	7/1	701–	6/30	700		4	7/1	657–	6/30	656
20,	1	7/1	700–	6/30	699	31,	1	7/1	656–	6/30	655
	2	7/1	699–	6/30	698		2	7/1	655–	6/30	654
	3	7/1	698–	6/30	697		3	7/1	654–	6/30	653
	4	7/1	697–	6/30	696		4	7/1	653–	6/30	652

Ol.		B.C.					Ol.		B.C.				
		Month Day	*Year*	*Month Day*	*Year*				*Month Day*	*Year*	*Month Day*	*Year*	
32,	1	7/1	652–6/30	651			43,	1	7/1	608–6/30	607		
	2	7/1	651–6/30	650				2	7/1	607–6/30	606		
	3	7/1	650–6/30	649				3	7/1	606–6/30	605		
	4	7/1	649–6/30	648				4	7/1	605–6/30	604		
33,	1	7/1	648–6/30	647			44,	1	7/1	604–6/30	603		
	2	7/1	647–6/30	646				2	7/1	603–6/30	602		
	3	7/1	646–6/30	645				3	7/1	602–6/30	601		
	4	7/1	645–6/30	644				4	7/1	601–6/30	600		
34,	1	7/1	644–6/30	643			45,	1	7/1	600–6/30	599		
	2	7/1	643–6/30	642				2	7/1	599–6/30	598		
	3	7/1	642–6/30	641				3	7/1	598–6/30	597		
	4	7/1	641–6/30	640				4	7/1	597–6/30	596		
35,	1	7/1	640–6/30	639			46,	1	7/1	596–6/30	595		
	2	7/1	639–6/30	638				2	7/1	595–6/30	594		
	3	7/1	638–6/30	637				3	7/1	594–6/30	593		
	4	7/1	637–6/30	636				4	7/1	593–6/30	592		
36,	1	7/1	636–6/30	635			47,	1	7/1	592–6/30	591		
	2	7/1	635–6/30	634				2	7/1	591–6/30	590		
	3	7/1	634–6/30	633				3	7/1	590–6/30	589		
	4	7/1	644–6/30	632				4	7/1	589–6/30	588		
37,	1	7/1	632–6/30	631			48,	1	7/1	588–6/30	587		
	2	7/1	631–6/30	630				2	7/1	587–6/30	586		
	3	7/1	630–6/30	629				3	7/1	586–6/30	585		
	4	7/1	629–6/30	628				4	7/1	585–6/30	584		
38,	1	7/1	628–6/30	627			49,	1	7/1	584–6/30	583		
	2	7/1	627–6/30	626				2	7/1	583–6/30	582		
	3	7/1	626–6/30	625				3	7/1	582–6/30	581		
	4	7/1	625–6/30	624				4	7/1	581–6/30	580		
39,	1	7/1	624–6/30	623			50,	1	7/1	580–6/30	579		
	2	7/1	623–6/30	622				2	7/1	579–6/30	578		
	3	7/1	622–6/30	621				3	7/1	578–6/30	577		
	4	7/1	621–6/30	620				4	7/1	577–6/30	576		
40,	1	7/1	620–6/30	619			51,	1	7/1	576–6/30	575		
	2	7/1	619–6/30	618				2	7/1	575–6/30	574		
	3	7/1	618–6/30	617				3	7/1	574–6/30	573		
	4	7/1	617–6/30	616				4	7/1	573–6/30	572		
41,	1	7/1	616–6/30	615			52,	1	7/1	572–6/30	571		
	2	7/1	615–6/30	614				2	7/1	571–6/30	570		
	3	7/1	614–6/30	613				3	7/1	570–6/30	569		
	4	7/1	613–6/30	612				4	7/1	569–6/30	568		
42,	1	7/1	612–6/30	611			53,	1	7/1	568–6/30	567		
	2	7/1	611–6/30	610				2	7/1	567–6/30	566		
	3	7/1	610–6/30	609				3	7/1	566–6/30	565		
	4	7/1	609–6/30	608				4	7/1	565–6/30	564		

Ol.		B.C.				Ol.		B.C.			
		Month Day	Year	Month Day	Year			Month Day	Year	Month Day	Year
54,	1	7/1	564	–6/30	563	65,	1	7/1	520	–6/30	519
	2	7/1	563	–6/30	562		2	7/1	519	–6/30	518
	3	7/1	562	–6/30	561		3	7/1	518	–6/30	517
	4	7/1	561	–6/30	560		4	7/1	517	–6/30	516
55,	1	7/1	560	–6/30	559	66,	1	7/1	516	–6/30	515
	2	7/1	559	–6/30	558		2	7/1	515	–6/30	514
	3	7/1	558	–6/30	557		3	7/1	514	–6/30	513
	4	7/1	557	–6/30	556		4	7/1	513	–6/30	512
56,	1	7/1	556	–6/30	555						
	2	7/1	555	–6/30	554	....					
	3	7/1	554	–6/30	553						
	4	7/1	553	–6/30	552	....					
57,	1	7/1	552	–6/30	551	110,	1	7/1	340	–6/30	339
	2	7/1	551	–6/30	550		2	7/1	339	–6/30	338
	3	7/1	550	–6/30	549		3	7/1	338	–6/30	337
	4	7/1	549	–6/30	548		4	7/1	337	–6/30	336
58,	1	7/1	548	–6/30	547	111,	1	7/1	336	–6/30	335
	2	7/1	547	–6/30	546		2	7/1	335	–6/30	334
	3	7/1	546	–6/30	545		3	7/1	334	–6/30	333
	4	7/1	545	–6/30	544		4	7/1	333	–6/30	332
59,	1	7/1	544	–6/30	543	112,	1	7/1	332	–6/30	331
	2	7/1	543	–6/30	542		2	7/1	331	–6/30	330
	3	7/1	542	–6/30	541		3	7/1	330	–6/30	329
	4	7/1	541	–6/30	540		4	7/1	329	–6/30	328
60,	1	7/1	540	–6/30	539	113,	1	7/1	328	–6/30	327
	2	7/1	539	–6/30	538		2	7/1	327	–6/30	326
	3	7/1	538	–6/30	537		3	7/1	326	–6/30	325
	4	7/1	537	–6/30	536		4	7/1	325	–6/30	324
61,	1	7/1	536	–6/30	535	114,	1	7/1	324	–6/30	323
	2	7/1	535	–6/30	534		2	7/1	323	–6/30	322
	3	7/1	534	–6/30	533		3	7/1	322	–6/30	321
	4	7/1	533	–6/30	532		4	7/1	321	–6/30	320
62,	1	7/1	532	–6/30	531	115,	1	7/1	320	–6/30	319
	2	7/1	531	–6/30	530		2	7/1	319	–6/30	318
	3	7/1	530	–6/30	529		3	7/1	318	–6/30	317
	4	7/1	529	–6/30	528		4	7/1	317	–6/30	316
63,	1	7/1	528	–6/30	527	116,	1	7/1	316	–6/30	315
	2	7/1	527	–6/30	526		2	7/1	315	–6/30	314
	3	7/1	526	–6/30	525		3	7/1	314	–6/30	313
	4	7/1	525	–6/30	524		4	7/1	313	–6/30	312
64,	1	7/1	524	–6/30	523	117,	1	7/1	312	–6/30	311
	2	7/1	523	–6/30	522		2	7/1	311	–6/30	310
	3	7/1	522	–6/30	521		3	7/1	310	–6/30	309
	4	7/1	521	–6/30	520		4	7/1	309	–6/30	308

Ol.		B.C.				Ol.		B.C.			
		Month Day	Year	Month Day	Year			Month Day	Year	Month Day	Year
118,	1	7/1	308–	6/30	307	181,	1	7/1	56–	6/30	55
	2	7/1	307–	6/30	306		2	7/1	55–	6/30	54
	3	7/1	306–	6/30	305		3	7/1	54–	6/30	53
	4	7/1	305–	6/30	304		4	7/1	53–	6/30	52
119,	1	7/1	304–	6/30	303	182,	1	7/1	52–	6/30	51
	2	7/1	303–	6/30	302		2	7/1	51–	6/30	50
	3	7/1	302–	6/30	301		3	7/1	50–	6/30	49
	4	7/1	301–	6/30	300		4	7/1	49–	6/30	48
120,	1	7/1	300–	6/30	299	183,	1	7/1	48–	6/30	47
	2	7/1	299–	6/30	298		2	7/1	47–	6/30	46
	3	7/1	298–	6/30	297		3	7/1	46–	6/30	45
	4	7/1	297–	6/30	296		4	7/1	45–	6/30	44
....						184,	1	7/1	44–	6/30	43
....							2	7/1	43–	6/30	42
150,	1	7/1	180–	6/30	179		3	7/1	42–	6/30	41
	2	7/1	179–	6/30	178		4	7/1	41–	6/30	40
	3	7/1	178–	6/30	177	185,	1	7/1	40–	6/30	39
	4	7/1	177–	6/30	176		2	7/1	39–	6/30	38
151,	1	7/1	176–	6/30	175		3	7/1	38–	6/30	37
	2	7/1	175–	6/30	174		4	7/1	37–	6/30	36
	3	7/1	174–	6/30	173	186,	1	7/1	36–	6/30	35
	4	7/1	173–	6/30	172		2	7/1	35–	6/30	34
152,	1	7/1	172–	6/30	171		3	7/1	34–	6/30	33
	2	7/1	171–	6/30	170		4	7/1	33–	6/30	32
	3	7/1	170–	6/30	169	187,	1	7/1	32–	6/30	31
	4	7/1	169–	6/30	168		2	7/1	31–	6/30	30
153,	1	7/1	168–	6/30	167		3	7/1	30–	6/30	29
	2	7/1	167–	6/30	166		4	7/1	29–	6/30	28
	3	7/1	166–	6/30	165	188,	1	7/1	28–	6/30	27
	4	7/1	165–	6/30	164		2	7/1	27–	6/30	26
154,	1	7/1	164–	6/30	163		3	7/1	26–	6/30	25
	2	7/1	163–	6/30	162		4	7/1	25–	6/30	24
	3	7/1	162–	6/30	161	189,	1	7/1	24–	6/30	23
	4	7/1	161–	6/30	160		2	7/1	23–	6/30	22
155,	1	7/1	160–	6/30	159		3	7/1	22–	6/30	21
	2	7/1	159–	6/30	158		4	7/1	21–	6/30	20
	3	7/1	158–	6/30	157	190,	1	7/1	20–	6/30	19
	4	7/1	157–	6/30	156		2	7/1	19–	6/30	18
....							3	7/1	18–	6/30	17
....							4	7/1	17–	6/30	16
180,	1	7/1	60–	6/30	59	191,	1	7/1	16–	6/30	15
	2	7/1	59–	6/30	58		2	7/1	15–	6/30	14
	3	7/1	58–	6/30	57		3	7/1	14–	6/30	13
	4	7/1	57–	6/30	56		4	7/1	13–	6/30	12

Ol.		B.C.				Ol.		A.D.			
		Month Day	*Year*	*Month Day*	*Year*			*Month Day*	*Year*	*Month Day*	*Year*
192,	1	7/1	12–	6/30	11	202,	1	7/1	29–	6/30	30
	2	7/1	11–	6/30	10		2	7/1	30–	6/30	31
	3	7/1	10–	6/30	9		3	7/1	31–	6/30	32
	4	7/1	9–	6/30	8		4	7/1	32–	6/30	33
193,	1	7/1	8–	6/30	7	203,	1	7/1	33–	6/30	34
	2	7/1	7–	6/30	6		2	7/1	34–	6/30	35
	3	7/1	6–	6/30	5		3	7/1	35–	6/30	36
	4	7/1	5–	6/30	4		4	7/1	36–	6/30	37
194,	1	7/1	4–	6/30	3	204,	1	7/1	37–	6/30	38
	2	7/1	3–	6/30	2		2	7/1	38–	6/30	39
	3	7/1	2–	6/30	1		3	7/1	39–	6/30	40
	4	7/1 B.C.–		6/30 A.D.	1*		4	7/1	40–	6/30	41
						205,	1	7/1	41–	6/30	42
							2	7/1	42–	6/30	43
			A.D.				3	7/1	43–	6/30	44
							4	7/1	44–	6/30	45
195,	1	7/1	1–	6/30	2	206,	1	7/1	45–	6/30	46
	2	7/1	2–	6/30	3		2	7/1	46–	6/30	47
	3	7/1	3–	6/30	4		3	7/1	47–	6/30	48
	4	7/1	4–	6/30	5		4	7/1	48–	6/30	49
196,	1	7/1	5–	6/30	6	207,	1	7/1	49–	6/30	50
	2	7/1	6–	6/30	7		2	7/1	50–	6/30	51
	3	7/1	7–	6/30	8		3	7/1	51–	6/30	52
	4	7/1	8–	6/30	9		4	7/1	52–	6/30	53
197,	1	7/1	9–	6/30	10	208,	1	7/1	53–	6/30	54
	2	7/1	10–	6/30	11		2	7/1	54–	6/30	55
	3	7/1	11–	6/30	12		3	7/1	55–	6/30	56
	4	7/1	12–	6/30	13		4	7/1	56–	6/30	57
198,	1	7/1	13–	6/30	14	209,	1	7/1	57–	6/30	58
	2	7/1	14–	6/30	15		2	7/1	58–	6/30	59
	3	7/1	15–	6/30	16		3	7/1	59–	6/30	60
	4	7/1	16–	6/30	17		4	7/1	60–	6/30	61
199,	1	7/1	17–	6/30	18	210,	1	7/1	61–	6/30	62
	2	7/1	18–	6/30	19		2	7/1	62–	6/30	63
	3	7/1	19–	6/30	20		3	7/1	63–	6/30	64
	4	7/1	20–	6/30	21		4	7/1	64–	6/30	65
200,	1	7/1	21–	6/30	22	211,	1	7/1	65–	6/30	66
	2	7/1	22–	6/30	23		2	7/1	66–	6/30	67
	3	7/1	23–	6/30	24		3	7/1	67–	6/30	68
	4	7/1	24–	6/30	25		4	7/1	68–	6/30	69
201,	1	7/1	25–	6/30	26	212,	1	7/1	69–	6/30	70
	2	7/1	26–	6/30	27		2	7/1	70–	6/30	71
	3	7/1	27–	6/30	28		3	7/1	71–	6/30	72
	4	7/1	28–	6/30	29		4	7/1	72–	6/30	73

* A.D. 1 equals Ol. 194, 4 Jan-Jun, plus Ol. 195, 1 Jul-Dec.

2. THE ERA OF THE CITY OF ROME

LITERATURE: Ludwig Ideler, *Handbuch der mathematischen und technischen Chronologie*, II, 1826, pp.150ff.; J. S. Reid, "Chronology," in *A Companion to Latin Studies*, ed. John E. Sandys. 1925, pp.105f.; Hans Lietzmann, *Zeitrechnung der römischen Kaiserzeit, des Mittelalters und der Neuzeit für die Jahre 1-2000 nach Christus*. 1934, pp.12f.

([188. The era distinctively used among the Romans took for its epoch the foundation of the city of Rome, and the reckoning was *ab urbe condita*, "from the foundation of the city," or *anno urbis conditae*, "in the year of the founded city" (abbreviated A.U.C.). As to when Rome was founded, however, there were different opinions. Dionysius of Halicarnassus (54?-7? B.C.), the Greek historian who wrote a work on Ῥωμαϊκὴ Ἀρχαιολογία or "Roman Antiquities" in twenty books and also a lost work on chronology called Χρόνοι or "Times" which is cited by Clement of Alexandria,[1] discusses the problem at length, citing a number of authorities and several variant opinions.[2] He says that the Greek historian Timaeus of Sicily thought that Rome and Carthage were founded at the same time in the thirty-eighth year before the first Olympiad, which would be in 814/813 B.C. Lucius Cincius, a member of the senate, put it about the fourth year of the twelfth Olympiad, or 729/728 B.C.; and Quintus Fabius placed it in the first year of the eighth Olympiad, or 748/747 B.C. Porcius Cato used a different type of reference and put the founding of Rome four hundred and thirty-two years after the Trojan war. At this point Dionysius cites the *Chronicles* of Eratosthenes, for which he expresses high regard. This work began with the fall of Troy, which Eratosthenes placed in 1183 B.C. Four hundred and thirty-two years after that brings us to 751 B.C. or to the Roman year which began in the first year of the seventh Olympiad, and this is the date which Dionysius himself accepts for the foundation of Rome.

([189. A yet slightly variant date, however, was calculated by the Roman antiquarian and writer, Varro (116-27 B.C.). From the middle of the first century B.C. onward, the era based on Varro's date (and hence known as the Varronian era) was the most widely accepted reckoning and that used by the chief Roman writers. In the twelfth chapter of his *Life of Romulus* Plutarch says that it was

[1] *Stromata.* I, xxi, 102.   [2] *Roman Antiquities.* I, 74-75.

agreed that the city was founded on the twenty-first of April; mentions the third year of the sixth Olympiad; and describes the work of Varro in relation to the dating. Censorinus[3] also tells about Varro and then gives the date of his own writing in terms of both the Olympic games and the founding of Rome. In this double citation the 1014th Olympiadic year is equated with the 991st year from the founding of Rome, making a difference of twenty-three years between the two eras. Since the Olympiadic year began about Jul 1 and the founding of Rome, as we have just seen, on Apr 21, the period between the epochs of the two eras was actually less than twenty-three full years. Twenty-three full years from the beginning of the first Olympiad would only have passed at the end of Ol. 6, 3, i.e., about Jun 30, 753 B.C. Therefore Varro must have put the founding of Rome in Ol. 6, 3 (= 754/753), and to be exact on Apr 21, 753 B.C.

⟨ 190.   Strictly speaking, therefore, we should reckon A.U.C. from Apr 21, 753 B.C. By this factual reckoning A.U.C. 1 extended from Apr 21, 753 B.C. to Apr 20, 752 B.C.; and if A.U.C. 1 is set parallel with 753 B.C. it means that A.U.C. 1 began in the year 753 B.C. But the Roman year came to be reckoned from Jan 1 (¶142), therefore in practice the A.U.C. reckoning was also often counted from Jan 1. By this manner of reckoning A.U.C. 1 extended from Jan 1 to Dec 31, 753 B.C.; and in this case we have simple and exact equations, A.U.C. 1 = 753 B.C., A.U.C. 753 = 1 B.C., A.U.C. 754 = A.D. 1, and so on. Unless otherwise stated it is this latter manner of equation which may be assumed in the present handbook. In either case a table of parallel years will show A.U.C. 1 in parallel with 753 B.C., and so on.

⟨ 191.   In making or interpreting an equation between a given Roman year and an Olympiadic year, or contrariwise between an Olympiadic year and a Roman year, it is also necessary to be clear as to the method followed. The Roman year (and the corresponding year of the Christian era) may be set parallel with the Olympiadic year in the course of which it began or with the year in the course of which it ended. For example the Roman year A.U.C. 1 = 753 B.C. began in Ol. 6, 3 and ended in Ol. 6, 4, and hence might be set parallel with either. Stating the matter the other way around,

[3] *De die natali liber.* 21; ed. F. Hultsch. 1867, p.45.

the Olympiadic year may be set parallel with the Roman year in the course of which it began or with the year in the course of which it ended. Thus Ol. 6, 3 began in 754 B.C. and ended in 753 B.C., and might be set parallel with either. It was apparently the practice of Dionysius of Halicarnassus and probably also of other writers such as Polybius and Diodorus to identify the Roman year with the Olympiadic year in the course of which it began.[4] In this case Ol. 6, 3 and A.U.C. 1 (= 753 B.C.) stand in parallel; and further parallelisms follow according to the same pattern, e.g. Ol. 151, 1 – A.U.C. 579 – 175 B.C.; Ol. 194, 3 – A.U.C. 753 – 1 B.C.; Ol. 194, 4 – A.U.C. 754 – A.D. 1; and so on. But modern custom is to put the Olympiadic year parallel with the year of the Christian era (and hence of the era of the city of Rome) in which it begins. This results in parallelisms according to this pattern, e.g., Ol. 1, 1 – 776 B.C.; Ol. 6, 4 – A.U.C. 1 – 753 B.C.; Ol. 151, 1 – A.U.C. 578 – 176 B.C.; Ol. 194, 4 – A.U.C. 753 – 1 B.C.; Ol. 195, 1 – A.U.C. 754 – A.D. 1. The modern custom appears, e.g., in the tables of parallel years in Schürer[5] and in Helm's edition of the *Chronicle* of Eusebius in Jerome's translation.[6] Table 45 is intended to present the relationships without ambiguity and to facilitate the understanding of either type of parallelism just described. While relatively short periods are covered, by reference back to Table 44 other sections of such a tabulation (Table 45) can readily be prepared.

3. THE SELEUCID ERA

LITERATURE: A. Bouché-Leclercq, *Histoire des Séleucides.* 2 vols. 1913-14; Walther Kolbe, *Beiträge zur syrischen und jüdischen Geschichte.* 1926; Wilhelm Kubitschek, *Grundriss der antiken Zeitrechnung.* Handbuch der Altertumswissenschaft, I, 7. 1928, pp.70-73; F.-M. Abel, *Les livres des Maccabées.* 1949; Sidney Tedesche and Solomon Zeitlin, *The First Book of Maccabees.* 1950; J. C. Dancy, *A Commentary on I Maccabees.* 1954.

¶192.   The establishment of the Seleucid era is connected with the founding of the Seleucid empire. After the death of Alexander the Great (323 B.C.) his empire fell to his generals, known as the Diadochi or "successors." In the long and complex struggle which ensued Antigonus Cyclops (323-301 B.C.) claimed all of Asia, Ptolemy I Soter I (323-285 B.C.) was satrap of Egypt, and Seleu-

[4] Earnest Cary, *The Roman Antiquities of Dionysius of Halicarnassus.* LCL, I (1937), p.xxxi.
[5] SHJP I, ii, pp.393ff.   [6] See below ¶¶269f.

TABLE 45. YEARS FROM THE FOUNDING OF THE CITY OF ROME
(VARRONIAN ERA)

Olympiadic Year	A.U.C.	B.C.	Olympiadic Year	A.U.C.	B.C.
		755		24	730
6, 2 = Jul 1, 755-Jun 30, 754			3 = Jul 1, 730-Jun 30, 729		
		754		25	729
3 = Jul 1, 754-Jun 30, 753			4 = Jul 1, 729-Jun 30, 728		
	1	753		26	728
4 = Jul 1, 753-Jun 30, 752			....		
	2	752	....		
7, 1 = Jul 1, 752-Jun 30, 751					
	3	751		166	588
2 = Jul 1, 751-Jun 30, 750			48, 1 = Jul 1, 588-Jun 30, 587		
	4	750		167	587
3 = Jul 1, 750-Jun 30, 749			2 = Jul 1, 587-Jun 30, 586		
	5	749		168	586
4 = Jul 1, 749-Jun 30, 748			3 = Jul 1, 586-Jun 30, 585		
	6	748		169	585
8, 1 = Jul 1, 748-Jun 30, 747			4 = Jul 1, 585-Jun 30, 584		
	7	747		170	584
2 = Jul 1, 747-Jun 30, 746			49, 1 = Jul 1, 584-Jun 30, 583		
	8	746		171	583
3 = Jul 1, 746-Jun 30, 745			2 = Jul 1, 583-Jun 30, 582		
	9	745		172	582
4 = Jul 1, 745-Jun 30, 744			3 = Jul 1, 582-Jun 30, 581		
	10	744		173	581
9, 1 = Jul 1, 744-Jun 30, 743			4 = Jul 1, 581-Jun 30, 580		
	11	743		174	580
2 = Jul 1, 743-Jun 30, 742			50, 1 = Jul 1, 580-Jun 30, 579		
	12	742		175	579
3 = Jul 1, 742-Jun 30, 741			2 = Jul 1, 579-Jun 30, 578		
	13	741		176	578
4 = Jul 1, 741-Jun 30, 740			3 = Jul 1, 578-Jun 30, 577		
	14	740		177	577
10, 1 = Jul 1, 740-Jun 30, 739			4 = Jul 1, 577-Jun 30, 576		
	15	739		178	576
2 = Jul 1, 739-Jun 30, 738			51, 1 = Jul 1, 576-Jun 30, 575		
	16	738		179	575
3 = Jul 1, 738-Jun 30, 737			2 = Jul 1, 575-Jun 30, 574		
	17	737		180	574
4 = Jul 1, 737-Jun 30, 736			3 = Jul 1, 574-Jun 30, 573		
	18	736		181	573
11, 1 = Jul 1, 736-Jun 30, 735			4 = Jul 1, 573-Jun 30, 572		
	19	735		182	572
2 = Jul 1, 735-Jun 30, 734			52, 1 = Jul 1, 572-Jun 30, 571		
	20	734		183	571
3 = Jul 1, 734-Jun 30, 733			2 = Jul 1, 571-Jun 30, 570		
	21	733		184	570
4 = Jul 1, 733-Jun 30, 732			3 = Jul 1, 570-Jun 30, 569		
	22	732		185	569
12, 1 = Jul 1, 732-Jun 30, 731			4 = Jul 1, 569-Jun 30, 568		
	23	731		186	568
2 = Jul 1, 731-Jun 30, 730			53, 1 = Jul 1, 568-Jun 30, 567		

Olympiadic Year	A.U.C.	B.C.	Olympiadic Year	A.U.C.	A.D.
	187	567		578	176
2 = Jul 1, 567-Jun 30, 566			151, 1 = Jul 1, 176-Jun 30, 175		
	188	566		579	175
3 = Jul 1, 566-Jun 30, 565			2 = Jul 1, 175-Jun 30, 174		
	189	565		580	174
4 = Jul 1, 565-Jun 30, 564			3 = Jul 1, 174-Jun 30, 173		
	190	564		581	173
54, 1 = Jul 1, 564-Jun 30, 563			4 = Jul 1, 173-Jun 30, 172		
	191	563			
2 = Jul 1, 563-Jun 30, 562			....		
	192	562	....		
3 = Jul 1, 562-Jun 30, 561				750	4
	193	561	194, 1 = Jul 1, 4-Jun 30, 3		
4 = Jul 1, 561-Jun 30, 560				751	3
	194	560	2 = Jul 1, 3-Jun 30, 2		
55, 1 = Jul 1, 560-Jun 30, 559				752	2
	195	559	3 = Jul 1, 2 B.C.-Jun 30, 1 B.C.		
2 = Jul 1, 559-Jun 30, 558				753	1 B.C.
	196	558	4 = Jul 1, 1 B.C.-Jun 30, A.D. 1		
3 = Jul 1, 558-Jun 30, 557				754	A.D. 1
	197	557	195, 1 = Jul 1, A.D. 1-Jun 30, A.D. 2		
4 = Jul 1, 557-Jun 30, 556				755	2
			2 = Jul 1, 2-Jun 30, 3		
....				756	3
....			3 = Jul 1, 3-Jun 30, 4		
	442	312		757	4
117, 1 = Jul 1, 312-Jun 30, 311			4 = Jul 1, 4-Jun 30, 5		
	443	311			
2 = Jul 1, 311-Jun 30, 310			....		
	444	310	....		
3 = Jul 1, 310-Jun 30, 309				A.U.C.	A.D.
	445	309			
4 = Jul 1, 309-Jun 30, 308				778	25
	446	308	201, 1 = Jul 1, 25-Jun 30, 26		
118, 1 = Jul 1, 308-Jun 30, 307				779	26
	447	307	2 = Jul 1, 26-Jun 30, 27		
2 = Jul 1, 307-Jun 30, 306				780	27
	448	306	3 = Jul 1, 27-Jun 30, 28		
3 = Jul 1, 306-Jun 30, 305				781	28
	449	305	4 = Jul 1, 28-Jun 30, 29		
4 = Jul 1, 305-Jun 30, 304				782	29
			202, 1 = Jul 1, 29-Jun 30, 30		
....				783	30
....			2 = Jul 1, 30-Jun 30, 31		
	574	180		784	31
150, 1 = Jul 1, 180-Jun 30, 179			3 = Jul 1, 31-Jun 30, 32		
	575	179		785	32
2 = Jul 1, 179-Jun 30, 178			4 = Jul 1, 32-Jun 30, 33		
	576	178		786	33
3 = Jul 1, 178-Jun 30, 177			203, 1 = Jul 1, 33-Jun 30, 34		
	577	177		787	34
4 = Jul 1, 177-Jun 30, 176			2 = Jul 1, 34-Jun 30, 35		

Olympiadic Year	A.U.C.	A.D.	Olympiadic Year	A.U.C.	A.D.
	788	35		820	67
3 = Jul 1, 35-Jun 30, 36			3 = Jul 1, 67-Jun 30, 68		
	789	36		821	68
4 = Jul 1, 36-Jun 30, 37			4 = Jul 1, 68-Jun 30, 69		
				822	69
....			212, 1 = Jul 1, 69-Jun 30, 70		
....				823	70
			2 = Jul 1, 70-Jun 30, 71		
	818	65		824	71
211, 1 = Jul 1, 65-Jun 30, 66			3 = Jul 1, 71-Jun 30, 72		
	819	66		825	72
2 = Jul 1, 66-Jun 30, 67			4 = Jul 1, 72-Jun 30, 73		

cus I Nicator (323-281 B.C.) was satrap of Babylon but fled to Egypt. In 312 B.C. Ptolemy and Seleucus together defeated Demetrius Poliorcetes, son of Antigonus, at Gaza, and Seleucus returned triumphantly to Babylon. In his account of the decisive battle Diodorus mentions[1] that Demetrius had summoned his soldiers to Gaza from their winter quarters and thus awaited the approach of his opponents. Therefore the victory of Seleucus was presumably in the spring of the year, and his return to Babylon subsequent to that. The victory and triumphant return to Babylon were evidently considered to mark the real beginning of his reign; the first regnal year of Seleucus was dated accordingly as beginning with the ensuing New Year's day in Babylon, namely the following Nisanu 1, which was Apr 3, 311 B.C.

《 193.   When the Seleucid rule was later centered in Syria, this beginning point was taken as the immediately preceding New Year's day in the Macedonian calendar. In what we have called its earlier correlation (¶121), the Macedonian calendar began with the month Dios, equivalent to Tishri. In this year Dios 1 was Oct 7, 312 B.C., a date which was closer than the Babylonian New Year's day to the date of the victory at Gaza and return to Babylon. After the death of Seleucus, instead of starting a new reckoning with the next king, the first year of Seleucus continued to be used as the fixed point from which to count. Thus the Seleucid era was instituted. Its designation is *Anno Seleucidarum* (abbreviated A.S.), "in the year of the Seleucids," i.e., "in the Seleucidan era," and it is reckoned from the two points as explained, from Dios 1 = Oct 7, 312 B.C. in the Mace-

[1] XIX, 80, 5; cf. Plutarch, *Demetrius.* 5.

donian calendar, from Nisanu 1 = Apr 3, 311 B.C. in the Babylonian calendar. Tables 46 and 47 show, for a few years at the beginning of the era, how the years are counted in terms of the two
calendars respectively.

TABLE 46. THE BEGINNING OF THE SELEUCID ERA
ACCORDING TO THE MACEDONIAN CALENDAR

Year of the Seleucid Era	New Year's Day, Dios 1 = Tishri 1	Calendar Year
1	Oct 7, 312	312/311
2	Sep 26, 311	311/310
3	Oct 15, 310	310/309
4	Oct 4, 309	309/308
5	Sep 23, 308	308/307

TABLE 47. THE BEGINNING OF THE SELEUCID ERA
ACCORDING TO THE BABYLONIAN CALENDAR

Year of the Seleucid Era	New Year's Day, Nisanu 1	Calendar Year
1	Apr 3, 311	311/310
2	Apr 22, 310	310/309
3	Apr 10, 309	309/308
4	Mar 30, 308	308/307
5	Apr 18, 307	307/306

⟨ 194.   The Seleucid era is used in I Maccabees in many notations
of date from 1:10 on. The reference in 1:10 states that Antiochus
Epiphanes "began to reign in the one hundred and thirty-seventh
year of the kingdom of the Greeks." Other references also give days
and months. The months are sometimes designated by name (e.g.,
1:54), sometimes by number (e.g., 9:3), and sometimes by both,
e.g., 4:52—"on the twenty-fifth day of the ninth month, which is
the month of Kislev, in the one hundred and forty-eighth year";
and 16:14—"in the one hundred and seventy-seventh year, in the
eleventh month, which is the month of Shebat." Here where both
number and name are cited it is evident that the months are numbered from the spring and it may be supposed that the year references in the same verses are also reckoned from the spring, i.e.,
are years of the Seleucid era according to the Babylonian-Jewish

calendar. Then Kislev 25, in the year 148 (4:52), for example, will be interpreted thus: A.S. 148 = 164/163 B.C.; in this year Kislev 1 fell on Nov. 20; therefore Kislev 25 was Dec 14, 164 B.C. If 1:10 is to be interpreted in the same way then the beginning of the reign of Antiochus Epiphanes in the one hundred and thirty-seventh year was in the year beginning Mar 30, 175 B.C.

【 195.   Some think, however, that while dates derived from a Jewish source are indeed reckoned in this way (namely: 1:29; 1:54; 1:59; 2:70; 4:52; 7:43; 9:3; 9:54; 10:21; 13:41; 13:51; 14:27; 16:14), other dates come from an official Seleucid source and are years of the Seleucid era as reckoned according to the Macedonian calendar, i.e., from a first year beginning Oct 7, 312 B.C. Dates which may come from such a source are 1:10; 3:37; 6:16; 7:1; 10:1; 10:57; 10:67; 11:19; 14:1; 15:10. In this case the beginning of the reign of Antiochus Epiphanes (1:10) would be in the year beginning Oct 3, 176. In the same view,[2] four dates could fall in either class (namely: 1:20; 4:28; 6:20; 9:58); and one (6:20) is regarded as erroneous in either case. In II Maccabees similar problems are found and are presumably to be dealt with along the same lines.

【 196.   Josephus likewise gives dates in the Seleucid era, and in two passages equates these with Olympiads:

> "in the hundred and forty-fifth year, on the twenty-fifth day of the month which by us is called Chasleu ($X\alpha\sigma\lambda\epsilon\acute{\upsilon}$ = Kislev), and by the Macedonians Apellaios ('$A\pi\epsilon\lambda\lambda\alpha\hat{\iota}os$), in the hundred and fifty-third Olympiad";[3]
> "the twenty-fifth of the month Apellaios, in the hundred and forty-eighth year, in the hundred and fifty-fourth Olympiad."[4]

The year A.S. 145 extended by the Macedonian reckoning from the fall of 168 B.C. to the fall of 167 B.C.; by the Babylonian reckoning from the spring of 167 B.C. to the spring of 166 B.C. Therefore Kislev 25 was Dec 27, 168, in the Macedonian reckoning; Dec 16, 167, in the Babylonian. Olympiad 153 began in the summer of 168 B.C. Therefore the equivalence stated by Josephus is correct on either reckoning. The year A.S. 148 extended by the Macedonian reckoning from the fall of 165 B.C. to the fall of 164 B.C.; by the Babylonian reckoning from the spring of 164 B.C. to the spring of

---

[2] Dancy, *A Commentary on I Maccabees*, pp.50-51.
[3] *Ant.* XII, 248 (= XII, v, 4).   [4] *Ant.* XII, 321 (= XII, vii, 6).

163 B.C. Therefore Kislev 25 was Dec 24, 165 B.C., in the Macedonian reckoning; Dec 14, 164 B.C., in the Babylonian. Olympiad 154 began in the summer of 164 B.C. Therefore the equivalence stated by Josephus is correct only on the Babylonian reckoning and, assuming such reckoning, he is correct in both synchronisms.

¶ 197.   In the *Chronicle* of Eusebius as translated by Jerome (¶¶256ff.),[5] the beginning of the reign of Seleucus Nicanor, as he is called, is placed in Ol. 117, 1. This Olympiadic year began Jul 1, 312 B.C., and the date is correct.

¶ 198.   Of all the ancient eras the Seleucid became probably the one most widely and longest used. Examples of its employment in Jewish literature were given above (¶¶194-196), and among the Jews it continued in use for a long time. They called it not only "the Greek era" (מנין יונית, *minyan yewanit*), but also "the era of contracts" (מנין שטרות, *minyan sheṭarot*) because legal documents were dated by it. The era was also used by the followers of Muhammad, and it has continued in use by the Syrian Christians in Lebanon until the present.[6]

4. THE JEWISH ERAS

LITERATURE: Eduard Mahler, *Handbuch der jüdischen Chronologie.* 1916; Arthur Spier, *The Comprehensive Hebrew Calendar, Its Structure, History, and One Hundred Years of Corresponding Dates 5660-5760, 1900-2000.* 1952; *Sefer Seder 'Olam. The Book of the Order of the World, being the Book Seder 'Olam Rabbah by Rabbi Jose ben Halafta, with comments and emendations by Rabbi Jacob Emden and Rabbi Elijah of Vilna . . . and now added to this edition Seder 'Olam Zuta and the Sefer ha-Kabalah of Rabad,* prepared for publication by Rabbi Samuel Waxman. [5]712 = 1953; Edgar Frank, *Talmudic and Rabbinical Chronology.* 1956.

(1) THE ERA OF THE DESTRUCTION OF
THE SECOND TEMPLE

¶ 199.   The Jews employed the Seleucid era (¶¶192ff.). They also developed distinctive eras of their own. Of these one was that which took as its epoch the destruction of the Second Temple. In this era dates are given as in a certain year of "the destruction of the Temple" (לחרבן הבית, *leḥorban habayit*) or "from the destruction"

[5] ed. Helm, p.126.
[6] Kubitschek, *Grundriss der antiken Zeitrechnung*, p.70.

(אחר החורבן‎, *aḥar haḥurban*). The era was used in Palestine and is still mentioned in Hebrew writings of the Middle Ages.

【200.   In the Seleucid era the year of the destruction of the Temple was 381, which corresponds to the year from the fall of A.D. 69 to the fall of A.D. 70 according to the Macedonian calendar; or to the year from the spring of A.D. 70, to the spring of A.D. 71 according to the Babylonian calendar. As to the month and day, the Jewish sources claim a striking identity between the destruction of the Second Temple and of the First Temple. II K 25:8 states that the First Temple was burned by Nebuzaradan on the seventh day of the fifth month, while Jer 52:12 gives the tenth day of the fifth month. The rabbis reconciled these data by explaining that the Babylonians entered the Temple on the seventh day of Ab (which is the fifth month), ate and did damage in it on that day and the eighth, and on the ninth day toward dusk set fire to it; it then continued to burn through the whole of that day which is presumably extended through the tenth.[1] As to the reoccurrence of disaster at the identical time they said, "The same thing too happened in the Second Temple."[2] For a single day, the ninth of Ab was taken as the exact date: "On the ninth of Ab . . . the Temple was destroyed the first and the second time."[3]

【201.   In his account of the second destruction Josephus gives the following sequence of events. On Xanthikos 14 Titus encamped before the city.[4] On Panemos 17 the daily sacrifices ceased.[5] On Loos 8 the Roman armies completed their earthworks[6] and Titus ordered the gates of the temple area set afire.[7] On the following day, which was Loos 9, Titus resolved to spare the Temple.[8] On the yet following day, which was Loos 10, amidst the fighting a soldier cast a firebrand into the Temple and it was burned.[9] The date of the burning is stated explicitly by Josephus: "the tenth of the month Loos, the day on which of old it had been burnt by the king of Babylon."[10] In the later correlation of the Macedonian calendar as it was used

---

[1] *Taanith.* 29a; SBT II, 7, pp.153-154.   [2] *ibid.*
[3] *Taanith.* IV, 6; DM p.200.
[4] *War.* V, 99 (= V, iii, 1); V, 133 (= V, iii, 5); V, 567 (= V, xiii, 7).
[5] *War.* VI, 94 (= VI, ii, 1).   [6] *War.* VI, 220 (=VI, iv, 1).
[7] *War.* VI, 228 (=VI, iv, 1).   [8] *War.* VI, 241 (= VI, iv, 3).
[9] *War.* VI, 244, 252 (=VI, iv, 4-5).   [10] *War.* VI, 250 (= VI, iv, 5).

in Palestine (Table 29), Loos was parallel to Ab, the fifth month. Therefore Josephus' date of Loos = Ab 10 is identical with Jeremiah's (52:12) date of the tenth day of the fifth month for the first destruction, and just one day later than the ninth day of Ab taken as the official date by the rabbis.

¶ 202.   Taking the ninth day of Ab as the standard date, in A.S. 381 this was equivalent to Aug 5, A.D. 70, and this was accordingly the epoch of the era of Destruction. The first year of the era would extend from this beginning point to the end of the then current calendar year. According to the passage already cited (¶¶164, 168) from Rosh Hashanah, the year which was used "for years"—which should include the reckoning of years in eras—was the year beginning on Tishri 1. Therefore Year 1 of the Destruction era extended from Ab 9 = Aug 5, A.D. 70, to the last day of Elul = Sep 24, A.D. 70; Year 2 extended from Tishri 1 = Sep 25, A.D. 70, to the last day of the following Elul = Oct 13, A.D. 71; and so on. The first several years of the era were accordingly as shown in Table 48 from which any further years may also be calculated.

TABLE 48. THE BEGINNING OF THE ERA OF
THE DESTRUCTION OF THE SECOND TEMPLE

Year of the Destruction Era	Beginning of the Year	End of the Year	Calendar Year in the Christian Era
1	Ab 9 = Aug 5, 70	Elul 30 = Sep 24, 70	70
2	Tishri 1 = Sep 25, 70	Elul 29 = Oct 13, 71	70/71
3	Tishri 1 = Oct 14, 71	Elul 30 = Oct 2, 72	71/72
4	Tishri 1 = Oct 3, 72	Elul 29 = Sep 21, 73	72/73
5	Tishri 1 = Sep 22, 73	Elul 29 = Oct 10, 74	73/74

¶ 203.   An example of the use of this era is found in a Geniza fragment in the British Museum dated Tammuz 13, 987, after the destruction of the Temple.[11] Since Year 2 of this era equals A.D. 70/71, Year 987 equals A.D. 1055/1056, and Tammuz 13 of that year was June 28, A.D. 1056.[12]

[11] A. Marmorstein in *Zeitschrift der Deutschen Morgenländischen Gesellschaft* 67 (1913), p.640 n.4, p.643.
[12] Mahler, *Handbuch der jüdischen Chronologie*, p.152.

(2) THE ERA OF THE WORLD

❲ 204.   The more universally employed Jewish era is called the "era of creation" (מנין ליצירה, *minyan liyeṣirah*) or the "era of the world" (מנין העולם, *minyan ha'olam*) or of the "creation of the world" (לבריאת העולם, *libriat ha'olam*). The epoch is the creation of the world, and dates are given "in the year of the world," often abbreviated A.M. for *anno mundi*.

❲ 205.   The earliest mention of this era is in a Baraitha cited in the tractate Abodah Zarah in the Babylonian Talmud.[1] The whole passage, to which reference will be made again later (¶208), begins with a quotation from Rabbi Hanina (third Christian century), who also employs this era and then cites the Baraitha for comparison.

> "Said R. Hanina: From the year 400 after the destruction onwards, if one says unto you, 'Buy a field that is worth one thousand denarii for one denar'—do not buy it. In a Baraitha it is taught: From the year four thousand two hundred and thirty-one of the Creation of the World onward, if one says unto you, 'Buy thee a field that is worth a thousand denarii for one denar,' do not buy it. What difference is there between these two [given periods]?—There is a difference of three years between them, the one of the Baraitha being three years longer."

❲ 206.   In the tractate Niddah,[2] there is mention of a work called Seder Olam and of its author Rabbi Jose. Rabbi Jose is Jose ben Halafta who died about A.D. 160, and the Seder Olam Rabbah or "Book of the Order of the World" is the oldest Jewish chronicle, a work listing events of Old Testament and later history down to Bar Kokhba. A further and supplementary work of the eighth century, the Seder Olam Zutta, supplies the numbers of the years for the skeleton outline of Seder Olam Rabbah and continues it to around A.D. 800. Seder Olam Rabbah begins[3] with a tabulation from Gen 5, of which the opening lines are:

אדם	ק״ל	= 130
שת	ק״ה	= 105
אנוש	צ׳	= 90

These and the subsequent notations may be represented by Table 49.[4]

---

[1] *Abodah Zarah.* 9b; SBT IV, 7, p.47.   [2] *Niddah*, 46b; SBT VI, 1, p.325.
[3] ed. Waxman, p.1.
[4] Frank, *Talmudic and Rabbinical Chronology*, pp.11-12.

TABLE 49. FROM ADAM TO NOAH IN SEDER OLAM RABBAH

		Born in the Year of the World	Became the father of the son at the age of
1.	Adam	0	130
2.	Seth	130	105
3.	Enosh	235	90
4.	Kenan	325	70
5.	Mahalalel	395	65
6.	Jared	460	162
7.	Enoch	622	65
8.	Methuselah	687	187
9.	Lamech	874	182
10.	Noah	1056	

¶207. Without giving these details, the Seder Olam Zutta begins at this point with the summary statement: "From Adam to Noah are 1056 years." From here on Table 50 shows the main divisions of the chronicle (where Seder Olam Rabbah and Seder Olam Zutta diverge—as they sometimes do by a year—we follow Seder Olam Rabbah).

¶208. Returning to the passage quoted above (¶205) from Abodah Zarah, we are now prepared to show that A.M. 3828 (the year of the second destruction) plus 400 (as in the formula of Rabbi Hanina) equals A.M. 4228; and that A.M. 4231 (cited in the Baraitha) minus 3 equals A.M. 4228. In other words Rabbi Hanina and the Baraitha are in agreement in dating the second destruction in Anno Mundi 3828 as does also Seder Olam Rabbah.

¶209. Since "the first of Tishri is New Year for years" (¶¶164, 168) and since the world was held by many to have been created in Tishri (¶169), this year 3828 from the creation of the world was presumably reckoned as a year beginning on Tishri 1. Beginning thus in the fall, this year corresponds with year 381 of the Seleucid era also reckoned, by Macedonian custom, from the fall and extending from the fall of A.D. 69 to the fall of 70. The following synchronism is thereby established: A.M. 3828 = A.S. 381 = A.D. 69/70 = Year 1 of the era of Destruction.

¶210. The foregoing tabulation presumably places the creation of Adam near the beginning of the year zero (Table 49) and makes him one year old one year later, thus the years one, two, three, and

TABLE 50. FROM THE FLOOD TO THE DESTRUCTION
OF THE SECOND TEMPLE IN SEDER OLAM RABBAH

	In the Year of the World	Number of Years
10. (Continued from Table 49)		600 years, the age of Noah when the Flood came (Gen 7:6)
11. Flood	1656	340 years until the confusion of languages
12. Confusion of languages	1996	52 years until the birth of Isaac
13. Birth of Isaac	2048	400 years until the exodus from Egypt (Nisan 15) and the revelation on Sinai (seven weeks later)
14. Exodus from Egypt (Nisan 15) and revelation on Sinai (seven weeks later)	2448	40 years of wandering in the wilderness until the entry into Canaan (Moses died [Dt 34:5] on Adar 7; the people mourned 30 days, then after three days [Jos 1:11; 3:2] passed over Jordan on Nisan 10)
15. Entry into Canaan	2488	480 years from the exodus to the foundation of the Temple (I K 6:1); therefore 440 years from the entry into Canaan to the foundation of the Temple
16. Foundation of the First Temple	2928	410 years the First Temple stood
17. Destruction of the First Temple	3338	70 years of Babylonian captivity
18. Consecration of the Second Temple	3408	420 years the Second Temple stood
19. Destruction of the Second Temple	3828	

so on, actually indicate the age of Adam[5] and after him the age of mankind. It would also be possible, however, to assign the number one to the year in which Adam was created rather than to the year when he became one year old. In that case the year in which Adam was one year old would actually be Year 2 of the era; and then the year of the second destruction would be Anno Mundi 3829. But it would also be possible to assign the year one to the time when "the earth was without form and void" (Gen 1:2). In this case Adam would be created near the beginning of Year 2 and would be one year old in Year 3; and then the year of the second destruction would be Anno Mundi 3830.

⟨ 211.   Depending, therefore, upon which starting point is selected, the year of the destruction of the second Temple is A.M. 3830, 3829, or 3828, and all three designations refer to the same year. Accordingly the preceding tabulation (Tables 49, 50) may be expanded now to take account of these three possibilities (Table 51). The number of years to be added in the several steps, grouped here into larger units, may still be seen in Tables 49, 50; the three ways of counting are labeled Creation Era I, II, and III; and the correlation with the Christian, Seleucid, and Destruction eras is shown.[6]

⟨ 212.   It was also a concern of rabbinical chronology to establish the exact point of beginning of the first year of the era of Creation. In the language of these reckonings the time of the new moon (the mean astronomical new moon, i.e., when the moon is in conjunction with the sun and its phase is new) is called the מולד, molad (plural moladoth). The day begins at our six o'clock p.m. which is called 0 h or 24 h, i.e., Hour zero or Hour twenty-four. So what we call Sunday 6 p.m. is by this system called Monday 0 h. The hour is divided into 1080 חלקים, halakim (from a word meaning "to divide"), or parts, so that each helek equals 3 1/3 seconds.

⟨ 213.   Using this system the molad which marked the beginning of Year 1 in Creation Era I is called Molad Tohu referring to the time when the earth was "without form" (תהו) (Gen 1:2). It is also called Molad Beharad (בהר״ד). The latter name is derived as follows: ב = 2 and means the second day of the week, i.e., Monday.

---

[5] Cf. Parah. VIII, 9, cited above in ¶165.
[6] Frank, Talmudic and Rabbinical Chronology, p.19.

TABLE 51. THE ERA OF CREATION OR THE ERA OF THE WORLD

		Creation Era			Christian Era	Seleucid Era	Destruction Era
		I	II	III	B.C.		
1.	Earth without form and void	1			3761/3760		
2.	Creation of Adam	2	1		3760/3759		
3.	Adam one year old	3	2	1	3759/3758		
4.	Flood	1658	1657	1656	2104/2103		
5.	Exodus	2450	2449	2448	1312/1311		
6.	Foundation of the First Temple	2930	2929	2928	832/831		
7.	Destruction of the First Temple	3340	3339	3338	422/421		
8.	Consecration of the Second Temple	3410	3409	3408	352/351		
9.	Beginning of the Seleucid Era	3450	3449	3448	312/311	1	
10.	Beginning of the Christian Era	3760 3761 3762	3759 3760 3761	3758 3759 3760	2/1 1 B.C./A.D. 1 A.D. 1/2	311 312 313	
11.	Destruction of the Second Temple and Beginning of the Destruction Era	3830	3829	3828	69/70	381	1

ה = 5 and means five hours after the beginning of Monday or what we would call Sunday 11 p.m. ר״ד = 204 and means 204 ḥalakim or 11 minutes and 20 seconds.

〖 214.   Astronomically the moon actually was in conjunction (new phase) on Sunday Oct 6 at eleven minutes after six o'clock in the morning, Jerusalem time, in the year 3761 B.C. Therefore the crescent of the new moon would have been in the sky that evening to mark the first of Tishri and the beginning of the new year. By modern reckoning this was still Sunday evening but by Jewish reckoning it was the early hours of Monday Oct 7. So the Molad Beharad or Molad Tohu, the exact point of beginning of the first day of the first month (Tishri 1) of the first year of Creation Era I was placed on what present reckoning would give as Sunday Oct 6, 3761 B.C., at eleven o'clock and eleven and one-third minutes p.m., but which Jewish reckoning specifies as on Monday Oct 7 of the same year at five hours and 204 ḥalakim.[7]

([215.   The point corresponding to Tishri 1, 3761 B.C., has continued to be that from which the World era is reckoned among the Jews. Accordingly the formula for changing a date in the World era into the Christian era is to subtract 3761 between the Jewish New Year's day (Tishri 1) and December 31, and to subtract 3760 between Jan 1 and the Jewish New Year's day.[8] Thus Tishri 1, Anno Mundi 5721, began at sundown at the time which the civil calendar calls Wednesday 6 p.m. but which the Jewish calendar calls Thursday 0 h, on Sep 21, Anno Domini 1960. To apply the formula: $5721 - 3761 = 1960$; after Jan 1, $5721 - 3760 = 1961$; in other words A.M. 5721 = A.D. 1960/1961.

([216.   In writing such a year date in Hebrew the 5 (ה) of the thousands is simply understood and not written. Next, for the date just given (¶215) come ת and ש which have the numerical values of 400 and 300 respectively and total 700. Then come כ = 20 and א = 1. Thus תשכ״א[ה] = [5] 721.

5. THE ERA OF DIOCLETIAN

LITERATURE: Carl Bertheau, "Era," in NSH IV, pp.162-163.

([217.   Among eras with later epochs one may be mentioned briefly in transition to treatment of the Christian era. The reign of Diocletian (A.D. 284-305) was considered so important as to mark an era. Diocletian was proclaimed emperor by his troops at Chalcedon on Sep 17, A.D. 284. The reckoning of an era of Diocletian origi-

[7] Mahler, *Handbuch der jüdischen Chronologie*, pp.466-467.
[8] Frank, *Talmudic and Rabbinical Chronology*, p.13.

nated in Egypt and the epoch was taken as the Egyptian New Year's day immediately preceding his accession, namely Thoth 1 = Aug 29, A.D. 284. Accordingly Anno Diocletiani 1 was Aug 29, 284 — Aug 28, 285; Anno Diocletiani 100 was Aug 29, 383 — Aug 28, 384, and so on. The era was often employed in the Christian church where, since Diocletian was the great persecutor of the Christians, it was also known as the *aera martyrum*, "era of the martyrs." Wide use of the era continued until in the eighth century, and it is still found among the Abyssinians and Copts in Egypt.

6. THE CHRISTIAN ERA

LITERATURE: Walter F. Wislicenus, *Der Kalender in gemeinverständlicher Darstellung*. 1905, pp.14ff.; H. Achelis, "Dionysius Exiguus," in NSH III, pp.441-442.

❰ 218.   When Cyril of Alexandria (died A.D. 444) computed his Easter-table he employed the era just described (¶217) and designated the separate years as so many years after Diocletian and his persecution. But when the prominent scholar of the next century, the Roman monk Dionysius Exiguus ("Dionysius the Little"), in A.D. 525 prepared a continuation of Cyril's Easter-table he did not count from Diocletian but *ab incarnatione Domini*. Feeling it inappropriate to reckon from the reign of the imperial enemy of Christianity, he explained:

> "We have been unwilling to connect our cycle with the name of an impious persecutor, but have chosen rather to note the years from the incarnation of our Lord Jesus Christ."

❰ 219.   In the time of Dionysius the annunciation to Mary was celebrated on Mar 25 and the birth of Jesus on Dec 25. Following a reckoning which was evidently current in his time, Dionysius placed these events in A.U.C. 754 and for the beginning point of the era went back to Jan 1 of that year. While he used the phrase *ab incarnatione Domini*, "from the incarnation of the Lord," other designations of the era also were used and the best known is that which we still employ, *anno Domini*, "in the year of the Lord," abbreviated A.D. Thus A.D. 1 in the Dionysian reckoning was the same as A.U.C. 754 in the Varronian reckoning. In the summer of that year Ol. 194, 4 ended and Ol. 195, 1 began. In the spring of that year, by Babylonian reckoning, A.S. 312 began; in the fall, by Macedonian reckoning, A.S. 313 began. These relationships are shown below in Table 53.

([220. With the use of the Christian era and the reckoning Anno Domini there arose also the possibility of counting backward from this beginning point as well as forward. While this possibility now seems obvious, it actually remained the custom for a long time to designate dates prior to the Christian era in terms of some of the older eras. But from the eighteenth century onward the use of a reckoning prior to the Christian epoch as well as following it became customary, and the designations *ante Christum* (A.C.), *anno ante Christum* (A.A.C.), and "before Christ" (B.C.) were employed.

([221. In carrying the reckoning backward as well as forward, no Year zero was established but the first year of the period prior to Christ was placed immediately before the first year of the Christian era, that is the years 1 B.C. and A.D. 1 followed each other in immediate succession. Mathematically speaking the omission of zero in a sequence of numbers involves an error and accordingly, in astronomical reckoning, the first year before A.D. 1 is designated as Year zero and from there on back the years are marked with a minus sign, while the years moving forward from Year zero are marked with a plus sign. Thus in the two systems, which we may call the historical and the astronomical, the years run as follows at the point of transition (Table 52).

TABLE 52. THE TRANSITION FROM B.C. TO A.D.
IN HISTORICAL AND IN ASTRONOMICAL RECKONING

Historical		Astronomical
A.D. 4	=	+4
A.D. 3	=	+3
A.D. 2	=	+2
A.D. 1	=	+1
1 B.C.	=	0
2 B.C.	=	−1
3 B.C.	=	−2
4 B.C.	=	−3

([222. Mathematically, reckoning from B.C. to A.D. is simplified by the astronomical system. If we ask, for example, how many years there are from Jan 1, A.D. 2 to Jan 1, A.D. 4 simple subtraction gives the correct answer of 2 by either system. But if we ask how many years there are from Jan 1, 2 B.C. to Jan 1, A.D. 4 simple addition of these figures would give an answer of 6 which is incorrect. According to the astronomical system, however, one would still subtract the temporally prior date from the temporally following date. To subtract a negative number from a positive number their positive values are added. Accordingly −1 subtracted from +4 is the same as 1 plus 4 equals 5, which is the correct answer.

⟨223.   In a table of parallel years (Table 53), which covers only a relatively few years at the transition from B.C. to A.D. but which can readily be extended as desired in either direction, the years of the Christian reckoning are shown as the standard and are of course years counted from Jan 1. The years reckoned from the founding of the city of Rome are considered to be counted from Jan 1 also and are therefore identical with the years B.C.—A.D. The Olympiadic years are years beginning on Jul 1 in the year B.C. or A.D. with which they are parallel, i.e., Ol. 184, 1 begins Jul 1, 44 B.C. and

TABLE 53. PARALLEL YEARS OF THE OLYMPIADIC,
SELEUCIDAN, ROMAN, AND CHRISTIAN ERAS

Ol.		A.S.	A.U.C.	B.C.	Ol.		A.S.	A.U.C.	B.C.
184,	1	269	710	44	188,	1	285	726	28
	2	270	711	43		2	286	727	27
	3	271	712	42		3	287	728	26
	4	272	713	41		4	288	729	25
185,	1	273	714	40	189,	1	289	730	24
	2	274	715	39		2	290	731	23
	3	275	716	38		3	291	732	22
	4	276	717	37		4	292	733	21
186,	1	277	718	36	190,	1	293	734	20
	2	278	719	35		2	294	735	19
	3	279	720	34		3	295	736	18
	4	280	721	33		4	296	737	17
187,	1	281	722	32	191,	1	297	738	16
	2	282	723	31		2	298	739	15
	3	283	724	30		3	299	740	14
	4	284	725	29		4	300	741	13

Ol.		A.S.	A.U.C.	B.C.	Ol.		A.S.	A.U.C.	A.D.
192,	1	301	742	12		3	343	784	31
	2	302	743	11		4	344	785	32
	3	303	744	10	203,	1	345	786	33
	4	304	745	9		2	346	787	34
193,	1	305	746	8		3	347	788	35
	2	306	747	7		4	348	789	36
	3	307	748	6	204,	1	349	790	37
	4	308	749	5		2	350	791	38
194,	1	309	750	4		3	351	792	39
	2	310	751	3		4	352	793	40
	3	311	752	2	205,	1	353	794	41
	4	312	753	1		2	354	795	42
195,	1	313	754	A.D. 1		3	355	796	43
	2	314	755	2		4	356	797	44
	3	315	756	3	206,	1	357	798	45
	4	316	757	4		2	358	799	46
196,	1	317	758	5		3	359	800	47
	2	318	759	6		4	360	801	48
	3	319	760	7	207,	1	361	802	49
	4	320	761	8		2	362	803	50
197,	1	321	762	9		3	363	804	51
	2	322	763	10		4	364	805	52
	3	323	764	11	208,	1	365	806	53
	4	324	765	12		2	366	807	54
198,	1	325	766	13		3	367	808	55
	2	326	767	14		4	368	809	56
	3	327	768	15	209,	1	369	810	57
	4	328	769	16		2	370	811	58
199,	1	329	770	17		3	371	812	59
	2	330	771	18		4	372	813	60
	3	331	772	19	210,	1	373	814	61
	4	332	773	20		2	374	815	62
200,	1	333	774	21		3	375	816	63
	2	334	775	22		4	376	817	64
	3	335	776	23	211,	1	377	818	65
	4	336	777	24		2	378	819	66
201,	1	337	778	25		3	379	820	67
	2	338	779	26		4	380	821	68
	3	339	780	27	212,	1	381	822	69
	4	340	781	28		2	382	823	70
202,	1	341	782	29		3	383	824	71
	2	342	783	30		4	384	825	72

extends through Jun 30, 43 B.C. The years of the Seleucid era are considered to be reckoned according to the Macedonian system from Oct 1, i.e., A.S. 269 begins Oct 1, 44 B.C. and extends through Sep 30, 43 B.C. (by Babylonian reckoning A.S. 269 begins in the spring of 43 B.C. and extends to the spring of 42 B.C.).[1]

[1] SHJP I, ii, pp.393ff.

III. EARLY CHRISTIAN CHRONOGRAPHERS

1. CHRONICLES AND CHRONOGRAPHERS

(1) GREEK AND ROMAN

¶ 224. Works devoted to chronology were familiar in the Greek and Roman world and are frequently referred to under names often related to the Greek word χρονικός or χρονικόν. Derived from the noun χρόνος (¶i in the Preface) these are adjectives which mean "concerning time" and they in turn give us names such as the following: τὰ χρονικά, with which βιβλία may be understood, are "chronological books" and are mentioned by Plutarch.[1] αἱ χρονικαί, with which γραφαί may be understood, are "chronological writings" and are mentioned by Dionysius of Halicarnassus.[2] χρονικοὶ κανόνες are "chronological canons" and are mentioned by Plutarch.[3] A χρονογραφία is a "chronography," and Dionysius of Halicarnassus[4] gives χρονογραφίαι, "chronographies," as the title of a work of Eratosthenes. Similarly a χρονογράφος (Latin *chronographus*) is a writer of chronology, a chronographer, or a chronicler, and Strabo[5] mentions the writers of chronicles (οἱ χρονογράφοι) whose works he used.

¶ 225. In Latin τὰ χρονικά were *chronica* and Pliny,[6] for example, speaks of "the chronicles undoubtedly being in error" (*chronicorum errore non dubio*). Likewise Aulus Gellius[7] mentions a work of Apollodorus entitled with the same plural, *Chronica*, and tells of making notes for his own work "from the books known as Chronicles" (*ex libris qui chronici appellantur*). In Latin the same word came to be used as a singular form, and Aulus Gellius[8] cites a passage, for example, in the first chronicle of Cornelius Nepos (*in primo Chronico*). So χρονικά or *chronica* (*-orum*) are chronological treatises or chronicles, and a χρονικόν or *chronica* (*-ae*) is also such a work, and in English we may speak of chronicles or of a chronicle or a chronicon.

---

[1] *Themistocles.* 27.
[2] I, 8, 3.
[3] *Solon.* 27.
[4] I, 74, 2.
[5] I. 2. 9.
[6] *Natural History.* xxxv, xxxiv, 58.
[7] *Attic Nights.* xvii, iv. 5; xvii, xxi, 1.
[8] *Attic Nights.* xvii, xxi, 3.

⟨ 226.   As for the word "canon" (κανών, *canon*) found in Plutarch's mention (¶224) of "chronological canons" (χρονικοὶ κανόνες), it could apply to the whole work or might apply particularly to the tabular summary or "table" which might follow upon introductory materials. Also in the singular or plural the word could have the sense of a whole system of chronology, as when Dionysius of Halicarnassus,[9] in parallelism with his mention of the Chronographies (χρονογραφίαι) of Eratosthenes, says that "the canons (οἱ κανόνες) of Eratosthenes are sound."

(2) JEWISH

⟨ 227.   Also a Jewish writer such as Josephus was interested in chronology in relation to the history he wrote, and the more so because he particularly wished to demonstrate the high antiquity of Jewish traditions in comparison with pagan, presumably on the hypothesis that priority implies superiority. In *Against Apion*[1] he makes it plain that such a demonstration of the great age of the Jewish race was a prime purpose in the writing of the *Antiquities*, and he claims that the history of his people embraces in fact a period of five thousand years. Josephus there says:

> "In my history of our *Antiquities*, most excellent Epaphroditus, I have, I think, made sufficiently clear to any who may peruse that work the extreme antiquity of our Jewish race, the purity of the original stock, and the manner in which it established itself in the country which we occupy today. That history embraces a period of five thousand years, and was written by me in Greek on the basis of our sacred books."

⟨ 228.   As for specifically chronological works as such, we have already had occasion (¶¶206f.) to deal with the relatively old and very important Seder Olam Rabbah of the second Christian century and also with the eighth century continuation of the same, the Seder Olam Zutta. In proceeding shortly (¶¶229ff.) to consider certain early Christian chronicles we will find that they tabulate Old Testament data in much the same manner as the Seder Olam.

(3) EARLY CHRISTIAN

⟨ 229.   As for the early Christian writers, there was a not improper reticence about chronology and an awareness of its uncertainties.

---

[9] I, 74, 2.

[1] I, 1.

As noted earlier (¶v in the Preface), this attitude was expressed by Eusebius even in the introduction to his *Chronicle* where he quoted Ac 1:7—"it is not for you to know times or seasons"—and applied this saying not only to the eschatological end-time but also to all times, thus emphasizing the factor of uncertainty in all chronological reckoning. Nevertheless early Christian writers, including Eusebius himself, were led to be interested in chronology for various reasons.

¶230. There was concern to comprehend the whole sweep of God's administration of the world and the time of the world's end. The *Epistle of Barnabas*[1] observes that God made the works of his hands in six days (Gen 1), recalls that with him one day is as a thousand years (Ps 90:4; II Pet 3:8), and concludes that he will finish all things in six thousand years.

¶231. As was true of Josephus (¶227) and presumably for similar reasons, there was also an interest among the Christians in demonstrating the high antiquity of biblical traditions over against pagan ones. In his *Address to the Greeks*[2] Tatian undertakes to show by chronological considerations that "our philosophy [i.e., the Christian] is older than the system of the Greeks." Clement of Alexandria also wishes to prove that biblical institutions and laws are far more ancient than the philosophy of the Greeks. He cites the work of Tatian in this regard, and devotes a long section of his own *Stromata*[3] to an outline of history with tables of dates.

¶232. Chronological studies were pursued in connection with trying to show the fulfillment of prophecy. In *An Answer to the Jews*[4] Tertullian inquires into "the times . . . of the predicted and future nativity of the Christ, and of his passion, and of the extermination of the city of Jerusalem."

¶233. And chronological investigation was necessary in relation to the determination of the date of church festivals, particularly of Easter. Eusebius[5] states that Hippolytus of Rome (A.D. 170-236) wrote a work on the passover in which he gave a chronological table and set forth a paschal canon of sixteen years. Jerome[6] like-

---

[1] 15.
[2] 31-41, specially 31.
[3] I, xxi.
[4] 8.
[5] *Ch. Hist.* VI, xxii, 1; NPNFSS I, p.270 n.2.
[6] *Lives of Illustrious Men.* 61.

wise says that Hippolytus wrote *A Reckoning of the Paschal Feast and Chronological Tables,* in which he discussed the cycle of sixteen years, which the Greeks knew, and through which he gave the cue to Eusebius for the construction of a cycle of nineteen years. In 1551 a marble statue was found on the Via Tiburtina at Rome of a person (the upper part of the body missing) seated on a chair, probably none other than Hippolytus, for on the back of the chair is inscribed a list of works agreeing well with what he is known to have written, and on either side is an Easter canon. The latter gives astronomical full moons and Easter dates as calculated for the sixteen years from A.D. 222 to 237.[7]

◀ 234. Thus chronological statements and passages are to be found in various early Christian writers such as those we have cited and others, and eventually longer and entire works on chronology arose. Among the earliest and most important are those of Africanus (¶¶235ff.) and Eusebius (¶¶246ff.).

2. THE *CHRONOGRAPHIES* OF AFRICANUS

LITERATURE: M. J. Routh, *Reliquiae Sacrae.* 1846, pp.238-309, 357-509 (*cited as Routh*); George Salmon, "Africanus, Julius," in SWDCB I, pp.53-57; E. Schwartz, "Die Königslisten des Eratosthenes und Kastor mit Excursen über die Interpolationen bei Africanus und Eusebios," in *Abhandlungen der königlichen Gesellschaft der Wissenschaften zu Göttingen* (abbreviated AKGWG), Mathematisch-physikalische Klasse. 40 (1894-95), pp.1-96, specially, pp.22-54.

◀ 235. Julius Africanus was a Christian writer who spent much of his life (A.D. c.170-c.240) at Emmaus (Nicopolis, not the Emmaus of Lk 24:16) in Palestine. The church historian Socrates[1] mentions him along with Clement and Origen as "eminent for . . . information in every department of literature and science." Eusebius[2] says that among his numerous writings were "five books of Chronographies (πέντε Χρονογραφιῶν), a monument of labor and accuracy." The title of the work was therefore presumably Χρονογραφίαι, *Chronographies.* As a whole it has been lost, but there are quotations and extracts from it in Eusebius and other writers, while Eusebius himself probably based his own *Chronicle* upon it. The fragments,

[7] DACL VI, 2, cols. 2425-2428.

[1] *Ch. Hist.* II, 35.   [2] *Ch. Hist.* VI, xxxi, 2.

in all quite extensive, are edited by Routh, *Reliquiae Sacrae* (cited as Routh).

《236.   As his starting point Africanus takes the creation of Adam, and he reckons his years ἀπὸ 'Αδάμ, "from Adam." In references we may use the designation A. Ad., Anno Adam, "in the year of Adam." As he deals with the Old Testament Africanus uses the Septuagint text. The first interval is from the creation of Adam to the time when he became the father of Seth. Gen 5:3 states in the Hebrew text that "When Adam had lived a hundred and thirty years he became the father of . . . Seth"; but the Septuagint gives the figure as "two hundred and thirty years." Here it is unnecessary to decide whether the time of the conception or the time of the birth of the child is meant, but there are chronological computations (¶¶394, 399, 400) where the distinction must be taken into account. Seth in turn (Gen 5:6) was a hundred and five years old, according to the Hebrew, when he became the father of Enosh, but two hundred and five according to the Septuagint. Following the Septuagint, Africanus begins:[3]

'Αδὰμ γενόμενος ἐτῶν σλ' γεννᾷ τὸν Σήθ . . .
When Adam is two hundred and thirty years old he begets Seth . . .

Σὴθ γενόμενος ἐτῶν σε' ἐγέννησεν τὸν 'Ενώς.
When Seth was two hundred and five years old he begot Enosh.

'Απὸ 'Αδὰμ τοίνυν μέχρι γενέσεως
'Ενὼς ἔτη τὰ σύμπαντα υλε'

From Adam, therefore, to the begetting (*or* birth)
of Enosh was all together four hundred and thirty-
five years.

This gives us the following tabulation at the outset:

TABLE 54. FROM ADAM TO ENOSH IN THE *Chronographies* OF AFRICANUS

		Born in Anno Adam	Became the father of the son at the age of
1.	Adam	0	σλ' = 230
2.	Seth	230	σε' = 205
3.	Enosh	υλέ = 435	

《237.   Africanus then goes on in this same manner, makes certain adjustments in his data, and arrives at these dates:

[3] Excerpt VI Routh p.240.

TABLE 55. FROM THE FLOOD TO THE DEATH OF JOSEPH
IN THE *Chronographies* OF AFRICANUS

		Anno Adam
4.	Flood[4]	͵βσξβ′ = 2262
5.	Entry of Abraham into the Promised Land[5]	͵γσοζ′ = 3277
6.	Death of Joseph[6]	͵γφξγ′ = 3563

⟨ 238.   After that Africanus puts Moses and the exodus from Egypt (which he also equates with the time of the flood of Ogygos in Greek legend[7]) under the first king of the Egyptian Eighteenth Dynasty whom he calls Amos.[8] The year of the exodus is not preserved in the fragments of Africanus, but he gives the final year of the period of the Judges as ͵δσϞβ′ = 4292, and from the intervals involved the date of the exodus can be calculated as having been Anno Adam 3707 in the system of Africanus.[9] From the exodus (and the flood of Ogygos) to the first Olympiad was ͵ακ′ = 1020 years,[10] therefore in the reckoning of Africanus A. Ad. 4727 = Ol. 1, 1.

⟨ 239.   Here and from this point onward Africanus could correlate his dates with the well-established Greek system of dating by Olympiads (¶¶185ff.). In the Greek calendar, it will be remembered (§185), the year began in the summer and Ol. 1, 1, was the year from approximately Jul 1, 776 to Jun 30, 775 B.C. In the case of Africanus, writing in Palestine, it seems likely that he would have used the Syro-Macedonian calendar with the year beginning on Oct 1 (¶130).[11] If he took the Oct 1 nearest Jul 1, 776, it would be Oct 1, 776, and would make Ol. 1, 1, equivalent to Oct 1, 776–Sep 30, 775 B.C. At all events for present purposes it will suffice to indicate the equivalent year as 776/775 B.C. So the synchronism is: A. Ad. 4727 = Ol. 1, 1 = 776/775 B.C.

⟨ 240.   Also in terms of Olympiads it was possible to indicate a positive synchronism with secular history. Citing Diodorus and

---

[4] Excerpt VIII Routh p.243 cf. p.507.   [5] Excerpt IX Routh p.245 cf. p.507.
[6] Excerpt XXI Routh p.269 cf. p.508.
[7] Ogygos (Ὤγυγος) was first king of Thebes (chief city of Boeotia). In his reign came a great deluge. The account is one of the two Greek versions of the flood, the other being the story of Deucalion.
[8] Excerpt XXVIII Routh p.281.
[9] Schwartz in AKGWG 40 (1894-95), pp.22-23.
[10] Excerpt XXII Routh pp.273, 275.   [11] Schwartz, AKGWG, p.24.

others as his authorities, Africanus places the first year of Cyrus in Ol. 55, 1. In his own *Library of History* Diodorus of Sicily does in fact say:[12] "Cyrus became king of the Persians in the opening year of the fifty-fifth Olympiad." Africanus says:[13] Κῦρος δ' οὖν τῷ πρώτῳ τῆς ἀρχῆς ἔτει, ὅπερ ἦν 'Ολυμπιάδος νε΄ ἔτος τὸ πρῶτον; "Cyrus was in the first year of his reign which was the fifty-fifth Olympiad the first year." Therefore the synchronism exists: Cyrus Year 1 = Ol. 55, 1 = 560/559 B.C. Recapitulating, Africanus says in the same passage[14] that from the first Olympiad (i.e., Ol. 1, 1) to Ol. 55, 1 and the first year of Cyrus is σιζ΄ = 217 years which is correct (i.e., 54 × 4 = 216 + 55, 1 = 217, counted inclusively). So, since Ol. 1, 1 = A. Ad. 4727 (¶239), Ol. 55, 1 = A. Ad. 4943. Likewise Africanus says that from Ogygos (= from Moses and the exodus) to Cyrus is ͺασλζ΄ = 1237 years.[15] If the exodus was in A. Ad. 3707 and if we count these 1237 years inclusively (as we saw we had to do with the 217 years just above) then we reach the figure of 4943. Accordingly Cyrus Year 1 = Ol. 55, 1 = A. Ad. 4943, and Ol. 55, 1 = 560/559 B.C.

❡241.   This point where Africanus is able to synchronize his system with a well-fixed point in secular history is also a very important point in biblical history since Cyrus was the king who terminated the captivity of the Jews in Babylonia. In the same passage from which we have just been quoting, Africanus brings his reckoning to the first year of Cyrus with the words: ἐπὶ Κύρου βασιλείας ἔτος πρῶτον, ὅπερ ἦν αἰχμαλωσίας τέλος; "to the first year of the reign of Cyrus when there was an end to the captivity." Actually 560/559 B.C. is the year when Cyrus became king of Persia but he did not take Babylon and free the Jewish captives until 539 B.C. From the dates just surveyed (¶¶238-241) our tabulation representing Africanus may be continued as shown in Table 56.

❡242.   Fortunately the fragments of Africanus also preserve his dates for the life of Jesus. Counting as usual from Adam, he says that the number of years to the appearing of the Savior is 5500 (ἀριθμὸν ἐτῶν πεντάκις χιλίων πεντακοσίων [in alphabetical numerals the figure would be written ͵εφ΄] εἰς τὴν ἐπιφάνειαν τοῦ Σωτηρίου Λό-

[12] IX, 21.   [13] Excerpt XXII Routh p.271.
[14] Excerpt XXII Routh p.273.
[15] Excerpt XXII Routh pp.273, 274, 275.

TABLE 56. FROM THE EXODUS TO THE FIRST YEAR OF CYRUS
IN THE *Chronographies* OF AFRICANUS

	Anno Adam	Ol.	B.C.
7. Exodus under Moses and Flood of Ogygos	3707		
8. End of the period of the Judges	4292		
9. First Olympiad	4727	1, 1	776/775
10. First year of Cyrus	4943	55, 1	560/559

γου);[16] and the number to the presence of the Lord and the resurrection is 5531 (Συνάγονται δὲ τοίνυν οἱ χρόνοι ἐπὶ τὴν τοῦ Κυρίου παρουσίαν ἀπὸ 'Αδὰμ, καὶ τῆς ἀναστάσεως ἔτη ͵εφλα').[17] In view of the synchronism previously established (¶240) for the first year of Cyrus where A. Ad. 4943 = Ol. 55, 1 = 560/559 B.C. we can also establish that A. Ad. 5500 = Ol. 194, 2 = 3/2 B.C. which must be Africanus' date for the birth of Jesus; and that A. Ad. 5531 = Ol. 202, 1 = A.D. 29/30 which must be Africanus' date for the death and resurrection of Christ.

❨ 243.   The understanding just stated (¶242) of the dates of Africanus for the death and resurrection of Christ is confirmed by another statement which Africanus makes. Following the date given for the resurrection he says:[18] ἀφ' οὗ χρόνου ἐπὶ 'Ολυμπιάδα σν' ἔτη ρϞβ'; *a qua temporis epocha ad Olympiadem 250 anni 192*; that is, it was one hundred and ninety-two years from the resurrection of Christ to the two hundred and fiftieth Olympiad. This terminal point of Ol. 250 is presumably given because Africanus was closing his work at that time, perhaps in the last days of Ol. 249, 4 = A.D. 220/221. If we add 192 years to A. Ad. 5531 we get A. Ad. 5723 and this, by the statement just quoted, has to equal Ol. 250, 1 = A.D. 221/222. Therefore, as the next table shows, Africanus' date for the resurrection in A. Ad. 5531 must equal Ol. 202, 1 = A.D. 29/30; and his date for the birth of Jesus in A. Ad. 5500 must equal Ol. 194, 2 = 3/2 B.C.[19] The years of the life of Jesus must then appear as shown in Table 57 according to the chronology of Africanus.

[16] Excerpt x Routh p.246.   [17] Excerpt L Routh p.306.
[18] *Ibid.*
[19] Eduard Schwartz, *Eusebius* II, iii (GCS), p.CCXXII n.1.

TABLE 57. THE YEARS OF THE LIFE OF JESUS
ACCORDING TO THE *Chronographies* OF AFRICANUS

Ol.	B.C.-A.D.	A.Ad.	Ol.	B.C.-A.D.	A.Ad.
194, 1	4/3 B.C.		199, 1	17/18	5519
2	3/2	5500	2	18/19	5520
			3	19/20	5521
	Birth of Jesus		4	20/21	5522
3	2/1	5501			
4	1 B.C./A.D. 1	5502			
195, 1	A.D. 1/2	5503	200, 1	21/22	5523
2	2/3	5504	2	22/23	5524
3	3/4	5505	3	23/24	5525
4	4/5	5506	4	24/25	5526
196, 1	5/6	5507	201, 1	25/26	5527
2	6/7	5508	2	26/27	5528
3	7/8	5509	3	27/28	5529
4	8/9	5510	4	28/29	5530
197, 1	9/10	5511	202, 1	29/30	5531
2	10/11	5512	*Death and resurrection of Christ*		
3	11/12	5513	2	30/31	5532
4	12/13	5514	3	31/32	5533
			4	32/33	5534
			....		
			....		
			249, 4	220/221	5722
198, 1	13/14	5515	250, 1	221/222	5723
2	14/15	5516			
3	15/16	5517			
4	16/17	5518			

《244. In a recapitulatory table (58) we may now bring together the major points which we have determined in the *Chronographies* of Africanus. Since in this scheme 4726 years lie before Ol. 1, 1 = 776/775 B.C. we conclude that the date of Africanus for Year 1 of Adam is equivalent to 5502/5501 B.C.[20]

《245. In comparison with the foregoing scheme (Table 58) of Africanus (A.D. c.170-c.240), the work of his contemporary, Hippolytus of Rome (A.D. c.170-236) may be mentioned only briefly. The *Chronicle* of Hippolytus was published in Rome in the thirteenth year of Severus Alexander, the date to which its tables are carried.

20 Schwartz in AKGWG 40 (1894-95), p.23.

TABLE 58. RECAPITULATION OF MAJOR POINTS
IN THE *Chronographies* OF AFRICANUS

		Anno Adam	Ol.	B.C.-A.D.
1.	Adam	0		
2.	Seth	230		
3.	Enosh	435		
4.	Flood	2262		
5.	Entry of Abraham into the Promised Land	3277		
6.	Death of Joseph	3563		
7.	Exodus under Moses and Flood of Ogygos	3707		
8.	End of the period of the Judges	4292		
9.	First Olympiad	4727	1, 1	776/775 B.C.
10.	First year of Cyrus	4943	55, 1	560/559 B.C.
11.	Birth of Jesus	5500	194, 2	3/2 B.C.
12.	Resurrection of Christ	5531	202, 1	A.D. 29/30

Severus Alexander began to reign on Mar 11, A.D. 222,[21] and his thirteenth factual year of reign extended from Mar 11, A.D. 234, to Mar 10, A.D. 235. The original work of Hippolytus is probably preserved only in one incomplete manuscript (Codex Matritensis 4701), but is also transmitted in various translations and revisions, some of which in particular represent the work of later chronographers in Alexandria. As reconstructed from these sources, the chronological system of Hippolytus appears in its presumed original form as shown in Table 59A.[22] Since the year 5738 reckoned from Adam falls in the thirteenth year of Severus Alexander, i.e., in A.D. 234/235, the year 5502 (to which the birth of Jesus is assigned) must have been equivalent to 3/2 B.C. In terms of the Christian era this is the same date for the birth of Christ which we found the chronology of Africanus to indicate (Table 58), although it is there equivalent to the Year 5500 (rather than 5502) from Adam. In another text which goes under the name of "Hippolytus of Thebes" and presumably represents one of the Egyptian revisions of the work of Hippolytus of Rome, the figures are adjusted as shown in Table 59B to total 5500 years to the birth of Christ just as in Africanus:[23]

[21] Liebenam, *Fasti Consulares Imperii Romani*, p.111.
[22] *Hippolytus Werke* (GCS), IV, *Die Chronik*, by Adolf Bauer, 2d ed. by Rudolf Helm. 1955, pp.193-196.
[23] ed. Jo. Albertus Fabricius. 1716, p.46.

TABLE 59A. The Chronology of Hippolytus of Rome

		Number of Years in the Period	Cumulative Years from Adam
1.	From Adam to the Flood	2242	
2.	From the Flood to Abraham's Entry into Canaan	1141	3383
3.	From Abraham's Entry into Canaan to the Death of Joshua	501	3884
4.	From the Death of Joshua through the Reign of Zedekiah	958	4842
5.	From the Exile to the Birth of Christ	660	5502
6.	From the Birth of Christ to the Passion	30	5532
7.	From the Passion to the Thirteenth Year of Severus Alexander	206	5738

TABLE 59B. The Chronology of "Hippolytus of Thebes"

		Years
1.	From Adam to Noah	2242
2.	From Noah to Abraham	1170
3.	From Abraham to Moses	444
4.	From Moses to David	599
5.	From David to Christ	1045
	Total	5500

3. THE *CHRONICLE* OF EUSEBIUS

LITERATURE: Alfred Schoene, *Eusebi Chronicorum libri duo.* 2 vols. 1866-75; George Salmon, "Eusebius, Chronicle of," in SWDCB II, pp.348-355; Alfred Schöne, *Die Weltchronik des Eusebius in ihrer Bearbeitung durch Hieronymus.* 1900; John K. Fotheringham, *The Bodleian Manuscript of Jerome's Version of the Chronicle of Eusebius reproduced in Collotype with an Introduction.* 1905; Eduard Schwartz, *Eusebius,* II, iii. GCS, 1909, pp.CCXV-CCXLVIII; Josef Karst, *Die Chronik aus dem Armenischen übersetzt mit text-kritischem Commentar.* GCS, Eusebius V, 1911 (*cited as* Karst); John K. Fotheringham, *Eusebii Pamphili Chronici Canones latine vertit, adauxit, ad sua tempora produxit.* 1923; Rudolf Helm, "Eusebius' Chronik und ihre Ta-bellenform," in *Abhandlungen der preussischen Akademie der Wissenschaften.* 1923, Philosophisch-historische Klasse, 4, 1924; Helm, "Hieronymus' Zusätze in Eusebius' Chronik und ihr Wert für die Literaturgeschichte," in *Philologus*, Supplementband XXI, Heft II, 1929; Helm, "Die neuesten Hypothesen zu Eusebius' (Hieronymus') Chronik," in *Sitzungsberichte der preussischen Akademie der Wissenschaften*. 1929, Phil.-hist. Kl., pp.371-408; Helm, *Die Chronik des Hieronymus*. GCS, Eusebius VII, 2d ed. 1956 (*cited as* Helm).

⟨246. In his *Eclogae Propheticae*[1] Eusebius mentions a work of his own which he calls Χρονικοὶ κανόνες, "Chronological Canons," and speaks of as ἐπιτομὴ παντοδαπῆς ἱστορίας, an "epitome of universal history." In his *Praeparatio Evangelica*[2] he refers to the same work and uses some material from it. As he begins his *Church History*[3] and explains the plan of it he says in effect that the *Church History* is an expansion of the same earlier work:

> "I have already given an epitome of these things in the *Chronological Canons* which I have composed, but notwithstanding that, I have undertaken in the present work to write as full an account of them as I am able."

In the *Church History* Eusebius also refers in very complimentary terms, as we have seen (¶235), to the *Chronographies* of Africanus, and his acquaintance with and high regard for that work make it probable that it provided much of the basis for his own *Chronicle*. From his own work in the *Chronicle* and the *Church History* it is evident that he also drew directly from the Scriptures, from Josephus, and from other sources.

(1) CHRONOLOGY IN THE *CHURCH HISTORY*

⟨247. Of the Χρονικοὶ κανόνες of Eusebius the Greek text unfortunately has been lost but there are extant Armenian and Latin versions, which will be discussed below (¶¶255ff.). Since the *Church History* is preserved in Greek text and since it is—as Eusebius himself says—based upon the *Chronicle*, it may be useful to look briefly at the *Church History* to see how the author uses his chronological sources.[1] In the *Church History*[2] he mentions "those Greek historians who have recorded the Olympiads, together with the respective events which have taken place in each period." Therefore he was familiar with this manner of reckoning and with sources which employed it. In the *Chronicle* he cites the Olympiads regu-

---

[1] I. MPG XXII, col. 1024.
[2] X, 9, 11. ed. Karl Mras, GCS, *Eusebius* VIII, 1, p.587.
[3] I, i, 6.

---

[1] E. Schwartz, GCS, *Eusebius*. II, iii, pp.CCXV-CCXLVIII.
[2] II, vii, 1.

larly; that he does not do so in the *Church History* may be because he thought it unnecessary to weight this narrative with a repetition of the citations.

⟨ 248.   In quoting the supposed correspondence of Abgar, ruler of Edessa, and Jesus, and also a further Syriac account of how, after the Ascension, the apostle Thaddaeus came to preach at Edessa, Eusebius reproduces a date in this way: "These things were done in the three hundred and fortieth year."[3] This is presumably a date in the Seleucid era,[4] but he does not regularly employ this era.

⟨ 249.   A regular practice of Eusebius in the *Church History* is to give dates in terms of rulers, particularly the Roman emperors. When he cites documents and sources of a particular local area we may suppose that he reproduces the system there in use. When he quotes an Easter letter of the Alexandrian bishop Dionysius,[5] for example, with a date in the ninth year of the emperor Gallienus, we may suppose that this date is to be interpreted according to Egyptian practice. In Egypt the calendar year began Aug 29 (¶49) and the non-accession-year system prevailed, that is the period from accession to the end of the then current calendar year was counted as Year 1, the ensuing calendar year was Year 2, and so on (¶152). Since Gallienus was declared Augustus about September A.D. 253,[6] his first nine regnal years would be reckoned in the Egyptian system as shown in Table 60. According to this reckoning, then, an Easter letter dated in the ninth year of Gallienus would belong at Easter in A.D. 262. Likewise not a few other citations by Eusebius appear

TABLE 60. REGNAL YEARS OF GALLIENUS IN EGYPTIAN RECKONING

Egyptian Regnal Years	A.D.
1	Sep 253 – Aug 28, 254
2	Aug 29, 254 – Aug 28, 255
3	Aug 29, 255 – Aug 28, 256
4	Aug 29, 256 – Aug 28, 257
5	Aug 29, 257 – Aug 28, 258
6	Aug 29, 258 – Aug 28, 259
7	Aug 29, 259 – Aug 28, 260
8	Aug 29, 260 – Aug 28, 261
9	Aug 29, 261 – Aug 28, 262

[3] *Ch. Hist.* I, xiii, 22.   [4] Schwartz, *op.cit.*, p.CCXVII n.3.
[5] *Ch. Hist.* VII, xxiii, 4.   [6] CAH XII, p.169.

to give dates in accordance with the local systems in the areas represented by the sources.[7]

⟨ 250.   The residence of Eusebius himself, however, was in Caesarea in Palestine and there one would presume he was accustomed to use the Syro-Macedonian calendar with the new year beginning Oct 1 (Table 25). Like many other dates, that which he gives for the birth of Jesus is stated in terms of years of Roman emperors; and it provides a good opportunity to see if the manner in which he reckons can be ascertained. It has just been surmised that Eusebius might follow the Syro-Macedonian calendar; it is also believed (¶246) that he based his work on that of Africanus and in that case for so important an event as the birth of Jesus it would seem likely that he would have the same date as Africanus. According to Africanus, as we saw (¶¶242, 243), the date of the birth of Jesus is A. Ad. 5500 = Ol. 194, 2 = 3/2 B.C.; and we judged it probable (¶239) that he counted an Olympiadic year as running from Oct. 1 to Sep 30, so that the year just given was in fact the year from Oct. 1, 3 B.C., to Sep 30, 2 B.C.

⟨ 251.   In the *Church History*[8] Eusebius gives the date of the birth of Jesus thus:

"It was in the forty-second year of the reign of Augustus and the twenty-eighth after the subjugation of Egypt and the death of Antony and Cleopatra, with whom the dynasty of the Ptolemies in Egypt came to an end, that our Savior and Lord Jesus Christ was born in Bethlehem of Judea."

In this statement the twenty-eighth year has to do with the rule of Egypt by Augustus after the death of Antony and Cleopatra and is presumably to be computed according to the same principles just used in establishing the regnal years of Gallienus in Egyptian reckoning (¶249). The death of Antony was on Aug 1, 30 B.C., and that of Cleopatra followed later in the same month.[9] Year 1 of Augustus was therefore, in Egyptian reckoning, only the balance of that calendar year, namely Aug 1 to Aug 28, 30 B.C., and the new calendar year then ensuing was already Year 2 of the reign. The beginning of the reign and the resultant date for Year 28 are shown in Table 61.

[7] Schwartz, *op.cit.*, pp.ccxix-ccxx.   [8] I, v, 2.
[9] CAH X, p.108.

TABLE 61. REGNAL YEARS OF AUGUSTUS IN EGYPTIAN RECKONING

Egyptian Regnal Years	B.C.
1	Aug 1, 30 – Aug 28, 30
2	Aug 29, 30 – Aug 28, 29
....	
....	
28	Aug 29, 3 – Aug 28, 2

❲252.   According to the same passage in Eusebius (¶251) this twenty-eighth year after the subjugation of Egypt was parallel with the forty-second year of the reign of Augustus. In the absence of full information as to how Roman regnal years were reckoned (¶182) let us establish first how the factual years of the reign of Augustus ran. Presumably the beginning point was provided by the death of Julius Caesar on Mar 15, 44 B.C. (Table 39). Counted from this point, factual years of reign went as shown in Table 62, where the resultant date for Year 42 is also given.

TABLE 62. FACTUAL YEARS OF REIGN OF AUGUSTUS

Factual Regnal Years	B.C.
1	Mar 15, 44 – Mar 14, 43
2	Mar 15, 43 – Mar 14, 42
....	
....	
42	Mar 15, 3 – Mar 14, 2

❲253.   Already the manner of counting just given satisfies, with an equivalence during a considerable part of the two years, the equation of the twenty-eighth year in Egyptian reckoning and the forty-second year of the reign. We have surmised (¶250), however, that Eusebius, living in Caesarea, might probably have been accustomed to use the Syro-Macedonian calendar. If he did so, and equated regnal years with calendar years in that calendar, the regnal years would have been counted from Oct 1 (Table 35). If they were counted from Oct 1 prior to Mar 15, 44 B.C. (i.e., from Oct 1, 45 B.C.) the equation of the forty-second year (which would then be Oct 1, 4 – Sep 30, 3 B.C.) with the twenty-eighth year in Egyptian reckoning would be almost destroyed. The alternate possibility is, therefore, to be preferred, namely that the regnal years were counted from Oct 1 following Mar 15, 44 B.C. (i.e., from Oct 1, 44 B.C.). In this case the period from Mar 15 to Oct 1, 44 B.C. constituted in effect an accession year (¶163), and the ensuing regnal years ran as in Table 63 with a resultant date for the forty-second year as shown there too.

TABLE 63. REGNAL YEARS OF AUGUSTUS IN THE SYRO-MACEDONIAN CALENDAR AS PRESUMED USED BY EUSEBIUS

Regnal Years	B.C.
Accession year	Mar 15, 44 – Sep 30, 44
Year 1	Oct 1, 44 – Sep 30, 43
....	
....	
Year 42	Oct 1, 3 – Sep 30, 2

In this case Year 42 (Oct 1, 3 – Sep 30, 2 B.C.) coincides even more extensively with Year 28 in the Egyptian reckoning (Aug 29, 3-Aug 28, 2 B.C.) than the factual Year 42 (Mar 15, 3 – Mar 14, 2 B.C.). Either the calendar year just described or the factual year must be what Eusebius means by the forty-second year of Augustus. In either case the date of Eusebius for the birth of Jesus is 3/2 B.C., the same as that given by Africanus (¶¶242-243).

⟨254.   A further check on this date is possible from two other references of Eusebius in the *Church History*. Referring to the action of Diocletian against the Christian church, he says[10] that "from the birth of our Savior to the destruction of the places of worship" was "a period of three hundred and five years"; and later he dates the persecution and the destruction of churches by Diocletian as follows:[11]

> "It was in the nineteenth year of the reign of Diocletian, in the month Dystros, called March by the Romans, when the feast of the Savior's passion was near at hand, that royal edicts were published everywhere, commanding that the churches be leveled to the ground. . . ."

Diocletian became emperor in the late autumn—probably Nov 17—in A.D. 284; he celebrated his *vicennalia* (a festival on the twentieth anniversary of reign) in Rome on Nov 20, 303.[12] In this case factual years (from November to November) and Syro-Macedonian calen-

[10] VII, xxxii, 32.   [11] VIII, ii, 4.
[12] CAH XII, pp.323, 340.

dar years (Oct 1 to Sep 30) were not far apart and there is little doubt that Eusebius would have normally counted the regnal years of Diocletian as extending from autumn to autumn, beginning with the autumn of his accession. If, to be precise, he used the Syro-Macedonian calendar years, they would have run as shown in Table 64 and Year 19 would be that indicated:

TABLE 64. REGNAL YEARS OF DIOCLETIAN IN THE
SYRO-MACEDONIAN CALENDAR

Regnal Years	A.D.
1	Nov 17, 284 – Sep 30, 285
2	Oct 1, 285 – Sep 30, 286
....	....
....	....
19	Oct 1, 302 – Sep 30, 303

The month Dystros = March, mentioned by Eusebius, in this nineteenth year of Diocletian was therefore March A.D. 303. A date for the birth of Jesus in 3/2 B.C. means that approximately two years— slightly more or slightly less—had elapsed at the turn of the era; here at the point of the persecution we are in the three hundred and third year after the beginning of the Christian era; together, counting inclusively, the total is three hundred and five years, and a date by Eusebius for the birth of Jesus in 3/2 B.C. is confirmed.[13]

(2) THE ARMENIAN VERSION OF THE CHRONICLE

《255.   Turning now to the Chronicle itself, we have already noted (¶247) that the Greek text is lost but that Armenian and Latin versions are extant. The Armenian version is found in two late codices of the thirteenth-fourteenth centuries, and has been edited by Karst (GCS, Eusebius V, 1911). This version contains a lengthy introductory portion, often spoken of as the Chronicle proper, which deals with the chronology of the Chaldeans, Hebrews, Egyptians, Greeks, and Romans; and the chronological tables themselves, often called

[13] Schwartz in AKGWG 40 (1894-95), p.30. It must be noticed however that in the consecutive tabulation of the Chronicle itself, at least as edited by Jerome (Helm pp.225-228), the beginning of the reign of Diocletian is placed in A.D. 285, his first regnal year is equated with A.D. 286, and his nineteenth year and the first year of the persecution is equated with A.D. 304. The historically correct date of the inauguration of the persecution, however, is A.D. 303 and probably on Feb. 23 (CAH XII, p.666).

the Canon. As found in the Armenian, the tables are confined within the horizontal limits of the breadth of a page. On each side of the page is a column in which events are listed. Events in biblical history are almost always on the left side; events in secular history are distributed on both sides. In the center of the page are several narrow columns of dates. One of these numbers the years from Abraham. Another column, after that point is reached, gives the Olympiadic dates. Other columns, as many as are needed, list the successive years of kings of various nations. As now preserved the Armenian Canon begins with Year 344 of Abraham, which is equated with the time of Joseph in Egypt, and comes down to Constantine and Maximian, that is to the time of Eusebius himself.

(3) THE LATIN VERSION OF THE CHRONICLE BY JEROME

‹[256.   The Latin version of the *Chronicle* was the work of Jerome. In his Letter 57 to Pammachius written in A.D. 395 Jerome refers to what he had done "in translating the Chronicle of Eusebius of Caesarea into Latin"; and there is reason to think the translation was made in Constantinople in A.D. 381.[1] The version is represented in nearly a dozen manuscripts, the two earliest probably from the fifth century, and has been edited by Helm (GCS, Eusebius VII, 2d ed. 1956).

‹[257.   In this version Jerome made additions of his own, particularly enlarging the notices which pertained to Roman history and continuing the tables to Valentinian and Valens, that is to his own time. The long introductory section dealing with the chronology of the various nations, found in the Armenian, is not in the Latin version. It opens instead with only a brief introduction by Jerome and the Latin translation of a brief introduction by Eusebius. The chronological tables themselves have a somewhat different arrangement from the Armenian. Down to the end of the Jewish captivity the columns are spread over two adjacent pages. On each page there is a column of events in the center place which is sometimes called the *spatium historicum*. On each side thereof is a column or columns of dates. Since these consist for the most part of successive years of

[1] Schoene, *Die Weltchronik des Eusebius in ihrer Bearbeitung durch Hieronymus*, pp.249-252.

successive kings they are sometimes called *fila regnorum*. After the point indicated there is only one column of events, with columns of dates on either side of it, and the whole is kept within the limits of one page. After the fall of Jerusalem (A.D. 70) there is no longer a column of dates on the right side.

([258.   Since the form of the tables is more complex and more carefully arranged in the Latin than in the Armenian, and since Jerome says in his preface[2] that he dictated his translation to a stenographer (*notarius*) at very high speed (*velocissime*), we can hardly think that he was responsible for the invention of this complicated form, and we must suppose that the Latin version in fact represents the original arrangement of the Canon better than the more simply arranged Armenian.[3] Also when compared with the *Church History* of Eusebius, the figures in the Armenian version are found to diverge more widely than those in the Latin, so from this point of view also the translation by Jerome may be taken, as far as it extends, as the preferred source.[4]

([259.   In connection with the dates found in the two versions there is, in particular, a difference in the treatment of the important Olympiadic dates. In the Armenian version the numbers of the Olympiads are set directly against years of Abraham evenly divisible by four. In most of the Latin manuscripts the Olympiadic numbers are normally set in the farthest column of regnal years at the left side of the page or the two pages; and the number is not set against a year of Abraham or a regnal year but is always put in the space between two regnal years. If the latter was the original arrangement made by Eusebius it would be explicable that, on the one hand, the Armenian translator, in bringing the *Chronicle* into smaller compass as he did, placed the Olympiadic notation against the year above; and that, on the other hand, in at least one Latin manuscript (L, or Londinensis, of the tenth century) also, for the sake of conciseness, the notation was placed in the year below (with the result that it was opposite a year of Abraham divisible by four with a remainder of one).[5]

[2] Helm p.2.
[3] Helm in *Abh. d. preuss. Akad. d. Wiss.* 1923. Phil.-hist. Kl. 4, p.45.
[4] Schwartz, *Eusebius* II, iii (GCS), p.CCXXXVIII; and in AKGWG 40 (1894-95), pp.27, 44.
[5] Fotheringham, *The Bodleian Manuscript of Jerome's Version of the Chronicle of Eusebius*, p.15.

Again the conclusion is supported that the Latin version of Jerome, in the oldest and best manuscripts, is the best representative we have of the original *Chronicle* of Eusebius.

(4) FROM ADAM TO ABRAHAM IN THE *CHRONICLE*

⟦260. For the biblical chronology prior to Abraham we have what is in the long introductory portion of the Armenian version and what is in the very brief introduction of Eusebius, translated by Jerome, in the Latin version. According to the Armenian version Eusebius notices that there are differences in the figures in the Hebrew, Septuagint, and Samaritan texts. In general he thinks that mistakes and inconsistencies are evident in the extant Hebrew text and that the Septuagint was translated from ancient and accurate copies of the Hebrew text and was therefore to be preferred.[1] The Septuagint text used by Eusebius must have differed from that available now, however, as may be noted for example in its omission of Elon in the list of Judges (Table 68). From Adam to the Flood[2] the figures given by the several texts are: LXX—2242 years; Hebrew—1656 years; Samaritan—1307 years. Africanus, who also followed the Septuagint, has 2262 years here (Table 55), the difference perhaps being due to different figures for Methuselah. In the brief Latin introduction[3] the figure is also 2242. From the Flood to Abraham, as the Armenian version notes,[4] the several texts give these figures: LXX—942; Hebrew—292; Samaritan—942. Again the Latin introduction gives 942 years from the Flood to the nativity of Abraham. The several totals from Adam to Abraham are therefore: LXX—3184; Hebrew—1948; and Samaritan—2249. Accepting the Septuagint as the standard, the skeletal tabulation in Table 65 results.

⟦261. As distinguished from the long introductory portion sometimes called the Chronicle, the chronological tables themselves, sometimes called the Canon, begin with Abraham. Here Eusebius numbers consecutive years of Abraham, and in occasional summaries also gives recapitulations from Adam. In the extant manuscripts the Canon begins in the Armenian with Anno Abraham 344, the Latin with Anno Abraham 1. Since it has been established

[1] Karst p.45.
[3] Helm p.15.
[2] Karst pp.38-41.
[4] Karst pp.41-45.

TABLE 65. FROM ADAM TO ABRAHAM IN THE *Chronicle* OF EUSEBIUS

		Anno Adam	Number of Years Intervening
1.	Adam	0	2242
2.	Flood	2242	942
3.	Birth of Abraham	3184	

(¶¶258-259) that the Latin is probably the closer to the Greek original of Eusebius we will follow the Latin from here on with only occasional references to the Armenian.

(5) FROM ABRAHAM THROUGH THE EGYPTIAN SERVITUDE

❰262. At this initial point the tables of the Canon are spread across two adjacent pages and in the four columns of successively numbered years the first year of Abraham is synchronized with the years of reign of Assyrian, Greek, and Egyptian kings.[1] The first column at the left hand side gives the years of rule of the Assyrian kings. In the view of Greek writers the first historical king of Asia was Ninus. Herodotus[2] names Ninus (Νίνος) as the son of Belus, and Diodorus[3] gives an extended account of his life and accomplishments. Opening his record of "the events which took place in Asia in the ancient period, beginning with the time when the Assyrians were the dominant power," Diodorus writes: "The first to be handed down by tradition to history and memory for us as one who achieved great deeds is Ninus, king of the Assyrians." He goes on to tell how Ninus conquered most of Asia between the Tanaïs or Don River and the Nile, and then founded a very great city to which he gave his own name, Ninus. Eusebius is, therefore, simply following the standard Greek view of the history of Asia when he begins the first column of the Canon with Ninus son of Belus and says that he ruled all of Asia except India. He also notes that he founded the city of Ninus in the region of the Assyrians, which the Hebrews call Nineveh. To Ninus he attributes a reign of fifty-two years and he says, presumably following some further established tradition, that it was in the forty-third year of Ninus that Abraham was born. Thus he places the beginning of Hebrew history against

[1] Helm pp.20 a-b.　　　[2] I, 7.　　　[3] II, 1-7.

the backdrop of the history of Asia and in fact at the beginning of that history.

¶ 263.   In his second column, accordingly, Eusebius shows this beginning of Hebrew history by placing Year 1 of Abraham over against Year 43 of Ninus. Extending the correlation to Greece and to Egypt he shows in the third column the rule of the Sicyonians and in the fourth column the rule of the Egyptians. At Sicyon, a city of the Peloponnesus also known as Aegialeia ("beach-town"), the second king of the dynasty ranked as the ruler of Europe and was in the twenty-second year of a forty-five year reign. In Egypt the identical year was the first of the first king of the Sixteenth Dynasty, a dynasty which Eusebius says reigned in Thebes for one hundred and ninety years and was followed by the Seventeenth Dynasty of "shepherd kings." This first year of the Canon, which is the first year of Abraham, appears, therefore, as in Table 66.

TABLE 66. YEAR 1 OF ABRAHAM IN THE *Chronicle* OF EUSEBIUS

Kingdom of the Assyrians	Beginning of the Hebrew people	Kingdom of the Sicyonians	Kingdom of the Egyptians
Ninus, son of Belus XLIII = Year 43	Abraham I = Year 1	The second king of Sicyon XXII = Year 22	The Sixteenth Dynasty I = Year 1

From here on the cumulative years of Abraham are also marked in the left margin at ten year intervals (x, xx, etc.), and this reckoning is continued throughout the entire Canon as if Abraham had continued to live the entire time and one were giving the years of his life.

¶ 264.   From Abraham to Moses and the exodus from Egypt Eusebius finds that the Septuagint, Hebrew, and Samaritan texts all agree on a total of five hundred and five years, and he gives this figure (DV) in the Latin introduction.[5] This is counted as follows: In the seventy-fifth year of Abraham God made the promise (Gen 12:1-4) to him.[6] This "first year of the promise of God to Abraham" is also used as a point of cumulative reckoning, and ten years later the "tenth year of the promise" is noted, and so on for some

4 Helm p.28 b.   5 Karst pp.45-46, 156-161; Helm p.17.
6 Helm p.23 a.

time.[7] When Abraham was one hundred years old he became the father of Isaac.[8] When Isaac was sixty years old he became the father of Jacob.[9] When Jacob was one hundred and twenty-one years old, Joseph became the chief of the land of Egypt and continued in that position for eighty years.[10] After the death of Joseph the servitude of the Israelites in Egypt began and continued for one hundred and forty-four years.[11] Moses was born in the sixty-fourth year of the servitude, which was also the three hundred and fiftieth year of the promise $(25 + 60 + 121 + 80 + 64 = 350)$.[12] At this point a cumulative reckoning from Moses is also introduced, and is noted at ten year intervals.[13] Here we notice that Moses was eighty years old in the one hundred forty-fourth and last year of the servitude, which was also the four hundred thirtieth year of the promise,[14] a figure likewise used by Paul (Gal 3:17). This portion of the Canon may therefore be recapitulated in brief (Table 67).

(6) FROM THE WANDERING IN THE WILDERNESS TO THE FOUNDATION OF THE TEMPLE IN THE FOURTH YEAR OF SOLOMON

⟨ 265.   The next portion of the Canon continues from the forty years in the wilderness to the fourth year of Solomon in which the building of the Temple in Jerusalem was begun.[1] In brief, and continuing of the cumulative reckonings only the Years of Abraham, this portion of the tabulation provides the outline in Table 68.

⟨ 266.   The period just summarized totals four hundred and seventy-nine years and in the Latin introduction Eusebius gives the same figure (CCCCLXXVIIII) as the time from Moses to Solomon and the first building of the Temple.[2] At the beginning of this part of the tabulation there is a note in the Canon,[3] however, which gives the period as four hundred and eighty years. In I K 6:1 the Hebrew text says that it was in the four hundred and eightieth year after the people came out of Egypt and in the fourth year of Solomon's reign that he began to build the Temple. In the same passage the Septuagint, as available today, has the four hundred and fortieth year, one

---

[7] Helm pp.23 a, 24 a, etc. [8] Helm p.24 a.
[9] Helm p.27 a.   [10] Helm p.32 a.   [11] Helm p.36 a.
[12] Helm p.39 a.   [13] Helm p.40 a, etc.   [14] Helm p.43 a.

---

[1] Helm pp.43-70.   [2] Helm p.17.   [3] Helm p.43 a.

TABLE 67. FROM ABRAHAM THROUGH THE SERVITUDE IN EGYPT
IN THE *Chronicle* OF EUSEBIUS

Year of Abraham	Year of the Promise	Year of Moses	Year of Hebrew History	Events	Number of Years Intervening
			Abraham		
1			1		
					} 75
75	1		75	Promise	
					} 25
100	25		100	Abraham becomes father of Isaac	
			Isaac		
			1		
					} 60
160	85		60	Isaac becomes father of Jacob	
			Jacob		
			1		
					} 121
281	206		121	Joseph becomes chief of Egypt	
			Joseph the Chief of Egypt		
			1		
					} 80
361	286		80		
			Servitude of the Hebrews in Egypt		
			1		
					} 64
425	350	1	64	Birth of Moses	
					} 80
505	430	80	144	Last year of servitude	
					505

manuscript has the four hundred and eightieth.[4] If one counts inclusively from Anno Abraham 505, the last year of the servitude, to A. Abr. 984, the fourth year of Solomon, the period was indeed four hundred and eighty years long. But the note in the Canon ap-

[4] LXX ed. Rahlfs, I, p.638.

TABLE 68. FROM THE WANDERING IN THE WILDERNESS TO THE
BUILDING OF THE TEMPLE IN THE *Chronicle* OF EUSEBIUS

Year of Abraham	Year of Hebrew History	Events	Number of Years Intervening
	Moses leads the Hebrew people in wilderness for forty years		
506	1		40
545	40	Death of Moses	
	After Moses, Joshua leads the people for twenty-seven years		
	1		27
572	27		
	The Judges Othniel 40 years Ehud 80 years Deborah and Barak 40 years Gideon 40 years Abimelech 3 years Tola 22 years Jair 22 years Jephthah 6 years Ibzan 7 years Here it is noted that the Hebrew text (Jg 12:11-12) has Elon 10 years, but that this is not in the LXX, hence is omitted in the table (cf. above ¶260). Abdon 8 years Samson 20 years		328
900	Eli 40 years		
	Samuel and Saul forty years		
	1		40
940	40		
	David is king for forty years		
	1		40
980	40		

Year of Abraham	Year of Hebrew History	Events	Number of Years Intervening
	Solomon is king for forty years		
	1		
	2		
	3		
984	4	Foundation of the Temple	4
			479

pears to be intended as reckoning from the first year in the wilderness (A. Abr. 506) and in that case the four hundred and eighty years total is one in excess of what the tabulation actually shows. Also at the end of this period there is a note in the Canon[5] which recapitulates the years from Adam to this point and uses the figure of 480 years in the same way. It gives the figures in Table 69.

TABLE 69. A SUMMARY NOTE IN THE *Chronicle* OF EUSEBIUS FROM ADAM TO THE BUILDING OF THE TEMPLE

	Number of Years
1. From Adam to the Flood	2242
2. From the Flood to Moses (942 + 505)	1447
3. From Moses and the egress of the Israelites from Egypt to the fourth year of Solomon and the building of the Temple	480
	4169

According to our understanding of the tabulation the summary figures should be those shown in Table 70. Since the two notes with the figure of 480 years are thus in disagreement with the actual tables by one year, they may be editorial and in error to this extent.

[5] Helm p.70 a.

TABLE 70. A CORRECTED SUMMARY NOTE IN THE *Chronicle* OF EUSEBIUS
FROM ADAM TO THE BUILDING OF THE TEMPLE

		Number of Years
1.	From Adam to the Flood	2242
2.	From the Flood to Moses	1447
3.	From Moses and the egress of the Israelites from Egypt to the fourth year of Solomon and the building of the Temple	479
		4168

(7) FROM THE FIFTH YEAR OF SOLOMON TO THE DESTRUCTION OF THE TEMPLE

¶ 267.   From the fifth year of Solomon, with which the Canon continues, down to the eleventh year of Zedekiah and the destruction in that year of the Temple, the years of reign of the kings of Judah are given in Table 71.[1] The eleventh year of Zedekiah, with which the foregoing list closes, was the year in which the Temple was destroyed (II K 25:2ff.; Jer 52:5ff.). Without listing these individual reigns, our main tabulation may be continued in brief in Table 72. At this point in the text of the *Chronicle*[2] it is correctly noted that from its first erection to its burning by Nebuchadrezzar the Temple had endured for 442 years (*Nabuchodonosor rex Chaldaeorum Hierosolymis captis templum incendit. Quod ab initio aedificationis suae permanserat annis CCCCXLII*).

¶ 268.   Within the period just summarized (¶267) we come to the point where the Greek era of the Olympiads (¶¶185ff.) begins. The way this is shown, at the outset, in the Canon[3] may be indicated in Table 73. As stated already (¶259), the Olympiadic number is regularly set at the left side of the page and in the space between two regnal years. The B.C. dates, shown in the right hand column, will be explained in ¶269.

¶ 269.   In the standard Greek reckoning, Ol. 1, 1 began about Jul 1, 776 B.C., and extended to about Jun 30, 775 B.C. (¶185). The fact that the Olympiad is marked between two regnal years

---

[1] Helm pp.70a-99a.   [2] Helm p.100 a.   [3] Helm p.86 a.

TABLE 71. THE YEARS OF THE KINGS OF JUDAH
IN THE *Chronicle* OF EUSEBIUS

		Number of Years of Reign
1.	Solomon (beginning, inclusively, with his fifth year)	36
2.	Rehoboam	17
3.	Abijam	3
4.	Asa	41
5.	Jehoshaphat	25
6.	Jehoram	8
7.	Ahaziah	1
8.	Athaliah	7
9.	Joash	40
10.	Amaziah	29
11.	Azariah, or Uzziah	52
12.	Jotham	16
13.	Ahaz	16
14.	Hezekiah	29
15.	Manasseh	55
16.	Amon	12
17.	Josiah	32
18.	Jehoahaz (three months)	1
19.	Jehoiakim	11
20.	Jehoiachin (three months)	} 11
21.	Zedekiah	
		442

would seem to indicate that the Olympiad did not necessarily begin at the same point as the regnal year.[4] In the case of Africanus, living in Palestine, we surmised (¶239) that he probably used the Syro-Macedonian calendar with the year beginning Oct 1, and per-

TABLE 72. FROM THE FIFTH YEAR OF SOLOMON TO THE
ELEVENTH YEAR OF ZEDEKIAH IN THE *Chronicle* OF EUSEBIUS

Year of Abraham	Year of Hebrew History	Number of Years Intervening
985	Solomon 5	} 442
1426	Zedekiah 11	

[4] Fotheringham, *The Bodleian Manuscript of Jerome's Version of the Chronicle of Eusebius*, p.16.

TABLE 73. THE FIRST OLYMPIADIC NOTATIONS
IN THE *Chronicle* OF EUSEBIUS

Year of Abraham	Olympiad	Year of Hebrew History	B.C.
		Azariah, or Uzziah, is king for fifty-two years	
....			
....			
1240		49	777
	Ol. 1		
1241		50	776
1242		51	775
1243		52	774
		Jotham is king for sixteen years	
1244		1	773
	Ol. 2		
1245		2	772
1246		3	771
1247		4	770
1248		5	769
	Ol. 3		
1249		6	768
1250		7	767
		etc.	

haps cited Olympiads in terms of that calendar, so that Ol. 1, 1 =
Oct 1, 776-Sep 30, 775 B.C., and so on. The same surmise might
be made with respect to Eusebius, bishop of Caesarea in Palestine.
But in fact Eusebius, at least as translated by Jerome, seems to have
made a different adjustment, perhaps for the purpose of simplicity
in the construction of his tables. He seems to begin the Olympiadic
year on Jan 1, i.e., on the New Year's day of the Julian calendar,
so that the Olympiadic year simply corresponds to the Julian year;
and on the Jan 1 prior to the Jul 1 of the Greek reckoning, so that
Ol. 1, 1 began Jan 1, 776 B.C., and extended to Dec 31, 776 B.C.,
and so on.[5] Therefore we read Table 73 to mean the following, for
example: Ol. 1, 1 equals 776 B.C. and was the year in which the
fiftieth year of Azariah began or ended; Ol. 1, 2 equals 775 B.C.
and was the year in which the fifty-first year of Azariah began or
ended; Ol. 2, 1 equals 772 B.C. and was the year in which the second

[5] George Salmon in SWDCB II, p.353 col. 2.

year of Jotham began or ended; and so on. These and the other B.C. dates for the years in question are shown in the right-hand column of Table 73. In Helm's edition of the *Chronicle* the dates B.C. and A.D. are shown in exactly the same way throughout the entire Canon.

¶270.   The correctness of this understanding of the Olympiadic notations in the Canon appears demonstrable, for example, at the point of Olympiad 184 where we have a date relatively near to the time of Eusebius and Jerome and presumably very well fixed and known, namely the date of the death of Julius Caesar. This date is historically fixed as on the Ides of March (in the language of the Roman calendar [¶141]), i.e., on Mar 15 (in the language of our calendar), in the year 44 B.C.[6] In the Canon the listing of the last years of Julius Caesar, together with the Olympiadic notation, is demonstrated in Table 74.[7]

TABLE 74. THE OLYMPIADIC DATE OF THE DEATH OF JULIUS CAESAR IN THE *Chronicle* OF EUSEBIUS

Rulers of the Romans
C. Julius Caesar, four years, seven months
....
....
4
Ol. 184
5

There is also a note in the Canon, opposite Caesar's Year 5, mentioning that he was killed in the senate house on the Ides of March (*Idibus Martiis C. Iulius Caesar in curia occiditur*). So the death of Julius Caesar in his fifth and last year on Mar 15, 44 B.C. fell in Ol. 184, 1. According to the standard Greek reckoning, Ol. 184, 1 would be Jul 1, 44, to Jun 30, 43 B.C.; according to the reckoning we attributed to Africanus (¶239) it would be Oct 1, 44, to Sep 30, 43 B.C. On neither reckoning would the assassination of Julius Caesar on Mar 15, 44 B.C., be in Ol. 184, 1. But if the Olympiadic dates were reckoned by Eusebius as suggested above (¶269), Ol.

[6] CAH IX, pp.735-738.   [7] Helm p.157.

184, 1 would be Jan 1 to Dec 31, 44 B.C., and would include the date of the death of Julius Caesar precisely as it should. We will accordingly equate the Olympiadic dates of the *Chronicle* with dates B.C.-A.D. in this manner throughout, which is exactly the way they are shown in Helm's edition.

❨271. At the same time we note that in the Armenian version of the *Chronicle* Year 5 of Julius Caesar is equated with Ol. 184, 2.[8] Here too the simplest explanation seems to be that this version also makes the Olympiadic year begin on Jan 1 but, in moving the notation up to a position directly opposite a regnal year (¶259), places the beginning not just six months prior to the true Greek beginning (as Eusebius did) but a full year and six months prior.[9] We will of course continue to follow what we regard as the true usage of Eusebius, as preserved by Jerome.

❨272. If the Olympiadic years in the Canon are equivalent to Julian years so that Ol. 1, 1 = Jan 1–Dec 31, 776 B.C., and so on, it does not necessarily follow that regnal years are also equivalent to Julian years. Presumably they coincide at least in some part with the Julian year indicated but in particular cases we may still try to determine if possible, within those limits, the beginning and ending points of the regnal year. It is for this reason that we have said, for example, that the notation of Azariah's Year 50 in Table 73 means that that year of that king must have either begun or ended in Ol. 1, 1 = 776 B.C.

❨273. If we continue the enumeration of the years of Abraham, as we have done in Table 73, down to Year 50 of Azariah we have the equation: A. Abr. 1241 = Azariah Year 50 = Ol. 1, 1 = 776 B.C. From this point it is possible to reckon backwards and establish the equivalent B.C. dates of earlier events. Doing this, we establish that A. Abr. 1 = 2016 B.C. From Adam to Abraham was 3184 years according to the figures of the Septuagint (1948 according to the Hebrew text) (¶260). This would place the creation of Adam in 5200 B.C. (3964 according to the Hebrew).

[8] Karst p.209.
[9] Salmon in SWDCB II, p.353 col. 2.

(8) THE SEVENTY YEARS OF CAPTIVITY

⟨ 274.   The portion of the *Chronicle* which we have just discussed brought us to Year 11 of Zedekiah, the year in which the Temple was destroyed by Nebuchadrezzar (Table 72). In his major left-hand column of secular history, in succession to the Assyrians, Eusebius has now for some time been showing the rule of the Medes and will shortly go on with the Persians. Thus Year 11 of Zedekiah was equated with Year 8 of Astyages the Median king.[1] Continuing from this point the *Chronicle* covers next the seventy years of captivity (Jer 25:11-12; 29:10; Dan 9:2).[2] The period may be summarized as shown in Table 75.

⟨ 275.   The reign of Cyrus falls within the preceding tabulation (Table 75), and it may be recalled (¶240) that Africanus took from Diodorus the equation of Year 1 of Cyrus with Ol. 55, 1. Eusebius elsewhere[3] quotes Africanus and Diodorus in the same respect, and in the Canon makes the same equation. This also means that he shows the thirtieth and last year of the reign of Cyrus in relation to Ol. 62, 2. The tabulation of the *Chronicle* at these two points may be reproduced as in Table 76:[4]

⟨ 276.   By the reckoning of Olympiadic dates which we have accepted (¶270) as probably used by Eusebius, Ol. 55, 1 equals 560 B.C., Ol. 62, 2 equals 531 B.C. For the reign of Cyrus quite precise information is now available from the cuneiform sources and in terms of the Babylonian calendar.[5] The latest date attested in his reign is the twenty-third day of Abu in his ninth year (mentioned on a tablet from Borsippa), which (counting his years of reign in Babylon) is equivalent to Aug 12, 530 B.C. The earliest date attested in the reign of his successor Cambyses is the twelfth day of Ululu in the latter's accession year, and this is equivalent to Aug 31, 530. It is to be concluded that the death of Cyrus, fighting on the northeastern frontier, was reported in Babylon in August 530 B.C.

⟨ 277.   According to the *Chronicle*, the reign of Cyrus ended in his thirtieth and last year and this year was related to Ol. 62, 2, i.e.,

[1] Helm p.99 a.   [2] Helm pp.100-105.
[3] *Praepar. evang.* x, 10, 4. GCS, *Eusebius* VIII, 1, p.591.
[4] Helm pp.102 a, 104 a.   [5] PDBC p.14.

TABLE 75. THE SEVENTY YEARS OF CAPTIVITY
IN THE *Chronicle* OF EUSEBIUS

Year of Abraham	Kingdom of the Medes	Year of Hebrew History	Number of Years Intervening	
	Astyages reigns for thirty-eight years			
....				
		The people of Judea are in captivity for seventy years		
1427	9	1	⎫	
1456	38	30	⎬	30
	Kingdom of the Persians			
	Cyrus reigns for thirty years			
1457	1	31	⎫	
1486	30	60	⎬	30
	Cambyses reigns for eight years			
1487	1	61	⎫	
1494	8	68	⎬	8
	The Magi brothers reign seven months after whom Darius reigns thirty-six years			
1495	1	69	⎫	
1496	2	70	⎬	2
				──
				70

to 531 B.C. If the regnal year of Cyrus was considered to begin in the spring, in line with Mesopotamian custom, his Year 30 could extend from Mar/Apr 531 to Mar/Apr 530, and it would end a few months ahead of his actual death as just established (¶276). But if the regnal year was counted as beginning on the following Oct 1 (in the manner in which we have seen [¶253] reason to think Eusebius reckoned elsewhere), then Year 30 extended from Oct 1, 531, to Sep 30, 530 B.C. and included the time when the death of

[169]

TABLE 76. THE BEGINNING AND THE END OF THE REIGN
OF CYRUS IN THE *Chronicle* OF EUSEBIUS

	Kingdom of the Persians
	Astyages Year 38
Ol. 55	
	Cyrus Year 1
···	
···	
Ol. 62	
	Cyrus Year 29
	Cyrus Year 30
	Cambyses Year 1

Cyrus became known in Babylon in August 530 B.C. By the same interpretation Year 1 of Cyrus, related to Ol. 55, 1 = 560 B.C., would mean more exactly the year from Oct 1, 560, to Sep 30, 559 B.C.

〔278.   The biblical references to the first year of Cyrus when he made the proclamation which allowed the Jewish exiles to return from Babylon to Jerusalem (II Ch 36:22f.; Ezr 1:1ff.) are presumably stated in terms of his reign in Babylon since they deal with an event in that city. According to the cuneiform evidence and the Babylonian calendar, Babylon fell on Tashritu 16 = Oct 12, 539 B.C., and Cyrus entered the city two and one-half weeks later on Arahsamnu 3 = Oct 29. His Babylonian regnal years began, therefore, as shown in Table 77.[6]

TABLE 77. BABYLONIAN REGNAL YEARS OF CYRUS
AT THE BEGINNING OF HIS REIGN

Accession	539/538
Year 1	538/537
Year 2	537/536

Accordingly his first year, in which he made the proclamation, was 538/537 B.C.

〔279.   In the second year of the return of the exiles to Jerusalem Zerubbabel began the rebuilding of the Temple (Ezr 3:8). Then

[6] PDBC p.29.

the work was interrupted and not resumed until the second year of
Darius (Ezr 4:24) and it was completed in the sixth year of Darius
on the third day of the month Adar (Ezr 6:15). The same dates
are also given by Josephus.[7] The beginning of the reign of Darius
has been shown in Table 75. If we now expand and continue our
summary of the *Chronicle* at the point of the transition to and beginning of the reign of Darius, we have Table 78.[8]

TABLE 78. The Beginning of the Reign of Darius I
in the *Chronicle* of Eusebius

Year of Abraham	Olympiad	Kingdom of the Persians	B.C.
		Cambyses reigns for eight years	
....	....	....	....
....	....	....	....
	Ol. 64		
1493		7	524
1494		8	523
		The Magi brothers reign seven months after whom Darius reigns thirty-six years	
1495		1	522
1496		2	521
	Ol. 65		
1497		2	520
1498		3	519
1499		4	518
1500		5	517
	Ol. 66		
1501		6	516

¶ 280.   In Table 78 the unusual fact is that Year 2 of Darius is
shown twice in succession. At this point a note in the Canon[9] calls
attention to this fact and explains that it is because one of the years
is comprised with the seven months of the Magi. Actually, according to the Behistun inscription,[10] the Magian Gaumata, who claimed
to be Bardiya, son of Cyrus, and who is also known as Smerdis,

[7] *Against Apion.* I, 154.   [8] Helm pp.104 a – 106.
[9] Helm p.105 a.   [10] §§11, 13.

seized the entire Persian empire on Duzu 9 = Jul 1, 522 B.C., and was killed by Darius on Tashritu 10 = Sep 29, 522.[11] Cambyses himself is still mentioned in a text of Nisanu 23 = Apr 18, 522, and may not have died until after Jul 1, 522. Therefore in Babylonian chronology the transition from Cambyses to Darius I and the early years of reign of the latter are usually shown as in Table 79.[12]

TABLE 79. THE BEGINNING OF THE REIGN OF DARIUS I
IN BABYLONIAN CHRONOLOGY

Cambyses Year 8 (including the reign of Gaumata)	522/521
Darius Year 1	521/520
Year 2	520/519
Year 3	519/518
Year 4...	518/517
Year 5	517/516
Year 6	516/515

﴿ 281.   Since the arrangement of the *Chronicle* reflected in Table 78 with two successive listings of "Year 2" of Darius is obviously confusing, it is not surprising to find that this arrangement has been altered in the Armenian version. Here[13] the Magi are allowed a separate year to themselves as is shown in Table 80.

﴿ 282.   Year 1 of Darius (= A. Abr. 1496) in the Armenian version of the *Chronicle* (Table 80) and the first Year 2 of Darius (= A. Abr. 1496) in the Latin version (Table 75) are evidently considered as the last year of the captivity, rounding out seventy years of captivity (Table 75), presumably because the people were not considered to be really free until they were free to rebuild their Temple. This last year of the seventy years of captivity, which is Year 1 of Darius in the Armenian version and the first Year 2 in the Latin version, is related in the Latin version to Ol. 64, 4 = 521 B.C. If Eusebius was thinking of a regnal year beginning in the spring or fall (¶277) this Year 1 (or first Year 2) of Darius was actually equivalent to 521/520 B.C., and this is in agreement with the date given for Year 1 of Darius in Table 79 representing our best present knowledge of the chronology of his reign. The seventy

[11] Arno Poebel in AJSL 55 (1938), pp.142-165, 285-314; 56 (1939), pp.121-145.
[12] PDBC p.30.   [13] Karst pp.189-190.

TABLE 80. THE BEGINNING OF THE REIGN OF DARIUS I
IN THE ARMENIAN VERSION OF THE *Chronicle* OF EUSEBIUS

Year of Abraham	Kingdom of the Persians
	Cambyses reigns for eight years
....	....
....	....
1494	8
	The Magi, two brothers, rule for seven months
1495	1
	Darius reigns for thirty-six years
1496	1
1497	2
1498	3
1499	4
1500	5
1501	6

years of captivity (Anni Abraham 1427-1496) are therefore represented in the *Chronicle* as equivalent to 590 to 521 (or 521/520) B.C.

(9) FROM THE REBUILDING OF THE TEMPLE TO THE BIRTH OF JESUS

《 283.   The resumption of the rebuilding of the Temple (Ezr 3:8) marks the beginning of the next period. The year of this event appears in the Armenian version of the *Chronicle* as Year 2 of Darius, and in the Latin version as the second Year 2 of Darius, and in both cases the equivalent Year of Abraham is 1497. In the Latin version this year is also related to Ol. 65, 1 = 520 B.C. which in line with our previous reasoning (¶282) presumably means a regnal year equivalent to 520/519 and is the same as Year 2 of Darius in terms of Babylonian chronology (Table 79). The year 520 B.C., or more exactly 520/519, is therefore the year of the resumption of the rebuilding of the Temple. Likewise Year 6 of Darius is related to Ol. 66, 1 = 516 B.C. (Table 78). In similar fashion this presumably means 516/515 and is again in agreement with the same date in Table 79. In this year the Temple was completed on Adar 3 (Ezr 6:15) and this date is equivalent to Mar 12, 515 B.C.

¶ 284.   Beginning with the resumption of the rebuilding of the Temple (¶283) the next period covered by the *Chronicle* may be taken as extending to the birth of Jesus which is placed in the forty-second year of Augustus. The numbering of the intervening years may be seen in Table 81, which takes consecutive years from several parallel columns in the *Chronicle* in succession.[1]

¶ 285.   As Table 81 shows, the period from the second year of Darius to the forty-second year of Augustus comprised five hundred and nineteen years and extended from A. Abr. 1497 to 2015, and at this point in the *Chronicle* a note indicates correctly that the years from Abraham to the nativity of Christ are $\overline{\text{II}}.\text{XV} = 2015$.

TABLE 81. FROM THE REBUILDING OF THE TEMPLE IN THE SECOND YEAR OF DARIUS TO THE BIRTH OF JESUS IN THE FORTY-SECOND YEAR OF AUGUSTUS IN THE *Chronicle* OF EUSEBIUS

Year of Abraham	Kingdom of the Persians	Number of Years Intervening	B.C.
	Darius		
1497	Year 2	} 35	520
	Year 36		
	Xerxes, 20 years	20	
	Artabanus, 7 months	1	
	Artaxerxes Longimanus, 40 years	40	
	Darius Nothus, 19 years	19	} 191
	Artaxerxes Mnemon, 40 years	40	
	Artaxerxes Ochus, 26 years	26	
	Arses, 4 years	4	
	Darius son of Arsames, 6 years	6	
	Kingdom of the Macedonians		
	Alexander had already reigned seven years (his Year 1 = Arses Year 4 = 336 B.C.) and the tabulation continues now with his		
1688	Year 8	} 5	329
	Year 12		
	Thereafter the table continues with the Ptolemaic dynasty		
	Kingdom of the Alexandrians		

[1] Helm pp.106-169.

[174]

Year of Abraham	Kingdom of the Persians	Number of Years Intervening	B.C.
1693	Ptolemy Lagus, 40 years		324
	Ptolemy Philadelphus, 38 years		
	Ptolemy Euergetes, 26 years		
	Ptolemy Philopator, 17 years		
	Ptolemy Epiphanes, 24 years		
	Ptolemy Philometor, 35 years		
	Ptolemy Euergetes, 29 years		
	Ptolemy Physkon, 17 years	276	
	Ptolemy Alexander, 10 years		
	Ptolemy who was exiled by his mother, 8 years		
	Ptolemy Dionysos, 30 years		
	Cleopatra then reigned for twenty-two years, but of those years we will here count only 2		

Year 3 of Cleopatra is equated
with Year 1 of Julius Caesar
and from here on we follow the
column of the Romans, also
adding again the Olympiads

*Kingdom of
the Romans*

C. Julius Caesar, four years,
seven months

Ol. 183

1969	Year 1		48
1970	Year 2		47
1971	Year 3		46
1972	Year 4	5	45
Ol. 184			
1973	Year 5		44

In this year Julius Caesar
was killed on the Ides of
March = Mar 15

Octavian Caesar Augustus,
fifty-six years, six months

1974	Year 1		43
Ol. 194			
2013	Year 40	42	4
2014	Year 41		3
2015	Year 42		2

Jesus Christ the Son of God
is born in Bethlehem of Judea

519

⟨ 286.   If, as previously surmised (¶253), Eusebius was reckoning regnal years in terms of the Syro-Macedonian calendar, the period from Mar 15 to Sep 30, 44 B.C., may be considered in the foregoing tabulation (Table 81) to represent an "accession year" of Augustus, and his Year 1 is really Oct 1, 44, to Sep 30, 43 B.C. This means that his Year 42 is Oct 1, 3, to Sep 30, 2 B.C., and Eusebius, like Africanus (¶243), is giving the date of 3/2 B.C. for the birth of Jesus.

(10) THE PERIOD OF THE LIFE OF JESUS

⟨ 287.   The *Chronicle* now continues[1] from the year after the birth of Jesus, i.e., from the forty-third year of Augustus, to the fifteenth year of Tiberius when John the Baptist began to preach and Jesus began his public ministry (Lk 3:1ff.), and to the eighteenth year of Tiberius in which year Eusebius places the death of Jesus. Table 82 is an outline of the Canon for this period:

TABLE 82. THE PERIOD OF THE LIFE OF JESUS FROM THE FORTY-THIRD YEAR OF AUGUSTUS TO THE EIGHTEENTH YEAR OF TIBERIUS IN THE *Chronicle* OF EUSEBIUS

Year of Abraham	Romans	Number of Years Intervening	B.C.–A.D.
	Augustus		
2016	Year 43	⎫	1 B.C.
		⎬ 14	
2029	Year 56	⎭	A.D. 13
	Tiberius, twenty-three years		
2030	Year 1	⎫	14
....			
....		⎬ 15	
Ol. 201, 4			
2044	Year 15	⎭	28
	John the Baptist preaches in the wilderness		
Ol. 202			
2045	Year 16	⎫	29
2046	Year 17	⎬ 3	30
2047	Year 18	⎭	31
	The death of Jesus Christ		
		────	
		32	

[1] Helm pp.169-174.

(11) FROM AFTER THE DEATH OF JESUS
TO THE FINAL DESTRUCTION OF JERUSALEM IN THE
SECOND YEAR OF VESPASIAN

❪ 288.   From the nineteenth year of Tiberius, which was the first year after the death of Jesus, to the second year of Vespasian, which was the year in which Jerusalem was finally destroyed, the *Chronicle* may be outlined as shown in Table 83:[1]

TABLE 83. FROM THE NINETEENTH YEAR OF TIBERIUS TO THE SECOND YEAR OF VESPASIAN AND THE FINAL DESTRUCTION OF JERUSALEM IN THE *Chronicle* OF EUSEBIUS

Year of Abraham	Romans	Number of Years Intervening	A.D.
	Tiberius		
2048	Year 19		32
		5	
2052	Year 23		36
	Gaius, three years, ten months		
2053	Year 1		37
		4	
2056	Year 4		40
	Claudius, thirteen years, eight months, twenty-eight days		
2057	Year 1		41
		14	
2070	Year 14		54
	Nero, thirteen years, seven months, twenty-eight days		
2071	Year 1		55
		14	
2084	Year 14		68
	Vespasian, nine years, eleven months, twenty-two days		
2085	Year 1		69
		2	
2086	Year 2		70
		39	

[1] Helm pp.174-187.

(12) THE TABLES OF THE *CHRONICLE* FROM
JULIUS CAESAR TO VESPASIAN

〔289. The period from Julius Caesar to Vespasian, outlined in brief in the foregoing Tables 81, 82, and 83, is of special interest in relation to the New Testament and may now be shown (Table 84) somewhat more fully as it actually appears in the tables of the *Chronicle*.[1] Julius Caesar was in power for four years and seven months, and we will begin with his last year, shown as his fifth. The same year is shown as the seventh of Cleopatra (who reigned for twenty-two years) and the twenty-fourth of Hyrcanus (who held the high priesthood of the Jews for thirty-four years). After Hyrcanus comes the thirty-seven year reign of Herod the Great, the beginning of the reign being placed several years too late (¶¶362f.) with a consequent displacement of his successors too. The Years of Abraham are shown in the left-hand margin at ten-year intervals, the Olympiads are noted between regnal years, and the brief historical notices follow the years to which they appear to relate. Our understanding of the interrelationships of the Olympiadic dates, regnal years, and dates before and after the Christian era has been set forth above (¶¶269-270, etc.).

TABLE 84. THE TABLES OF THE *Chronicle* FROM
JULIUS CAESAR TO VESPASIAN

Year of Abraham	Olympiad	Romans	Alexandrians	Jews	B.C.
	Ol. 184	(I) Julius Caesar	Cleopatra	Hyrcanus	
		5	7	24	44
		Julius Caesar is killed on the Ides of March (II) Octavian Caesar Augustus reigns fifty-six years, six months			
		1	8	25	43
		2	9	26	42
		3	10	27	41
	Ol. 185				
		4	11	28	40
		5	12	29	39
		6	13	30	38

[1] Helm pp.157-187.

Year of Abraham	Olympiad	Romans	Alexandrians	Jews	B.C.
1980		7	14	31	37
	Ol. 186				
		8	15	32	36
		9	16	33	35
		10	17	34	34
			Herod reigns thirty-seven years		
		11	18	1	33
	Ol. 187				
		12	19	2	32
		13	20	3	31
		14	21	4	30
		15	22	5	29
			End of the empire of the Alexandrians		
	Ol. 188				
		16		6	28
1990		17		7	27
		18		8	26
		19		9	25
	Ol. 189				
		20		10	24
		21		11	23
		22		12	22
		23		13	21
	Ol. 190				
		24		14	20
		25		15	19
		26		16	18
2000		27		17	17
	Ol. 191				
		28		18	16
		29		19	15
		30		20	14
		31		21	13
	Ol. 192				
		32		22	12
		33		23	11
		34		24	10
		35		25	9
	Ol. 193				
		36		26	8

Year of Abraham	*Olympiad*	*Romans*	*Alexandrians*	*Jews*	*B.C.*
2010		37		27	7
		38		28	6
		39		29	5
	Ol. 194				
		40		30	4
		41		31	3
		42		32	2
		Jesus Christ the Son of God is born in Bethlehem of Judea			
		All the years from Abraham to the birth of Christ total 2015			
		43		33	1
					A.D.
	Ol. 195				
		44		34	1
		45		35	2
		46		36	3
2020		47		37	4
			Archelaus leader of the Jews for nine years		
	Ol. 196				
		48		1	5
		49		2	6
		50		3	7
		51		4	8
	Ol. 197				
		52		5	9
		53		6	10
		54		7	11
		55		8	12
	Ol. 198				
		56		9	13
		(III) Tiberius reigns twenty-three years	Herod the tetrarch holds chief place for twenty-four years		

Year of Abraham	Olympiad	Romans	Alexandrians	Jews	A.D.
2030		1		1	14
		2		2	15
		3		3	16
	Ol. 199				
		4		4	17
		5		5	18
		6		6	19
		7		7	20
	Ol. 200				
		8		8	21
		9		9	22
		10		10	23
2040		11		11	24
	Ol. 201				
		12		12	25
		13		13	26
		Pilate is sent by Tiberius as procurator of Judea			
		14		14	27
		15		15	28

John the son of Zechariah preaches in the desert by the Jordan river

From the second year of Darius and the rebuilding of the Temple, five hundred and forty-eight years

From Solomon and the first building of the Temple, one thousand and sixty years

From Moses and the exodus of the Israelites from Egypt, one thousand five hundred and thirty-nine years

From Abraham, two thousand and forty-four years

From the Flood to Abraham, nine hundred and forty-two years

From Adam to the Flood, two thousand, two hundred and forty-two years

Year of Abraham	Olympiad	Romans	Alexandrians	Jews	A.D.
	Ol. 202				
		16		16	29
		17		17	30
		18		18	31
		Jesus Christ, according to the prophecies which were spoken ahead of time concerning him, comes to his passion in the eighteenth year of Tiberius			
		19		19	32
	Ol. 203				
		20		20	33
2050		21		21	34
		22		22	35
		23		23	36
	Ol. 204				
		(IIII) Gaius (Caligula) reigns three years, ten months			
		1		24	37
				Agrippa chief of the Jews, seven years	
		2		1	38
		3		2	39
		4		3	40
		(v) Claudius reigns thirteen years, eight months, twenty-eight days			
	Ol. 205				
		1		4	41
		2		5	42
		3		6	43
2060		4		7	44
				Agrippa king of the Jews, twenty-six years	
	Ol. 206				
		5		1	45
		6		2	46
		7		3	47
		8		4	48
	Ol. 207				
		9		5	49
		10		6	50
		11		7	51
		12		8	52

Year of Abraham	Olympiad	Romans	Alexandrians	Jews	A.D.
	Ol. 208				
		13		9	53
2070		14		10	54
		(VI) Nero reigns thirteen years, seven months, twenty-eight days			
		1		11	55
		2		12	56
		Festus succeeds Felix			
	Ol. 209				
		3		13	57
		4		14	58
		5		15	59
		6		16	60
	Ol. 210				
		7		17	61
		8		18	62
		9		19	63
2080		10		20	64
		Nero burns the larger part of the city of Rome			
	Ol. 211				
		11		21	65
		12		22	66
		13		23	67
		14		24	68
		First persecution of the Christians by Nero in which Peter and Paul die			
	Ol. 212				
		(VII) Vespasian reigns nine years, eleven months, twenty-two days			
		1		25	69
		2		26	70
		Titus destroys Jerusalem			

From the fifteenth year of the reign of Tiberius Caesar and from the beginning of the preaching of the gospel, forty-two years

From the second year of Darius, under whom the Temple was built again, five hundred and ninety years

[183]

Year of Abraham	Olympiad	Romans	Alexandrians	Jews	A.D.
		From the first building of the Temple under Solomon to the most recent destruction of it which was carried out under Vespasian, one thousand, one hundred and two years			

(13) SUMMARY OF THE *CHRONICLE*

❨ 290.   In accordance with the foregoing analysis we may summarize the *Chronicle* in abbreviated form from Adam to the final destruction of the Temple as it stands in the Latin version of Jerome (Table 85). We give the number of years in the several major periods, cumulative reckonings from Adam and from Abraham, the Olympiadic dates of Eusebius, and equivalents in B.C.-A.D. according to our interpretation as given above.

TABLE 85. SUMMARY OF THE *Chronicle* OF EUSEBIUS
IN THE LATIN VERSION OF JEROME

	Number of Years	Years from Adam	Years from Abraham	Olympiadic Years	Years B.C.-A.D.
					B.C.
1. Adam		0			5200
2. Flood	2242	2242			
3. First Year after the Flood		2243			
4. Birth of Abraham	942	3184	0		
5. First Year of Abraham		3185	1		2016
6. Last Year of Servitude in Egypt	505	3689	505		1512
7. First Year in the Wilderness		3690	506		1511
8. Foundation of the Temple in the Fourth Year of Solomon	479	4168	984		1033

	Number of Years	Years from Adam	Years from Abraham	Olympiadic Years	Years B.C.- A.D.
9. Fifth Year of Solomon		4169	985		1032
10. Fiftieth Year of Azariah, or Uzziah	442			1, 1	776
11. Destruction of the Temple in the Eleventh Year of Zedekiah		4610	1426	47, 2	591
12. First Year of the Captivity		4611	1427	47, 3	590
13. Seventieth Year of the Captivity and (First) Second Year of Darius	70	4680	1496	64, 4	521
14. Rebuilding of the Temple in the (Second) Second Year of Darius		4681	1497	65, 1	520
15. Birth of Jesus in the Forty-second Year of Augustus	519	5199	2015	194, 3	2
16. Forty-third Year of Augustus		5200	2016	194, 4	1
17. Beginning of the Public Ministry of Jesus in the Fifteenth Year of Tiberius	29	5228	2044	201, 4	A.D. 28
18. Sixteenth Year of Tiberius		5229	2045	202, 1	29
19. Death of Jesus in the Eighteenth Year of Tiberius	3	5231	2047	202, 3	31
20. Nineteenth Year of Tiberius		5232	2048	202, 4	32
21. Final Destruction of Jerusalem in the Second Year of Vespasian	39	5270	2086	212, 2	70

([291. That Table 85 does in fact represent correctly the way Eusebius counts the years from Adam to the final destruction of Jerusalem is confirmed by comparison with cumulative summaries of years contained in the *Chronicle*, typical examples of which were reproduced in Table 84. The figures given in several of these summaries are shown in the following tables, and the correspondence of them with the figures in Table 85 may be seen at a glance.

¶ 292.   In the Introduction of Eusebius as translated by Jerome the figures in Table 86 are included:[1]

TABLE 86. CUMULATIVE SUMMARY FIGURES IN THE INTRODUCTION
OF THE *Chronicle* OF EUSEBIUS

	NUMBER OF YEARS
1. From Adam to the Flood	2242
2. From the Flood to the Nativity of Abraham	942
3. From Abraham to Moses and the exodus from Egypt	505
4. From Moses to Solomon and the building of the Temple	479
5. From Solomon to the restoration of the Temple under Darius	512 (442 + 70 = 512)
6. From Darius to the preaching of Jesus Christ in the fifteenth year of Tiberius	548 (519 + 29 = 548)
7. From Abraham to the fifteenth year of Tiberius	2044

¶ 293.   At the fourth year of Solomon the figures in Table 87 are given.[2]

TABLE 87. CUMULATIVE SUMMARY AT THE FOURTH YEAR OF SOLOMON
IN THE *Chronicle* OF EUSEBIUS

	NUMBER OF YEARS
1. From Adam to the Flood	2242
2. From the Flood to Moses	1447 (942 + 505 = 1447)
3. From Moses to Solomon and the building of the Temple	480
4. Total	4169

It has already been explained (¶266) that while this note gives the conventional figure of four hundred and eighty years (I K 6:1) from Moses to Solomon and the building of the Temple, the figure in the Introduction (Table 86) and the actual listing of the sequential years in the Canon give four hundred and seventy-nine, and the total therefore should really be 4168 (Table 85) instead of 4169.

¶294.   At the birth of Jesus the cumulative figure is a total of 2015 years from Abraham to the Nativity.[3]

[1] Helm pp.15, 17.   [2] Helm p.70 a.   [3] Helm p.169.

⟨ 295.   At the beginning of the public ministry of Jesus in the fifteenth year of Tiberius it is marked that this point was removed, as shown in Table 88, from certain earlier historic points.[4]

TABLE 88. CUMULATIVE SUMMARY AT THE FIFTEENTH YEAR OF TIBERIUS
IN THE *Chronicle* OF EUSEBIUS

	NUMBER OF YEARS
1. From the rebuilding of the Temple under Darius	548 (519 + 29 = 548)
2. From Solomon and the first building of the Temple	1060 (442 + 70 + 548 = 1060)
3. From Moses and the exodus from Egypt	1539 (479 + 1060 = 1539)
4. From Abraham	2044 (505 + 1539 = 2044)

Here it is also recalled that from the Flood to Abraham was 942 years, and from Adam to the Flood 2242 years. Therefore, although the total is not given, from Adam to the beginning of the public ministry of Jesus Christ must have been 5228 (2242 + 942 + 2044 = 5228) years.

⟨ 296.   At the final destruction of the Temple there is this brief recapitulation of the number of years of this point from previous points:[5]

TABLE 89. CUMULATIVE SUMMARY AT THE FINAL DESTRUCTION
OF THE TEMPLE IN THE *Chronicle* OF EUSEBIUS

	NUMBER OF YEARS
1. From the fifteenth year of Tiberius	42 (39 + 3 = 42)
2. From the second year of Darius and the rebuilding of the Temple	590 (519 + 29 + 42 = 590)
3. From Solomon and the first building of the Temple	1102 (442 + 70 + 590 = 1102)

[4] Helm pp.173-174.   [5] Helm p.187.

PART TWO
PROBLEMS OF CHRONOLOGY
IN THE BIBLE

I. MODERN SYSTEMS OF BIBLICAL CHRONOLOGY

I. THE *ANNALES VETERIS ET NOVI TESTAMENTI*
OF JAMES USSHER

LITERATURE: Charles R. Elrington and James H. Todd, *The Whole Works of the Most Rev. James Ussher, D.D.* 17 vols. 1847-64. vols. 8-11, *Annales Veteris et Novi Testamenti*, and *Chronologia sacra*; J. A. Carr, *The Life and Times of James Ussher.* 1895; "Ussher, James," in NSH XII, pp.114-115; "Usher (or Ussher), James," in EB XXII, p.907.

¶ 297. Of systems of biblical chronology which have become widely known in modern times the most famous is that of James Ussher (1581-1656), who was archbishop of Armagh in Ireland. His chronology was published in 1650-54 in a work entitled *Annales Veteris et Novi Testamenti*, and was inserted by an unknown authority in the margin of reference editions of the English translation of the Bible which was first issued in 1611 under the authority of King James I.[1] The computation of Ussher consists essentially of adding the successive figures found in the biblical text. In the Old Testament, the Hebrew text is followed and the Flood comes, for example, in 2349 B.C., 1656 years (¶260) after the creation of Adam in 4004 B.C. Since these figures are still available in many editions of the King James Version of the Bible it is not necessary to deal with them further here. Somewhat similar figures are also to be found in *The Berkeley Version* of the Bible.[2]

¶ 298. At the present time much chronological study of the Bible attempts not only to tabulate and interpret the figures which are provided by the biblical text but also to bring them into relationship to what is known otherwise of ancient times through history and archaeology. That this is not dissimilar from what even Eusebius did will be realized when we recall his extended tables of historical parallels and synchronisms (¶¶262ff.). Examples will appear in some detail in what follows in relation to both the Old Testament and the New Testament.

[1] The dates appear, for example, in the margins of *The Holy Bible* (KJV) printed in London by Charles Bill in 1703.
[2] 1959. E.g., p.5 n.e.

II. THE OLD TESTAMENT

1. ABRAHAM

LITERATURE: Y. Aharoni, "The Land of Gerar," a paper published in Hebrew in *Eretz-Israel*. 3 (1954), pp.108-111, and in English in IEJ 6 (1956), pp.26-32, see especially p.31; Nelson Glueck in *The Holy Land, New Light on the Prehistory and Early History of Israel*, published in cooperation with the Hebrew University, Department of Antiquities, Israel Exploration Society, *Antiquity and Survival*, II:2-3, 1957, p.275; F. Cornelius, "Chronology, Eine Erwiderung," in JCS 12 (1958), pp.101-104; Nelson Glueck, *Rivers in the Desert, A History of the Negev*. 1959, pp.68-69; Friedrich Cornelius, "Genesis XIV," in ZAW 72 (1960), pp.1-7.

¶299. At least as early as the time of Abraham (Gen 11:27ff.) the attempt may be made to establish the kind of correlation just referred to (¶298). In the Bible record the entry of Abraham into Canaan appears to be put by the figures in the Hebrew text at about 1921 B.C. (Ussher), by the figures in the Septuagint at around 1700 B.C.[1] Historically it is at least possible that the Amraphel of Gen 14:1 is to be identified with King Hammurabi of Babylon, and the latter is now probably to be dated about 1728-1686 B.C. Archeologically, conditions in the Negeb in general and at Gerar in particular appear to be such as are presupposed in the biblical narrative concerning Abraham either in the period known as Middle Bronze I (twenty-first to nineteenth centuries B.C.) or in Middle Bronze II (nineteenth to sixteenth centuries B.C.), perhaps the latter.

2. THE EXODUS

LITERATURE: J. S. Griffiths, *The Exodus in the Light of Archaeology*. 1923; J. W. Jack, *The Date of the Exodus*. 1925; W. M. F. Petrie, *Palestine and Israel*. 1934, pp.54-58; William F. Albright, *From the Stone Age to Christianity*. 2d ed. 1946, pp.194ff.; H. H. Rowley, *From Joseph to Joshua*. 1950, pp.129ff.; M. B. Rowton, "The Background of the Treaty between Ramesses II and Ḫattušiliš III," in JCS 13 (1959), pp.1-11; "Comparative Chronology at the Time of Dynasty XIX," in JNES 19 (1960), pp.15-22.

¶300. The statement in I K 6:1 that it was in the four hundred and eightieth year after the people came out of Egypt that Solomon began, in the fourth year of his reign, to build the Temple, appears to provide a relatively precise date for the exodus. Computation on this basis leads to dates for the exodus from 1491 (Ussher) to

[1] FLP pp.71-73; Jack Finegan, *In the Beginning, A Journey through Genesis*. 1962, pp.87ff.

1446 B.C. The statement of Ex 1:11 that the Israelites built for Pharaoh the store cities of Pithom and Raamses seems to require, however, that the enslavement immediately prior to the exodus be placed under the famous Pharaoh Ramses II. According to the best information presently available the reign of Ramses II is probably to be dated 1304-1237 B.C., and a date for the exodus not too long after 1300 B.C. seems more probable.[1]

3. THE KINGS OF JUDAH AND ISRAEL

LITERATURE: Joachim Begrich, *Die Chronologie der Könige von Israel und Juda und die Quellen des Rahmens der Königsbücher.* 1929; Edwin R. Thiele, "The Chronology of the Kings of Judah and Israel," in JNES 3 (1944), pp.137-186; W. F. Albright, "The Chronology of the Divided Monarchy of Israel," in BASOR 100 (Dec. 1945), pp.16-22; M. B. Rowton, "The Date of the Founding of Solomon's Temple," in BASOR 119 (Oct. 1950), pp.20-22; Edwin R. Thiele, *The Mysterious Numbers of the Hebrew Kings.* 1951 (abbreviated TMN); W. F. Albright, "Alternative Chronology" (review of TMN) in *Interpretation.* 6 (1952), pp.101-103; J. Liver, "The Chronology of Tyre at the Beginning of the First Millennium B.C.," in IEJ 3 (1953), pp.113-122; Edwin R. Thiele, "A Comparison of the Chronological Data of Israel and Judah," in *Vetus Testamentum.* 4 (1954), pp.187-191; Hayim Tadmor, "The Campaigns of Sargon II of Assur: A Chronological-Historical Study," in JCS 12 (1958), pp.22-40, 77-100; William W. Hallo, "From Qarqar to Carchemish: Assyria and Israel in the Light of New Discoveries," in BA 23 (1960), pp.34-61.

¶ 301.　　The biblical records of reign of the kings of Judah and Israel provide more detailed chronological information than is available for earlier periods. In attempting to interpret the data here provided it is essential to keep in mind many of the principles of time reckoning in the ancient world already discussed (specially ¶163). Even so it is often difficult to determine which manner of reckoning is employed in a given case. As to the calendar year in terms of which the reigns were described: From I K 6:1, 37, 38 Edwin R. Thiele[1] deduces that the regnal year in the time of Solomon was counted from the first of Tishri in the fall, although the year beginning the first of Nisan was used for reckoning ordinary and ecclesiastical dates; but Julian Morgenstern[2] finds that the same passages indicate a regnal year beginning with Nisan 1. Again when

---

[1] FLP pp.117ff.; Jack Finegan, *Let My People Go, A Journey through Exodus.* 1963, ch. 2.

---

[1] TMN p.31.
[2] In *Occident and Orient, Gaster Anniversary Volume,* p.446.

Neh 1:1 and 2:1 refer to the month Kislev and the following Nisan, both in the twentieth year of Artaxerxes, Morgenstern[3] thinks Nehemiah was using a year beginning in Tishri (cf. ¶167), but Hayim Tadmor[4] suggests that Nehemiah simply carried over "the twentieth year" by mistake when the month of Nisan was actually the beginning of the twenty-first year or, alternatively, that the text should read "the twenty-fifth year" as in Josephus,[5] although the latter mistakenly changes the ruler to Xerxes. Thiele[6] thinks that the regnal year was counted from Tishri in Judah but from Nisan in Northern Israel; moreover, that while the books of Kings and Jeremiah use a regnal year beginning in Tishri for the kings of Judah, in references to Babylonian or Persian kings the writers of Kings, Jeremiah, Haggai, and Zechariah use a year reckoned from Nisan, as Ezekiel also does in giving the years of the captivity of Jehoiachin; but W. F. Albright[7] finds this system too elaborate.

¶302. As to the question of whether reigns were described in terms of the accession-year or the nonaccession-year system: In Hebrew the word ראש, *rosh*, means "head" or "front" and in relation to time it and the related noun ראשית, *reshiyt*, and adjective ראשני, *roshony*, mean "beginning" or "first." The phrase מלכות בראשית, *bereshiyt malkut*, occurs in Jer 26:1 in relation to Jehoiakim and in Jer 27:1; 28:1; and 49:34 in relation to Zedekiah. The phrase is commonly translated "in the beginning of the reign of . . ." (RSV) and is doubtless to be recognized as the Hebrew equivalent of the Babylonian *resh sharruti* (¶160) and the normal designation of an accession year. Related but variant forms are found in Jer 25:1 and in II K 25:27 = Jer 52:31 and will require special notice later to determine, if possible, whether they mean "beginning" and refer to an accession year (¶314), or mean "first" and refer to an official first year of reign. In general, it is the opinion of Thiele[8] that the kings of Judah followed the accession-year system from Rehoboam to Jehoshaphat, the nonaccession-year system from Jehoram to Joash, and the accession-year system again from Amaziah to Zedekiah; and that the kings of Israel followed the nonaccession-year system from Jeroboam I to Jehoahaz, and the accession-year system from Jehoash to Hoshea. If this is correct, then in the later

[3] *Op.cit.*, p.441.
[5] *Ant.* XI, v, 7.
[7] In BASOR 100 (Dec 1945), pp.17f.
[4] In JNES 15 (1956), p.227 n.10.
[6] TMN pp.32f., 157.
[8] TMN pp.157, 281f.

period of the two monarchies both were using the accession-year system, and at the same time the biblical writers would presumably also use the accession-year system in their references to Babylonian or Persian kings. It is in that later period to which we will shortly turn (¶¶309ff.) that the application of the principles to which we have devoted so much attention now makes possible the attainment of relative precision and probable accuracy in the interpretation of certain crucial dates.

⟨ 303.   Within even the earlier part of the period of the kings, certain synchronisms are now available. On any reckoning, Ahab king of Israel, must have been on the throne about the middle of the ninth century B.C. In the Monolith Inscription[9] of Shalmaneser III (858-824 B.C.) his victory over a Syrian coalition of twelve kings at Qarqar on the Orontes River is recorded and "Ahab, the Israelite" is named among the allied leaders. The battle is placed in the sixth year of the Assyrian king and it is stated that he left Nineveh on the fourteenth day of Aiaru (Apr/May) and crossed the Euphrates at its (spring) flood, hence the event at Qarqar is probably to be placed in the summer of 853 B.C. This provides independent confirmation of the rule of Ahab at this time.

⟨ 304.   On the Black Obelisk of Shalmaneser III the Assyrian king records the taking of tribute from Jehu king of Israel,[10] and in a fragment of his annals dates this event in the eighteenth year of his reign, 841 B.C.[11] Between Ahab who fought with Shalmaneser III at Qarqar in 853 (¶303) and Jehu who paid tribute to him in 841, the rulers of Israel were Ahaziah and Joram who are credited with reigns of two years and twelve years respectively in I K 22:51 and II K 3:1. By the nonaccession-year system these two reigns actually total twelve years, which is the time between Qarqar and the paying of tribute by Jehu. Therefore the death of Ahab at Ramoth-gilead (I K 22:3, 35) must have taken place in 853 B.C. soon after Qarqar, and the accession of Jehu have been in 841 B.C.[12]

⟨ 305.   Counting backward from the battle of Qarqar and the death of Ahab (¶304), if the reigns of the kings of Israel are reck-

9 ARAB I, §§610-611; ANET pp.278-279; ANEA p.188.
10 ARAB I, §590; ANET p.281; ANEA p.192.
11 ARAB I, §672; ANET p.280; ANEA p.192.
12 TMN pp.48-53, 62.

oned according to the nonaccession-year system, and those of the kings of Judah according to the accession-year system, the period to the division of the kingdom under Rehoboam and Jeroboam totals seventy-eight years and leads to placing the disruption in 931/930 B.C.[13] If the first year of Rehoboam and Jeroboam I in the separated kingdoms was 931/930, then Solomon's fortieth and last year was 932/931, his first year was 971/970, and his fourth year in which the Temple was founded was 968/967.[14]

〖306. In one of his inscriptions Tiglath-pileser III (744-727 B.C.) mentions receiving tribute from a number of kings including Azariah of Judah.[15] The reference belongs to the third year of the reign of Tiglath-pileser; since he departed from the traditional system of counting regnal years and included his accession year (745 B.C.) in the numbering, his third year was 743 B.C.[16] In another text, dated according to the eponym lists in 732 B.C., he speaks of the defeat of Rezon.[17] This is probably the same event as that mentioned in II K 16:9 and provides a date for the deportation of Northern Israelites by Tiglath-pileser, the change in rule from Pekah to Hoshea, and the submission of Ahaz to the Assyrian king.

〖307. A Babylonian chronicle written in the twenty-second year of King Darius (500/499 B.C.), covering Assyrian and Babylonian history from Tiglath-pileser III to Ashurbanipal, states that Shalmaneser V (726-722 B.C.) died in the tenth month, Tebetu, of his fifth year of reign, and that his successor, Sargon II (721-705 B.C.), ascended the throne on the twelfth day of the same month, which

---

[13] Thiele in JNES 3 (1944), pp.147, 184; TMN pp.54f.; and in *Vetus Testamentum*. 4 (1954), pp.187-191.

[14] Begrich (*Die Chronologie der Könige von Israel und Juda*, p.155) places the division of the kingdom in 926 B.C. Albright (in BASOR 100 [Dec. 1945], pp.16-22; and in *Interpretation*. 6 [1952], pp.101-103) puts it in 922 B.C. The latter date, with a correlative of 959 B.C. for the founding of Solomon's temple, is supported by M. B. Rowton (in BASOR 119 [Oct. 1950], pp.20-22) from evidence in the king list of Tyre as cited by Josephus from Menander of Ephesus. Dealing with the same materials, however, Liver (in IEJ 3 [1953], pp.113-122) accepts the date of 825 B.C. for the foundation of Carthage as given by Pompeius Trogus (rather than 814 B.C. as given by Timaeus), puts the beginning of the reign of Hiram of Tyre in 979/978 B.C., and arrives at the date of 968/967 for the commencement of work on the Temple, and 931/930 for the separation of the kingdom.

[15] ARAB I, §770; ANET p.282; ANEA p.193.

[16] A. Poebel in JNES 2 (1943), p.89 n.23.

[17] ARAB I, §779; ANET p.283; ANEA p.194; cf. TMN pp.90, 106, 121; Albright in BASOR 100 (Dec. 1945), p.22 n.26.

was late in December 722 B.C.[18] The calendar year from Nisan 1, 722, to the end of Addaru 721 B.C. was, accordingly, both the last regnal year of Shalmaneser V and the accession year of Sargon II. The same Babylonian chronicle also records as the noteworthy event of the reign of Shalmaneser that he destroyed the city of Shamarain. This is probably the biblical Samaria, capital of Northern Israel, and means that the fall of that city in the ninth year of King Hoshea (II K 17:6) is to be placed in the fighting season of 722 B.C., that is sometime between spring and summer of that year. In his inscriptions Sargon II also claims the honor of the taking of the city at the beginning of his reign,[19] and it might of course be the case that he did participate in some phase of the campaign or subsequent deportation of the Israelites, but the date of 722 B.C. remains probable for the fall of Samaria.[20]

❡ 308.   In the annals of Sennacherib (704-681 B.C.) the record of his "third campaign" (701 B.C.) describes a siege of Jerusalem, doubtless conducted during the summer of that year, which may be the same as the siege which II K 18:13 and Is 36:1 put in the fourteenth year of King Hezekiah.[21]

4. THE CLOSING PERIOD OF THE KINGDOM OF JUDAH

LITERATURE: C. J. Gadd, *The Fall of Nineveh*. 1923; W. F. Albright, "The Seal of Eliakim and the Latest Preëxilic History of Judah, With Some Observations on Ezekiel," in JBL 51 (1932), pp.77-106; Waldo H. Dubberstein, "Assyrian-Babylonian Chronology (669-612 B.C.)," in JNES 3 (1944), pp.38-42; W. F. Albright, "A Brief History of Judah from the Days of Josiah to Alexander the Great," in BA 9 (1946), pp.1-16; D. Winton Thomas, "The Age of Jeremiah in the Light of Recent Archaeological Discovery," in PEQ 1950, pp.1-15; D. J. Wiseman, *Chronicles of Chaldaean Kings (626-556 B.C.) in the British Museum*. 1956 (abbreviated WCCK); J. Philip Hyatt, "New Light on Nebuchadrezzar and Judean History," in JBL 75 (1956), pp.277-284; A. Malamat, "A New Record of Nebuchadrezzar's Palestinian Campaigns," in IEJ 6 (1956), pp.246-256; Hayim Tadmor, "Chronology of the Last Kings of Judah," in JNES 15 (1956), pp.226-230; Edwin R. Thiele, "New Evidence on the Chronology of the Last Kings of

[18] *Babylonian Chronicle*. I, 27-31; Hugo Winckler, *Keilinschriftliches Textbuch zum Alten Testament*. 2d ed. 1903, p.61; TMN pp.122-128.
[19] ARAB II, §§4, 55; ANET pp.284f.; ANEA pp.195f.
[20] Tadmor in JCS 12 (1958), pp.22-40.
[21] ARAB II, §240; ANET p.288; ANEA p.200; cf. TMN pp.101, 110; Albright in BASOR 100 (Dec 1945), p.22 n.28.

Judah," in BASOR 143 (Oct. 1956), pp.22-27; Martin Noth, "Die Einnahme von Jerusalem im Jahre 597 v. Chr.," in ZDPV 74 (1958), pp.133-157; Elias Auerbach, "Der Wechsel des Jahres-Anfangs in Juda im Lichte der neugefundenen babylonischen Chronik," in VT 9 (1959), pp.113-121; E. Auerbach, "Die Umschaltung vom judäischen auf den babylonischen Kalender," in VT 10 (1960), pp.69-70.

⟨ 309. Assyria, which had deported Northern Israelites (¶¶306, 307) and threatened Jerusalem (¶308), fell but was replaced by the Chaldean or New Babylonian empire, which ultimately destroyed the kingdom of Judah. A number of cuneiform texts from Babylon in the British Museum, some only recently published, make available portions of a Babylonian chronicle with annals covering much of what was the closing period of the kingdom of Judah. By the correlation of such extra-biblical evidence with biblical data it is possible to state dates in this period with relatively great precision and assurance.

⟨ 310. British Museum Tablet No. 25127 records the accession of the Chaldean Nabopolassar to the throne of Babylon: "On the twenty-sixth day of the month of Arahsamnu, Nabopolassar sat upon the throne in Babylon. This was the 'beginning of reign' of Nabopolassar."[1] The date of this "beginning of reign" or accession of Nabopolassar corresponds to Nov 23, 626 B.C., and the ensuing twenty-one regnal years of Nabopolassar extend from 625/624 to 605/604.[2] British Museum Tablet No. 21901 records the destruction of Nineveh, the great Assyrian capital, by Nabopolassar and his allies (cf. Zph 2:13-15; Nah 3:1-3).[3] This was in the fourteenth year of Nabopolassar, in the month Abu, but the day is missing in a gap in the text. The date was therefore sometime in Jul/Aug 612 B.C.

⟨ 311. In the western city of Haran a remnant of Assyrian empire was maintained a few years longer by Ashur-uballit II (611-608 B.C.). British Museum Tablet No. 21901 records that in his sixteenth year (610/609 B.C.) Nabopolassar drove Ashur-uballit out of Haran; in the next year (609/608) between Duzu (Jun/Jul) and Ululu (Aug/Sep) Ashur-uballit and "a large army of Egypt" tried to reconquer Haran.[4] The "army of Egypt" is probably the

[1] WCCK pp.50f., cf. 7, 93.　　　　[2] PDBC p.27.
[3] ARAB II, §§1177f.; ANET p.304; ANEA p.202.
[4] ARAB II, §1183; ANET p.305; ANEA p.202.

expeditionary force of Pharaoh Necho II (609-595) mentioned also in II K 23:29 and II Ch 35:21, which King Josiah tried vainly to oppose at Megiddo. The purpose of Necho was evidently to assist the Assyrians and resist the New Babylonians; the intent of Josiah was to keep help from reaching the Assyrians, the old enemy of Judah. The death of Josiah in his ill-fated attempt is to be dated shortly before Duzu (Jun/Jul) in the seventeenth year of Nabopolassar, that is approximately in Simanu = May/Jun 609 B.C.[5]

⟪312.   The Egyptians stayed in the north for some years. British Museum Tablet No. 22047 reports that in the twentieth year of Nabopolassar (606/605 B.C.) they successfully attacked a Babylonian garrison in the city of Kimuhu on the Euphrates.[6] British Museum Tablet No. 21946 tells how, in the twenty-first year of Nabopolassar (605/604), the Babylonian king sent his son Nebuchadrezzar against the Egyptians. Nebuchadrezzar met the Egyptian army in Carchemish on the bank of the Euphrates, accomplished their defeat, and conquered the whole area of "the Hatti-country." In the record of Nebuchadrezzar's seventh year, soon to be quoted (¶319), "the Hatti-land" includes "the city of Judah," therefore the term is a general designation for Syria-Palestine. Soon after the victory at Carchemish and in the Hatti-country, Nebuchadrezzar learned that his father had died and returned to Babylon to ascend the throne. The chronicle puts the death of Nabopolassar on Abu 8 = Aug 15, and the accession of Nebuchadrezzar on Ululu 1 = Sep 7, 605 B.C. The crucial battle of Carchemish must have taken place between Nisanu 1 (= Apr 12) when Nabopolassar's twenty-first year began and Abu 8 (= Aug 15) when he died, therefore in the late spring or early summer, say perhaps in Simanu (May/Jun), 605 B.C. The accession year of Nebuchadrezzar extended from Ululu 1 = Sep 7, 605, to the end of the current calendar year. His first regnal year began on the next Nisanu 1 = Apr 2, 604 (cf. Table 10). In his first regnal year (604/603) in the month Simanu (May/Jun) the new king of Babylon returned to the West to cement his supremacy, and "all the kings of the Hatti-land came before him and he received their heavy tribute."[7]

⟪313.   According to the contemporary prophet Jeremiah, the battle of Carchemish took place in the fourth year of King Jehoiakim

<hr/>

[5] Tadmor in JNES 15 (1956), pp.228f.   [6] WCCK p.67.
[7] WCCK pp.67-69, cf. 25.

of Judah (Jer 46:2).[8] The assumption has already been noted that in Judah the regnal year was reckoned in terms of the old calendar year which began in the fall in the month of Tishri (¶301), and that the accession-year system was in use from Jehoash to Hoshea (¶302). Confirmation of reckoning by the fall year is found as late as in the eighteenth year of King Josiah. In his eighteenth year (II K 22:3) the "book of the law" was found in the house of the Lord (II K 22:8) and in the selfsame eighteenth year the passover was celebrated (II K 23:23). The numerous intervening events between the finding of the law book and the observance of the passover could hardly have been concentrated within the two weeks between Nisan 1 and Nisan 14 as would have been necessary if Josiah's eighteenth year had only begun on Nisan 1; therefore his eighteenth year must have begun the preceding Tishri 1. We have dated the death of Josiah at Megiddo approximately in Simanu (May/Jun) 609 B.C. (¶311). After him the people put on the throne his son Jehoahaz, and the latter reigned three months (II K 23:31). These three months were therefore approximately Sivan (Babylonian Simanu) = May/Jun, Tammuz (Duzu) = Jun/Jul, and Ab (Abu) = Jul/Aug. Pharaoh Necho then deposed Jehoahaz and installed Eliakim, son of Josiah, in the kingship, changing his name to Jehoiakim, and he reigned for eleven years (II K 23:36). The accession year of Jehoiakim was, therefore, approximately the month of Elul (Ululu) = Aug/Sep, and his first regnal year began on the first of Tishri (Tashritu) = Sep/Oct. The transition in reign from Josiah to Jehoahaz and to Jehoiakim and the early years of reign of Jehoiakim may therefore be shown in Table 90. The battle of Carchemish took place in the late spring or early summer, perhaps in Simanu (Sivan = May/Jun 605 B.C. (¶312). This was in fact in the fourth year of King Jehoiakim as stated in Jer 46:2.

¶ 314. We have already seen (¶312) that Nebuchadrezzar returned to Babylon soon after the battle of Carchemish and there ascended the throne on Ululu 1 = Sep 7, 605 B.C. His accession year extended from that date to the end of the then current calendar year; his first regnal year began on the next Nisanu 1 = Apr 2, 604 B.C. As shown in our Table 90, the fourth year of Jehoiakim

[8] Cf. Josephus, *Ant.* x, 84 (= x, vi, 1).

TABLE 90. The Transition from Josiah to Jehoahaz and to Jehoiakim
and the Early Years of Reign of Jehoiakim

Josiah: Died approximately	Sivan (May/Jun) 609 B.C.
Jehoahaz: Three months reign, approximately	Sivan (May/Jun)
	Tammuz (Jun/Jul)
	Ab (Jul/Aug)
Jehoiakim: Accession year, approximately	Elul (Aug/Sep)
Year 1	Tishri (Sep/Oct) 609 –
	Elul (Aug/Sep) 608
Year 2	Tishri (Sep/Oct) 608 –
	Elul (Aug/Sep) 607
Year 3	Tishri (Sep/Oct) 607 –
	Elul (Aug/Sep) 606
Year 4	Tishri (Sep/Oct) 606 –
	Elul (Aug/Sep) 605

includes the battle of Carchemish, in agreement with Jer 46:2, and
also the accession of Nebuchadrezzar. But Jer 25:1 also mentions
the fourth year of Jehoiakim and says, in the usual translation,
"that was the first year of Nebuchadrezzar king of Babylon" (RSV).
That is manifestly incorrect, at least according to our results in
Table 90, for the fourth year of Jehoiakim does not include the
first regnal year of Nebuchadrezzar, i.e., 604/603 B.C. In Hebrew
the words are השנה הראשנית, *hashshanah haroshniyt*. The phrase
is not found elsewhere but we recognize, modifying the word "year,"
the feminine singular form of the adjective which can mean either
"first" or "beginning." Since a related noun is used in the standard
designation of an accession year (¶302), the phrase in Jer 25:1
probably also means the "beginning year," i.e., the accession year,
of Nebuchadrezzar.[9] Accepting this as the correct translation, the
synchronism in Jer 25:1 is correct and in agreement with that in
Jer 46:2. The fourth year of Jehoiakim included the battle of Carchemish and the accession of Nebuchadrezzar to the throne of Babylon.

¶ 315.   The first regnal year of Nebuchadrezzar was 604/603 B.C.
and in that year in the month Simanu, i.e., in May/Jun 604 B.C.,
he returned to the Hatti-land and received the tribute of all the kings
of that region (¶312). Jehoiakim was probably among the kings
making submission at that time (II K 24:1). At that time and

[9] Cf. Albright in JBL 51 (1932), p.102.

in connection with that submission Jehoiakim may very well have accepted the Babylonian calendar.[10] As late as the eighteenth year of Josiah the old Israelite year was still in use and the regnal year began in the fall (¶313), and the same was probably true up to the present point in the reign of Jehoiakim. But with the acceptance of the Babylonian calendar the regnal year would begin in the spring. In view of the return of Nebuchadrezzar to the Hatti-land in Simanu = May/Jun 604 B.C. the submission of the kings, including Jehoiakim, was probably approximately in Duzu = Tammuz = Jun/Jul 604. At this time Jehoiakim was in his fifth year of reign (cf. Table 90). By the old system, this fifth year would have ended in the fall of 604. With the adoption of the new system the fifth regnal year was presumably extended to the following spring, i.e., to the spring of 603. In accordance with this reconstruction of events, the regnal years of Jehoiakim at the point of the calendrical change and immediately following may be shown in Table 91.

TABLE 91. THE REGNAL YEARS OF JEHOIAKIM WHEN THE BABYLONIAN CALENDAR WAS ADOPTED AND IMMEDIATELY FOLLOWING

Year 5	Tishri (Sep/Oct) 605 — Adar (Feb/Mar) 603
Year 6	Nisan (Mar/Apr) 603 — Adar (Feb/Mar) 602
Year 7	Nisan (Mar/Apr) 602 — Adar (Feb/Mar) 601
Year 8	Nisan (Mar/Apr) 601 — Adar (Feb/Mar) 600

([316. In the narrative of the eighteenth year of Josiah in II K chapters 22-23 the sequence of events required the assumption of the old Israelite year beginning in the fall (¶313). In the narrative of the fifth year of Jehoiakim (Jer 36) the sequence of events just as plainly requires the assumption of the new Babylonian year beginning in the spring. Here in the fifth year of Jehoiakim (Jer 36:9) the ninth month falls in the winter (Jer 36:22) as it would only in a calendar year reckoned from the spring. This first employment at this point in historical narrative of the year beginning in the spring is confirmatory of the theory that Jehoiakim adopted the Babylonian calendar in his fifth year of reign.

([317. By the reconstruction thus adopted (Table 91) the eighth year of Jehoiakim was identical with the fourth year of Nebuchad-

[10] Auerbach in VT 9 (1959), pp.113-121.

rezzar, 601/600 B.C. In his fourth year, according to British Museum Tablet No. 21946, Nebuchadrezzar suffered a virtual defeat on the borders of Egypt.[11] According to II K 24:1 Jehoiakim was the servant of the king of Babylon for three years, then turned and rebelled against him. By our reconstruction, the three years of servitude were Jehoiakim's Years 5, 6, and 7, and the act of rebellion would have fallen in Year 8. This was precisely the time when Nebuchadrezzar was defeated in Egypt and it may well be supposed that that defeat was the event which caused Jehoiakim to venture upon rebellion. The venture was, of course, ultimately disastrous to Jehoiakim and Judah.

⟪ 318.   According to II K 23:36 and II Ch 36:5 Jehoiakim reigned eleven years. Continuing the foregoing tabulation (Tables 90, 91) the remaining years of his reign were:

TABLE 92. THE LAST YEARS OF THE REIGN OF JEHOIAKIM

Year 9	Nisan (Mar/Apr)	600 — Adar (Feb/Mar)	599
Year 10	Nisan (Mar/Apr)	599 — Adar (Feb/Mar)	598
Year 11	Nisan (Mar/Apr)	598 — Adar (Feb/Mar)	597

⟪ 319.   The eleventh year of Jehoiakim corresponds with the seventh year of Nebuchadrezzar, 598/597 B.C. British Museum Tablet No. 21946 records:

"In the seventh year, the month of Kislimu, the king of Akkad mustered his troops, marched to the Hatti-land, and encamped against the city of Judah and on the second day of the month of Addaru he seized the city and captured the king. He appointed there a king of his own choice, received its heavy tribute and sent them to Babylon."[12]

The "city of Judah" must be Jerusalem and this, accordingly, is the Babylonian record of the first fall of Jerusalem to Nebuchadrezzar, corresponding to the account in II K chapter 24. The seventh year of Nebuchadrezzar began on Nisanu 1 (= Mar 27), 598 B.C. The month of Kislimu began on Dec 18, 598. The second day of the month of Addaru was Mar 16, 597 B.C. The last is the exact date of the first fall of Jerusalem to Nebuchadrezzar.

[11] WCCK p.71.   [12] WCCK p.73.

❪ 320.   When Jerusalem fell, Jehoiachin, young son of Jehoiakim, was king. He had reigned three months (II K 24:8) or, more exactly, three months and ten days (II Ch 36:9). Therefore Jehoiakim had died (II K 24:6) or otherwise been removed from the throne (II Ch 36:6; Jer 22:19; 36:30)[13] on Arahsamnu (Heshvan) 22 = Dec 9, 598 B.C.

❪ 321.   According to II Ch 36:10 the capture of Jerusalem and deportation of Jehoiachin took place "in the spring of the year" (RSV) or "at the turn of the year" (Berkeley Version). The Hebrew used here, לתשובת השנה, *litshubat hashshanah*, probably means the time shortly before the end of the year and agrees exactly with the date in Addaru, the last month of the calendar year, given by the Babylonian chronicle (¶319).[14]

❪ 322.   The Babylonian chronicle (¶319) states that in place of the king he captured in the city of Judah Nebuchadrezzar appointed there a king of his own choice. The latter must have been the uncle (II K 24:17) or brother (II Ch 36:10) of Jehoiachin, Mattaniah, whose name was changed to Zedekiah. Zedekiah's accession year was the balance of the month in which Nebuchadrezzar installed him in his position, i.e., from Adar 2 (= Mar 16, 597 B.C.) to the end of the same month; his first regnal year began with the beginning of the new calendar year, i.e., with Nisan 1 (= Apr 13, 597). In all he reigned eleven years (II K 24:18; II Ch 36:11). The transition to his reign and his own regnal years may be shown, therefore, as in Table 93. These years correspond to a number of the years of Nebuchadrezzar shown in Table 10, and the same form of the Babylonian calendar is assumed with its intercalated months and observationally determined dates of Nisanu 1.[15]

❪ 323.   In the biblical records of the second siege and fall of Jerusalem, exact dates are given in terms of the reign of Zedekiah. If the reconstruction of his regnal years set forth in Table 93 is correct, these dates may be translated as follows. II K 25:1 states that the siege began in the ninth year of Zedekiah, in the tenth month, on the tenth day of the month; and Jer 39:1 gives the same information, lacking the day. This date was equivalent to Jan 15, 588 B.C.

13 Cf. Josephus, *Ant.* x, 97 (= x, vi, 3).
14 Noth in ZDPV 74 (1958), pp.133-157.
15 PDBC pp.27-28.

TABLE 93. THE TRANSITION TO THE REIGN OF ZEDEKIAH AND THE REGNAL YEARS OF ZEDEKIAH

Removal of Jehoiakim and accession of Jehoiachin	Heshvan 22 = Dec 9, 598 B.C.
Fall of Jerusalem and capture of Jehoiachin	Adar 2 = Mar 16, 597

Zedekiah

Accession year	Adar	2 = Mar 16, 597, to Adar 29 = Apr 12, 597
Year 1	Nisan	1 = Apr 13, 597, to Adar 29 = Apr 2, 596
Year 2	Nisan	1 = Apr 3, 596, to Adar 29 = Apr 21, 595
Year 3	Nisan	1 = Apr 22, 595, to Adar 30 = Apr 11, 594
Year 4	Nisan	1 = Apr 12, 594, to Adar II 30 = Apr 29, 593
Year 5	Nisan	1 = Apr 30, 593, to Adar 29 = Apr 18, 592
Year 6	Nisan	1 = Apr 19, 592, to Adar 29 = Apr 7, 591
Year 7	Nisan	1 = Apr 8, 591, to Adar II 30 = Apr 26, 590
Year 8	Nisan	1 = Apr 27, 590, to Adar 30 = Apr 14, 589
Year 9	Nisan	1 = Apr 15, 589, to Adar 29 = Apr 3, 588
Year 10	Nisan	1 = Apr 4, 588, to Adar II 29 = Apr 22, 587
Year 11	Nisan	1 = Apr 23, 587, to Adar 29 = Apr 12, 586

Jer 32:1-2 states that the siege was still in progress and the prophet Jeremiah was in custody in the tenth year of Zedekiah. This regnal year was 588/587. II K 25:2-4 and Jer 39:2 record that a breach was made in the city in the eleventh year of Zedekiah, in the fourth month, on the ninth day. This was Jul 29, 587. On the seventh day of the fifth month according to II K 25:8, or on the tenth day of the fifth month according to Jer 52:12, Nebuzaradan, servant of Nebuchadrezzar, came and burned Jerusalem and the Temple. These dates were Aug 25 and 28, 587 B.C.

❰ 324.   According to the foregoing reconstruction of events (¶¶314ff.) Jehoiakim adjusted his regnal year to the Babylonian calendar in the fifth year of his reign and from then on the regnal years of the kings of Judah were reckoned by the same calendar year as the regnal years of the king of Babylon. The correspondence implied in our reconstruction (cf. Tables 91, 92, 93) is shown in Table 94.

TABLE 94. THE REGNAL YEARS OF THE LAST KINGS OF JUDAH
IN EQUATION WITH THE REGNAL YEARS OF NEBUCHADREZZAR

Kings of Judah	King of Babylon	B.C.
Jehoiakim	Nebuchadrezzar	
6	2	603/602
7	3	602/601
8	4	601/600
9	5	600/599
10	6	599/598
11		
Jehoiachin		
Three months and ten days	7	598/597
Zedekiah		
Accession year		
1	8	597/596
2	9	596/595
3	10	595/594
4	11	594/593
5	12	593/592
6	13	592/591
7	14	591/590
8	15	590/589
9	16	589/588
10	17	588/587
11	18	587/586

⟨[325. The correspondences indicated in the foregoing tabulation (Table 94) place the first fall of Jerusalem at the end of the brief reign of Jehoiachin in the seventh year of Nebuchadrezzar, and the second fall in the eleventh year of Zedekiah in the eighteenth year of Nebuchadrezzar. That the first fall took place in the seventh year of Nebuchadrezzar is established by the Babylonian chronicle (¶319) and in our reconstruction the biblical data point to the same date. That the second fall took place in the eighteenth year of Nebuchadrezzar follows from the equation of regnal years of Zedekiah and of Nebuchadrezzar shown in Table 94. British Museum Tablet No. 21946 itself, however, which began with the twenty-first year of Nabopolassar and provided the exact date of the first fall, extends only to the eleventh year of Nebuchadrezzar, hence ceases too soon to give the date of the second fall. For this reason the date of the second fall (¶323) is not yet as well estab-

lished as that of the first, yet appears highly probable. The first fall
was in the seventh year of Nebuchadrezzar, on Mar 16, 597 B.C.—
this appears to be an exact date. The second fall was in the eighteenth
year of Nebuchadrezzar, the city being breached on Jul 29 and
burned between Aug 25 and 28, 587 B.C.—these dates are very
probable.

⟨ 326.   A historical notice preserved in Jer 52:28-30 gives the
number of people whom Nebuchadrezzar carried away captive on
three occasions: in the seventh year, in the eighteenth year, and in
the twenty-third year. The last occasion (the twenty-third year =
582/581 B.C.) may have been in punishment for disturbances in
connection with the assassination of Gedaliah (II K 25:25). The
first two occasions in the seventh and in the eighteenth years correspond with the dates of the first fall and the second fall of Jerusalem as just established (¶325).

⟨ 327.   Thus far we have spoken of the regnal years of Nebuchadrezzar in terms of the standard Babylonian accession-year system.
By the nonaccession-year system (which would consider the time
from his accession on Ululu 1 = Sep 7, 605 B.C. to Addaru 30 =
Apr 1, 604, as already his first year, and the new year beginning
Nisanu 1 = Apr 2, 604, as his second year) the seventh and eighteenth years of Nebuchadrezzar (as we have spoken of them hither-
to) would be counted as his eighth and nineteenth years respectively. In II K 24:12 the first fall of Jerusalem is put in the eighth
year of Nebuchadrezzar; in II K 25:8 the second fall is placed in
his nineteenth year. The latter date is also repeated in Jer 52:12,
but Jer chapter 52 (with the exception of verses 28-30 which are
recognizably separate and are also omitted in the LXX) is almost
identical with II K 24:18-25:30 and probably derived from it or
from the same source as it. In general, therefore, these references
to the "eighth year" and the "nineteenth year" probably represent
a view of Nebuchadrezzar's regnal years in terms of something like
a nonaccession-year system. In particular they may represent a method of citing Nebuchadrezzar's regnal years which was used in Syria-
Palestine where it was considered that he was already king (since
he was really acting in that capacity) when he came for the battle
of Carchemish (¶312) in 605 B.C. and where, accordingly, 605/604

was counted as his first regnal year rather than 604/603.[16] But what in this Syrian-Palestinian usage were called the eighth and nineteenth years of Nebuchadrezzar were in standard Babylonian usage his seventh and eighteenth years.[17]

5. THE EXILE OF JEHOIACHIN

LITERATURE: Ernst F. Weidner, "Jojachin, König von Juda, in babylonischen Keilschrifttexten," in *Mélanges Syriens offerts a Monsieur René Dussaud.* II, 1939, pp.923-927; W. F. Albright, "King Joiachin in Exile," in BA 5 (1942), pp.49-55.

¶ 328.   Nebuchadrezzar took Jerusalem the first time on Addaru 2 = Mar 16, 597 B.C. (¶317), and carried the young king Jehoiachin into captivity from Jerusalem to Babylon (II K 24:15). The time was shortly before the end of the year (*litshubat hashshanah*) (¶319). Therefore the first full year of the exile of Jehoiachin began with the ensuing Nisan 1 = Apr 13, 597, and extended to Adar 29 = Apr 2, 596. This and the subsequent years of the exile of Jehoiachin up to the thirty-seventh may be shown in brief as in Table 95, the year in each case being understood to extend from the first day of Nisan to the last day of Adar.

TABLE 95. THE YEARS OF EXILE OF JEHOIACHIN

Fall of Jerusalem and deportation of Jehoiachin, Addaru 2 = Mar 16, 597 B.C.
Full Years of Exile

1.	597/596	14.	584/583	27.	571/570
2.	596/595	15.	583/582	28.	570/569
3.	595/594	16.	582/581	29.	569/568
4.	594/593	17.	581/580	30.	568/567
5.	593/592	18.	580/579	31.	567/566
6.	592/591	19.	579/578	32.	566/565
7.	591/590	20.	578/577	33.	565/564
8.	590/589	21.	577/576	34.	564/563
9.	589/588	22.	576/575	35.	563/562
10.	588/587	23.	575/574	36.	562/561
11.	587/586	24.	574/573	37.	561/560
12.	586/585	25.	573/572		
13.	585/584	26.	572/571		

[16] Noth in ZDPV 74 (1958), pp.133-157.
[17] For a discussion of other possibilities of interpretation see FLP pp.590ff.

¶ 329. According to Table 95 the thirty-seventh year of the exile corresponds to 561/560 B.C. According to II K 25:27 and Jer 52:31 it was in his thirty-seventh year of exile that Jehoiachin was freed from prison and treated kindly at the Babylonian court. This was done by Evil-merodach, or Amel-Marduk, the immediate successor of Nebuchadrezzar. With reference to Evil-merodach the time is given, in the usual translation (RSV), as "in the year that he began to reign" (II K 25:27) or "in the year that he became king" (Jer 52:31), which presumably means his accession year. The Hebrew in the two passages (בשנת מלכו את-ראש, *bishnat malkow 'et-rosh*) is not the same, however, as what we have recognized as the normal designation of an accession year (¶302) or as a special form for the same designation in Jer 25:1 (¶314). Rather the present phrase is most probably to be translated as James Moffatt does, "in the first year of his reign."[1] The synchronism, therefore, is between the thirty-seventh year of the exile of Jehoiachin and the first regnal year of Amel-Marduk. As far as available cuneiform evidence is concerned,[2] the last tablet dated in the reign of Nebuchadrezzar is from Uruk with the date Ululu 26 in his forty-third year, which is equivalent to Oct 8, 562 B.C. The first tablet dated to Amel-Marduk is perhaps from Sippar and has the same date equivalent to Oct 8, 562. The death of Nebuchadrezzar and the accession of Amel-Marduk were therefore in the early days of Oct 562. Therefore the accession year of Amel-Marduk was 562/561, and the first year of his reign was 561/560. The synchronism of Jehoiachin's thirty-seventh year of captivity and Amel-Marduk's first regnal year is correct and indicates 561/560 B.C. In this year the lifting up of Jehoiachin took place in the twelfth month, on the twenty-seventh day according to II K 25:27, or on the twenty-fifth day according to Jer 52:31. The dates are respectively Mar 23 or Mar 21, 560 B.C.

6. THE DATES IN EZEKIEL

LITERATURE: Julius A. Bewer, "Das Datum in Hes 33:21," in ZAW 54 (1936), pp.114-115; C. F. Whitley, "The 'Thirtieth' Year in Ezekiel I, 1," in VT 9 (1959), pp.326-330.

¶ 330. Ezk 1:2 refers to the fifth year of the exile of King Jehoiachin, and a series of dates follows in the same book (8:1; 20:1;

[1] Cf. Albright in JBL 51 (1932), pp.101-102.
[2] PDBC p.12.

24:1; 26:1; 29:1, 17; 30:21; 31:1; 32:1, 17; 33:21; 40:1) which are evidently stated likewise in terms of the years of Jehoiachin's exile. We have already made a tabulation of the years of exile of Jehoiachin (Table 95) from the point of view of the history at the time he was carried into captivity. There we considered that his years of exile ran parallel, at the outset, with the regnal years of Zedekiah (Table 94), his successor in Jerusalem. Here we may check several of Ezekiel's dates to see if they are in harmony with the results already obtained.

❴331.   Referring presumably to the exile of Jehoiachin, Ezk 24:1 dates the beginning of the siege of Jerusalem by the king of Babylon in the ninth year, in the tenth month, on the tenth day of the month. Exactly the same date is given in II K 25:1 and Jer 39:1 (where the day is lacking) in terms of the regnal years of Zedekiah. The references agree, and the date is Jan 15, 588 B.C. (¶323).

❴332.   The second and final fall of Jerusalem to Nebuchadrezzar was probably on Jul 29, 587 B.C. (¶¶323, 325). Ezk 33:21 tells how a man who had escaped from Jerusalem came to Ezekiel and told him that the city had fallen. In the Hebrew text represented by the RSV translation the date is "in the twelfth year of our exile, in the tenth month, on the fifth day of the month." This would give the date of Jan 8, 585 B.C., and would mean that the fugitive took about one and one-half years to get to Babylon, which is manifestly incorrect. In a number of Hebrew, Greek, and Syriac manuscripts, however, the date is in the eleventh year, in the tenth month, on the fifth day of the month. This gives the date of Jan 19, 586, and allows somewhat less than six months for the journey. Under the disturbed conditions undoubtedly prevailing, this compares not unfavorably with the full four months required by Ezra for a journey under peaceful circumstances (Ezr 7:9) (¶336).

❴333.   Ezk 40:1 gives a date "in the twenty-fifth year of our exile, at the beginning of the year, on the tenth day of the month, in the fourteenth year after the city was conquered, on that very day." The phrase "at the beginning of the year" (בראש השנה, berosh hashshanah) must mean the first month, hence the date in terms of the exile is Year 25, Month 1, Day 10. By our reckoning (Table 95) this is equivalent to Apr 28, 573 B.C. The date stated in terms of the exile is equated with "the fourteenth year after the city was captured." Since Jerusalem was captured the second time by Nebuchadrezzar on Jul 29, 587 B.C. (¶¶323, 325), the first factual year "after the city was captured" was Jul 29, 587-Jul 28, 586. By the same reckoning the fourteenth year after the capture was Jul 29, 574-Jul 28, 573. The date of Apr 28, 573, falls in this "fourteenth year." The mention of "that very day" is simply a reference back to Year 25 (in terms of the exilic dating), Month 1, Day 10, the important day when the prophet experienced the important vision related in Chapter 40.

7. POST-EXILIC DATES

LITERATURE: R. P. Dougherty, *Nabonidus and Belshazzar.* 1929; Norman H. Snaith, "The Date of Ezra's Arrival in Jerusalem," in ZAW 63 (1951), pp.53-66; H. H. Rowley, "The Chronological Order of Ezra and Nehemiah," in *The Servant of the Lord and Other Essays on the Old Testament.* 1952, pp.131-159; Kurt Galling, "Von Naboned zu Darius," in ZDPV 69 (1953), pp.42-64; 70 (1954), pp.4-32; Peter R. Ackroyd, "Two Old Testament Historical Problems of the Early Persian Period," in JNES 17 (1958), pp.13-27; J. Morgenstern, "The dates of Ezra and Nehemiah," in JSS 7 (1962), pp.1-11.

❨ 334.   The fall of Babylon to Cyrus the Persian led to the return of the Jewish exiles to their homeland. The fall of Babylon is recorded in a cuneiform document known as the Nabonidus Chronicle.[1] Referring to the seventeenth and last year of King Nabunaid (Nabonidus) of Babylon, this source gives dates which may be summarized, with their equivalents, as follows: The Persian forces took Sippar on Tashritu 14 = Oct 10, 539 B.C.; they took Babylon on Tashritu 16 = Oct 12; and Cyrus entered the city on Arahsamnu 3 = Oct 29. The decree allowing the exiles to return to Jerusalem was published in the first year of Cyrus (II Ch 36:22; Ezr 1:1; 6:3). His first official year as king of Babylon was 538/537.

❨ 335.   In the second year of Darius the rebuilding of the Temple was resumed (Ezr 4:24). The second regnal year of Darius I was 520/519 B.C. In that year in the sixth month, on the first day of the month, the prophet Haggai exhorted Zerubbabel to rebuild the house of the Lord (Hag 1:1f.). This date was Aug 29, 520. The beginning of the work was in the sixth month, on the twenty-fourth day

[1] ANET pp.305f.; ANEA pp.203f.

of the month (Hag 1:15). This was Sep 21, 520. In the same year in the eighth month the first address of Zechariah was given (Zec 1:1). This was in Oct/Nov 520. The completion of the rebuilding of the Temple was on the third day of the month of Adar in the sixth year of the reign of Darius (Ezr 6:15). The date was Mar 12, 515.

¶ 336.   Ezra went to Jerusalem in the seventh year of Artaxerxes (Ezr 7:1, 8-9). If this was Artaxerxes I, the year was 458/457 B.C. Departure from Babylon on the first day of the first month was on Apr 8, 458; arrival in Jerusalem on the first day of the fifth month was on Aug 4, 458. Nehemiah obtained permission to return to Jerusalem in the month of Nisan, in the twentieth year of Artaxerxes (Neh 2:1). If this was Artaxerxes I, the year was 445/444 B.C. In that year the first day of the month of Nisan was Apr 13, 445. Under Nehemiah the wall of Jerusalem was finished on the twenty-fifth day of the month Elul, fifty-two days after the task was started (Neh 6:15). The completion date was Oct 2, 445 B.C.

III. THE NEW TESTAMENT

A. THE LIFE OF JESUS

LITERATURE: Urbanus Holzmeister, *Chronologia Vitae Christi*. 1933; Damianus Lazzarato, *Chronologia Christi seu discordantium fontium concordantia ad juris normam*. 1952.

1. THE BIRTH OF JESUS

(1) CAESAR AUGUSTUS

¶ 337. According to Lk 2:1 Jesus was born under the rule of Caesar Augustus, but the year is not given. Early Christian sources give specific years of Augustus, but the way in which the years are reckoned is not always evident. There are in fact various possibilities. In our earlier Table 39 chief events and honors in the life and reign of Augustus were shown. In Table 96 a preliminary numbering of regnal years is given, following three possible starting points. Julius Caesar died on the Ides of March, i.e., Mar 15, in A.U.C. 710 = 44 B.C., and Octavian, his grand-nephew and adopted heir, succeeded him. Regnal years beginning with that date are numbered in Column 1, and with the first full year after that date in Column 2. Octavian defeated Antony at Actium on Sep 2 in A.U.C. 723 = 31 B.C. Years beginning with that date are numbered in Column 3. Antony and Cleopatra died sometime in the month of August in A.U.C. 724 = 30 B.C., and this date was presumably determinative of the beginning of the reign of Augustus in Egypt. Regnal years beginning with this date are numbered in Column 4, and with the first full year after that date in Column 5.

TABLE 96. REGNAL YEARS OF CAESAR OCTAVIAN AUGUSTUS

A.U.C.	B.C.		Col. 1	Col. 2	Col. 3	Col. 4	Col. 5
710	44	Mar 15, death of Julius Caesar	1				
711	43		2	1			
712	42		3	2			
713	41		4	3			
714	40		5	4			
715	39		6	5			
716	38		7	6			
717	37		8	7			
718	36		9	8			
719	35		10	9			

A.U.C.	B.C.		Col. 1	Col. 2	Col. 3	Col. 4	Col. 5
720	34		11	10			
721	33		12	11			
722	32		13	12			
723	31	Sep 2, defeat of Antony at Actium	14	13	1		
724	30	Aug, death of Antony and Cleopatra	15	14	2	1	
725	29		16	15	3	2	1
726	28		17	16	4	3	2
727	27		18	17	5	4	3
728	26		19	18	6	5	4
729	25		20	19	7	6	5
730	24		21	20	8	7	6
731	23		22	21	9	8	7
732	22		23	22	10	9	8
733	21		24	23	11	10	9
734	20		25	24	12	11	10
735	19		26	25	13	12	11
736	18		27	26	14	13	12
737	17		28	27	15	14	13
738	16		29	28	16	15	14
739	15		30	29	17	16	15
740	14		31	30	18	17	16
741	13		32	31	19	18	17
742	12		33	32	20	19	18
743	11		34	33	21	20	19
744	10		35	34	22	21	20
745	9		36	35	23	22	21
746	8		37	36	24	23	22
747	7		38	37	25	24	23
748	6		39	38	26	25	24
749	5		40	39	27	26	25
750	4		41	40	28	27	26
751	3		42	41	29	28	27
752	2		43	42	30	29	28
753	1		44	43	31	30	29
754	A.D. 1		45	44	32	31	30
755	2		46	45	33	32	31
756	3		47	46	34	33	32
757	4		48	47	35	34	33
758	5		49	48	36	35	34
759	6		50	49	37	36	35
760	7		51	50	38	37	36
761	8		52	51	39	38	37
762	9		53	52	40	39	38
763	10		54	53	41	40	39
764	11		55	54	42	41	40

A.U.C.	B.C.		Col. 1	Col. 2	Col. 3	Col. 4	Col. 5
765	12		56	55	43	42	41
766	13		57	56	44	43	42
767	14	Aug 19, death of Augustus	58	57	45	44	43

⟨338. Referring to Columns 1 and 2 of Table 96 and counting from the death of Julius Caesar on Mar 15, 44 B.C., to the death of Augustus on Aug 19, A.D. 14, it would appear that Augustus had a factual reign of fifty-seven years, five months, and four days. The fact that reckoning was actually made in this way is shown by Josephus, who states that Augustus reigned fifty-seven years, six months, and two days.[1] The figure of six months can hardly be correct and may occur in the present text of Josephus because some copyist confused the Greek numeral five (ε′) for the numeral six (ς′). The figure of two days, on the other hand, is probably more precise than the four days of our preliminary reckoning for the will of Julius Caesar was not opened until Mar 17 and that date therefore, rather than Mar 15, should probably be taken as the starting point of the reign.[2] Fifty-seven years, five months, and two days is, accordingly, the factual length of the reign of Augustus in Rome, and his factual regnal years were as indicated in Table 97.

⟨339. Similarly, referring to Columns 4 and 5 of Table 96 and counting from the death of Antony and Cleopatra in August, 30 B.C., to the death of Augustus on Aug 19, A.D. 14, it would appear that Augustus had a factual reign in Egypt of very close to forty-three years. The forty-second year of his reign is mentioned in Oxyrhynchus Papyrus No. 2277 ([ἔτους] μβ Καίσαρος). The factual regnal years would be as shown in Table 98. Since the exact day in August which was taken as the beginning of the reign is unknown it is possible only to show each regnal year as extending from an undetermined date in August of one year to an undetermined date in August of the next year. If the exact beginning date of the regnal year in the month of August was later than Aug 19 (the date of the death of Augustus in the year 14), then the forty-third regnal year was that much short of a full year; if the exact beginning date of the regnal year was prior to Aug 19, then the forty-third regnal

[1] War. II, 168 (= II, ix, 1); Ant. XVIII, 32 (= XVIII, ii, 2).
[2] LCL, Josephus II, p.388 note a.

year came to a close and there were some additional days before Aug 19. In reading the table observe, therefore, that "Aug, 30-Aug, 29 B.C.," means from an undetermined date in the month of August in the year 30 B.C. to an undetermined date in the month of August in the year 29 B.C., and so on; but at the end "Aug, 13-Aug 19, A.D. 14," means from an undetermined date in the month of August in the year A.D. 13 to the exact date of Aug 19 in the year A.D. 14.

TABLE 97. FACTUAL REGNAL YEARS
OF AUGUSTUS IN ROME

Number of Regnal Year	Duration of Regnal Year
1	Mar 17, 44 – Mar 16, 43 B.C.
2	Mar 17, 43 – Mar 16, 42
....	....
36	Mar 17, 9 – Mar 16, 8
37	Mar 17, 8 – Mar 16, 7
38	Mar 17, 7 – Mar 16, 6
39	Mar 17, 6 – Mar 16, 5
40	Mar 17, 5 – Mar 16, 4
41	Mar 17, 4 – Mar 16, 3
42	Mar 17, 3 – Mar 16, 2
43	Mar 17, 2 – Mar 16, 1
44	Mar 17, 1 B.C. – Mar 16, A.D. 1
45	Mar 17, A.D. 1 – Mar 16, 2
....	....
56	Mar 17, 12 – Mar 16, 13
57	Mar 17, 13 – Mar 16, 14
Additional Months and Days	Mar 17, 14 – Aug 19, 14

¶ 340. Instead of counting factual regnal years, however, it was also possible as we have seen (¶163) to reckon regnal years as equivalents of calendar years. To use the Julian calendar in initial example, this would mean counting the regnal year as coterminous with the calendar year which extends from Jan 1 to Dec 31. If the reckoning was by what we have called the nonaccession-year system, the first regnal year of Augustus in Rome comprised the period from Mar 17 to Dec 31, 44 B.C., the second regnal year was the calendar year from Jan 1 to Dec 31, 43 B.C., and so on, in other words Column 1 of Table 96 may be used directly for the reckoning. If the reckoning was by what we have called the accession-year system, the period from Mar 17 to Dec 31, 44 B.C., was only an "accession year," and the first regnal year of Augustus in Rome was the ensuing calendar year, namely the year from Jan 1 to Dec 31, 43 B.C., and so on, in other words Column 2 in Table 96 may be used directly for the reckoning.

TABLE 98. FACTUAL REGNAL YEARS
OF AUGUSTUS IN EGYPT

Number of Regnal Year	Duration of Regnal Year
1	Aug, 30 – Aug, 29 B.C.
2	Aug, 29 – Aug, 28
. . . . . .	. . . . . .
22	Aug, 9 – Aug, 8
23	Aug, 8 – Aug, 7
24	Aug, 7 – Aug, 6
25	Aug, 6 – Aug, 5
26	Aug, 5 – Aug, 4
27	Aug, 4 – Aug, 3
28	Aug, 3 – Aug, 2
29	Aug, 2 – Aug, 1
30	Aug, 1 B.C. – Aug, A.D. 1
31	Aug, A.D. 1 – Aug, 2
. . . . . .	. . . . . .
42	Aug, 12 – Aug, 13
43	Aug, 13 – Aug 19, A.D. 14

([341. In terms of the Julian calendar and the nonaccession-year system, then, the regnal years of Augustus in Rome may be shown as in Table 99.

([342. In terms of the Julian calendar and the accession-year system, the regnal years of Augustus in Rome may be shown as in Table 100.

([343. In Egypt a reckoning of regnal years as calendar years would presumably have been in terms of the Egyptian calendar.

In its standardized form (Table 8) and in a common year this calendar year began on Thoth 1 = Aug 29. The deaths of Antony and Cleopatra took place at a not precisely determined time in the month of August, 30 B.C., and it may be assumed that it was at least some time prior to Aug 29. Therefore, in terms of the Egyptian

TABLE 99. REGNAL YEARS OF AUGUSTUS COUNTED AS
CALENDAR YEARS OF THE JULIAN CALENDAR
ACCORDING TO THE NONACCESSION-YEAR SYSTEM

Number of Regnal Year	Duration of Regnal Year
1	Mar 17 – Dec 31, 44 B.C.
2	Jan 1 – Dec 31, 43
....	....
36	Jan 1 – Dec 31, 9
37	Jan 1 – Dec 31, 8
38	Jan 1 – Dec 31, 7
39	Jan 1 – Dec 31, 6
40	Jan 1 – Dec 31, 5
41	Jan 1 – Dec 31, 4
42	Jan 1 – Dec 31, 3
43	Jan 1 – Dec 31, 2
44	Jan 1 – Dec 31, 1 B.C.
45	Jan 1 – Dec 31, A.D. 1
46	Jan 1 – Dec 31, 2
....	....
57	Jan 1 – Dec 31, 13
58	Jan 1 – Aug 19, 14

calendar and the nonaccession-year system the regnal years of Augustus must have appeared as in Table 101.

⟨ 344.   In terms of the Egyptian calendar and the accession-year system, the regnal years of Augustus would appear as shown in Table 102.

⟨ 345.   In Syria we believe (¶¶129-130. Table 25) that the Macedonian calendar was used from shortly before the middle of the first century of the Christian era onwards in its later correlation in which the year began on Hyperberetaios 1 = Oct 1. Counted as years of this calendar according to the nonaccession-year system the regnal years of Augustus would be as shown in Table 103.

〔346. In terms of the same Macedonian calendar in Syria but according to the accession-year system the regnal years of Augustus would be as shown in Table 104.

〔347. In the Jewish calendar (Table 13) the year began with the month Nisan, equivalent to Mar/Apr of the Julian calendar. In 44 B.C. when Julius Caesar was killed on Mar 15 and Octavian succeeded him on Mar 17, the first day of Nisan should have fallen

TABLE 100. REGNAL YEARS OF AUGUSTUS COUNTED AS CALENDAR YEARS OF THE JULIAN CALENDAR ACCORDING TO THE ACCESSION-YEAR SYSTEM

Number of Regnal Year	Duration of Regnal Year
Accession Year	Mar 17 – Dec 31, 44 B.C.
1	Jan 1 – Dec 31, 43
2	Jan 1 – Dec 31, 42
....	....
36	Jan 1 – Dec 31, 8
37	Jan 1 – Dec 31, 7
38	Jan 1 – Dec 31, 6
39	Jan 1 – Dec 31, 5
40	Jan 1 – Dec 31, 4
41	Jan 1 – Dec 31, 3
42	Jan 1 – Dec 31, 2
43	Jan 1 – Dec 31, 1 B.C.
44	Jan 1 – Dec 31, A.D. 1
45	Jan 1 – Dec 31, 2
....	....
56	Jan 1 – Dec 31, 13
57	Jan 1 – Aug 19, 14

by lunar observation on Apr 20.[3] By the nonaccession-year system, therefore, the first regnal year of Augustus would have extended from Mar 17 to Apr 19, with his second regnal year beginning on Apr 20, 44 B.C. In the accession-year system the same period, Mar 17 to Apr 19, 44 B.C., would have constituted the "accession year"

[3] PDBC p.44.

and the first regnal year would have begun on Apr 20, 44 B.C. After that, in Tables 105 and 106 to allow for the variation from year to year in the exact date of Nisan 1, we simply show the regnal year as extending from Mar/Apr to Mar/Apr.

TABLE 101. REGNAL YEARS OF AUGUSTUS COUNTED AS CALENDAR YEARS OF THE EGYPTIAN CALENDAR ACCORDING TO THE NONACCESSION-YEAR SYSTEM

Number of Regnal Year	Duration of Regnal Year
1	From the deaths of Antony and Cleopatra sometime in Aug to Aug 28, 30 B.C.
2	Aug 29, 30 – Aug 28, 29
....	....
22	Aug 29, 10 – Aug 28, 9
23	Aug 29, 9 – Aug 28, 8
24	Aug 29, 8 – Aug 28, 7
25	Aug 29, 7 – Aug 28, 6
26	Aug 29, 6 – Aug 28, 5
27	Aug 29, 5 – Aug 28, 4
28	Aug 29, 4 – Aug 28, 3
29	Aug 29, 3 – Aug 28, 2
30	Aug 29, 2 – Aug 28, 1
31	Aug 29, 1 B.C. – Aug 28, A.D. 1
32	Aug 29, A.D. 1 – Aug 28, 2
....	....
42	Aug 29, 11 – Aug 28, 12
43	Aug 29, 12 – Aug 28, 13
44	Aug 29, 13 – Aug 19, 14

⟨ 348.   In the Jewish calendar and according to the accession-year system the regnal years of Augustus would be shown as in Table 106.

⟨ 349.   Writing *Against Heresies* in approximately A.D. 180, Irenaeus states: "Our Lord was born about the forty-first year of the reign of Augustus."[4] Assuming factual regnal years (Table 97) this would be 4/3 B.C.; assuming Julian calendar years it would be either 4 B.C. by the nonaccession-year system (Table 99) or 3 B.C. by the accession-year system (Table 100).

[4] III, xxi, 3.

⟨ 350. In the *Stromata*, written about A.D. 194,[5] Clement of Alexandria says: "And our Lord was born in the twenty-eighth year . . . in the reign of Augustus."[6] In the same passage he also says very precisely: "From the birth of Christ . . . to the death of Commodus are, in all, a hundred and ninety-four years, one month, thir-

TABLE 102. REGNAL YEARS OF AUGUSTUS COUNTED AS CALENDAR YEARS OF THE EGYPTIAN CALENDAR ACCORDING TO THE ACCESSION-YEAR SYSTEM

Number of Regnal Year	Duration of Regnal Year
Accession Year	From the deaths of Antony and Cleopatra sometime in Aug to Aug 28, 30 B.C.
1	Aug 29, 30 – Aug 28, 29
2	Aug 29, 29 – Aug 28, 28
. . .	. . .
22	Aug 29, 9 – Aug 28, 8
23	Aug 29, 8 – Aug 28, 7
24	Aug 29, 7 – Aug 28, 6
25	Aug 29, 6 – Aug 28, 5
26	Aug 29, 5 – Aug 28, 4
27	Aug 29, 4 – Aug 28, 3
28	Aug 29, 3 – Aug 28, 2
29	Aug 29, 2 – Aug 28, 1 B.C.
30	Aug 29, 1 B.C. – Aug 28, A.D. 1
31	Aug 29, A.D. 1 – Aug 28, 2
. . .	. . .
42	Aug 29, 12 – Aug 28, 13
43	Aug 29, 13 – Aug 19, 14

teen days." The emperor Commodus was murdered Dec 31, A.D. 192.[7] From Jan 1, 2 B.C., to Dec 31, A.D. 192, are one hundred and ninety-four years. One month before Jan 1, 2 B.C., is Dec 1, 3 B.C. Thirteen days before that is Nov 18, 3 B.C.[8] This is Clement's date for the birth of Christ. This date was in the twenty-eighth year of the Egyptian reign of Augustus, counting that reign either in factual regnal years (Table 98) or in Egyptian calendar years according to

[5] ANF II, p.168.   [6] I, xxi, 145.   [7] EB 6, p.122.
[8] Holzmeister, *Chronologia Vitae Christi*, p.43.

the accession-year system (Table 102), both of which reckonings are very close together.

〖 351.   In *An Answer to the Jews,* written about A.D. 198,[9] Tertullian makes these statements:[10]

> After Cleopatra, Augustus reigned forty-three years.
> All the years of the empire of Augustus were fifty-six years.
> In the forty-first year of the empire of Augustus, when he has been reigning for twenty-eight years after the death of Cleopatra, the Christ is born.
> And the same Augustus survived, after Christ is born, fifteen years.

TABLE 103. REGNAL YEARS OF AUGUSTUS COUNTED AS CALENDAR YEARS OF THE SYRO-MACEDONIAN CALENDAR ACCORDING TO THE NONACCESSION-YEAR SYSTEM

Number of Regnal Year	Duration of Regnal Year
1	Mar 17 – Sep 30, 44 B.C.
2	Oct 1, 44 – Sep 30, 43
....	....
36	Oct 1, 10 – Sep 30, 9
37	Oct 1, 9 – Sep 30, 8
38	Oct 1, 8 – Sep 30, 7
39	Oct 1, 7 – Sep 30, 6
40	Oct 1, 6 – Sep 30, 5
41	Oct 1, 5 – Sep 30, 4
42	Oct 1, 4 – Sep 30, 3
43	Oct 1, 3 – Sep 30, 2
44	Oct 1, 2 – Sep 30, 1
45	Oct 1, 1 B.C. – Sep 30, A.D. 1
46	Oct 1, 1 – Sep 30, 2
....	....
57	Oct 1, 12 – Sep 30, 13
58	Oct 1, 13 – Aug 19, 14

After the death of Cleopatra Augustus reigned almost exactly forty-three factual years in Egypt (Table 98) as well as forty-three Egyptian calendar years according to the accession-year system (Table 102). In Rome, after the part year in which Julius Caesar died and before the part year in which he himself died, Augustus reigned fifty-

[9] ANF III, p.151 n.1.   [10] Ch. 8.

six full calendar years (Table 100). By the reckoning just indicated (Table 100) the forty-first year of Augustus was the year 3 B.C.; the twenty-eighth Egyptian year (Tables 98 and 102) was 3/2 B.C. After the year 3 B.C. = A.U.C. 751 there were fifteen full years of reign remaining, namely A.U.C. 752-766 or 2 B.C.-A.D. 13 inclusive; after the twenty-eighth Egyptian year there were fifteen years remaining, namely the twenty-ninth to the forty-third inclusive.

TABLE 104. REGNAL YEARS OF AUGUSTUS COUNTED AS CALENDAR YEARS OF THE SYRO-MACEDONIAN CALENDAR ACCORDING TO THE ACCESSION-YEAR SYSTEM

Number of Regnal Year	Duration of Regnal Year
Accession Year	Mar 17 – Sep 30, 44 B.C.
1	Oct 1, 44 – Sep 30, 43
2	Oct 1, 43 – Sep 30, 42
. . . .	
36	Oct 1, 9 – Sep 30, 8
37	Oct 1, 8 – Sep 30, 7
38	Oct 1, 7 – Sep 30, 6
39	Oct 1, 6 – Sep 30, 5
40	Oct 1, 5 – Sep 30, 4
41	Oct 1, 4 – Sep 30, 3
42	Oct 1, 3 – Sep 30, 2
43	Oct 1, 2 – Sep 30, 1
44	Oct 1, 1 B.C. – Sep 30, A.D. 1
45	Oct 1, 1 – Sep 30, 2
. . . .	
56	Oct 1, 12 – Sep 30, 13
57	Oct 1, 13 – Aug 19, 14

❨ 352.   In his *Chronographies* Julius Africanus (A.D. c.170-c.240) (¶235) placed the birth of Christ in A. Ad. 5500 = Ol. 194, 2 = 3/2 B.C., as established above (¶243). His contemporary, Hippolytus of Rome (A.D. c.170-236) also indicates in his *Chronicle* the same date of 3/2 B.C., although in his scheme this is shown as the Year 5502 from Adam (¶245).

❨ 353.   Origen (A.D. c.185-c.253) left Alexandria for Caesarea in A.D. 231. He had perhaps written some of his *Homilies on Luke* by then; the rest were written later in Caesarea.[11] In a Greek fragment of the *Homilies* Origen says that Christ was born in the forty-first year of Caesar Augustus, that Augustus reigned fifty-six years, and that after the birth of Christ there remained fifteen years.[12] The figures seem to be the same as those of Tertullian and to give the same result (¶351).

TABLE 105. REGNAL YEARS OF AUGUSTUS COUNTED AS CALENDAR YEARS
OF THE JEWISH CALENDAR ACCORDING TO THE
NONACCESSION-YEAR SYSTEM

Number of Regnal Year	Duration of Regnal Year
1	Mar 17 – Apr 19, 44 B.C.
2	Apr 20, 44 – Mar/Apr, 43
. . .	. . .
36	Mar/Apr, 10 – Mar/Apr, 9
37	Mar/Apr, 9 – Mar/Apr, 8
38	Mar/Apr, 8 – Mar/Apr, 7
39	Mar/Apr, 7 – Mar/Apr, 6
40	Mar/Apr, 6 – Mar/Apr, 5
41	Mar/Apr, 5 – Mar/Apr, 4
42	Mar/Apr, 4 – Mar/Apr, 3
43	Mar/Apr, 3 – Mar/Apr, 2
44	Mar/Apr, 2 – Mar/Apr, 1
45	Mar/Apr, 1 B.C. – Mar/Apr, A.D. 1
46	Mar/Apr, 1 – Mar/Apr, 2
. . .	. . .
57	Mar/Apr, 12 – Mar/Apr, 13
58	Mar/Apr, 13 – Mar/Apr, 14 with the death of Augustus on the following Aug 19

⟪ 354.   Eusebius of Caesarea (A.D. c.325) says in the *Church History*:[13]

"It was, then, the forty-second year of the reign of Augustus, and the twenty-eighth year after the submission of Egypt and the death of Antony and Cleopatra . . . when our Savior and Lord Jesus Christ . . . was born."

[11] F. C. Grant, *The Earliest Lives of Jesus*. 1962, p.52.
[12] Frag. 82 on Lk 3:1, ed. Max Rauer IX, 2d ed. 1959 (GCS 49), p.260.
[13] I, v, 2.

By both factual (Table 98) and accession-year calendar (Table 102) reckonings, the twenty-eighth Egyptian year of Augustus extends from August of 3 B.C. to August of 2 B.C. (cf. ¶351). Likewise in the Macedonian calendar in Syria according to the accession-year system the forty-second year of Augustus extends from Oct 1, 3 B.C. to Sep 30, 2 B.C. (Table 104). In the *Chronicle* as translated by Jerome[14] Eusebius says that Augustus reigned fifty-six years and six months, and places the birth of Jesus in the forty-second year. It has already been established (¶286) that this probably indicates the same year, 3/2 B.C.

TABLE 106. REGNAL YEARS OF AUGUSTUS COUNTED AS CALENDAR YEARS OF THE JEWISH CALENDAR ACCORDING TO THE ACCESSION-YEAR SYSTEM

Number of Regnal Year	Duration of Regnal Year
Accession Year	Mar 17 – Apr 19, 44 B.C.
1	Apr 20, 44 – Mar/Apr, 43
2	Mar/Apr, 43 – Mar/Apr, 42
. . . . . .	. . . . . .
36	Mar/Apr, 9 – Mar/Apr, 8
37	Mar/Apr, 8 – Mar/Apr, 7
38	Mar/Apr, 7 – Mar/Apr, 6
39	Mar/Apr, 6 – Mar/Apr, 5
40	Mar/Apr, 5 – Mar/Apr, 4
41	Mar/Apr, 4 – Mar/Apr, 3
42	Mar/Apr, 3 – Mar/Apr, 2
43	Mar/Apr, 2 – Mar/Apr, 1
44	Mar/Apr, 1 B.C. – Mar/Apr, A.D. 1
45	Mar/Apr, 1 – Mar/Apr, 2
. . . . . .	. . . . . .
56	Mar/Apr, 12 – Mar/Apr, 13
57	Mar/Apr, 13 – Mar/Apr, 14 with the death of Augustus on the following Aug 19

¶355.   Epiphanius (A.D. c.315-403) was born in Palestine and became bishop of Salamis or Constantia on the island of Cyprus in A.D. 357. In his *Panarion* or "medicine chest" for the healing of

[14] Helm p.157.

all heresies, he states, like Eusebius (¶354), that Augustus reigned fifty-six years and six months,[15] and that Jesus was born in his forty-second year.[16] He also says, however, that this was the year when the consuls were Octavian for the thirteenth time and Silvanus.[17] This indicates, therefore, the year 2 B.C., when the consul listing is: *Augusto XIII et Silvano* (Table 38).

⟨ 356. Epiphanius also mentions a different date for the birth of Christ which he says was given by the Alogi. The Alogi, as he calls them, were a group in Asia Minor around A.D. 180 who were opposed to the Montanists. Because the Montanists used the Johannine writings to support their doctrine of the Spirit, this group also opposed the books of John. Epiphanius explains the name he gives them: "They reject the books of John. Accordingly since they do not receive the Logos proclaimed by John they shall be called Alogi (Ἄλογοι)."[18] According to the Alogi, Christ was born around (περί) the fortieth year of Augustus.[19] Assuming the equation by Epiphanius of the forty-second year of Augustus with the year 2 B.C. (¶355), the fortieth year must have been the year 4 B.C. In the same passage,[20] however, he says that the Alogi put the birth of Christ under the consuls S. Camerinus and B. Pompeianus. Assuming that the latter name means Poppaeus Sabinus, these were the consuls of A.D. 9 (Table 38): *Camerino et Sabino*.

⟨ 357. In fragments of "Hippolytus of Thebes" (¶245) the birth of Christ is put one time in the forty-second year of Augustus,[21] but another time in the forty-third year of Augustus.[22] If the forty-second year means 3/2 B.C. (cf. ¶286), this is the same date given by Hippolytus of Rome (¶352). Then the forty-third year would presumably mean the year 2/1 B.C.

⟨ 358. The Chronographer of the Year 354 (¶176) lists as consuls Caius Caesar and Lucius Aemilius Paullus which indicates A.U.C. 754 = A.D. 1 (Table 38), and writes: *Hoc cons. dominus*

---

[15] *Ancoratus*. 60, 4. ed. Karl Holl I (GCS 25), p.71.
[16] *Panarion haer*. 20, 2 (*Chris*. 2, 1). ed. Holl I, p.228.
[17] *Panarion haer*. 51, 22, 3. ed. Holl II (GCS 31), p.284; for his list of consuls see 51, 22, 24. ed. Holl II, pp.290f.
[18] *Panarion haer*. 51, 3, 2. ed. Holl II, p.250.
[19] *Panarion haer*. 51, 29, 1. ed. Holl II, p.300.
[20] *Panarion haer*. 51, 29, 2. ed. Holl II, p.300.
[21] Ed. Jo. Albertus Fabricius. 1716, p.52.
[22] Frag. 13. MPG 117, col. 1056.

Iesus Christus natus, "When these were consuls the Lord Jesus Christ was born."

〔359. Cassiodorus Senator (A.D. c.490-585) (¶177) carries his list of consuls to C. Lentulus and M. Messala and then notes: *His conss. dominus noster Iesus Christus filius dei in Bethlehem nascitur anno imperii Augusti XLI*, "When these were consuls our Lord Jesus Christ the Son of God was born in Bethlehem in the forty-first year of the reign of Augustus." *Lentulo et Messalino* is the consular listing for A.U.C. 751 = 3 B.C. (Table 38), which was the forty-first year of Augustus in the Julian calendar according to the accession-year system (Table 100).

〔360. The dates given by these several early Christian writers (¶¶349-359) for the birth of Christ may therefore be tabulated in the chronological order of the dates as shown in Table 107.

〔361. In general the tendency exhibited by the foregoing dates seems to be to move the date of the birth of Christ later, that is,

TABLE 107. DATES OF THE BIRTH OF CHRIST IN EARLY CHRISTIAN SOURCES

Source	Year of Augustus	Consuls	A. Ad.	Ol.	A.U.C.	B.C.
Alogi	40					4
Irenaeus	41					4/3
Cassiodorus Senator	41	*Lentulo et Messalino*			751	3
Clement of Alexandria	28					3/2
Tertullian	41/28					3/2
Origen	41					3/2
Africanus				194, 2		3/2
Hippolytus of Rome			5502			3/2
"Hippolytus of Thebes" (one fragment)	42					3/2
Eusebius	42/28					3/2
Epiphanius	42	*Augusto XIII et Silvano*			752	2
"Hippolytus of Thebes" (another fragment)	43					2/1
Chronographer of the Year 354		*Caesare et Paulo*			754	A.D. 1

nearer to the authors themselves. Even the earliest preserved dates which we interpret to indicate 4 and 4/3 B.C., however, seem hardly early enough to be acceptable. In the *Chronicle*[23] Eusebius equates the forty-second year of Augustus, in which he places the birth of Jesus, with the thirty-second year of Herod the Great. In the *Panarion*[24] Epiphanius equates the forty-second year of Augustus, in which he also puts the birth of Jesus, with the thirty-third year of Herod. Both equations seem impossible as will appear in consideration of the dates of the reign of Herod the Great(¶¶362ff.), but both show a recognition of the fact that the birth of Jesus must be placed within the reign of Herod. This requirement is based upon the biblical references next to be considered (¶362), and it appears that it can be satisfied only by a date of 4 B.C. or probably earlier.

(2) HEROD THE GREAT

LITERATURE: Thomas Corbishley, "The Chronology of the Reign of Herod the Great," in JTS 36 (1935), pp.22-32; Stewart Perowne, *The Life and Times of Herod the Great.* 1956.

⟨ 362.   Mt 2:1 states that Jesus was born "in the days of Herod the king"; and Lk 1:5 likewise places the annunciations to Zechariah and to Mary "in the days of Herod, king of Judea." Josephus[1] states that Herod received the kingship from Antony and Octavian "in the hundred and eighty-fourth Olympiad, the consuls being Gnaeus Domitius Calvinus, for the second time, and Gaius Asinius Pollio." The consular date *Calvino et Pollione* corresponds with the year 40 B.C. (Table 38). Ol. 184, 4 ended on June 30, 40 B.C. (Table 44). Another reference of Josephus indicates, however, that Herod did not actually go to Rome until winter.[2] Therefore the date was actually in Ol. 185, 1. So Herod was named king late in 40 B.C.

⟨ 363.   Josephus[3] also states that Herod took Jerusalem and thus actually began his reign there, his rival Antigonus being slain, "during the consulship at Rome of Marcus Agrippa and Caninius Gallus, in the hundred and eighty-fifth Olympiad." The consular date *Agrippa et Gallo* signifies the year 37 B.C. (Table 38). Ol. 185, 4

---

[23] Helm p.169.
[24] *Panarion haer.* 51, 10, 1. ed. Holl II, p.261.

---

[1] *Ant.* XIV, 389 (= XIV, xiv, 5).
[2] *Ant.* XIV, 376 (= XIV, xiv, 2).
[3] *Ant.* XIV, 487 (= XIV, xvi, 4).

extended from Jul 1, 37, to June 30, 36 B.C., and the city was probably taken in the summer or fall. Dio Cassius[4] places the event in the consulship of Claudius and Norbanus who were the predecessors in his list of Agrippa and Gallus, hence in 38 B.C., but is probably less accurate in this than Josephus. Herod therefore became king in fact by residence in Jerusalem in the summer or fall of 37 B.C.

([364.   Josephus[5] says further that Herod died "after a reign of thirty-four years, reckoning from the date when, after putting Antigonus to death, he assumed control of the state; of thirty-seven years, from the date when he was proclaimed king by the Romans." From these two possible starting points Herod's years of reign may be numbered as follows (Table 108) to make the totals of thirty-seven and thirty-four years respectively.

([365.   In the narrative of Josephus[6] there is mention of an eclipse of the moon shortly before the death of Herod: "And that very night there was an eclipse of the moon." There is also mention shortly afterward of "the feast of unleavened bread, which the Jews call passover."[7] The reference to the passover indicates spring. In 4 B.C. the month of Nisan began on Mar 29 and Nisan 14 = Apr 11. As for the eclipse, this is the only eclipse of moon or sun mentioned by Josephus in any of his writings.[8] Only on the night of Mar 12/13, 4 B.C. was there a lunar eclipse, and there was no such phenomenon in 3 or 2 B.C.[9] Accordingly the death of Herod took place between Mar 12 and Apr 11 in the year 4 B.C.

([366.   The date of Herod's death seems thus firmly established (¶365). In the light of this date and of the references in Mt 2:1 and Lk 1:5 (¶362) it seems necessary to conclude that the birth of Jesus could not have been later than the spring of 4 B.C.

([367.   According to Mt 2:3 the visit of the wise men from the East came also while Herod was still alive. When they "saw the child with Mary his mother" (Mt 2:11) he is called in Greek τὸ παιδίον. This word often means "very young child," "infant." Therefore it may be held probable that the birth of Jesus, the visit of the

---

[4] XLIX, 22-23.
[5] *War.* I, 665 (=I, xxxiii, 8); *Ant.* XVII, 191 (= XVII, viii, 1).
[6] *Ant.* XVII, 167 (= XVII, vi, 4).
[7] *War.* II, 10 (= II, i, 3); *Ant.* XVII, 213 (= XVII, ix, 3).
[8] William Whiston, *The Works of Flavius Josephus.* p.514 n.†.
[9] SHJP I, i, p.465 n.1.

Magi, and the death of Herod all took place in fairly close succession, and in accordance with this evidence the birth of Jesus could be placed in the winter of 5/4 B.C. Justin Martyr[10] supports this idea

TABLE 108. REGNAL YEARS OF HEROD THE GREAT

B.C.	Col. 1 Years of reign from being named king	Col. 2 Years of reign from the taking of Jerusalem
40	1	
39	2	
38	3	
37	4	1
36	5	2
35	6	3
34	7	4
33	8	5
32	9	6
31	10	7
30	11	8
29	12	9
28	13	10
27	14	11
26	15	12
25	16	13
24	17	14
23	18	15
22	19	16
21	20	17
20	21	18
19	22	19
18	23	20
17	24	21
16	25	22
15	26	23
14	27	24
13	28	25
12	29	26
11	30	27
10	31	28
9	32	29
8	33	30
7	34	31
6	35	32
5	36	33
4	37	34

[10] Dialogue with Trypho. 88.

when he speaks of "the Magi from Arabia, who as soon as the Child was born came to worship Him."

❪ 368.   On the other hand Mt 2:16 states that Herod ordered killed all the male children in and around Bethlehem "who were two years old or under, according to the time which he had ascertained from the wise men." As to the likelihood of Herod's perpetrating such a crime a recent study affirms:

> "That Herod, in the awful physical and mental decay into which he had fallen, and in this atmosphere of fervid Messianism, should have ordered the massacre of the Innocents of Bethlehem is wholly in keeping with all that we know of him. Bethlehem was but a few miles distant from his palace-fortress of Herodium: there least of all could any subversive cell be tolerated. Such an act was by no means unheard of. In pagan antiquity, the life of a new-born child was at the mercy of its father or of the state. As Abel points out, a few months before the birth of Augustus, a prodigy having presaged the birth of a king for the Roman people, the affrighted Senate decreed that none of the children born that year were to be brought up. Later on Nero, fearing the consequences of the appearance of a comet, ordered the execution of leading aristocrats of Rome. Their children were driven from the city and died from hunger or poison."[11]

As to the bearing of the reference on the date of the birth of Jesus, it would suggest that what the wise men told Herod made him think that Jesus was already anything up to two years old, thus was born up to two years before. A two year period before the spring of 4 B.C. would extend back to 5 or 6 B.C.

❪ 369.   That the Magi came when Jesus was two years old was held by some of the early Christian writers. A passage found both in Origen[12] and in Eusebius[13] states that Jesus was two years old when the wise men came and when he was taken to Egypt, that he remained in Egypt for two years and was four years old when he returned from there, and that the return was in the first year of Archelaus and the forty-fifth year of Augustus. Since Origen put the birth of Jesus in the forty-first year of Augustus (= 3/2 B.C.) (¶353), these earliest events must have fallen into the following pattern (Table 109) in his view.

[11] Perowne, *The Life and Times of Herod the Great*, p.172.
[12] *Commentary on Matthew*. Frag. 23. ed. Erich Klostermann XII (GCS 41), p.25.
[13] *Quaestiones ad Stephanum*. XVI, 2. MPG 22, col. 934.

TABLE 109. THE EARLIEST EVENTS IN THE LIFE OF JESUS
ACCORDING TO ORIGEN

	Regnal Year of Augustus	B.C.–A.D.
Birth of Jesus	41	3/2 B.C.
	42	2/1
Flight to Egypt at Age of Two	43	1 B.C./A.D. 1
	44	A.D. 1/2
Return from Egypt at Age of Four	45	2/3

According to Mt 2:19, 22, however, the return from Egypt took place upon the death of Herod and the succession of Archelaus, therefore in the spring of 4 B.C. or later (¶365). Therefore there is confusion, such as has already been observed (¶361) in the equation of the reigns of Augustus and Herod on the part of Origen.

¶ 370.   The same confusion also vitiates the figures of Epiphanius,[14] which may be tabulated as shown in Table 110 (cf. ¶361).

TABLE 110. THE EARLIEST EVENTS IN THE LIFE OF JESUS
ACCORDING TO EPIPHANIUS

	Regnal Year of Augustus	Regnal Year of Herod
Birth of Jesus	44	33
Coming of the Magi	46	35
Death of Herod and Succession of Archelaus	48	37

Also according to Epiphanius[15] the star appeared in the East to the Magi in the hour when Jesus was born and two years before they arrived in Jerusalem and Bethlehem.

(3) THE ENROLLMENT OF QUIRINIUS

LITERATURE: W. M. Ramsay, *Was Christ Born at Bethlehem?* 1898; and *The Bearing of Recent Discovery on the Trustworthiness of the New Testament.* 1915; Lily R. Taylor, "Quirinius and the Census of Judaea," in AJP 54

[14] *Panarion haer.* 51, 10, 1. ed. Holl II, p.261.
[15] *Panarion haer.* 51, 22, 13. ed. Holl II, p.287.

(1933), pp.120-133; Egbert C. Hudson, "The Principal Family at Pisidian Antioch," in JNES 15 (1956), pp.103-107; Ethelbert Stauffer, *Jesus and His Story*. 1960, pp.21-32; A. N. Sherwin-White, *Roman Society and Roman Law in the New Testament*. 1963, pp.162-171.

([371. According to Lk 2:2 the birth of Jesus was at the time of "the first enrollment, when Quirinius was governor of Syria." The usually accepted sequence of governors of Syria runs as shown in Table 111.[1]

TABLE 111. GOVERNORS OF SYRIA

10-9 B.C.	M. Titius
9-6	C. Sentius Saturninus
6-4	P. Quinctilius Varus
3-2 (?)	P. Sulpicius Quirinius
1 B.C.-A.D. 4	C. Caesar
A.D. 4-5	L. Volusius Saturninus
6-7	P. Sulpicius Quirinius

([372. Of the life of P. Sulpicius Quirinius, Tacitus[2] gives a brief outline as he tells of his funeral which took place in A.D. 21.

"About this time Tiberius wrote to the senate, requesting that a public funeral might be decreed to Sulpicius Quirinius. . . . He was born at Lanuvium, a municipal town: he distinguished himself by his military services, had considerable talents for business, and was raised by Augustus to the honor of the consulship. Having afterwards stormed and taken the strongholds of the Homanadensians in Cilicia, he obtained triumphal honors. He attended Gaius Caesar in his expedition to Armenia. . . . But the character of Quirinius was held in no esteem . . . and the sordid avarice of the man, even in old age, and in the height of his power, left a stain upon his memory."

Chief points in this outline may be explicated as follows: (1) Quirinius was consul in 12 B.C. and appears in the list of consuls (Table 38) at this point: *Messala et Quirino*. (2) Sometime between 12 B.C. and A.D. 1 he conducted the Homanadensian War.[3] The resistance of the Homanadensians must have been broken by the time the net of Roman roads was laid out in the province of Galatia in 6 B.C., therefore at least the major part of this war must have been over by that date.[4] By around that date Quirinius could have been

[1] SHJP I, i, pp.350f.; PWRE Zweite Reihe IV, 2, col. 1629.
[2] *Annals*. III, 48.
[3] CAH X, p.271.
[4] Groag in PWRE Zweite Reihe, IV, i, col. 831.

free to attend to other business in the East. (3) In A.D. 2-3 Quirinius was adviser to Gaius Caesar in Armenia.[5]

¶ 373.   Josephus[6] records that Quirinius was sent to Syria as governor at the same time that Coponius was sent to Judea as procurator.

> "Now Cyrenius, a Roman senator, and one who had gone through other magistracies, and had passed through them till he had been consul, and one who, on other accounts, was of great dignity, came at this time into Syria, with a few others, being sent by Caesar to be a judge of that nation, and to take an account of their substance. Coponius also, a man of the equestrian order, was sent together with him, to have the supreme power over the Jews."

Upon the death of Herod the Great, Judea, Samaria, and Idumea were given to his son Archelaus who ruled 4 B.C.-A.D. 6. When Archelaus was deposed he was replaced by the first of the procurators, and this was Coponius who probably held office A.D. 6-9. Since Quirinius and he came out to their respective posts together, Quirinius must have assumed the governorship of Syria in A.D. 6, and thus appears in the list above (¶371) as governor in A.D. 6-7. The taxing for which Quirinius was responsible at this time was resisted by the Jews and a revolt was attempted by Judas the Gaulonite, as Josephus states.[7] The taxing was made "in the thirty-seventh year of Caesar's victory over Antony at Actium."[8] This year was A.D. 6 (Table 96 Column 3). It is probably this census which is referred to in Ac 5:37 along with "Judas the Galilean."

¶ 374.   The census just referred to (¶373) is certainly not the first which was ever taken by the Romans. A census of Roman citizens was held periodically under the Republic and was conducted by Augustus in 28 B.C. and on later occasions.[9] Also in his own reorganization of the empire in 27 B.C. Augustus undertook to acquire exact knowledge of the available resources, and it was necessary to obtain full information about the number and legal status of the inhabitants of each province and the amount and sources of their wealth. To do this he had to hold a census similar to but distinct from the old census of the Republican period. In Gaul, where there was much resistance to the procedure, there was a census in 27 B.C.,

[5] CAH X, p.276.
[6] *Ant.* XVIII, 1-2 (= XVIII, i, 1).
[7] *Ant.* XVIII, 4 (= XVIII, i, 1).
[8] *Ant.* XVIII, 26 (= XVIII, ii, 1).
[9] CAH X, p.192.

another in 12 B.C., and a third immediately after the death of Augustus.[10] In Cyrene exact information on the number and wealth of the inhabitants was available by 7 B.C.[11] In Egypt there are dated census returns from A.D. 34, 48, 62, and other years suggesting a regular census every fourteen years.[12]

〖375. The question has been raised whether the Romans would have instituted census and taxation procedures in Palestine while Herod the Great was ruling as king of the Jews. That they would not have hesitated to do so is suggested by comparison with Apamea on the Orontes in Syria. The autonomy of this city-state is shown by the fact that it minted its own coins,[13] yet Quirinius himself had a census taken there. A gravestone found in Venice carries the inscription of a Roman officer named Q. Aemilius Secundus. He states that by order of P. Sulpicius Quirinius, whom he calls *legatus Caesaris Syriae*, he himself conducted a census of Apamea, a city-state of 117,000 citizens.[14] As for Herod, Josephus reports that in the time when Saturninus and Volumnius were the presidents of Syria,[15] Caesar Augustus demoted him from "friend" ($\phi\iota\lambda o\varsigma = ami cus$) to "subject."[16] Saturninus was listed above as governor of Syria in 9-6 B.C., and Volumnius was evidently associated with him. By comparison with Apamea and specially from the time of Herod's demotion by Augustus, Palestine would scarcely be exempt from any census and taxation procedures the Romans wished to institute.

〖376. The question remains whether, at some time in the latter years of Herod, Quirinius might have been connected with such a census in Palestine. Since Quirinius was a high Roman official with important assignments in the East, and since at least by 6 B.C. the Homanadensian War was probably under control (¶372), this does not appear unlikely. Tertullian[17] says in fact that the census at the time of the birth of Jesus was "taken in Judea by Sentius Saturninus." According to the list of governors of Syria (¶371) this would mean sometime in the years 9-6 B.C. No reason is evident why Quirinius could not have been associated with Saturninus in such a

[10] CAH X, p.193.   [11] CAH X, pp.192f.   [12] FLP p.260.
[13] *The Excavations at Dura-Europos*, Final Report VI, The Coins, by A. R. Bellinger. 1949, p.86 Nos.1832, 1833.
[14] T. Mommsen, *Ephemeris epigraphica*. IV (1881), p.538.
[15] *Ant.* XVI, 277 (= XVI, ix, 1).
[16] *Ant.* XVI, 290 (= XVI, ix, 3).
[17] *Against Marcion*. IV, 19.

project. In view of the sequence of known events in his career (¶372) a likely time might have been in 6 or 5 B.C. That Quirinius actually took this census is still only concretely affirmed by Lk 2:2; under the circumstances as we have reconstructed them the affirmation is not unlikely.

¶ 377.   From relatively early times Christian writers declared that it was possible to verify the census in official Roman records. Justin Martyr (A.D. c.114-165) speaks of "the registers of the taxing made under Cyrenius";[18] and Tertullian (A.D. c.145-220) mentions the records of the census "kept in the archives of Rome."[19] These records have not been found.

(4) THE STAR

LITERATURE: John Williams, *Observations of Comets from B.C. 611 to A.D. 1640 Extracted from the Chinese Annals.* 1871; J. K. Fotheringham, "The New Star of Hipparchus and the Dates of Birth and Accession of Mithridates," in *Monthly Notices of the Royal Astronomical Society.* 79 (1919), pp.162-167; Knut Lundmark, "Suspected New Stars Recorded in Old Chronicles and Among Recent Meridian Observations," in *Publications of the Astronomical Society of the Pacific.* 33 (1921), pp.225-238; Paul Schnabel, "Der jüngste datierbare Keilschrifttext," in ZA 36 (1925), pp.66-70; Knut Lundmark, "The Messianic Ideas and Their Astronomical Background," in *Actes du VIIᵉ Congrès International d'Histoire des Sciences, Jerusalem (4-12 Aout 1953),* pp.436-439; *The Christmas Star* (Morrison Planetarium, California Academy of Sciences). 1954; Hsi Tsê-tsung, "A New Catalog of Ancient Novae," translated from *Acta Astronomica Sinica.* 3 (1955), p.183, and published in *Smithsonian Contributions to Astrophysics.* II, 6. 1958, pp.109-130; H. W. Montefiore, "Josephus and the New Testament," in *Novum Testamentum.* 4 (1960), pp.139-160.

¶ 378.   When Jesus was born in Bethlehem wise men from the East came asking for the king of the Jews and saying that they had seen his star in the East (Mt 2:1-2). Some may regard the star as entirely mythical, some as completely miraculous, but it is also possible to suppose and inquire after an actual celestial phenomenon back of the account.

¶ 379.   The study of the celestial bodies which we call astronomy was already advanced in the ancient world, and the idea that the heavenly bodies may provide portents of events upon earth, which idea is basic to what we term astrology, also existed from early times. That the two were often intermingled is not surprising. In

---

18 *Apology.* I, 34.
19 *Against Marcion.* IV, 7.

Mesopotamia the Sumerians identified the heavenly bodies with deities. The moon was Sin or Nanna, the sun was Utu, Venus was Inanna. The planets were "the big ones who walk about [the moon] like wild oxen"; the stars were "the little ones who are scattered about [the moon] like grain."[1] From the Old Babylonian period onward there are many available astrological and astronomical texts. In the reign of Ammisaduga the appearances and disappearances of Venus were recorded. In the Kassite period, texts describe a division of the sky into three zones and record the names of constellations and planets. In texts dated c.700 B.C. but doubtless copied from older material the fixed stars are arranged in three "roads" and the moon and planets are listed. By this time (c.700 B.C.) and under the Assyrian empire court astronomers were making and recording systematic observations. Summarizing the "prehistory" of Babylonian astronomy (from c.1800 to c.400 B.C.), Neugebauer enumerates the "tools" which had become available:

"The zodiac of 12 times 30 degrees as reference system for solar and planetary motion. A fixed luni-solar calendar and probably some of the basic period relations for the moon and the planets. An empirical insight into the main sequences of planetary and lunar phenomena and the variation of the length of daylight and night. The use of arithmetic progressions to describe periodically variable quantities. And, above all, a complete mastery of numerical methods which could immediately be applied to astronomical problems."[2]

With the availability of these "tools" came the great development of mathematical astronomy in the Hellenistic period and the last three centuries of the pre-Christian era.

⟨[380. In China more complete astronomical records exist than in Mesopotamia.[3] In the Shang period and the fourteenth and thirteenth centuries B.C. the famous oracle bones represent the practice

[1] Samuel N. Kramer, *From the Tablets of Sumer*. 1956, p.79.
[2] For the summary of Babylonian astronomy see Otto Neugebauer, *The Exact Sciences in Antiquity*. 2d ed. 1957, pp.97-144; for the Venus tablets see Arthur Ungnad, *Die Venustafeln und das neunte Jahr Samsuilunas (1741 v. Chr.)*. 1940; for Babylonian texts in astronomy and astrology see e.g., *The Cuneiform Inscriptions of Western Asia*. 3 (1870), Pls. LI-LXIV; and *Late Babylonian Astronomical and Related Texts*, copied by T. G. Pinches and J. N. Strassmeier. 1955; and for astrology see C. J. Gadd, *Ideas of Divine Rule in the Ancient East*. 1948, p.53.
[3] For Chinese astronomy see Joseph Needham, *Science and Civilisation in China* (3 vols. 1954-59), III, *Mathematics and the Sciences of the Heavens and the Earth*. 1959. Note that he uses minus and plus signs for B.C. and A.D., but does not insert a year zero as the astronomers do (¶221); his dates are historical and not astronomical, and −40 is 40 B.C. and so on.

of divination but also record astronomical observations. They report lunar and solar eclipses and other celestial phenomena. One inscription dating about 1300 B.C. gives this notice of a new star which is located in relation to Antares, the principal star in the constellation Scorpio: "On the seventh day of the month . . . a great new star appeared in company with Antares." In the succeeding Chou period (c.1100-221 B.C.) and particularly in its latter part observational work was continued and refined. In the Han period (202 B.C.-A.D. 220) cosmological theories were developed and astronomical records were carefully kept. One important source of the period is the *Shih Chi* or "Historical Records" of Ssu-ma Ch'ien who lived c.140-c.80 B.C. and completed this great work between 100 and 90 B.C.[4] Somewhat later this massive undertaking was continued in a further important historical treatise, the *Ch'ien-Han Shu* or "History of the Former Han Dynasty."[5] This was the work of the Pan family, father, son, and daughter. Revising and continuing the work of Ssu-ma Ch'ien, the father Pan Piao (A.D. 3-54) compiled annals of emperors and biographies of notable men. The son, Pan Ku (A.D. 32-92) used materials from his father and from Ssu-ma Ch'ien, compiled annals and biographies, and wrote nine of the ten treatises which make up the History. The daughter, Pan Chao (born A.D. 45-51, died 114-120), shared in the compilation of the tenth treatise, on astronomy.[6] Later still, toward the end of the thirteenth century of the Christian era, Ma Tuan-Lin (flourished A.D. 1240-1280) in his work *Wên-hsien t'ung-k'ao* in Chapter 286 dealt with observed comets down to A.D. 1222, and in Chapter 294 made a list of extraordinary stars. From these and other sources we have information on Chinese astronomical observations, including comets and novae, observations which have often proved to be of such accuracy that they are used seriously in present-day astronomy, e.g., in the search for radio stars.[7]

---

[4] Édouard Chavannes, *Les mémoires historiques de Se-Ma Ts'ien, traduits et annotés.* 5 vols. 1895-1905; Burton Watson, *Records of the Grand Historian of China translated from the Shih chi of Ssu-ma Ch'ien,* I, *Early Years of the Han Dynasty 209-141 B.C.* 1961.

[5] Homer H. Dubs, *The History of the Former Han Dynasty by Pan Ku.* 3 vols. 1938-1955.

[6] *Food and Money in Ancient China, The Earliest Economic History of China to A.D. 25, Han Shu 24, with Related Texts, Han Shu 91 and Shih-Chi 129.* Translated and Annotated by Nancy Lee Swann. 1950, p.3.

[7] W. Baade in *Astrophysical Journal.* 97 (1943), p.126.

([381. At this point we are interested in Chinese records of comets and novae. A nova is a star which suddenly, perhaps as a result of an explosion, increases very greatly in brightness, perhaps ten thousandfold or a millionfold. If the occurrence is exceptionally great the term supernova is used. The oracle bone inscription quoted above (¶380) presumably describes a nova and is the oldest record of such a phenomenon. The word used is *hsin hsing*, meaning "fire star." From the middle of the Han period the usual name for a nova is *kho hsing* or "guest star." A comet is known to us as a luminous heavenly body, often with a long tail. The English term is derived from the Greek κομήτης, "long haired." In China from early times the technical term was *hui hsing* or *sao hsing*, now translated "brush star" or "sweeping star," suggesting how it brushes past or sweeps by. When a comet is in opposition, i.e., in line with the earth and sun, its tail is not visible. For a comet in opposition the Chinese uses a special term, *po hsing*. Understandably enough, particularly with regard to tailless comets, a clear distinction is not always made between comets and novae. As to identifying the position of objects in the sky, the Chinese divided the visible heavens into thirty-one portions, of which twenty-eight were designated by the term *hsiu* or "stellar division." For example, the stellar division Fang is the part of the sky which includes our constellations Libra, Lupus, Ophiuchus, and Scorpio. As far as comets are concerned in the Chinese sources a list has been compiled of three hundred and seventy-two comets from 611 B.C. to A.D. 1640 by John Williams; and as far as novae are concerned a list was made by Knut Lundmark running from 134 B.C. to A.D. 1828, and a revised list was published by Hsi Tsê-tsung (see LITERATURE above).

([382. Now coming toward the mention of the star in Mt 2:2, it has been customary[8] to cite supposed parallels in pagan literature to suggest the mythical character of such an account. Virgil,[9] for example, tells how on one occasion "a star shot from heaven" and provided a significant omen. Even in pagan records, however, actual phenomena of nature may sometimes be involved. A good example is provided by the study by J. K. Fotheringham of the new star of

[8] E.g. Erich Klostermann, *Das Matthäusevangelium* (HZNT). 2d ed. 1927, p.16; Rudolf Bultmann, *Die Geschichte der synoptischen Tradition*. 2d ed. 1931, p.318.
[9] *Aeneid.* II, 692-704.

Hipparchus and the dates of the birth and accession of Mithridates.[10] Mithridates VI Eupator, famous king of Pontus and opponent of the Romans, died in 63 B.C. while Pompey was on the march toward Petra.[11] Pliny, who speaks of the fabulous achievements of Mithridates in linguistics and medicine, mentions that he reigned fifty-six years.[12] If these were full years of reign between the year of accession and the year of death, his accession was in 120 B.C. Memnon[13] states that he was thirteen years old at accession. Therefore his birth was in 133 B.C. and conception in the preceding year, 134 B.C. These events and dates in the life of Mithridates, including his fifty-six full years of reign, are shown in Table 112.

TABLE 112. THE LIFE OF MITHRIDATES VI EUPATOR

B.C.	Events	Years of Age	Regnal Years
134	Conception		
133	Birth	0	
132		1	
131		2	
130		3	
129		4	
128		5	
127		6	
126		7	
125		8	
124		9	
123		10	
122		11	
121		12	
120	Accession	13	
119			1
118			2
....			....
....			....
66			54
65			55
64			56
63	Death		

[10] In *Monthly Notices of the Royal Astronomical Society.* 79 (1919), pp.162-167.
[11] CAH IX, p.391.   [12] *Natural History.* xxv, iii, 6.
[13] Ch. 32, in the *Bibliotheca* of Photius (A.D. c.820-891), Cod. ccxxiv. MPG 103, 9050.

¶383.   Concerning Mithridates, Justin, Roman historian of the second century of the Christian era, quotes from the *Historiae Philippicae* or "Philippic Histories" of Pompeius Trogus, a Roman historian of the time of Augustus, as follows:[14]

> "His future greatness was also predicted by celestial portents. For both in the year in which he was begotten and in that in which he first began to reign, a star, a comet (*stella cometes*), so shone on each occasion for seventy days that the whole sky seemed to be on fire. For in its magnitude it occupied a fourth part of the sky, and in its brightness it overcame the brightness of the sun; and in rising and setting it took up a space of four hours."

¶384.   Such an account might easily be dismissed, and has been, as entirely imaginary. But the question naturally arises whether there really were comets at the times indicated, by our calculation in 134 and in 120 B.C. Actually there are relevant astronomical records in China. Since exact dates are involved, it may be explained that at this point in the Han period, in the reign of the emperor Wu (Mar 10, 141 B.C.-Mar 29, 87 2.3.),[15] a change was made in the calendar and names were given to periods of the reign signifying outstanding events of the respective periods. The first of these reign-periods included the following:

TABLE 113. REIGN-PERIODS IN THE REIGN
OF THE EMPEROR WU

	B.C.
chien-yüan	140-135
yüan-kuang	134-129
yüan-shou	122-117

¶385.   In the *Shih Chi* of Sssu-ma Ch'ien, mentioned above (¶380) as living c.140-c.80 B.C. and therefore at about the same time as Mithridates, there are these notices:

[14] Justin, *Pompei Trogi Hist. Phil. Epit.* xxxvii, ii, 1-3. ed. Otto Seel, 1935, p.252.

[15] These are the exact dates for Wu, but he is commonly shown as reigning 140-87 B.C. because the reign of a Han emperor was reckoned by the number of calendar years in which he was nominally on the throne. Even if he died immediately after the ceremonies he performed on the first day of the new year which declared him emperor, his successor would not begin to reign officially until the New Year's day of the following Han calendar year. The Chinese year, of course, did not begin and end at the times of the western world. For the dating see Swann, *Food and Money in Ancient China*, p.8.

> The Standard of Ch'ih-yu resembles a comet. . . .[16]
> In the years *yüan-kuang* and *yüan-shou* the Standard of Ch'ih-yu appeared twice; its size was such that it filled half the sky.[17]

So the *Shih Chi* records a comet which appeared twice, once in *yüan-kuang* = 134-129, and once in *yüan-shou* = 122-117 B.C. The two appearances comprise Comets No. 31 and No. 32 in Williams' list (¶381). Another reference probably describes Comet No. 31:

> In the first year of the epoch *yüan-kuang*, the sixth month, a strange star was seen in Stellar Division Fang.[18]

This provides the date, which is equivalent to June, 134 B.C., and indicates the part of the sky (¶381) where the phenomenon was visible. An additional reference in the *Ch'ien-Han Shu* (¶380) probably describes Comet No. 32. In the annals of the reign-period *yüan-shou* it is stated:

> In the third year, in the spring, there was a comet in the eastern quarter [of the sky].[19]

Here the date is spring 120 B.C. The dates of the two comets, therefore, the first (Williams No. 31) in 134 B.C. and the second (Williams No. 32) in 120 B.C., agree with the historically probable dates of the conception and the accession of Mithridates.

〔386. The position given for the comet of 134 B.C. in the stellar division Fang (¶385) locates it in the area of the sky marked by the constellation Scorpio and others (¶381). Astronomically, therefore, the appearance would have been visible also at Sinope, the birthplace of Mithridates. In fact there is evidence that this very phenomenon was observed in the Mediterranean world as well as in China. Pliny[20] states that the Greek astronomer Hipparchus (who flourished 146-126 B.C.) "detected a new star (*novam stellam*) that came into existence during his lifetime." Pliny also mentions "the movement of this star in its line of radiance," and the fact that it moved thus probably means that it was a comet. He also says that this experience led Hipparchus to undertake the construction of his famous catalogue of the stars. In this catalogue he recorded this

---

[16] Chavannes, *Les mémoires historiques de Se-Ma Ts'ien*, III (1898), p.392.
[17] *Ibid.*, p.408.
[18] Fotheringham in *Monthly Notices of the Royal Astronomical Society*. 79 (1919), p.163.
[19] Dubs, *The History of the Former Han Dynasty*, II, p.62.
[20] *Natural History*. II, xxiv, 95 .

"new star" in the constellation Scorpio even as the Chinese noted it in their equivalent stellar division Fang. This agreement and a consideration of the time when Hipparchus began his catalogue both point to identification of the "new star" of Hipparchus and the comet of 134 B.C. in the Chinese records. "In any case," writes Needham,[21] "it was carefully watched at both ends of the Old World." So a comet, precisely dated in Chinese sources, was visible in the Mediterranean in 134 B.C., and a comet in 120 B.C., precisely the years of the begetting and the accession to the kingship of Mithridates according to the historical evidence (¶382). The record of Pompeius Trogus (¶383) about the *stella cometes* which appeared to signalize those events, seems to be substantiated.

⟨ 387. Speaking now directly about the star connected with the birth of Christ (Mt 2:2), it may be noted that the thought of a star in connection with the Messiah is attested as anciently as in the oracle of Balaam (Num 24:17):

> I see him, but not now;
> I behold him, but not nigh:
> a star shall come forth out of Jacob,
> and a scepter shall rise out of Israel.

It is interesting to observe that the expression of this idea is attributed to a man whose home was "near the River" (Num 22:5), i.e., in Mesopotamia where, as we pointed out (¶379), there was such early and great interest in the heavenly bodies.

⟨ 388. In regard to a possible astronomical event to connect with the star (ἀστήρ) of Mt 2:2, a conjunction of planets has been considered. On Dec 17, A.D. 1603, the planets Jupiter and Saturn were in conjunction; the following spring Mars moved into the vicinity of the other two; and in the autumn of 1604 a nova appeared nearby. Stimulated by observation of these phenomena, Johannes Kepler suggested in a work published in 1606 that the star of the Magi had consisted of a combination of Jupiter, Saturn, and some other extraordinary star.[22] A conjunction such as Kepler observed has been calculated to occur once in 805 years and this would bring us back in steps of such magnitude to 7 B.C. Computations verified by the Astronomer Royal at Greenwich, England, have indeed con-

[21] *Science and Civilisation in China*, III, p.425.
[22] Ideler, *Handbuch der mathematischen und technischen Chronologie*, II, pp.400f.

firmed that there was a triple conjunction of Jupiter and Saturn in 7 B.C. on May 29, Sep 29, and Dec 4.[23] Also, in Feb, 6 B.C., Mars moved into the configuration and stood so as to form a triangle with the other two planets, a situation known as a massing of the planets.[24] The conjunction also took place in the constellation of Pisces, the Fishes, astrologically connected with the Jewish people. The planets were probably not close enough together, however, to present the appearance of a single star, and therefore it may be questioned whether they could represent the phenomenon of Mt 2:2.

(389.   It is interesting to note, however, that a calculation of this conjunction is probably preserved in a cuneiform source. A tablet in the Berlin Museum, found at Sippar in Mesopotamia, is a fragment of an ephemeris, that is a publication of the computed positions of celestial bodies during the year. That it is a matter of advance reckoning here is shown by the advice (in Line 16) to observe a solar eclipse, so the table was perhaps drawn up by the Babylonian astronomers at the beginning of the year. In Line 7 there is mention of a solstice which can be shown to be the summer solstice, and from this the sequence of months can be established from Nisanu (Mar/Apr) to Tashritu (Sep/Oct), that is for the first seven months of the Babylonian year. From Simanu (May/Jun) to Tashritu the planets Jupiter and Saturn are in the constellation of the Fishes. Since the text is dated positively in the year 305 of the Seleucid Era, which began on Nisanu 1 = Apr 2, 7 B.C., this is the very conjunction of which we have been speaking (¶388). This unusual celestial event was predicted and observed in Mesopotamia. If it was not itself the event back of Mt 2:2 it could at least have served to direct attention toward the land of the Jews.

(390.   While it may be questioned whether such a conjunction of planets could be the equivalent of the "star" of Mt 2:2, a comet or nova (which are not always distinguishable from each other in the Chinese sources) (¶381) would fit the designation very well. In the list of comets compiled by Williams (¶381) there are two which fall near the time with which we are concerned. The nearest one before this time is No. 51 of 12 B.C. which is too early; the

[23] C. Pritchard, in *Monthly Notices of the Royal Astronomical Society*. 16 (1856), pp.215-216; and in *Memoirs of the Royal Astronomical Society*. 25 (1856), pp.119-124.
[24] *The Christmas Star* (Morrison Planetarium), p.12.

nearest one after is No. 54 of A.D. 13 which is too late. The two in question fall in the reign of the Han emperor Ai-Ti (6-1 B.C.). Comet No. 52 in Williams' list is recorded by Ma Tuan-Lin (¶380):

> In the reign of the Emperor Ai-Ti, the second year of the epoch *chien-p'ing*, the second month, a comet appeared in *Ch'ien-niu* for about seventy days.

Also in the *Ch'ien-Han Shu* (Chap. XXVI, p. 34b) of Pan Ku (¶380) it is said to have appeared "for more than seventy days." The reign-period *chien-p'ing* is equivalent to 6-3 B.C., therefore the second year of the period is 5 B.C. The second month is March, so the appearance of the comet took place in March of 5 B.C. The *Ch'ien-niu* or stellar division Niu is the area of the sky including the constellation Capricorn.

¶ 391. The second comet in question is No. 53 in Williams' list. It is recorded in the *Tung Keen Kang Muh*, a compilation of Chinese history from the earliest times to the end of the Yüan dynasty (A.D. 1368). Referring again to the reign-period *chien-p'ing*, this record states:

> In the third year of the same epoch, the third month, there was a comet in Ho-ku.

Also in the *Ch'ien-Han Shu* (Chap. XI, p.6b)[25] it is recorded:

> In the third month, on [the day] *chi-yu*. . . . A comet appeared in the [constellation] Ho-ku.

The third year of the reign-period *chien-p'ing* (6-3 B.C.) is 4 B.C. The third month is April, so the date of the comet's appearing is April of 4 B.C. The stellar division Ho-ku corresponds with the constellation Aquila which is visible in Palestine and Babylonia for almost the entire year.

¶ 392. The object seen in March of 5 B.C. (Williams No. 52) (¶390) is called a *hui hsing* or "sweeping star" (¶381); that in April of 4 B.C. (Williams No. 53) (¶391) is called a *po hsing*, properly a comet without a tail (¶381). The latter, at least, it would seem, might have been a nova, and these objects are in fact taken account of by Hsi Tsê-tsung in "A New Catalog of Ancient Novae," as well as by Williams in *Observations of Comets* (see

[25] Dubs, *The History of the Former Han Dynasty*, III, Part I, p.33.

LITERATURE above). So in 5 B.C. and again in 4 B.C. a comet or a nova, certainly an unusual "star," appeared. The conjunctions of 7/6 B.C. could have attracted attention toward Palestine. The comets (or novae) of 5 and 4 B.C. could be the astronomical phenomenon back of the account of the Star of Bethlehem. The comet of March of 5 B.C. could have started the Magi on their journey. They must have reached Judea before the death of Herod which fell between Mar 12 and Apr 11, 4 B.C. (¶365). The comet of April of 4 B.C. could have been shining at that time. Since Herod's order for the slaughter of the children included those "two years old or under" (Mt 2:16), the birth of Jesus could have been as much as two years prior to the spring of 4 B.C. (¶¶368-370). Since, however, the wise men came "when Jesus was born" (Mt 2:1) and since when they saw him with Mary his mother (Mt 2:11) the word τὸ παιδίον is used which often means "a very young child" or "infant," it seems more probable that the birth was not long before (¶367). At or before this time Quirinius could well have been connected with a census in Judea (¶376). Perhaps a date for the birth of Jesus sometime in the winter of 5/4 B.C. best satisfies all the available evidence.[26]

(5) THE DAY

LITERATURE: Hermann Usener, *Das Weihnachtsfest*. 2d ed. 1911; Kirsopp Lake, "Christmas," in HERE III, pp.601-608; and "Epiphany," in HERE V, pp.330-332; L. Duchesne, *Christian Worship, Its Origin and Evolution*. 5th ed. 1919, pp.257-265A; Karl Holl, "Der Ursprung des Epiphanienfestes," in *Sitzungsberichte der königlich preussischen Akademie der Wissenschaften*.

[26] Cf. Lundmark in *Actes du VIIe Congrès International d'Histoire des Sciences*. 1953, p.438: "The hypothesis that the Star of the Magi was a nova gains much in strength when we learn that in the year 5 B.C. there appeared a nova, which has been observed by Chinese star-gazers. There are two different sources about this very likely splendid phenomenon: the one tells that the nova was seen during 70 days, the second that it was seen during more than 70 days. Thus the Magi could have proper time to make a trip from any Eastern country to Jerusalem during the time of visibility of this nova." And cf. Montefiore in *Novum Testamentum*. 4 (1960), pp.143-144: "It is certain that in B.C. 7 there were three conjunctions of Jupiter and Saturn in Pisces. It is certain that in B.C. 4 and B.C. 5 an unknown star or stars were visible in China and also in Babylonia or Palestine. It is possible that Babylonian astrologers, noting the conjunctions in B.C. 7, and moved by a prophecy of a coming world ruler in the East, possibly knowing the tradition that a star would appear two years before the birth of the Messiah, set out for Jerusalem. It is possible that, confirmed in their expectations by the appearance of a comet in B.C. 5 and guided by local information, they may have found the infant Jesus in a house in Bethlehem. Herod died in March B.C. 4, and Jesus, according to Matthew's story, must have been born before Herod's death. He may well have been born in B.C. 5 or early in B.C. 4."

1917, pp.402-438; Kirsopp Lake, *The Christmas Festival, An Address de-livered by Kirsopp Lake at the Pierpont Morgan Library 15 December 1935.* 1937; Hans Lietzmann, *Geschichte der Alten Kirche,* III, *Die Reichskirche.* 1938, pp.321-329; Leonhard Fendt, "Der heutige Stand der Forschung über das Geburtsfest Jesu am 25. XII. und über Epiphanias," in *Theologische Literaturzeitung.* 78 (1953), cols. 1-10; Roland H. Bainton, "The Origins of Epiphany," in *Collected Papers in Church History.* I (1962), pp.22-38.

¶ 393.   At least as early as in the second century dates were being given for the day of Jesus' birth. As we have seen (¶350), Clement of Alexandria says in the *Stromata* (A.D. c.194) that from the birth of Christ to the death of Commodus (ἀφ' οὗ ὁ κύριος ἐγεννήθη ἕως Κομόδου τελευτῆς) was one hundred ninety-four years, one month, and thirteen days,[1] which gives Nov 18, 3 B.C., as Clement's date for the birth of Christ. Even though he himself thus gives an exact date, he seems to speak somewhat disapprovingly when he says that there are also those who have determined not only the year but the day of the Savior's birth (τῇ γενέσει τοῦ Σωτῆρος). They put the birth, as Clement too did, in the twenty-eighth year of Augustus, i.e., 3/2 B.C. (¶¶350, 360), but on the twenty-fifth day of Pachon which is equivalent to May 20 (Table 8). After that Clement re-marks that the followers of Basilides (the famous Gnostic who flour-ished at Alexandria about A.D. 117-138) hold as a festival also the day of Christ's baptism (καὶ τοῦ βαπτίσματος αὐτοῦ τὴν ἡμέραν), which they say was in the fifteenth year of Tiberius and on the fifteenth day of the month Tybi (= Jan 10), while others say that it was on the eleventh day of the same month (= Jan 6). Continu-ing immediately to the passion, Clement reports that some say it took place in the sixteenth year of Tiberius on the twenty-fifth of Phame-noth, others on the twenty-fifth of Pharmuthi, and yet others on the nineteenth of Pharmuthi. Then returning to the birth he says that others declare that the Savior was born (γεγεννῆσθαι) on the twenty-fourth or twenty-fifth of Pharmuthi, which is equivalent to Apr 19 or 20.

(a) JANUARY 6

¶ 394.   Epiphanius (A.D. c.315-403) also reports dating which goes back into the second century. In the *Panarion* we remember (¶356) that he directs himself at one point against the Alogi as he calls them, known as a group in Asia Minor around A.D. 180. In the

[1] *Stromata.* I, xxi, 145.

same passage where he says the Alogi put the birth of Jesus under the consuls Sulpicius Camerinus and Poppaeus Sabinus (the latter name being somewhat distorted in Epiphanius), which means in A.D. 9, he also says that they put the date on: πρὸ δεκαδύο καλανδῶν Ἰουλίων ἢ Ἰουνίων.[1] In Latin this date would be written: *XII Kal. Julius vel Junius.* The twelfth day before the Kalends or first day of July is equivalent (counting inclusively) to Jun 20; the twelfth day before the Kalends or first day of June is equivalent to May 21. Because of the similarity of date this would appear to represent the same tradition reported by Clement of Alexandria (¶393) in connection with the followers of Basilides which gave Pachon 25 = May 20 as the date of the birth of Jesus. This date it is now stated by Epiphanius, however, was that of the day of the conception (σύλληψις) as announced by Gabriel to Mary (Lk 1:26ff.) (τὴν ἡμέραν τῆς συλλήψεως καὶ ὡς εὐηγγελίσατο ὁ Γαβριὴλ τὴν παρθένον) rather than of the birth of Jesus. Probably, therefore, although Clement of Alexandria did not make it plain, the same point of reference was that which was intended in the tradition which he reported.

⟨ 395.   As for the day of the birth of Christ, Epiphanius himself refers to the forty-second year of Augustus and the consular date *Augusto XIII et Silvano* (A.U.C. 752 = 2 B.C.) and quotes the tradition he accepts:

τούτων ὑπατευόντων δὲ Ὀκτανίου τὸ τρισκαιδέκατον καὶ Σιλανοῦ, ἐγεννήθη Χριστὸς τῇ πρὸ ὀκτὼ εἰδῶν Ἰανουαρίων μετὰ δεκατρεῖς ἡμέρας τῆς χειμερινῆς τροπῆς καὶ τῆς τοῦ φωτὸς καὶ ἡμέρας προσθήκης.

When these were consuls, Octavian for the thirteenth time and Silvanus, Christ was born on the eighth day before the Ides of January, thirteen days after the winter solstice and the beginning of the increase of the light and the day.[2]

The eighth day before the Ides or thirteenth day of January (¶141), counting inclusively, is Jan 6; this is thirteen days inclusively after the winter solstice, dated at that time on Dec 25. In another passage Epiphanius gives the same date even more exactly as, according to Roman reckoning, between the evening of Jan 5 and the morning of Jan 6.[3] Also in the same passage he gives the same date in its equivalents in no less than eight other calendars: according to the

---

[1] *Panarion haer.* 51, 29, 2. ed. Holl, II, p.300.
[2] *Panarion haer.* 51, 22, 4. ed. Holl, II, p.284; cf. also 51, 22, 18. ed. Holl, II, p.288.
[3] *Panarion haer.* 51, 24, 1. ed. Holl, II, p.293; cf. 51, 27, 5. ed. Holl, II, p.298.

Egyptians on Tybi 11 (Tybi 1 = Dec 27 [Table 8], therefore Tybi 11 = Jan 6); according to the Syrian Greeks on Audynaios 6 (Audynaios 1 = Jan 1 [Table 25], therefore Audynaios 6 = Jan 6); in the calendar of the Hebrews on the fifth day of Tebeth (Dec/Jan); etc.

¶ 396. In Greek the word ἡ ἐπιφάνεια, "the epiphany," means "the manifestation" or "the appearing." In Greek literature and inscriptions it is used for the visible manifestation of a deity. In II Tim 1:10 it is used for the appearing of the Savior on earth. Epiphanius employs the same word in the plural, τὰ ἐπιφάνεια, "the manifestations," as a name for the day of the birth of Jesus, and he also dated other "manifestations" of the divine glory of Jesus on the same day. Speaking of the birth, he writes, for example:

ἡ ἡμέρα τῶν Ἐπιφανείων, ἥ ἐστιν ἡμέρα τῆς αὐτοῦ κατὰ σάρκα γεννήσεως.

The day of the Epiphanies, which is the day of his birth according to the flesh.[4]

Alternatively with τὰ ἐπιφάνεια he also uses τὰ θεοφάνεια, "the theophanies."[5] This word is not in the Greek New Testament but is found in Greek literature in the singular, ἡ θεοφάνεια, "the theophany," for the "vision of God"; and in the plural, τὰ θεοφάνεια, for a festival at Delphi in which statues of the gods were displayed to the people. It was also on this day of "the Epiphanies" or "the Theophanies" that, according to Epiphanius as we have seen (¶370), the star shone in the East for the Magi two years before they arrived at Jerusalem and Bethlehem.

¶ 397. From the date of Jesus' birth given by Epiphanius (Tybi 11, the eighth day before the Ides of January, etc., all equaling Jan 6 [¶395]), he also counts forward to events of the public ministry of Jesus. Jesus was baptized, Epiphanius says,[6] according to Egyptian reckoning on Hathyr 12 and according to Roman reckoning on the sixth day before the Ides of November. These dates (see Table 8 and ¶141) are both equivalent to Nov 8. This date, Epiphanius observes, was exactly sixty days before "the Epiphanies,"

---

[4] *Panarion haer.* 51, 16, 1. ed. Holl, II, p.270; cf. 51, 22, 12. ed. Holl, II, p.287; 51, 27, 4. ed. Holl, II, p.298.
[5] *Panarion haer.* 51, 29, 4, ed. Holl. II, p.300.
[6] *Panarion haer.* 51, 16, 1. ed. Holl, II, p.270; 51, 30, 4. ed. Holl, II, p.302.

i.e., the birthday of Jesus. Then Epiphanius cites Lk 3:23.[7] In Codex Sinaiticus, Codex Vaticanus, and many other manuscripts, this reads: ἦν Ἰησοῦς ἀρχόμενος ὡσεὶ ἐτῶν τριάκοντα. The participle ἀρχόμενος, literally "beginning," is somewhat difficult to interpret, as is shown by changes made in other manuscripts where Codex Alexandrinus, Codex Bezae, and others move it to the end, and where the Sinaitic Syriac and other texts omit the word altogether. In the minuscules of the Ferrar Group (13, 69, 124, 346) the meaning is clarified, according to one possible understanding, by the addition of the word εἶναι, and this is the way the quotation is given by Epiphanius: ἦν Ἰησοῦς ἀρχόμενος εἶναι ὡς ἐτῶν τριάκοντα. With this interpretation the statement is that Jesus was "beginning to be about thirty years of age" at his baptism. Using this interpretation and in the light of the baptismal date given above, Epiphanius then explains that Jesus was in fact, at the time of his baptism, twenty-nine years and ten months of age, which might be called "thirty years, but not full (ἀλλ' οὐ πλήρης). The miracle which followed soon afterward at the wedding at Cana took place a full thirty years from the birth of Jesus (πλήρωμα τριάκοντα ἐτῶν ἀπὸ τῆς γεννήσεως τοῦ κυρίου), i.e., exactly on his thirtieth birthday.[8]

〔398.   Summarizing the ministry in round numbers, Epiphanius can then say that the thirtieth year of Jesus was that of his baptism, that after that he preached during his thirty-first year being accepted by the people, that he preached also during his thirty-second year but under opposition, and that in yet another year (his thirty-third) there remained still seventy-four days.[9] From his birthday on Tybi 11 = Jan 6 to the day of his death on the thirteenth day before the Kalends of April (¶141) or on the twenty-fourth day of Phamenoth (Table 8), both of which designations indicate Mar 20, was exactly seventy-four days. Therefore altogether the life of Jesus covered thirty-two years and seventy-four days. Also, Epiphanius says, the resurrection took place on Phamenoth 26 or the eleventh day before the Kalends of April, namely on Mar 22. The life of Jesus, as understood by Epiphanius, may therefore be outlined as in Table 114.

[7] Panarion haer. 51, 16, 2. ed. Holl, II, p.271.
[8] Panarion haer. 51, 16, 7-8. ed. Holl, II, p.272; cf. 51, 29, 7. ed. Holl, II, p.301.
[9] Panarion haer. 51, 27, 4-6. ed. Holl, II, pp.298-299.

TABLE 114. THE LIFE OF JESUS ACCORDING TO THE
CHRONOLOGY OF EPIPHANIUS

Year of Jesus' Life	Year B.C./A.D.	Event	Date	
	B.C.			
0	2	Birth	Jan 6	
1	1	First Birthday	Jan 6	
	A.D.			
2	1	Second Birthday	Jan 6	
		Arrival of the Magi	Jan 6	
3	2	Third Birthday	Jan 6	
4	3	Fourth Birthday	Jan 6	
. . . .				
28	27	Twenty-eighth Birthday	Jan 6	
29	28	Twenty-ninth Birthday	Jan 6	
		Baptism "about thirty"		Nov 8
30	29	Thirtieth Birthday	Jan 6	
		Sign at Cana	Jan 6	
31	30	Thirty-first Birthday	Jan 6	
		Preached, being accepted		
32	31	Thirty-second Birthday	Jan 6	
		Preached, being opposed		
33	32	Thirty-third Birthday	Jan 6	
		Death seventy-four days		
		later		Mar 20
		Resurrection		Mar 22

〖 399. Returning to the date of the conception which Epiphanius gave as fixed by the Alogi on Jun 20 or May 21 (¶394), he also reports in this connection the tradition that the birth followed seven months later or, more exactly, seven lunar months less four days (ἑπτὰ μηνῶν χρόνον κατὰ τὸν σεληνιακὸν δρόμον παρὰ ἡμέρας τέσσαρας).[10] Seven lunar months of 29.5 days each equals 206.5 days. If we say 206 days, minus four days, we have 202 days, and the number of days from Jun 20 to Jan 6 inclusive is 201 days. There-

[10] *Panarion haer.* 51, 29, 3-4. ed. Holl, II, p.300.

fore Epiphanius evidently intends to show that this tradition agrees
with the date of Jan 6 for the birth. He says that others, however,
declare that the duration of the period in question was ten months
less fourteen days and eight hours or, otherwise stated, nine months
plus fifteen days and four hours. The two ways of stating this figure
show that he reckoned one lunar month as equaling twenty-nine
days and twelve hours, i.e., 29.5 days. In this connection he also
cites Wisd 7:2 for the "ten months." Epiphanius does not state the
meaning of this dating, but it could be explained as follows. From
Mar 6 to Jan 6 is ten months. Fourteen days and eight hours forward
from Mar 6 brings one to the night of Mar 19/20. In other words
from Mar 19/20 to Jan 6 is ten months less fourteen days and
eight hours. In this way the date of conception would coincide with
the date of death (Mar 20). So Epiphanius is able to conclude that
from all sides ($\pi\alpha\nu\tau\alpha\chi\delta\theta\epsilon\nu$) the date of Tybi 11 ($=$ Jan 6) is agreed
upon for the birth of Jesus.[11]

((400.   Glancing back, then, at the tradition reported by Clement
of Alexandria (¶393), a tradition deriving probably from the followers of Basilides, which gave the date of Pachon 25 = May 20,
it seems probable (¶394) that they also intended by $\gamma\epsilon\nu\epsilon\sigma\iota s$ to point
to conception rather than birth.[12] In this case there was a rather
widespread opinion at least as early as in the second century that
the conception was in the spring and the birth of Jesus near the midwinter, in the areas represented by Epiphanius' report specifically
on Jan 6. The fact that in the same connection Clement of Alexandria (¶393) also mentions the festival of the Basilidians which
celebrated the day of Jesus' baptism on Tybi 15 or Tybi 11, i.e.,
on Jan 10 or Jan 6, suggests that although Epiphanius gave the
different date of Nov 8 for the baptism (¶397) there were many
who believed that this event which could be thought of as marking
a birth "according to the Spirit" fell on the anniversary of the birth
"according to the flesh." In that case the "manifestations" celebrated
on Jan 6 were indeed numerous, namely the birth of Jesus (¶396),
the appearing of the star to the wise men (¶396), the first sign at
Cana (¶397), and, in the view of some, the baptism (¶400).

((401.   As to why Jan 6 was fixed upon as the exact day, Epiphani-

[11] *Panarion haer.* 51, 29, 7. ed. Holl, II, p.301.
[12] Lake in HERE III, p.605.

us may also provide a clue. In the *Panarion*[13] he describes a ceremony held in the temple of Kore at Alexandria on the night of Jan 5
and morning of Jan 6. The participants stay awake all night, he
says, making music to the idol with songs and flutes. In the early
morning at cockcrow they descend by torchlight to a subterranean
shrine and bring forth a wooden image, marked with the sign of
a cross and a star of gold on hands, knees, and head. This image
they carry in procession to musical accompaniment, and then return it to the crypt. They explain the meaning of the ceremony to
the effect that in this hour this day Kore, the virgin, gave birth to
the Aion. Similar ceremonies are held, Epiphanius says, on the
same date at Petra and Elusa in Arabia. This may account for the
choice of the same date for observance in the attempt to replace
pagan ceremony by Christian.[14]

(b) DECEMBER 25

([402.   In the Roman city calendar for the year 354, edited by
Filocalus and described above (¶176), there is a list of the burial
places of the martyrs (*depositio martyrum*) arranged in the order
of the days of the year on which festivals were held in their honor.[1]
The list can of course not be later than the calendar itself which is
shown to belong to A.D. 354 by the facts that the lists of consuls
and prefects extend to 354, and that the list of bishops extends to
Liberius whose accession was in 352 but of whose banishment in
366 nothing is said. But the original *depositio episcoporum* was
probably compiled in 336 and revised in 354 for it runs in order
through the church year and through the death of Sylvester in 335,
and then Marcus (who died in 336) and his immediate successors
are added—out of order as far as the months of the church year
are concerned—at the end of the list. If the same is true of the
depositio martyrum, it may also be dated in A.D. 336.

([403.   In the *depositio martyrum* the sequence of festivals in the
church year begins with the item:

VIII Kal. Ian. natus Christus in Betleem Iudeae

The eighth day before the Kalends of January, on which day it was

---

[13] *Panarion haer.* 51, 22, 9-11. ed. Holl, II, pp.285-287.
[14] Lake in HERE V, p.332; Lietzmann, *Geschichte der alten Kirche*, III, p.327.

[1] Lietzmann, *The Three Oldest Martyrologies*. KLT 2, pp.3-5.

remembered that Christ was born in Bethlehem of Judea, was the twenty-fifth day of December. Since the list for the entire year begins with this date and since the following dates are those when festivals were held in honor of the persons named, it seems evident that in Rome in A.D. 336 the festival of the birth of Christ was held on Dec 25. Also the last item on the list is a festival on the Ides of December, i.e., on Dec 13. Therefore the beginning of the liturgical year was between Dec 13 and Dec 25. The *depositio episcoporum* agrees by making its last and first items respectively Dec 8 and Dec 27.[2]

⁅ 404.   At Antioch in A.D. 386[3] John Chrysostom (born at Antioch A.D. c.345, preacher at Antioch and later [A.D. 398] bishop of Constantinople, died A.D. 407) delivered two sermons with which we are here concerned. On Dec 20[4] he spoke in memory of Philogonius, a former bishop of Antioch. In this sermon he says that a festival is approaching, namely that of the bodily birth of Christ. This is basic in its significance, he says, to the other great festivals of the Christian year, for if Jesus had not been born he would not have been baptized as is celebrated on Epiphany, he would not have been crucified and raised as is celebrated at Easter, and he would not have sent the Spirit as is commemorated at Pentecost. To this festival which will be celebrated in five days he therefore looks forward eagerly and urges the congregation to do the same.

⁅ 405.   On the day itself, namely Dec 25 of the year 386, Chrysostom delivered the second sermon. Theodoret (A.D. c.393-453), bishop of Cyprus, later made two quotations from this sermon, saying that they were taken from the "birthday discourse" (ἐκ τοῦ γενεθλιακοῦ λόγου).[5] Herein Chrysostom says[6] that it would be wonderful if the sun could come down from heaven and send forth its light on earth, and it is more wonderful that in the incarnation the sun of righteousness does in fact send forth its light from human flesh. With "the sun of righteousness" he is doubtless referring to Mal 4:2. Then he tells how long he had desired not only to experience this day but to do so in the company of a large congrega-

[2] Duchesne, *Christian Worship, Its Origin and Evolution*, pp.258-259.
[3] Usener, *Das Weihnachtsfest*, p.245; and Lietzmann, *ibid.*, p.384.
[4] Usener, *ibid.*, pp.222-223.
[5] *Dialogue* I. NPNFSS, III, p.181.
[6] Usener, *ibid.*, pp.225-227.

tion. He states that it was not yet ten years that the festival had been known to them. It was, however, transmitted to them as from long ago and from many years (ὡς ἄνωθεν καὶ πρὸ πολλῶν ἡμῖν παραδο-θεῖσα ἐτῶν). From long ago it was known to those who dwell in the West (παρὰ μὲν τοῖς τὴν ἑσπέραν οἰκοῦσιν ἄνωθεν γνωριζομένη). And from long ago it was a festival that was very well known and famous to those who dwell from Thrace to Gades (καὶ ἄνωθεν τοῖς ἀπὸ Θράκης μέχρι Γαδείρων οἰκοῦσι κατάδηλος καὶ ἐπίσημος γέγονε).

〔406. Later in the sermon Chrysostom introduces an exegesis of scripture to support the date of Dec 25. This is based on Lk 1 and runs as follows.[7] The promise to the priest Zechariah that his wife Elizabeth would bear a son to be named John came at the time Zechariah had entered the temple to burn incense (Lk 1:9). Evidently assuming, incorrectly as far as we know, that Zechariah was the high priest and that this was the most important event possible, Chrysostom explains that this was the time of the Fast and of the Feast of Tabernacles. The Fast was the Day of Atonement, the one day of the year when the high priest entered the Holy of Holies, and the date of it was the tenth day of the seventh month (Lev 16:29), i.e., Tishri 10. The Feast of Tabernacles followed shortly on the fifteenth day of the seventh month and continued for seven days (Lev 23:34). This feast, says Chrysostom, the Jews celebrate toward the end of the month Gorpiaios. In A.D. 386 there was a new moon on Sep 10. Since the month Tishri falls normally in Sep/Oct this new moon presumably marked Tishri 1. Tishri 1 (the Day of Atonement) was therefore approximately Sep 20 in that year, and Tishri 15-21 (the Feast of Tabernacles) was approximately Sep 25-Oct 1. In the later correlation of the Syro-Macedonian calendar with the Julian (Table 25) the month of Gorpiaios began on Sep 1. The Feast of Tabernacles was accordingly celebrated toward the end of Gorpiaios exactly as Chrysostom says. This was the date, then, of the conception of John the Baptist as announced to Zechariah (Lk 1:13). Counting from this time (Gorpiaios = Sep), it was in the sixth month (Lk 1:26) that annunciation was made to Mary and the conception of Jesus is to be dated. Here Chrysostom carefully names and counts six intervening months (Hyperberetaios, Dios, Apellaios, Audynaios, Peritios, and Dystros) and concludes

[7] Ibid., pp.230-233.

that it was in the next month, Xanthikos (= Apr) that the conception of Jesus is to be placed. From that point he counts nine months inclusively to the birth of Jesus, namely the months Xanthikos, Artemisios, Daisios, Panemos, Loos, Gorpiaios, Hyperberetaios, Dios, and Apellaios. The last, Apellaios (= Dec), was the month in which the birthday celebration was even then being held at which Chrysostom was preaching.

⟨ 407.   As to the reason for the selection of this exact date, the reference by Chrysostom (¶405) to "the sun of righteousness" (Mal 4:2) may give a clue. As we saw from Epiphanius (¶395), Dec 25 was the date accepted at this time for the winter solstice. From this point began the increase of the light and the day. It was appropriate that the time that the light of the natural sun began to increase was also the time that the "sun of righteousness" came into the world. It was also not unimportant that the pagan feast of the *sol invictus*, the "invincible sun," was observed on this date, and the Christian festival could replace it.[8] Ultimately the full equation with the solar year was completed in that the conception and the crucifixion were both placed on Mar 25 as well as the birth on Dec 25. Thus Augustine writes:

> "For He is believed to have been conceived on the twenty-fifth of March, upon which day also he suffered. . . . But he was born, according to tradition, upon December the twenty-fifth."[9]

⟨ 408.   The chief reckonings attested by the oldest sources, then, put the conception of Jesus in the spring, and his birth in midwinter. In the East the birth was celebrated on Jan 6, a date to which also the star and the Magi, the baptism, and the sign at Cana were attached. In the West the birthday of Christ was Dec 25. From Chrysostom we learn that, although this date had been introduced to Antioch only ten years before he spoke, say about A.D. 375, it had long been known in the West. As the Western usage gradually spread to most places, Jan 6 was retained as the celebration of the three "manifestations" in the coming of the Magi, the baptism, and the sign at Cana. Although the exact dates of Jan 6 and Dec 25 may have been fixed because of the relationships to the festival of Kore and the winter solstice respectively (¶¶401, 407), the selection of

---

[8] Lake in HERE III, p.608.
[9] *On the Trinity*. IV, 5. NPNF III, p.74.

specific dates at this time of the year agrees with what we suppose was a relatively old tradition of a midwinter birth, therefore a date in December or January is not in itself unlikely.

2. THE PUBLIC MINISTRY OF JESUS

LITERATURE: Conrad Cichorius, "Chronologisches zum Leben Jesu," in ZNW 22 (1923), pp.16-20; George Ogg, *The Chronology of the Public Ministry of Jesus.* 1940; and "The Age of Jesus When He Taught," in NTS 5 (1958-59), pp.291-298; Norman Walker, "The Reckoning of Hours in the Fourth Gospel," in *Novum Testamentum.* 4 (1960), pp.69-73.

(1) THE BEGINNING OF THE PUBLIC MINISTRY

(a) "IN THE FIFTEENTH YEAR OF THE REIGN OF TIBERIUS CAESAR"

LITERATURE: H. Dessau, ed., *Prosopographia Imperii Romani.* II (1897), pp.182f., No. 150; CAH X, pp.607-612.

〖 409.   According to Lk 3:1ff. it was in the fifteenth year of the reign of Tiberius Caesar that the word of God came to John the son of Zechariah in the wilderness and that he went into the region about the Jordan preaching a baptism of repentance for the forgiveness of sins. And at the time when all the people were baptized Jesus also was baptized and thus made his initial public appearance. Events and honors in the life and reign of Tiberius have been set forth above in Table 40. Tiberius Claudius Nero was born on Nov 16, A.U.C. 712 = 42 B.C. On Jun 26, A.U.C. 757 = A.D. 4, he was adopted by Augustus and designated his successor,[1] from which time he was called Tiberius Julius Caesar. On Oct 23, A.U.C. 765 = A.D. 12, he celebrated a triumph for his military victories in Germany and Pannonia. Referring to this event, Suetonius[2] says that "the consuls caused a law to be passed soon after this that he should govern the provinces jointly with Augustus and hold the census with him." The date when Tiberius thus began to govern the provinces jointly with Augustus was probably A.D. 12,[3] although arguments have been presented for putting it in A.D. 11 or 13.[4] In this connection Tacitus describes Tiberius Nero as *collega imperii,* "colleague in the empire,"[5] and some consider him joint emperor with Augustus from this time on.[6] On Aug 19, A.U.C. 767 = A.D. 14,

---

[1] Dio, *Roman History.* 55, 13, 1.   [2] *Tiberius.* 21.
[3] Suetonius, ed. J. C. Rolfe, LCL, I, p.323.
[4] Holzmeister, *Chronologia Vitae Christi,* p.66.
[5] *Annals.* I, 3.   [6] EB 22, p.176.

Augustus died, with the funeral on or around Sep 12. On Sep 17 the Senate met, voted the deceased emperor deity, *Divus Augustus*, and voted his designated successor, Tiberius, the new head of state. As emperor he was known as Tiberius Caesar Augustus. So Tiberius ruled as colleague of Augustus from A.D. 12, and as successor of Augustus from Aug 19 (or from Sep 17 if you count from the vote of the Senate), A.D. 14, and his rule continued until his death on Mar 16, A.U.C. 790 = A.D. 37.[7] In Table 115 a preliminary numbering of his regnal years is given. Column 1 numbers from the time when Tiberius began to govern jointly with Augustus, and Column 2 from the first full calendar year after that. Column 3 numbers from the death of Augustus and the succession of Tiberius, and Column 4 from the first full calendar year after that.

⟨ 410.   If Tiberius began to govern the provinces jointly with Augustus soon after Oct 23, A.D. 12 (¶409), his first factual year of such rule extended from late October (let us say), A.D. 12 to late October A.D. 13, and this year and his succeeding years counted from the same point may be tabulated as in Table 116.

⟨ 411.   If the reckoning from the same initial point (¶410) was by Roman calendar years and what we have called the nonaccession-year system (cf. Column 1 in Table 115), the years would be as in Table 117.

⟨ 412.   If the reckoning was the same as the foregoing (¶411) but according to the accession-year system (cf. Column 2 in Table 115), the count would be as in Table 118.

⟨ 413.   In the Syro-Macedonian calendar (Table 25) the year began on Hyperberetaios 1 = Oct 1 (cf. ¶345). In this calendar and by the nonaccession-year method, still using the joint rule of the provinces as the initial point, the reckoning would be as in Table 119.

⟨ 414.   By the same reckoning (¶413) but by the accession-year system the years would be as in Table 120. It is to be remembered that the assumed initial point of Tiberius' joint rule is in late October, on or after the twenty-third day of that month (¶410), hence after the Syro-Macedonian New Year on Oct 1.

---

[7] Suetonius, *Tiberius*. 73.

⟨415. In the Jewish calendar (Table 13) the year began with the month Nisan, corresponding to Mar/Apr of the Julian calendar. Using this calendar, counting still from the joint rule of the prov-

TABLE 115. REGNAL YEARS OF TIBERIUS CAESAR

A.U.C.	A.D.		Col. 1	Col. 2	Col. 3	Col. 4
765	12	Tiberius governs jointly with Augustus	1			
766	13	....	2	1		
767	14	Aug 19, death of Augustus				
		Sep 17, Tiberius named head of state	3	2	1	
768	15	....	4	3	2	1
769	16	....	5	4	3	2
770	17	....	6	5	4	3
771	18	....	7	6	5	4
772	19	....	8	7	6	5
773	20	....	9	8	7	6
774	21	....	10	9	8	7
775	22	....	11	10	9	8
776	23	....	12	11	10	9
777	24	....	13	12	11	10
778	25	....	14	13	12	11
779	26	....	15	14	13	12
780	27	....	16	15	14	13
781	28	....	17	16	15	14
782	29	....	18	17	16	15
783	30	....	19	18	17	16
784	31	....	20	19	18	17
785	32	....	21	20	19	18
786	33	....	22	21	20	19
787	34	....	23	22	21	20
788	35	....	24	23	22	21
789	36	....	25	24	23	22
790	37	Mar 16, death of Tiberius	26	25	24	23

inces, and reckoning both by the nonaccession-year and accession-year methods, the results are as in Tables 121 and 122.

⟨416. If the point from which the regnal years of Tiberius were reckoned was, however, the death of Augustus on Aug 19, A.D. 14 (or the formal naming of Tiberius to succeed Augustus by the Senate less than a month later on Sep 17) (¶409), then different sets of figures result. Taking Aug 19, A.D. 14, as the point of reference and

TABLE 116. FACTUAL REGNAL YEARS OF TIBERIUS
COUNTED FROM HIS JOINT RULE OF THE
PROVINCES WITH AUGUSTUS

Number of Regnal Year	Duration of Regnal Year
	A.D.
1	Oct, 12 – Oct, 13
2	Oct, 13 – Oct, 14
....	....
14	Oct, 25 – Oct, 26
15	Oct, 26 – Oct, 27
....	....

reckoning both factual and calendar years according to alternate systems and various calendars we obtain the results shown in Tables 123-131.

〖417.   Referring to Tables 115-131, it is obvious that the earliest dates for the regnal years of Tiberius are obtained by reckoning from his joint rule of the provinces with Augustus (probably in the month of October in A.D. 12) as the initial point (Columns 1 and 2 in Table 115). It also seems not unlikely that in Judea (where the work of John the Baptist and the baptism of Jesus took place),

TABLE 117. REGNAL YEARS OF TIBERIUS
FROM HIS JOINT RULE OF THE PROVINCES, COUNTED AS
JULIAN CALENDAR YEARS ACCORDING TO THE NONACCESSION-YEAR SYSTEM

Number of Regnal Year	Duration of Regnal Year
	A.D.
1	Oct – Dec 31, 12
2	Jan 1 – Dec 31, 13
....	....
14	Jan 1 – Dec 31, 25
15	Jan 1 – Dec 31, 26
....	....

TABLE 118. REGNAL YEARS OF TIBERIUS
FROM HIS JOINT RULE OF THE PROVINCES, COUNTED AS
JULIAN CALENDAR YEARS ACCORDING TO THE ACCESSION-YEAR SYSTEM

Number of Regnal Year	Duration of Regnal Year
	A.D.
Accession Year	Oct – Dec 31, 12
1	Jan 1 – Dec 31, 13
14	Jan 1 – Dec 31, 26
15	Jan 1 – Dec 31, 27

which was a part of the province of Syria, it would be his rule of the provinces which would be the point of reference for reckoning the regnal years of Tiberius. Writing *Against Marcion* Tertullian says in one place that "the Lord has been revealed since the twelfth year of Tiberius Caesar";[8] and in another: "In the fifteenth year of Tiberius, Christ Jesus vouchsafed to come down from heaven."[9] This dual and at first sight apparently contradictory dating can be explained by supposing that the fifteen years are counted from the

TABLE 119. REGNAL YEARS OF TIBERIUS
FROM HIS JOINT RULE OF THE PROVINCES, COUNTED AS
SYRO-MACEDONIAN CALENDAR YEARS
ACCORDING TO THE NONACCESSION-YEAR SYSTEM

Number of Regnal Year	Duration of Regnal Year
	A.D.
1	Oct, 12 – Sep 30, 13
2	Oct 1, 13 – Sep 30, 14
14	Oct 1, 25 – Sep 30, 26
15	Oct 1, 26 – Sep 30, 27

[8] I, XV.   [9] I, xix.

TABLE 120. Regnal Years of Tiberius
from his Joint Rule of the Provinces, Counted as Syro-Macedonian
Calendar Years according to the Accession-Year System

Number of Regnal Year	Duration of Regnal Year
	A.D.
Accession Year	Oct, 12 – Sep 30, 13
1	Oct 1, 13 – Sep 30, 14
....	....
....	....
14	Oct 1, 26 – Sep 30, 27
15	Oct 1, 27 – Sep 30, 28
....	....
....	....

time of the joint rule of the provinces, and the twelve years are
reckoned as full calendar years after the death of Augustus (Columns 1 and 4 respectively in Table 115), both references therefore
indicating the same year, A.U.C. 779 = A.D. 26.

(| 418.   If "the fifteenth year of the reign of Tiberius Caesar" in
Lk 3:1 is counted in the same manner as has just been established
as probable for "the fifteenth year of Tiberius" in Tertullian (¶417),
then the Lukan reference also appears, at least by a preliminary
reckoning (Table 115 Column 1), to point to A.D. 26. In more precise terms, if it was a factual regnal year counted from Tiberius'

TABLE 121. Regnal Years of Tiberius
from His Joint Rule of the Provinces, Counted as
Jewish Calendar Years according to the Nonaccession-Year System

Number of Regnal Year	Duration of Regnal Year
	A.D.
1	Oct, 12 – Mar/Apr, 13
2	Mar/Apr, 13 – Mar/Apr, 14
....	....
....	....
14	Mar/Apr, 25 – Mar/Apr, 26
15	Mar/Apr, 26 – Mar/Apr, 27
....	....
....	....

TABLE 122. Regnal Years of Tiberius
from His Joint Rule of the Provinces, Counted as
Jewish Calendar Years according to the Accession-Year System

Number of Regnal Year	Duration of Regnal Year
	A.D.
Accession Year	Oct, 12 – Mar/Apr, 13
1	Mar/Apr, 13 – Mar/Apr, 14
....	....
14	Mar/Apr, 26 – Mar/Apr, 27
15	Mar/Apr, 27 – Mar/Apr, 28
....	....

joint rule of the provinces with Augustus (Table 116), the fifteenth year extended from late October, A.D. 26, to late October, A.D. 27. If it was a regnal year equated with a calendar year according to the nonaccession-year system, the fifteenth year would begin on Jan 1 in the Julian calendar (Table 117), in Mar/Apr in the Jewish calendar (Table 121), or on Oct 1 in the Syro-Macedonian calendar (Table 119), all in the year 26 of the Christian era. If the calendar years were counted according to the accession-year system, the dates were one year later, in A.D. 27.

TABLE 123. Factual Regnal Years of Tiberius
Counted from His Succession to Augustus

Number of Regnal Year	Duration of Regnal Year
	A.D.
1	Aug 19, 14 – Aug 18, 15
2	Aug 19, 15 – Aug 18, 16
....	....
14	Aug 19, 27 – Aug 18, 28
15	Aug 19, 28 – Aug 18, 29
....	....

TABLE 124. REGNAL YEARS OF TIBERIUS
FROM HIS SUCCESSION TO AUGUSTUS, COUNTED AS JULIAN CALENDAR YEARS
ACCORDING TO THE NONACCESSION-YEAR SYSTEM

Number of Regnal Year	Duration of Regnal Year
	A.D.
1	Aug 19 – Dec 31, 14
2	Jan 1 – Dec 31, 15
....	....
....	....
14	Jan 1 – Dec 31, 27
15	Jan 1 – Dec 31, 28
....	....
....	....

❲419. Let us then maintain the comparison made just above (¶418) with Tertullian and assume that Lk 3:1 also means the year 26 of the Christian era. Within that year of the Christian era the fifteenth regnal year of Tiberius might have begun as late as in late October (Table 116). Let us assume this latest possible beginning of the regnal year, for with the earlier beginnings which are theoretically possible there would be more leeway and the problem would be made easier rather than harder. If the fifteenth year of Tiberius

TABLE 125. REGNAL YEARS OF TIBERIUS
FROM HIS SUCCESSION TO AUGUSTUS, COUNTED AS JULIAN CALENDAR YEARS
ACCORDING TO THE ACCESSION-YEAR SYSTEM

Number of Regnal Year	Duration of Regnal Year
	A.D.
Accession Year	Aug 19 – Dec 31, 14
1	Jan 1 – Dec 31, 15
....	....
....	....
14	Jan 1 – Dec 31, 28
15	Jan 1 – Dec 31, 29
....	....
....	....

TABLE 126. REGNAL YEARS OF TIBERIUS
FROM HIS SUCCESSION TO AUGUSTUS, COUNTED AS CALENDAR YEARS OF THE
EGYPTIAN CALENDAR, ACCORDING TO THE NONACCESSION-YEAR SYSTEM

Number of Regnal Year	Duration of Regnal Year
	A.D.
1	Aug 19 – Aug 28, 14
2	Aug 29, 14 – Aug 28, 15
....	....
....	....
14	Aug 29, 26 – Aug 28, 27
15	Aug 29, 27 – Aug 28, 28
16	Aug 29, 28 – Aug 28, 29
....	....
....	....

began in late October and if Jesus was baptized not long afterward, as the Lukan record would certainly allow, then the baptism may be put, say, in November A.D. 26. It has also been seen already that there is at least some evidence for putting the birth of Jesus in mid-

TABLE 127. REGNAL YEARS OF TIBERIUS
FROM HIS SUCCESSION TO AUGUSTUS, COUNTED AS CALENDAR YEARS OF THE
EGYPTIAN CALENDAR, ACCORDING TO THE ACCESSION-YEAR SYSTEM

Number of Regnal Year	Duration of Regnal Year
	A.D.
Accession Year	Aug 19 – Aug 28, 14
1	Aug 29, 14 – Aug 28, 15
....	....
....	....
14	Aug 29, 27 – Aug 28, 28
15	Aug 29, 28 – Aug 28, 29
16	Aug 29, 29 – Aug 28, 30
....	....
....	....
19	Aug 29, 32 – Aug 28, 33
....	....
....	....

TABLE 128. REGNAL YEARS OF TIBERIUS
FROM HIS SUCCESSION TO AUGUSTUS, COUNTED AS
CALENDAR YEARS OF THE SYRO-MACEDONIAN CALENDAR,
ACCORDING TO THE NONACCESSION-YEAR SYSTEM

Number of Regnal Year	Duration of Regnal Year
	A.D.
1	Aug 19 – Sep 30, 14
2	Oct 1, 14 – Sep 30, 15
....	....
....	....
14	Oct 1, 26 – Sep 30, 27
15	Oct 1, 27 – Sep 30, 28
....	....
....	....

winter, 5/4 B.C., perhaps in December or January (¶408). In this case the later date, say January, would allow more leeway and make the problem easier, therefore let us take the earlier date and suppose that the birth was in December of 5 B.C. In this case the successive birthdays of Jesus would fall as shown in Table 132. Therewith we arrive at this result: Jesus was baptized in November A.D. 26 and presumably began his ministry very shortly thereafter; his thirtieth

TABLE 129. REGNAL YEARS OF TIBERIUS
FROM HIS SUCCESSION TO AUGUSTUS, COUNTED AS CALENDAR YEARS OF THE
SYRO-MACEDONIAN CALENDAR, ACCORDING TO THE ACCESSION-YEAR SYSTEM

Number of Regnal Year	Duration of Regnal Year
	A.D.
Accession Year	Aug 19 – Sep 30, 14
1	Oct 1, 14 – Sep 30, 15
....	....
....	....
14	Oct 1, 27 – Sep 30, 28
15	Oct 1, 28 – Sep 30, 29
....	....
....	....

TABLE 130. REGNAL YEARS OF TIBERIUS
FROM HIS SUCCESSION TO AUGUSTUS, COUNTED AS
CALENDAR YEARS OF THE JEWISH CALENDAR (BEGINNING WITH NISAN),
ACCORDING TO THE NONACCESSION-YEAR SYSTEM

Number of Regnal Year	Duration of Regnal Year
	A.D.
1	Aug 19, 14 – Mar/Apr, 15
2	Mar/Apr, 15 – Mar/Apr, 16
....	....
....	....
14	Mar/Apr, 27 – Mar/Apr, 28
15	Mar/Apr, 28 – Mar/Apr, 29
....	....
....	....

birthday was in December A.D. 26. At the time of his baptism and
the beginning of the ministry he was almost thirty years of age. This
is in exact agreement with Lk 3:23, understanding the Greek as in
the King James Version: "And Jesus himself began to be about thirty
years of age"; or as in Epiphanius (¶397): "Jesus was beginning
to be about thirty years of age."

TABLE 131. REGNAL YEARS OF TIBERIUS
FROM HIS SUCCESSION TO AUGUSTUS, COUNTED AS
CALENDAR YEARS OF THE JEWISH CALENDAR (BEGINNING WITH NISAN),
ACCORDING TO THE ACCESSION-YEAR SYSTEM

Number of Regnal Year	Duration of Regnal Year
	A.D.
Accession Year	Aug 19, 14 – Mar/Apr, 15
1	Mar/Apr, 15 – Mar/Apr, 16
....	....
....	....
14	Mar/Apr, 28 – Mar/Apr, 29
15	Mar/Apr, 29 – Mar/Apr, 30
....	....
....	....

⟨ 420.   The foregoing discussion (¶¶417-419) has operated with a reckoning of the regnal years of Tiberius from the date of his joint rule of the provinces with Augustus, probably in late October A.D. 12 (¶410 and Tables 116-122). It is also possible to count the regnal years of Tiberius from the death of Augustus on Aug 19,

TABLE 132. BIRTHDAYS OF JESUS FROM AN ASSUMED
BIRTH IN DECEMBER OF THE YEAR 5 B.C.

Date B.C.	Event
Dec, 5	Birth
Dec, 4	First Birthday
Dec, 3	Second Birthday
Dec, 2	Third Birthday
Dec, 1	Fourth Birthday
A.D.	
Dec, 1	Fifth Birthday
Dec, 2	Sixth Birthday
....	....
....	....
Dec, 24	Twenty-eighth Birthday
Dec, 25	Twenty-ninth Birthday
Dec, 26	Thirtieth Birthday
Dec, 27	Thirty-first Birthday
Dec, 28	Thirty-second Birthday
Dec, 29	Thirty-third Birthday
Dec, 30	Thirty-fourth Birthday

A.D. 14 and the subsequent accession of Tiberius (¶416 and Tables 123-131). Several Roman historians provide examples of reckoning from this beginning point. Dio puts the death of Tiberius on Mar 26 in the consulship of Gnaeus Proculus and Pontius Nigrinus, and states that he had been emperor for twenty-two years, seven months, and seven days.[10] Gnaeus Acerronius Proculus and Gaius Pontius Nigrinus were consuls in A.U.C. 790 = A.D. 37. Therefore Dio's date for the death of Tiberius is Mar 26 (actually this is an error for Mar 16, the date given by Suetonius [¶421]), A.D. 37. From Aug 19, A.D. 14, to Mar 26, A.D. 15, is a period of seven months and seven days. From the latter date to Mar 26, A.D. 37, is a period of twenty-

[10] *Roman History.* LVIII, 27, 1 - 28, 5.

two years. Therefore in his reckoning of the length of the reign of Tiberius Dio counted the exact number of years, months, and days from the death of Augustus.

([421. Tacitus and Suetonius count from the same point (¶420), namely the death of Augustus on Aug 19, A.D. 14, and state regnal years of Tiberius in terms of full calendar years after that point (Table 115 Column 4), as the following examples show. Tacitus tells of the death of Augustus in Nola and the arrival there of Tiberius Claudius Nero (cf. ¶409 for the name Nero), and says that "one report announced simultaneously that Augustus had passed away and that Nero was master of the empire."[11] Later Tacitus equates the ninth year of Tiberius with the consulate of Gaius Asinius and Gaius Antistius.[12] In a critical list of consuls (although not in our Table 38) *C. Asinius C. f. Pollio et C. Antistius C. f. Vetus* are the consuls of the year A.U.C. 776 = A.D. 23.[13] If we count full calendar years after the death of Augustus, the ninth year of Tiberius is A.U.C. 776 = A.D. 23. Suetonius dates the death of Tiberius *XVII Kal. Ap. Cn. Acerronio Proculo C. Pontio Nigrino conss.*, and states that this was in his twenty-third year of reign.[14] The seventeenth day before the Kalends of April was Mar 16. Gnaeus Acerronius Proculus and Gaius Pontius Nigrinus were consuls in A.U.C. 790 = A.D. 37. This date was in the twenty-third full calendar year after the death of Augustus.

([422. In the foregoing examples (¶421) we assume that the Roman historians were using the Julian calendar. In the provinces, when the regnal years of Tiberius were reckoned as full calendar years after the death of Augustus, we assume that the relevant provincial calendar would be used.[15] For example, Oxyrhynchus Papyrus No. 2353 contains a perfectly preserved letter with this date line at the end (Line 20):

(ἔτους) ιθ Τιβερίου Καίσαρ⟨αρ⟩ος Σεβαστοῦ μηνὸς Σεβαστοῦ ζ

This reads:

In the nineteenth year of Tiberius Caesar Augustus on the seventh day of the month Sebastos.

[11] *Annals.* I, 5.　　　　　　　[12] *Annals.* IV, 1.
[13] Liebenam, *Fasti Consulares Imperii Romani.* KLT 41-43, p.10.
[14] *Tiberius.* 73.
[15] Cf. J. K. Fotheringham quoted in Holzmeister, *Chronologia Vitae Christi*, p.59 n.2.

If the first regnal year of Tiberius, considered as an Egyptian calendar year according to the accession-year system (Table 127), began on Thoth 1 = Aug 29, A.D. 14, then the nineteenth year began on Thoth 1, A.D. 32. Sebastos is the Roman name of the Egyptian month Thoth (¶136 and Table 27) and since Thoth 1 = Aug 29, the seventh day of that month is Sep 4. Therefore the date of the letter is Sep 4, A.D. 32.[16]

⟨ 423.   If Lk 3:1 reckons the fifteenth year of Tiberius from his joint rule of the provinces with Augustus the date indicated is probably A.D. 26 (¶¶418-419). If the reckoning follows the pattern of examples just given (¶¶420-422), however, and counts in some manner from the death of Augustus and subsequent accession of Tiberius, then different results are possible. In searching the language of Lk 3:1 for any clue as to the manner of reckoning, it may be noticed that the Greek word ἡ ἡγεμονία, "the rule, or sovereignty," is used. In itself this word would seem compatible with either interpretation of when to count the beginning of the "rule" of Tiberius, whether over the provinces with Augustus, or over the empire by himself. Josephus, however, uses the same word when he tells how "the empire of the Romans (τῆς Ῥωμαίων ἡγεμονίας)" passed to Tiberius upon the death of Augustus.[17] In comparison with this usage there might seem to be a slight balance of probability in favor of the supposition that the fifteenth year "of the reign (τῆς ἡγεμονίας)" of Tiberius in Lk 3:1 also reflects a reckoning from the same point, i.e., from the death of Augustus and the succession of Tiberius. If the reckoning is from this point, it must still be determined, if possible, which calendar and manner of counting are used. Various possibilities appear in Tables 123-131. The two which appear most likely are discussed in the two following sections (¶¶424, 425).

⟨ 424.   Since the events dated in Lk 3:1ff. in the fifteenth year of Tiberius are events which transpired in Judea, it may be deemed probable that the date is derived from a Jewish source in which, presumably, the dating would be in terms of the Jewish calendar year.[18] According to the passage in Rosh Hashanah discussed above (¶¶164-165), this should mean a calendar year beginning on Nisan 1 and a reckoning according to the nonaccession-year system. In this case

---

[16] OP XXII (1954), p.156.   [17] War. II, 168.
[18] Ogg, The Chronology of the Public Ministry of Jesus, pp.199-201.

(Table 130) the fifteenth year of Tiberius extends from the first day of Nisan (Mar/Apr) in the year 28 to the last day before the first day of Nisan in the year 29 of the Christian era. The exact dates that year were probably from Apr 15, A.D. 28, to Apr 4, A.D. 29.[19] Considering the summer temperatures in the Jordan depression, it is probable that the major impact of John's work would be in the spring and the fall. Since great crowds had been attracted (Mk 1:5) before Jesus came, and since for whatever it is worth the tradition represented by Epiphanius (¶397) puts the baptism in the fall, indeed in the late fall, we may prefer the autumn for his baptism. On the interpretation explored in the present paragraph, then, the baptism of Jesus and the beginning of his ministry were in the fall of the year 28. If the birth and birthdays of Jesus were as shown in Table 132, his thirty-second birthday was approaching in December of the same year. He was "about thirty" (Lk 3:23) in the broad sense of the term.

¶425.   Since the combined work, Luke-Acts, is addressed to Theophilus (Lk 1:3) who is saluted as "most excellent" (κράτιστε), a form of address otherwise employed in the same work only of a Roman official (Ac 23:26; 24:2; 26:25), it may appear probable that the writing is addressed to Roman readers, or at any rate to readers out in the Roman world, to whom dating in terms of the Julian calendar would presumably be most familiar. In terms of Julian calendar years counted from the succession of Tiberius to Augustus (Table 115 Column 4), the fifteenth year would be A.D. 28 or 29, depending upon whether the nonaccession-year or accession-year system was followed (Tables 124, 125). Since Tacitus equates the ninth year of Tiberius with A.D. 23 and Suetonius equates the twenty-third year with A.D. 37 (¶421), we may consider this "accession-year" method the more probable. In that case the fifteenth regnal year of Tiberius was equivalent to the Julian year A.D. 29 (Table 125). The baptism and beginning of the public ministry were probably in the fall (¶424). The thirty-third birthday was approaching in December (Table 132). Jesus was "about thirty" (Lk 3:23) if we allow considerable latitude to this expression.

(b) "About thirty years of age"

¶426.   The statement in Lk 3:23 concerning the age of Jesus

[19] PDBC p.46.

when he was baptized (Lk 3:21) and began his ministry (Lk 3:23) (ἦν Ἰησοῦς ἀρχόμενος ὡσεὶ ἐτῶν τριάκοντα) has been dealt with in the preceding paragraphs, and at this point only a brief recapitulation, with the citation of one or two additional references, is necessary. It is possible to interpret the statement rather strictly in the sense of the KJV translation, "Jesus began to be about thirty years of age." Irenaeus follows this interpretation quite strictly when he writes: "For when he came to be baptized, he had not yet completed his thirtieth year, but was beginning to be about thirty years of age."[1] Epiphanius also (¶397) read Lk 3:23 to say that Jesus was "beginning to be about thirty years of age," put the baptism on Nov 8, sixty days before the thirtieth birthday of Jesus on Jan 6, and thus made him exactly twenty-nine years and ten months of age at the baptism. This age at this time, however, presupposes Epiphanius' date for the birth of Jesus on Jan 6, 2 B.C., and that date appears impossible in view of the established death of Herod the Great in 4 B.C. (¶365) and the consequent necessity of placing the birth of Jesus prior to that date (¶366). But if Jesus was born in midwinter, 5/4 B.C. (¶¶392, 408), perhaps in December, 5 B.C. (¶418), and baptized in, say, November A.D. 26 (counting the fifteenth year of Tiberius from his joint rule of the provinces and taking the latest reckoning in terms of the several possible calendars and methods of counting [¶419]), then an equally strict interpretation of Lk 3:23 is possible to the effect that Jesus was baptized probably only a month or two before his thirtieth birthday (Table 132), i.e., at the time when he quite literally "began to be about thirty years of age."

¶ 427. It is also possible to interpret the same statement in Lk 3:23 (¶426) rather loosely as is suggested by the RSV translation, "Jesus, when he began his ministry, was about thirty years of age," and to regard the word "about (ὡσεί)" as allowing a considerable leeway in years. Justin Martyr appears to allow some leeway when he says that Jesus had "waited for thirty years, more or less, until John appeared."[2] If the fifteenth year of Tiberius is counted from the death of Augustus by Jewish reckoning it signifies the year beginning in Mar/Apr, A.D. 28 (¶424). The baptism could have been in the fall of that year, with the thirty-second birthday (Table 132)

[1] *Against Heresies.* II, xxii, 5.
[2] *Dialogue with Trypho.* 88.

approaching in December. Jesus was "about thirty," broadly speaking. If the fifteenth year of Tiberius is counted after the death of Augustus by Roman reckoning it signifies the Julian year, A.D. 29 (¶425). The baptism could have been in the fall of that year, with the thirty-third birthday (Table 132) approaching in December. Jesus was "about thirty," somewhat more broadly speaking. Of course if the birth of Jesus should be placed in 7/6 B.C. (¶¶388, 389), then he was considerably more than a literal thirty years of age at any of the probable times for his baptism in A.D. 26 or 28 or 29, and relative to any of these points the words "about thirty" would have to be taken quite loosely. At the same time his age would be advanced at least somewhat in the direction of what is suggested in Jn 8:57 (¶428), although not yet as much as would be required by a literal interpretation of that saying.

(c) "NOT YET FIFTY YEARS OLD"

⟨ 428.   In Jn 8:57 the Jews say to Jesus, in the course of his ministry, "You are not yet fifty years old." Irenaeus insists that this must mean sometime in the decade leading up to the age of fifty:

> "Now, such language is fittingly applied to one who has already passed the age of forty, without having as yet reached his fiftieth year, yet is not far from this latter period. But to one who is only thirty years old it would unquestionably be said, 'Thou art not yet forty years old.' "[1]

Since Irenaeus put the baptism of Jesus just before he was thirty years of age (¶426), and interpreted Jn 8:57 to mean that Jesus was at that time in his forties, he must have considered that the public ministry lasted for more than ten years. If the ministry lasted at the most only a few years, as is more commonly assumed, then the birth must be pushed much earlier than is commonly done, if Jn 8:57 is to be interpreted as literally as Irenaeus requires. Perhaps even more latitude must be allowed in the interpretation of "not yet fifty," than in the case of "about thirty" (Lk 3:23). Some confirmation (if any were needed) that Jesus was at all events not more than fifty may be found in Mt 17:24-27, the story of the collection of the half-shekel tax from Jesus and Peter, for Josephus states that the half-shekel was contributed by men aged from twenty years up to fifty.[2]

[1] *Against Heresies*. II, xxii, 6.
[2] *Ant.* III, 196 (= III, viii, 1).

(d) "FORTY-SIX YEARS TO BUILD THIS TEMPLE"

◀ 429.   In Jn 2:20 the Jews say to Jesus when he is in Jerusalem at the first passover which the Fourth Gospel mentions: τεσσερά-κοντα καὶ ἓξ ἔτεσιν οἰκοδομήθη ὁ ναὸς οὗτος. With regard to the first aorist indicative passive verb, οἰκοδομήθη, this is translated, "It has taken forty-six years to build this temple," in the RSV; and, "This sanctuary took forty-six years to build," by Moffatt. If the statement refers to the original construction of the Temple by Solomon, or the rebuilding of it by Zerubbabel, the text has no bearing on the chronology of Jesus' life. But the word οὗτος, "this," appears to point to the actual structure standing there at that time.

◀ 430.   Four statements by Josephus provide information about the work of Herod in rebuilding the Temple as it stood in the time of Jesus. In *Ant.* xv, 354 Josephus says:[1]

Ἤδη δ᾽ αὐτοῦ τῆς βασιλείας ἑπτακαιδεκάτου προελθόντος ἔτους Καῖσαρ εἰς Συρίαν ἀφίκετο.

Now when Herod had already reigned seventeen years, Caesar came into Syria.

If Herod had already "gone forward" (προελθόντος) through seventeen years, it was then his eighteenth year. Evidently describing the same trip of Caesar Augustus to which Josephus refers, Dio[2] says that Augustus spent the winter in Samos, then "in the spring of the year when Marcus Apuleius and Publius Silius were consuls" went on into Asia and, after settling everything there and in Bithynia, came to Syria. M. Apuleius and P. Silius P. f. Nerva were the consuls of the year A.U.C. 734 = 20 B.C. (Table 38).[3] If the eighteenth year of Herod (beginning presumably on Nisan 1) corresponded with 20 B.C., Josephus was evidently numbering the regnal years of Herod from his taking of Jerusalem (Table 108 Column 2).

◀ 431.   In *Ant.* xv, 380 Josephus says:[4]

Τότε δ᾽ οὖν ὀκτωκαιδεκάτου τῆς Ἡρώδου βασιλείας γεγονότος ἐνιαυτοῦ μετὰ τὰς προειρημένας πράξεις ἔργον οὐ τὸ τυχὸν ἐπεβάλετο, τὸν νεὼν τοῦ θεοῦ δι᾽ αὐτοῦ κατασκευάσθαι.

---

[1] *Ant.* xv, 354 (= xv, x, 3).
[2] *Roman History.* LIV, 7, 4-6.
[3] Liebenam, *Fasti Consulares Imperii Romani.* KLT 41-43, p.7.
[4] *Ant.* xv, 380 (= xv, xi, 1).

This is ordinarily translated:

"And now Herod, in the eighteenth year of his reign, and after the acts already mentioned, undertook a very great work, that is, to build of himself the temple of God."

But this is the next time notation in sequence from that just considered (¶430). There we judged that the phrase ἑπτακαιδεκάτου προελθόντος ἔτους meant that Herod had passed through his seventeenth year and entered upon his eighteenth. Therefore in the present phrase ὀκτωκαιδεκάτου . . . γεγονότος ἐνιαυτοῦ the second perfect participle γεγονότος is probably a variant for the preceding προελθόντος (second aorist participle) and similarly means that the eighteenth year had already been and that Herod was now entered upon his nineteenth year. By the reckoning already established (¶430) Herod's nineteenth year began on Nisan 1, 19 B.C.

〔 432. In *War.* I, 401 Josephus states:[5]

Πεντεκαιδεκάτῳ γοῦν ἔτει τῆς βασιλείας αὐτόν τε τὸν ναὸν ἐπεσκεύασεν.
Thus, in the fifteenth year of his reign, he restored the temple.

If we were to take *Ant.* xv, 380 (¶431) as meaning "in the eighteenth year," the present reference to "in the fifteenth year" would represent a difference of three years. There is a difference of three years between the two possible beginning points for the reign of Herod, 40 B.C. when he was named king (¶362), and 37 B.C. when he actually took Jerusalem (¶363). If "the eighteenth year" (*Ant.* xv, 380) were reckoned from the former point, and "the fifteenth year" (*War.* I, 401) from the latter, both would agree in giving 23 B.C. (Table 108). But *Ant.* xv, 380 stands in sequence with *Ant.* xv, 354, and we have shown (¶430) that the reference in *Ant.* xv, 354 is reckoned from Herod's taking of Jerusalem. Furthermore we have shown that the reference in *Ant.* xv, 380 probably actually means the nineteenth year. Therefore we cannot, in the way just explored, reconcile the statement in *War.* I, 401 with that in *Ant.* xv, 380 but must recognize that as they stand they are in contradiction. Since *Ant.* xv, 380 is in sequence with *Ant.* xv, 354 and the latter is confirmed by Dio (¶430), it seems necessary to conclude that *War.* I, 401, at least in its present text, is in error. If, however, *Ant.* xv, 380 actually means, as we have concluded that it probably does, *after* the eighteenth year, i.e., in the nine-

[5] *War.* I, 401 (= I, xxi, 1).

teenth year, then an interesting conjecture is possible. The original text of *War*. I, 401 might have contained the numeral $\iota\theta = 19$. By damage to the θ this might have been read as $\iota\epsilon = 15$. This would account for the apparently erroneous reading of the present text, "in the fifteenth year," and would allow the supposition that in the original text the nineteenth year was given even as the nineteenth year is indicated by *Ant*. xv, 380.[6] We conclude that Josephus is to be understood as stating that Herod began to rebuild the Temple in the nineteenth year of his reign (counting from his taking of Jerusalem [Table 108 Column 2]), which means the regnal year which began with the Jewish calendar year on Nisan 1, 19 B.C. (¶431).

❡ 433. In *Ant*. xv, 420-421[7] Josephus describes the general layout of the Temple. Using the word περίβολος, he tells of the first enclosure into which all might come, the second into which foreigners were forbidden to come, and the third into which only the priests might enter and in which stood the altar and the temple edifice proper. Then he explains that Herod could not go into the third enclosure and the place of altar and sanctuary, which meant that the temple edifice proper had to be built by the priests. Herod did, however, take care of the cloisters and the outer enclosures (τὰ περὶ τὰς στοὰς καὶ τοὺς ἔξω περιβόλους), and these he built in eight years. Then Josephus says:

Τοῦ δὲ ναοῦ διὰ τῶν ἱερέων οἰκοδομηθέντος ἐνιαυτῷ καὶ μησὶν πέντε.
But the temple itself was built by the priests in a year and five months.

The word ὁ ναός (Ionic) or νεώς (Attic), "the temple," is used regularly in Greek for a temple in general, and also in particular for the inner part of a temple and, in paganism, for the shrine in which the image of the god was placed. In *Ant*. xv, 380 (¶431) and *War*. I, 401 (¶432) Josephus evidently used the word in its general sense in saying that Herod built the temple. In the present passage (*Ant*. xv, 421), however, he obviously uses it in its more restricted sense for the inner part, the temple edifice proper. Later in *Ant*. XVI, 132[8] when he describes Herod as making a speech to the people in the temple (ἐν τῷ ἱερῷ, which would necessarily have been

---

[6] This conjecture by J. van Bebber, *Zur Chronologie des Lebens Jesu*. 1898, p.126, is cited by Ogg, *The Chronology of the Public Ministry of Jesus*, pp.159-160.
[7] *Ant*. xv, 420-421 (= xv, xi, 5-6).
[8] *Ant*. XVI, 132 (= XVI, iv, 6).

in the outer courts, he uses a different word, τὸ ἱερόν, which was commonly used for a whole temple precinct. Precisely the same distinction is made in the Gospels: τὸ ἱερόν, the entire area, Mk 11:11, etc.; ὁ ναός, the temple edifice proper, Mk 15:38, etc. If, then, Herod began his work on the Temple in 19/18 B.C. (¶431) and built the outer enclosures in eight years, that part of the work was only completed in 12/11 B.C. If the priests began their part of the work on the inner temple (ὁ ναός) at the same time in 19/18 B.C. and built it in one year and five months, they must have finished the "temple itself" in 17 B.C.

〔434. Now we return to Jn 2:20 (¶429). This is usually translated in somewhat the fashion of the RSV, "It has taken forty-six years to build this temple," implying that work was still going on, a point that is made explicit in the Berkeley Version, "This temple has been in process of building for forty-six years." If this is the correct understanding of the text, we should presumably understand also that the forty-six years is the time from when Herod began the work (the year beginning Nisan 1, 19 B.C. [¶431]) to the time when the statement was addressed to Jesus. Counting inclusively (i.e., in the Jewish manner [¶165]), if the first year began on Nisan 1, 19 B.C., the forty-sixth year began on Nisan 1, A.D. 27. By this reckoning, the first Passover of Jn 2:13ff. was in the spring of the year 27 of the Christian era.

〔435. It is possible, however, that Jn 2:20 has a different meaning. Perhaps οἰκοδομήθη, which is an aorist indicative passive (¶429) meaning literally "was built," does not refer to a building enterprise that was still going on, as it had been for forty-six years, but to a building enterprise that had been completed long before so that it could be said that the building had stood for forty-six years. On this interpretation the Jews ask Jesus in effect, "How can you possibly raise in three days a Temple which has stood for forty-six years?"[9] In this connection it may also be noticed that there seems to be a clear distinction in the Fourth Gospel between ναός and ἱερόν (¶433). Ἱερόν is used in the following passages: Jn 2:14—"In the temple he found those who were selling oxen and sheep . . ."; 5:14—Jesus found the healed man "in the temple"; 7:28—"as he taught in the temple"; 8:20—"he spoke in the treasury, as he taught

[9] Corbishley in JTS 36 (1935), p.22.

in the temple"; 10:23—"Jesus was walking in the temple, in the portico of Solomon"; 11:56—"saying to one another as they stood in the temple"; 18:20—"I have spoken openly to the world; I have always taught in synagogues and in the temple." Every passage suggests the more open and public outer courts; in every passage Jn uses ἱερόν, the word meaning the entire temple area. Only in Jn 2:19-20 is the word ναός employed. Therefore this reference could be specifically to the temple edifice proper. This observation does not invalidate the manner of reckoning followed in ¶434. If the priests began to build the ναός at the same time that Herod began the construction of the entire ἱερόν (¶433), we still have the same point from which reckoning is made, namely, by our understanding, 19/18 B.C., and forty-six years still brings us to 27/26 B.C. But if the verb οἰκοδομήθη refers to the time when the ναός was completed by the priests, namely, by our understanding, 17 B.C. (¶433), and if the forty-six years are counted inclusively from that point we are brought to the year A.D. 29, or if they are counted as the number of calendar years that the ναός had stood *after* it was built we are brought to A.D. 30.

(2) THE DURATION OF THE MINISTRY

(436.   In the course of the Jewish religious year several annual feasts and one fast were held, as shown in Table 133. The Day of Atonement (cf. ¶12) is a fast, the other observances are feasts. As I K 8:2 and other references show, the Feast of Tabernacles was probably often referred to simply as "the Feast."[1] In the Gospels as they stand[2] there are references to some of these festivals, from which it may be possible to gather some information about the probable length of Jesus' ministry.

(a) THE SYNOPTIC GOSPELS

(437.   In their account of the ministry of Jesus, the Synoptic Gospels mention only one Passover, namely the final one at which time Jesus was put to death (Mk 14:12; Mt 26:17; Lk 22:7). Since this was an annual feast and only one occurrence of it is mentioned,

---

[1] HDB I, p.407 note *a*.

[2] In its analysis of the Gospel materials, *Formgeschichte* is generally skeptical of such *Zeitangaben* as the tradition contains (e.g., see Rudolf Bultmann, *Die Geschichte der synoptischen Tradition*. 2d ed. 1931, pp.67f., 258, 365).

as far as this evidence goes the ministry could have comprised only one year or even less. In the second book of *Against Heresies* Irenaeus writes against the school of Valentinus (this famous Gnostic was educated at Alexandria and taught at Rome about A.D. 136-155) in general, and against Ptolemy in particular, a chief follower of Valentinus who was still alive at the time of Irenaeus.

TABLE 133. ANNUAL OBSERVANCES IN THE JEWISH RELIGIOUS YEAR

Name	Date	Scripture Reference
1. Passover	Fourteenth day of the first month = Nisan (Mar/Apr)	Ex 12:6
2. Feast of Weeks, or Pentecost	Fifty days after the ceremony of the barley sheaf at Passover time	Lev 23:16; Dt 16:10
3. Day of Atonement	Tenth day of the seventh month = Tishri (Sep/Oct)	Lev 23:27
4. Tabernacles	Fifteenth day of the seventh month = Tishri (Sep/Oct), for seven days	Lev 23:34; I K 8:2
5. Dedication	Twenty-fifth day of the ninth month = Kislev (Nov/Dec)	I Macc 4:59
6. Purim	Fourteenth and fifteenth days of the twelfth month = Adar (Feb/Mar)	Est 9:17-18

Irenaeus states that they taught that Jesus conducted his ministry of preaching for only a single year, reckoning from his baptism.

"They, however, that they may establish their false opinion regarding that which is written, 'to proclaim the acceptable year of the Lord,' maintain that he preached for one year only, and then suffered in the twelfth month."[1]

Against this position Irenaeus himself argues in the same section that at his baptism Jesus "was beginning to be about thirty years of age" (Lk 3:23), that if he had only completed this thirtieth year when he died he was still a young man, and that he had therefore never reached the more advanced age of a Master qualified to teach others. Irenaeus explains, not with complete clarity:

[1] *Against Heresies*. II, xxii, 5.

> "The first stage of early life embraces thirty years, and that this ex-
> tends onwards to the fortieth year, every one will admit; but from the
> fortieth and fiftieth year a man begins to decline towards old age, which
> our Lord possessed while he still fulfilled the office of a Teacher, even as
> the Gospel and all the elders testify; those who were conversant in Asia
> with John, the disciple of the Lord, [affirming] that John conveyed to them
> that information."

On the basis of Jn 8:57, however, Irenaeus is sure that Jesus had
not reached his fiftieth year (¶428). He was, then, between forty
and fifty, Irenaeus holds, and thus (counting from baptism at about
thirty) must have had a ministry of between ten and twenty years.
Thus Irenaeus argues against the Valentinian view of a one-year
ministry.

⟨ 438.   The final Passover in the Synoptic record came, of course,
in the springtime. But another Synoptic passage (Mk 2:23; Mt 12:
1; Lk 6:1) appears plainly to refer to a springtime prior to that
final one, for it tells how the disciples plucked ears of grain, and
thus it implies the spring harvest time, perhaps Apr/May (¶58).
Since the baptism (Mk 1:9) was obviously prior to that, perhaps
in the preceding fall (¶424), the total ministry was at least somewhat over one year in length. As we have already seen (¶393),
Clement of Alexandria states that the followers of Basilides put the
baptism in the fifteenth year of Tiberius, on the eleventh or fifteenth
of Tybi (= Jan 6 or 10), and the passion in the sixteenth year of
Tiberius, on the twenty-fifth of Phamenoth (= Mar 21) or on the
nineteenth or twenty-fifth of Pharmuthi (= Apr 14 or 20). In Egypt
the first regnal year of Tiberius presumably began on Thoth 1 =
Aug 29, A.D. 14, and the fifteenth regnal year was accordingly
from Aug 29, A.D. 28, to Aug 28, A.D. 29 (Table 127). Jan 6 or
10 in the year 29 is therefore the indicated date of the baptism.
Likewise the sixteenth year of Tiberius extended from Aug 29,
A.D. 29, to Aug 28, A.D. 30. So May 21 or Apr 14 or 20 in the year
30 is the indicated date of the passion. From baptism to passion
is one year plus a few months, a period of time with which the
Synoptic record by itself could be considered at least roughly con-
sonant.

⟨ 439.   The Synoptic record does not necessarily, however, require as brief a ministry as that just indicated. A springtime is
indicated (Mk 2:23, etc.) without mention of a corresponding Pass-

over. Other Passovers could have gone unmentioned. Or the Synoptic record could cover only a part—perhaps the part deemed most important—of a longer ministry.

(b) THE FOURTH GOSPEL

❨ 440.　The Fourth Gospel refers to more Jewish feasts than the Synoptic Gospels and thereby probably suggests a longer ministry. As far as passover is concerned, three observances of this festival are specifically mentioned: (1) Jn 2:13—"The Passover of the Jews was at hand" (also verse 23); at this time Jesus cleanses the Temple; (2) Jn 6:4—"Now the Passover, the feast of the Jews, was at hand"; at this time the Feeding of the Five Thousand took place; (3) Jn 11:55—"Now the Passover of the Jews was at hand"; this was the final passover at which time Jesus was put to death (it is mentioned by name also in 12:1; 18:28, 39; 19:14). In the Synoptic Gospels the cleansing of the Temple occurs on the final visit of Jesus to Jerusalem and near the time of the final passover (Mk 11:15ff., etc.). It is possible that Jn transposed this event to a place near the beginning of the ministry for some symbolic reason. In that event there would be but two passovers in Jn's record: (1) that of Jn 6:4; and (2) that described in two different places, Jn 2:13 and 11:55ff. In this way Jn might be thought to fit the pattern of a ministry of one year and some months, even as perhaps the Synoptics indicate (¶438).

❨ 441.　But taking the Fourth Gospel as it stands, there are not only three Passovers mentioned but also certain other notes of time. These are: (1) Jn 2:13, 23—the first Passover; (2) 4:35—"yet four months, then comes the harvest"; with harvest probably in Apr/May (¶438), this saying should belong in Jan/Feb and a second and unmentioned Passover should fall in Mar/Apr; (3) 5:1— according to Codex Vaticanus and other manuscripts "a feast of the Jews" was at hand, according to Codex Sinaiticus and other manuscripts it was "the feast of the Jews"; if it was "a feast" it was hardly passover which is otherwise mentioned by name, but it could have been the Feast of Weeks; if it was "the feast" it was probably Tabernacles, often (¶436) referred to simply in this way (cf. Jn 7:2, 10, 14, 37); (4) 6:4—a third passover is at hand; (5) 7:2— the Feast of Tabernacles is at hand; (6) 10:22f.—it was the Feast of Dedication, and winter; (7) 11:55ff.—the final passover. This provides the outline shown in Table 134.

TABLE 134. NOTES OF TIME IN THE FOURTH GOSPEL

First Year		
Nisan (Mar/Apr)	First Passover	2:13, 23
Shebat (Jan/Feb)	"four months to harvest"	4:35
Second Year		
Nisan (Mar/Apr)	Second Passover	Unmentioned
Tishri (Sep/Oct)	"the feast," i.e., Tabernacles	5:1, Codex Sinaiticus
Third Year		
Nisan (Mar/Apr)	Third Passover	6:4
Tishri (Sep/Oct)	Tabernacles	7:2
Kislev (Nov/Dec)	Dedication	10:22
Nisan (Mar/Apr)	Fourth and Final Passover	11:55ff.

Since the baptism and beginning of the public ministry preceded the first passover in the above outline, with the baptism perhaps coming in the preceding fall (¶424), it seems that a total ministry of three years plus a number of months is indicated.

⟨ 442. As we have seen (Table 114), Epiphanius likewise considered that the ministry of Jesus covered three years plus several months. In the *Chronicle* of Eusebius as translated by Jerome, the preaching of John the Baptist is placed in the fifteenth year of Tiberius (= A.D. 28) and the death of Jesus in the eighteenth year (= A.D. 31), and thus the ministry appears to cover two years and a portion of a third (Table 82). But in the Armenian version[1] the death of Jesus is placed in the nineteenth year of Tiberius, which may allow an additional year. Actually a ministry of three years and a portion of a fourth appears to be the real view of Eusebius. In the *Church History*[2] he says (presumably with Lk 3:2; Jn 11:49, 51; 18:13 in mind) that Jesus passed his entire ministry under the high priests Annas and Caiaphas. It is ordinarily assumed that Annas (who was actually high priest in A.D. 6-15) is mentioned in Lk 3:2 and Jn 18:13 along with his son-in-law Caiaphas (who

[1] ed. Karst, p.213.
[2] I, x.

held the office in A.D. 18-36) because he was still influential in the time of the latter. As known from Josephus and with approximate dates the high priests between Annas and Caiaphas were: Ishmael (A.D. 15-16), Eleazar (16-17), and Simon (17-18). Although he also cites Josephus, Eusebius evidently assumes that these men constituted a series of high priests who held office during the ministry of Jesus, each for a one-year term. Eusebius writes:

> "Accordingly the whole time of our Savior's ministry is shown to have been not quite four full years, four high priests, from Annas to the accession of Caiaphas, having held office a year each."

⟨ 443. As far as the evidence in the Gospels goes, therefore, we appear to have two chief possibilities as to the duration of the public ministry of Jesus. On the basis of the Synoptic Gospels taken by themselves (¶438) the ministry could have been one year and some months in length. With a critical rearrangement of the Fourth Gospel it might possibly be brought into harmony with such a length of ministry (¶440), and there is some support for such a figure in the tradition of the followers of Basilides reported by Clement of Alexandria (¶438). Taken as it stands, the Fourth Gospel appears to require a ministry of three years plus a number of months (¶441), and there is some support for a duration of some such magnitude in Epiphanius and Eusebius (¶442).

3. THE DEATH OF JESUS

LITERATURE: J. K. Fotheringham, "The Evidence of Astronomy and Technical Chronology for the Date of the Crucifixion," in JTS 35 (1934), pp.146-162; A. T. Olmstead, "The Chronology of Jesus' Life," in ATR 24 (1942), pp.1-26; and *Jesus in the Light of History*. 1942; Carl H. Kraeling, "Olmstead's Chronology of the Life of Jesus," in ATR 24 (1942), pp.334-354; T. J. Meek, Review of Olmstead, *Jesus in the Light of History*, in JNES 2 (1943), pp.124-125; A. Jaubert, "La date de la dernière Cène," in RHR 146 (1954), pp.140-173; Julian Morgenstern, "The Calendar of the Book of Jubilees, Its Origin and Its Character," in VT 5 (1955), pp.34-76; A. Jaubert, *La date de la cène*. 1957; Josef Blinzler, "Qumran-Kalender und Passionschronologie," in ZNW 49 (1958), pp.238-251; E. Vogt, "Kalenderfragmente aus Qumran," in *Biblica*. 39 (1958), pp.72-77; James A. Walther, "The Chronology of Passion Week," in JBL 77 (1958), pp.116-122; George Ogg, Review of Jaubert, *La date de la cène*, in *Novum Testamentum*. 3 (1959), pp.149-160; Norman Walker, "Concerning the Jaubertian Chronology of the Passion," in *Novum Testamentum*. 3 (1959), pp.317-320; A. Jaubert, "Jesus et le calendrier de Qumran," in NTS 7(1960), pp.1-30; August Strobel, "Der Termin des Todes Jesu," in ZNW 51 (1960), pp.69-101; Karl G.

Kuhn, "Zum essenischen Kalender," in zNW 52 (1961), pp.65-73; Massey H. Shepherd, Jr., "Are Both the Synoptics and John Correct about the Date of Jesus' Death?" in JBL 80 (1961), pp.123-132; Julian Morgenstern, "The Time of the Passover in the Synoptics and in John," and "Palm Sunday and Easter Sunday," in "Three Studies in the New Testament" (unpublished).

(1) THE DAY OF THE WEEK

¶ 444. All four Gospels indicate that the day of the crucifixion of Jesus was a Friday (in our terminology), because they describe the following day as the sabbath (Mk 15:42; Mt 28:1; Lk 23:56; Jn 19:31), our Saturday, and because they state that the visit of the women to the tomb on the next day was on the first day of the week (Mk 16:2; Mt 28:1; Lk 24:1; Jn 20:1), our Sunday.

(2) THE DATE IN THE JEWISH MONTH

¶ 445. On an evening which appears (but cf. ¶449) to be the evening immediately before the day of the crucifixion Jesus ate a supper with his disciples (I Cor 11:23; Mk 14:17; Mt 26:20; Lk 22:14; Jn 13:2). In order to discuss this meal it is necessary to recall the sequence of events in the observance of the Jewish feast of Passover. On the tenth day of the first month (Nisan = Mar/Apr) a lamb was selected for a household (Ex 12:3). On the fourteenth day of the month it was slain "in the evening" (Ex 12:6; cf. Lev 23:5). As explained above (¶20), the Hebrew is literally "between the two evenings," and Josephus[1] says that the sacrifices were made from the ninth to the eleventh hour, i.e., from three to five o'clock in the afternoon. Then "that night" (Ex 12:8) the passover meal was eaten. If the day was reckoned according to the earlier practice (¶12) from sunrise to sunrise, then both the slaying of the lamb and the eating of the meal took place on one and the same day, namely on the fourteenth day of Nisan. But if the day was reckoned according to the later practice (¶12) from sunset to sunset, then the lamb was indeed slain on the fourteenth day of Nisan but the passover meal held "that night" was actually eaten on the fifteenth day of Nisan which had begun at sunset. Jub 49:1 explicitly describes the observance in terms of the latter manner of reckoning:

"Remember the commandment which the Lord commanded thee concerning the passover, that thou shouldst celebrate it in its season on the fourteenth of the first month, that thou shouldst kill it before it is evening,

[1] *War.* VI, 423 (= VI, ix, 3).

and that they should eat it by night on the evening of the fifteenth from the time of the setting of the sun."

With the roast lamb, unleavened bread was eaten in the passover meal (Ex 12:8), and unleavened bread continued to be eaten for seven days all together (Ex 12:15; cf. Num 28:17; Dt 16:3-4). If the day was reckoned from sunrise to sunrise, the unleavened bread, like the roast lamb, was eaten already on the fourteenth day. If the day was reckoned from sunset to sunset then the unleavened bread, like the roast lamb, was eaten only after the fifteenth day had begun. Lev 23:6 presumably presupposes the latter manner of reckoning when it gives the fifteenth day of the first month as the date of "the feast of unleavened bread." By the same reckoning the seven days of the feast would presumably be, counted inclusively, Nisan 15-21.

(a) THE SYNOPTIC REPRESENTATION

(446. According to Mk 14:12 it was "on the first day of Unleavened Bread, when they sacrificed the passover lamb," that the disciples went and prepared for Jesus "to eat the passover." The parallel passages in Mt 26:17 and Lk 22:7-8 also refer to the Unleavened Bread and the preparation of the passover. Therefore this supper was the passover meal, which followed the slaying of the lamb on the fourteenth day of Nisan. Likewise if the death of Jesus followed on the next day after that, it appears to fall on the fifteenth of Nisan.

(b) THE JOHANNINE REPRESENTATION

(447. In the Fourth Gospel, however, it is explicitly stated that the day of Jesus' trial and execution was "the day of Preparation for the Passover" (Jn 19:14). The day of Preparation ($\pi\alpha\rho\alpha\sigma\kappa\epsilon\upsilon\dot\eta$) means the day of getting ready for a festival. Josephus uses the word in connection with the sabbath, citing a decree of Caesar Augustus which allowed that the Jews "be not obliged to go before any judge on the sabbath day, nor on the day of preparation before it, after the ninth hour."[1] Therefore the day of Preparation for the passover must have been the day of getting ready for it, namely the day on which the passover lamb was slain, Nisan 14. This was the day on which Jesus also was put to death. Only on the evening of

[1] *Ant.* XVI, 163 (= XVI, vi, 2).

this day would the passover meal be eaten, and the Jews who took Jesus to the Praetorium did not go in, "so that they might not be defiled, but might eat the passover" (Jn 18:28). This day of preparation for the passover was also a day of preparation for the sabbath which in this case coincided with the passover day and thus was a "high day" (Jn 19:31). According to this representation of the Fourth Gospel, then, the death of Jesus took place on Nisan 14.

〖 448.   Support for the Johannine date is found in additional sources. The statement of Paul that "Christ, our paschal lamb, has been sacrificed" (I Cor 5:7) fits very well with the remembrance that Jesus was put to death at the same time that the passover lambs were slain. The apocryphal Gospel according to Peter (verse 3) states that Jesus was delivered to the people "on the day before the unleavened bread, their feast." The tractate Sanhedrin in the Babylonian Talmud records, doubtless with reference to the Founder of Christianity: "On the eve of Passover Yeshu was hanged."[2]

〖 449.   One suggestion for reconciliation of the apparent difference between the Synoptic and the Johannine accounts is based upon the calendar with which we have become acquainted (¶¶82ff.) at Qumran. If by any chance Jesus and the disciples had had reason to follow this calendar they would have eaten their passover already on the preceding Tuesday evening, for by that calendar that was the appointed time for it (¶93) and Wednesday was the first day of passover in this year as in every year. While the Gospel records are usually held (¶445) to place the Last Supper on Thursday evening and the crucifixion immediately thereafter on Friday, it may be that all the events of the taking into custody of Jesus and the holding of his trials before Jewish and Roman authorities would fit better within the longer period from Tuesday evening until Friday. Interestingly enough, in the early Christian work known as the Didascalia[3] the apostles are quoted as saying that it was on Tuesday evening that they ate the passover with Jesus, and on Wednesday that he was taken captive and held in custody in the house of Caia-

---

[2] *Sanhedrin*. 43a. GBT VII, p.181; SBT p.281.

[3] The Didascalia is preserved in Syriac but was probably written originally in Greek, perhaps in the second or third century A.D.; it is now incorporated as the first six books in the Apostolical Constitutions, a work of the fourth or fifth century (CAP I, p.613). It is edited by F. X. Funk, *Didascalia et Constitutiones Apostolorum*. 2 vols. 1905.

phas.[4] This is, however, a relatively late source, and the canonical gospels themselves seem most naturally to presuppose a sequence of days as commonly understood, namely: Sunday, the entry into Jerusalem; Wednesday, the plan to kill Jesus; Thursday, the last supper; Friday, the trial and crucifixion.[5]

❨ 450. Another suggestion appeals to the possibility of a difference in dating as between Palestine and the Diaspora. In Palestine the beginning of the month was determined by observation of the new moon (¶73), but perhaps in the Dispersion a fixed calendar was in use. If that were the case it could have happened in the year Jesus died that the Jews in Palestine observed passover on Saturday, while those in the Dispersion observed it on Friday. John could then be considered to have followed the testimony of Christians who were in touch with priestly circles in Judea in his report that the Friday when Jesus died was the Preparation for passover. Mark, on the other hand, as a Christian of the Roman church, could have followed the tradition of his own church that Jesus died on a Friday in a year when that Friday was observed in the Dispersion as the passover.[6]

❨ 451. Again it is possible that it was simply by deliberate choice and in view of the ominous developments of those days that Jesus moved his observance of the passover ahead one day. In this connection his statement in Lk 22:15-16 may be significant. He speaks of how earnestly he has desired to eat this passover with his disciples before he suffers, then according to Codex Bezae, the Washington Codex, certain minuscules and Syriac versions, and the Koine Text, he says: "for I tell you I shall never eat it again until it is fulfilled in the kingdom of God." But according to Codex Vaticanus, Codex Sinaiticus, Codex Alexandrinus, Codex Ephraemi rescriptus, and some minuscules and Egyptian versions, he said: "for I tell you I shall not eat it until it is fulfilled in the kingdom of God." The first and less well attested form of the saying supposes that he was actually then eating the real passover meal. The second and much

[4] *Didascalia.* xxi = v, 4-6; ed. Funk, I, p.272.
[5] For the theory presented in this paragraph see in the LITERATURE under 3 (The Death of Jesus) the writings of Jaubert and the supporting article by Walker; against the theory see the listed articles of Blinzler, Ogg, Strobel, and Kuhn, and also A. J. B. Higgins, *The Historicity of the Fourth Gospel.* 1960, p.61.
[6] See the article by Shepherd listed in the LITERATURE.

better attested form of the saying supposes that he wanted to do so, but was unable. If the latter form of the saying represents the actual situation at the time, we may think that the Johannine record is literally correct in picturing the last supper as a meal held one evening prior to the real passover meal, and we could also surmise that the Synoptics were led to present the last supper as itself the passover meal because it was held so close to the time when the passover meal was to be held.

¶ 452.   But the simplest and therefore most convincing solution of the apparent discrepancy lies in the difference between the alternate ways of reckoning the day and accordingly the date. We have seen (¶¶ 12-13) that the earlier Israelite reckoning counted the day as beginning at sunrise, and that this reckoning is usually employed in the Synoptic Gospels, perhaps because it was the way followed by Jesus and his disciples; and that the later Jewish reckoning counted the day as beginning at sunset, and is found in the Fourth Gospel. The latter was undoubtedly the official manner of reckoning in the time of Jesus, and even in the Synoptic Gospels (Mk 1:32 = Lk 4:40) the sabbath begins and ends at sunset. Let us suppose that Jesus and his disciples, who came from Galilee, followed the old custom and counted the day as beginning at sunrise. Then the day when the passover lamb was slain and the day when the unleavened bread was eaten were indeed the same day (¶445), as Mk 14:12 states. So, by this way of reckoning, this day which began at sunrise on Thursday and continued until sunrise on Friday was the fourteenth day of Nisan, the day on which in the afternoon the passover lamb should be sacrificed and on which in the evening the passover meal, with its roast lamb and unleavened bread, should be eaten. By the same reckoning the next day began at sunrise on Friday morning and was already the fifteenth day of Nisan. This was the day on which Jesus was crucified. But, let us suppose, by official Jewish reckoning, the fourteenth day of Nisan did not begin at sunrise on Thursday morning but only at sunset on Thursday evening. Then, according to official usage, it would only be on the next afternoon, namely the afternoon of the official fourteenth day of Nisan, that the passover lamb would be slain. This was the very time that Jesus died, exactly as represented in the Fourth Gospel. The Fourth Gospel is, therefore, stating the event in terms of the official Jewish calendar, and in terms of that calendar the date of the death of Jesus was Friday, Nisan 14.[7]

(3) THE HOUR OF THE DAY

LITERATURE: Norman Walker, "The Reckoning of Hours in the Fourth Gospel," in *Novum Testamentum*. 4 (1960), pp.69-73.

¶453.　There is also an apparent discrepancy in the hour of the crucifixion between the Synoptic Gospels and the Fourth Gospel, but there is a probable reconciliation in terms of different methods of reckoning. According to Mk 15:25 it was the "third hour" when they crucified him. Assuming the common reckoning (¶18) from dawn or from six a.m., the third hour was what we would call nine o'clock in the morning. According to Jn 19:14 it was the "sixth hour" when Jesus was before Pilate. If the reckoning were the same as in Mk, there would be a large discrepancy. But if Jn is counting by the Roman method from midnight (¶19), the time is six o'clock in the morning. This gives adequate time for the various stages of the trial and mistreatment of Jesus, and for the sending of him to be crucified by nine o'clock.

(4) THE CALENDAR DATE

¶454.　In the foregoing it has been established that the death of Jesus was probably on a Friday (¶444) and probably on Nisan 14 in the official Jewish calendar (¶452). This is the clear representation of the Fourth Gospel (¶447). We have also established that the Synoptic Gospels probably do not place the death of Jesus at a different time, but simply reflect the observance by Jesus and his disciples of the Passover according to a different manner of time reckoning (¶452). Nevertheless, at first appearance the Synoptic Gospels may seem to place the crucifixion on Friday, Nisan 15, and accordingly the possibilities of this as an alternate date may also be explored in what follows. The problem at this point, therefore, is to determine within the range of years which come into consideration in general, in which year or years the Jewish month date of Nisan

[7] Morgenstern in VT 5 (1955), p.64 n.2; and "The Time of the Passover in the Synoptics and in John," in "Three Studies in the New Testament" (unpublished); cf. Sherman E. Johnson in IB 7, p.574; and *Jesus in His Homeland*, p.19. I express appreciation to Rev. Dr. Julian Morgenstern for his kindness in making available to me his unpublished "Three Studies."

14 or 15 fell on the week day which we call Friday, and to translate the date into terms of the Julian calendar.

〖 455.   The earliest probable date for the baptism of Jesus is A.D. 26 (¶419), and the shortest probable duration of his ministry is one year or a little more (¶¶437, 438). The latest probable date for the baptism of Jesus is A.D. 29 (¶425), and the longest probable duration of his ministry is three or four years (¶¶441, 442). The range of years from A.D. 27 to 34 should, therefore, cover the span of time within which to look for the date of the death of Jesus. The dates of Nisan 1 (from which the dates of Nisan 14 and 15 can readily be obtained) have been calculated astronomically for this range of years by J. K. Fotheringham,[1] and his results may now be compared with the corresponding results of Parker and Dubberstein,[2] for the accuracy of which there is a very high degree of probability.[3] In the tables the dates as given are civil days, from midnight to midnight, although as we know the Babylonian (¶11) or Jewish (¶12) day actually began with the preceding sunset.[4] As an example of the use of the tables, in the year 30 of the Christian era Nisan 1 probably fell on Mar 25; accordingly Nisan 14 was Apr 7.

〖 456.   When a date has thus been translated into the Julian calendar, the day of the week on which it fell can also be determined. This is done by consulting a table of what are called the Dominical Letters or Sunday Letters.[5] In the system represented by such a table the letters A, B, C, D, E, F, G are used to designate the first seven days of January and the "Sunday Letter" for the year tells which day is Sunday. Thus if the Sunday Letter is C, for example, we may show the beginning of the year as in Table 135. Thus we know that in this year not only is Jan 3 a Sunday but so also is each succeeding date against which the letter C is written in the recurring sequence of these letters, namely Jan 10, 17, 24, 31, Feb. 7, 14, 21, 28, Mar 7, 14, 21, 28, etc. Likewise if the Sunday Letter is D the year starts as in Table 136.

[1] In JTS 35 (1934), pp.158-160.
[2] PDBC p.46.
[3] PDBC p.25.
[4] PDBC p.26.
[5] Lietzmann, *Zeitrechnung*, pp.7f., 14ff.; cf. EB 4, p.570.

TABLE 135. THE BEGINNING OF
A YEAR WITH THE SUNDAY LETTER C

Jan	1	A	
	2	B	
	3	C	Sun,
	4	D	Mon
	5	E	Tues
	6	F	Wed
	7	G	Thu
	8	A	Fri
	9	B	Sat
	10	C	Sun

TABLE 136. THE BEGINNING OF A
YEAR WITH THE SUNDAY LETTER D

Jan	1	A	
	2	B	
	3	C	
	4	D	Sun,
	5	E	Mon
	6	F	Tues
	7	G	Wed
	8	A	Thu
	9	B	Fri
	10	C	Sat
	11	D	Sun

Thus we know that in this year not only is Jan 4 a Sunday but also Jan 11, 18, 25, Feb 1, 8, 15, 22, Mar 1, 8, 15, 22, 29, etc. In a leap year, however, the Sunday Letter applies as just explained only to January and February, for on or after Feb 29 all the following Sundays fall one day earlier. This may be seen in Table 137 if we continue the example just begun above (Table 136) of a year with the Sunday Letter D. In this year Feb 22 is still a Sunday, but is followed by Feb 29 as the next Sunday, after which the further Sundays are Mar 7, 14, 21, 28, etc., which is the way they fall in a common year with the Sunday Letter C (Table 135). Therefore this leap year is given the two Sunday Letters, DC, and D applies to Jan-Feb, while C applies to Mar-Dec.

[293]

TABLE 137. A PORTION OF A LEAP YEAR
WITH THE SUNDAY LETTERS DC

Feb	22	D	Sun	Mar	1	E	Mon
	23	E	Mon		2	F	Tues
	24	F	Tues		3	G	Wed
	25	G	Wed		4	A	Thu
	26	A	Thu		5	B	Fri
	27	B	Fri		6	C	Sat
	28	C	Sat		7	D	Sun
	29	D	Sun				

¶ 457.   In the example given above (¶455) Nisan 14 was determined to have fallen, most probably, on Apr 7 in the year 30 of the Christian era. For the year 30 the Sunday Letter is A.[6] This year therefore begins as in Table 138.

TABLE 138. THE BEGINNING OF A.D. 30
(SUNDAY LETTER A)

Jan	1	A	Sun
	2	B	Mon
	3	C	Tues
	4	D	Wed
	5	E	Thu
	6	F	Fri
	7	G	Sat
	8	A	Sun

Subsequent Sundays are Jan 15, 22, 29, Feb 5, 12, 19, 26, Mar 5, 12, 19, 26, Apr 2, etc. For a period of interest in March and April the days run as in Table 139. Accordingly, in the year 30 of the Christian era the Julian calendar date of Apr 7 (equivalent to the Jewish month date of Nisan 14) fell on a Friday.

¶ 458.   Utilizing the methods just explained (¶¶455-457), we may tabulate (Table 140) the dates of Nisan 14 and 15 (¶454) in the years 27-34 of the Christian era (¶455). In the table we show under (1) the results of Fotheringham (¶455) which are in exact agreement with Parker and Dubberstein (¶455), only supposing that several Babylonian intercalations (¶53) which the latter show

---

[6] Lietzmann, *Zeitrechnung*, p.14.

were *not* made in Jerusalem; and under (2) we show the results which follow from Parker and Dubberstein *with* the intercalations required by the Babylonian system.

TABLE 139. SOME DAYS IN MARCH AND APRIL, A.D. 30
(SUNDAY LETTER A)

Mar	19	A	Sun	Apr	1	G	Sat
	20	B	Mon		2	A	Sun
	21	C	Tues		3	B	Mon
	22	D	Wed		4	C	Tues
	23	E	Thu		5	D	Wed
	24	F	Fri		6	E	Thu
	25	G	Sat		7	F	Fri
	26	A	Sun		8	G	Sat
	27	B	Mon		9	A	Sun
	28	C	Tues		10	B	Mon
	29	D	Wed		11	C	Tues
	30	E	Thu		12	D	Wed
	31	F	Fri		13	E	Thu
					14	F	Fri
					15	G	Sat
					16	A	Sun
					17	B	Mon
					18	C	Tues
					19	D	Wed
					20	E	Thu

TABLE 140. THE DATES OF NISAN 14 AND 15 IN THE YEARS 27-34
OF THE CHRISTIAN ERA

	(1) As calculated by Fotheringham		(2) Or, supposing the intercalation of a month in the preceding year, as shown by Parker and Dubberstein, so that Nisan came one month late, then	
In the Year	Nisan 14 fell on	Nisan 15 fell on	Nisan 14 fell on	Nisan 15 fell on
27	Apr 10 Thu	Apr 11 Fri		Apr 29 Thu
28	Mar 30 Tue	Mar 31 Wed	Apr 28 Wed	
29	Apr 18 Mon	Apr 19 Tue		
30	Apr 7 Fri	Apr 8 Sat		
31	Mar 27 Tue	Mar 28 Wed	Apr 25 Wed	Apr 26 Thu
32	Apr 14 Mon	Apr 15 Tue		
33	Apr 3 Fri	Apr 4 Sat	May 2 Sat	May 3 Sun
34	Mar 24 Wed	Mar 25 Thu	Apr 22 Thu	Apr 23 Fri

¶ 459.   In the range of years considered in Table 140 the apparent Synoptic requirement of having Nisan 15 fall on a Friday (and Nisan 14 on a Thursday), is satisfied only in A.D. 27 under (1), and in A.D. 34 under (2). These years, however, represent the extreme limits of probability within which the death of Jesus might be expected to fall (¶455), and are therefore not likely. The Johannine requirement of having Nisan 14 fall on a Friday (and Nisan 15 on a Saturday) can be satisfied in A.D. 30 under (1) and in A.D. 33 under (1), both of which years seem to be well within the range of likelihood. Astronomically calculated, therefore, the likely dates for the crucifixion of Jesus appear to be either Friday Apr 7, A.D. 30, or Friday Apr 3, A.D. 33. Therewith, in terms of the standard Jewish calendar, the representation of the day in the Fourth Gospel appears to be confirmed.

¶ 460.   According to Clement of Alexandria[7] (¶¶393, 438) the followers of Basilides put the passion in the sixteenth year of Tiberius on the twenty-fifth of Phamenoth (= Mar 21) or on the nineteenth or twenty-fifth of Pharmuthi (= Apr 14 or 20). If by any chance the month of Phamenoth (which was properly from Feb 25 or 26 to Mar 26 [Table 8]) was later taken as simply equivalent to March, then Phamenoth 25 could be the same as Mar 25, and the latter is a date which is later found cited by various authorities including Tertullian and Augustine as quoted in the next paragraph (¶461). Since Basilides was a Gnostic of Alexandria (¶393) we have assumed (¶438) that his followers would use the Egyptian calendar, probably as shown in Table 127, and that the sixteenth year of Tiberius would therefore be the year from Aug 29, A.D. 29, to Aug 28, A.D. 30. Of the specific dates in that year just given, namely Mar 21, Mar 25, Apr 14, and Apr 20, only the date of Apr 14 falls on a Friday, as a glance at Table 139 will show. But it is the preceding Friday, Apr 7, A.D. 30, which corresponds with Nisan 14 (Table 140). Therefore none of the specific dates cited by Clement from the followers of Basilides checks out satisfactorily. But the fact that all of the dates cluster around the date in that year which is confirmed astronomically, namely the date of Friday Apr 7 (¶459), lends a measure of support to that date.

[7] *Stromata.* I, xxi.

⟮461. Of course if the sixteenth year of Tiberius were reckoned in the Egyptian calendar according to the nonaccession-year system (Table 126), it would correspond to Aug 29, A.D. 28, to Aug 28, A.D. 29, and the dates Mar 21, Mar 25, Apr 14, and Apr 20 (⟮460), would fall in the year 29 of the Christian era. The Sunday Letter for the year 29 is B,[8] and the days would fall as shown in Table 141.

TABLE 141. SOME DAYS IN MARCH AND APRIL, A.D. 29
(SUNDAY LETTER B)

Mar 20	B	Sun		Apr 1	G	Fri
21	C	Mon		2	A	Sat
22	D	Tue		3	B	Sun
23	E	Wed		4	C	Mon
24	F	Thu		5	D	Tue
25	G	Fri		6	E	Wed
26	A	Sat		7	F	Thu
27	B	Sun		8	G	Fri
28	C	Mon		9	A	Sat
29	D	Tue		10	B	Sun
30	E	Wed		11	C	Mon
31	F	Thu		12	D	Tue
				13	E	Wed
				14	F	Thu
				15	G	Fri
				16	A	Sat
				17	B	Sun
				18	C	Mon
				19	D	Tue
				20	E	Wed

⟮462. From a glance at Table 141 it is evident that none of the dates cited by Clement (⟮460), namely Mar 21, Apr 14, and Apr 20 fulfills the requirement (⟮454) of falling on a Friday. It was surmised (⟮460), however, that Phamenoth 25 (which is properly equivalent to Mar 21) might later have been considered equivalent to Mar 25, and it is at once notable that the latter date does fall on a Friday (Table 141). Whether or not it was derived from the tradition found among the followers of Basilides (⟮460), the date of Mar 25, A.D. 29, was later widely accepted. Thus Tertullian defines the date of the death of Jesus as follows:

". . . under Tiberius Caesar, in the consulate of Rubellius Geminus and Fufius Geminus, in the month of March, at the times of the passover,

[8] Lietzmann, *Zeitrechnung*, p.14.

on the eighth day before the Kalends of April, on the first day of unleavened bread, on which they slew the lamb at even."[9]

The consular date *Gemino et Gemino* indicates the year 29 (Table 38); the eighth day before the Kalends (¶141) of April = Mar 25. Augustine gives the same date:

"Now Christ died when the Gemini were consuls, on the eighth day before the Kalends of April."[10]

But in spite of this attestation for the date it seems impossible to accept it. Mar 25, A.D. 29 was a Friday, but Mar 25, A.D. 29 does not correspond with either Nisan 14 or Nisan 15 in the Jewish calendar (Table 140).

4. SUMMARY AND POSSIBLE CHRONOLOGICAL SCHEMES OF THE LIFE OF JESUS

¶ 463.   In the foregoing survey (¶¶337-462) of relevant evidence the following conclusions have been found probable: The birth of Jesus must have been before the death of Herod (Table 108) in the spring of 4 B.C. (¶¶365-366), and it might have been in midwinter 5/4 B.C. (¶¶392, 408), say perhaps in December 5 B.C. (¶418).

¶ 464.   The fifteenth year of Tiberius (Lk 3:1) may be reckoned from Tiberius' joint rule of the provinces with Augustus and be equivalent approximately to A.D. 26 (Table 115). Within that calendar year the fifteenth regnal year of Tiberius might have begun as late as in late October (Table 116). If the baptism was in, say, November A.D. 26, and if the thirtieth birthday of Jesus (Table 132) was in December A.D. 26, he was at the time of the baptism quite literally beginning to be "about thirty" (Lk 3:23) years of age (¶419). The fifteenth year of Tiberius may also be counted from the death of Augustus, however, and by Jewish reckoning it is then probably equivalent to Mar/Apr A.D. 28-Mar/Apr A.D. 29 (Table 130). If the baptism was in the fall of A.D. 28 and the thirty-second birthday of Jesus in December A.D. 28, he was at the time of baptism "about thirty" in a rather broad sense of the term (¶424). Counting from the death of Augustus the fifteenth year of Tiberius may also be reckoned by the Roman method, and is then probably

[9] *An Answer to the Jews.* 8.   [10] *The City of God.* XVIII, 54, 1.

equivalent to the Julian year A.D. 29 (Table 125). If the baptism was in the fall of A.D. 29 and the thirty-third birthday of Jesus in December A.D. 29, he was at the time of baptism "about thirty" in a yet broader sense of the term (¶425).

⟪465. At the first passover recorded in the Fourth Gospel the Jews say to Jesus, according to the usual translation, "It has taken forty-six years to build this temple" (Jn 2:20 RSV). Herod probably began to rebuild the Temple in the nineteenth year of his reign, the year which began Nisan 1, 19 B.C. (¶431). The priests probably began to build the inner temple edifice (ὁ ναός proper) at the same time, and finished it in one and one-half years, therefore in 17 B.C. (¶433). If the "forty-six years" are counted from when Herod began the work, the first passover of Jn 2:13ff. must have been the passover in the spring of A.D. 27 (¶434). But if Jn 2:20 refers specifically to the temple edifice proper (ὁ ναός) and means that it was built forty-six years before and thus has at this time stood for forty-six years, then this first passover would be in A.D. 29 (counting inclusively from 17 B.C.) or in A.D. 30 (counting full years after 17 B.C.) (¶435).

⟪466. A number of Jewish annual festivals (¶436) are mentioned in the Gospels and provide some data for an estimate of the length of the public ministry of Jesus. According to the Synoptic record the ministry might have been only one year and some months in length, but was not necessarily that brief (¶¶437-439). According to the Fourth Gospel the duration was probably three years plus a number of months (¶¶440f.).

⟪467. According to all four Gospels the sequence of events at the end of the life of Jesus appears to have been as follows in terms of days of the week: Thursday evening, the last supper; Friday, the crucifixion; Saturday, the day of rest; Sunday, the resurrection (¶¶444-445). According to the Johannine representation (¶¶447f.), with which we think the Synoptic (¶446) is reconcilable (¶¶449ff.), the last meal of Jesus and the disciples took place on the evening before the evening of the passover meal as celebrated by official Judaism, and the death of Jesus took place on the same day as the slaying of the passover lambs in official Jerusalem practice, namely on the fourteenth day of Nisan, a calendar date which in that year fell on a Friday. Given these two facts, that the crucifixion was on Nisan 14 and on a Friday (¶452), it is possible by astronomical (¶455) and calendrical (¶456) calculation to determine the years, within the probable range of years in question (¶455), in which the Jewish calendar date of Nisan 14 would fall on the day of the week which we call Friday. The result of this investigation (Table 140) is that the two dates which are possible, astronomically and calendrically, for the crucifixion are: Friday Apr 7, A.D. 30, and Friday Apr 3, A.D. 33.

¶ 468.   The data summarized in the preceding paragraphs (¶¶463-467) are capable of being incorporated in three different chronological schemes of the life of Jesus (Tables 142-144). Of the three the first makes it possible to take Lk 3:23 in the most exact sense of the words "about thirty" (¶419), and to take Jn 2:20 in what may be the most natural sense of these words as counting forty-six years from the time when Herod began the rebuilding of the Temple in 19/18 B.C. (¶434). The second scheme fits the Synoptic requirement of one year and some months for the duration of the ministry (¶¶437-438), but is insufficient for the requirements of the Fourth Gospel which, unless its materials are critically rearranged (¶440), supposes a longer ministry (¶441). The third scheme, again, allows for the longer ministry but makes it necessary to take "about thirty" (Lk 3:23) with considerable latitude (¶425), and to take Jn 2:20 as counting forty-six years after the priests completed the temple edifice proper (¶435), an interpretation which is possible but perhaps not quite as natural as that which counts from Herod's inauguration of the entire project in the nineteenth year of his reign (¶434). All together it appears that some preference may be given to the first chronological scheme of the life of Jesus. If the birth of Jesus should be placed earlier, say in 7/6 B.C. (¶¶388, 389), rather than in 5/4 B.C. (¶463), the foregoing schemes (Tables 142, 143, 144) could still hold as far as the public ministry is concerned, only the phrase "about thirty" would have to be taken with more latitude (¶427).

TABLE 142. First Chronological Scheme of the Life of Jesus

A.D.

26 Fifteenth year of Tiberius from his joint rule of the provinces with the regnal year beginning at the latest in late Oct (¶419)

Baptism and beginning of the public ministry of Jesus in Nov, when he was beginning to be about thirty (¶419)

Thirtieth birthday of Jesus in Dec (¶419)

27 First passover, forty-six years from when Herod began to re-build the Temple (¶434)

28 Second passover

29 Third passover

30 Final passover

Crucifixion on Nisan 14 = Fri, Apr 7 (¶459)

TABLE 143. Second Chronological Scheme of the Life of Jesus

A.D.

28 Fifteenth year of Tiberius after the death of Augustus, by Jewish reckoning extending from Apr 15, A.D. 28 to Apr 4, A.D. 29 (¶424)

Baptism and beginning of the public ministry of Jesus in the fall, when he was about thirty, broadly speaking (¶424)

Thirty-second birthday of Jesus in Dec (¶424)

29 First passover, forty-six years inclusively from when the priests finished the temple edifice proper (¶435)

30 Final passover

Crucifixion on Nisan 14 = Fri, Apr 7 (¶459)

TABLE 144. Third Chronological Scheme of the Life of Jesus

A.D.

29 Fifteenth year of Tiberius after the death of Augustus, by Roman reckoning extending from Jan 1 to Dec 31, A.D. 29 (¶425)

Baptism and beginning of the public ministry of Jesus in the fall, when he was about thirty, very broadly speaking (¶425)

Thirty-third birthday of Jesus in Dec (¶425)

30 First passover, forty-six years after the priests finished the temple edifice proper (¶435)

31 Second passover

32 Third passover

33 Final passover

Crucifixion on Nisan 14 = Fri, Apr 3 (¶459)

B. THE LIFE OF PETER

LITERATURE: Hans Lietzmann, *Petrus und Paulus in Rom.* 1915; James T. Shotwell and Louise R. Loomis, *The See of Peter* (Records of Civilization, Sources and Studies). 1927; Oscar Cullmann, *Peter, Disciple, Apostle, Martyr.* 1953; Theodor Klauser, *Die römische Petrustradition im Lichte der neuen Ausgrabungen unter der Peterskirche* (Arbeitsgemeinschaft für Forschung des Landes Nordrhein-Westfalen, Heft 24). 1956; Engelbert Kirschbaum, *The Tombs of St. Peter and St. Paul.* 1957; Ludwig Hertling and Engelbert Kirschbaum, *The Roman Catacombs and Their Martyrs.* rev. ed. 1960; Margherita Guarducci, *The Tomb of St. Peter.* 1960.

1. "HE DEPARTED AND WENT TO ANOTHER PLACE"

⟨ 469.   In Ac 12:1-3 it is recorded that Herod the king killed James the brother of John with the sword and then imprisoned Peter. This king is Herod Agrippa I, grandson of Herod the Great (¶¶362ff.). He was educated in Rome and became a close friend of Gaius (Caligula). Upon the death of the emperor Tiberius on Mar 16, A.D. 37, and the accession of Caligula (Table 41), the latter conferred upon Agrippa the tetrarchy of Philip (Lk 3:1), which lay to the north and east of the Sea of Galilee, together with the title of king. After Herod Antipas was banished (A.D. 39) his tetrarchy (Lk 3:1), which covered Galilee and Perea, was also given (probably in A.D. 40) to Agrippa. When Caligula was murdered (Jan 24, A.D. 41), Agrippa was in Rome and helped to secure the succession for Claudius (A.D. 41-54) (Table 42), who now gave him also Judea and Samaria. At this juncture Agrippa ruled the entire territory of Herod the Great. This was not to be for long, however, for Agrippa was to die suddenly.[1]

⟨ 470.   Josephus[2] relates that Agrippa came to Caesarea for games in honor of the emperor, appeared in the theater in a garment made wholly of silver, was flattered by the cry of admirers that he was a god, but soon afterward was seized with violent stomach pains and in five days was dead at the age of fifty-four. He had reigned seven years, four under Caligula, three under Claudius. In the *Chronicle* of Eusebius as translated by Jerome the reign of Herod Agrippa is paralleled with the reigns of Gaius (Caligula) and Claudius as shown in Table 145. (cf. Table 83)[3]

[1] SHJP I, ii, pp.153-154.   [2] *Ant.* XIX, 343-352 (= XIX, viii, 2).
[3] Helm pp.177-179.

TABLE 145. The Reign of Herod Agrippa I in the
Chronicle of Eusebius

Romans	Jews	A.D.
Gaius, three years, ten months	Herod Agrippa I, seven years	
Year 1	(Accession Year)	37
Year 2	Year 1	38
Year 3	Year 2	39
Year 4	Year 3	40
Claudius, thirteen years, eight months, twenty-eight days		
Year 1	Year 4	41
Year 2	Year 5	42
Year 3	Year 6	43
Year 4	Year 7	44

This agrees with the data of Josephus except that by putting four of Herod's years under Gaius and three under Claudius Josephus is evidently reckoning the year in which Gaius died (A.D. 41) to his reign rather than making it the first year of Claudius as is done in the table of Eusebius. The death of Herod Agrippa I is therefore to be assigned to the year 44 of the Christian era.

([471.   According to Ac 12:3-4 the imprisonment and deliverance of Peter took place near passover time, and according to Ac. 12:20-23 the death of Herod Agrippa came soon afterward. Therefore the date of the deliverance of Peter and his departure "to another place" (Ac 12:17) was in the spring of the year 44.

2. PETER IN ROME

([472.   The statement in I Pet 5:13, "She who is at Babylon . . . sends you greetings," is presumably an expression of greetings on behalf of the church where Peter is, or is represented as being, at the time. Taken literally and as the original famous city of this name, this would mean Babylon in Mesopotamia. According to Josephus[1] Babylon was still an inhabited place in the New Testament period, for he tells how, about the middle of the first century, many of the Jews left there to settle in Seleucia. Aside from this

[1] *Ant.* XVIII, 372 (= XVIII, ix, 8).

interpretation of I Pet 5:13 other evidence is not known that Peter went to Mesopotamia.

(473. Babylon was also the name of a place in Egypt. This Egyptian Babylon is mentioned by Josephus[2] as having been founded by Cambyses when he subjugated Egypt; by Diodorus of Sicily[3] as being a colony founded by Babylonian captive laborers in Egypt; and by Strabo[4] as founded by Babylonian emigrants and, in his day, the camp of one of the three Roman legions in Egypt. This Babylon is identified with still impressive Roman ruins in Old Cairo. Again it is possible that Peter could have been here, but confirmatory evidence is needed.

(474. In Rev 14:8; 16:19; 17:5; 18:2, 10, 21, the name Babylon is plainly used as a designation for Rome, the city which in that time appears as the enemy of the Christians even as in Old Testament times the city of Babylon was the enemy of the Jews. It seems probable that I Pet 5:13 uses the name in the same way and is in fact a reference to Rome. Eusebius[5] cites Clement of Alexandria, confirmed by Papias, for information about Peter and says that they stated that Peter wrote the First Epistle in Rome and referred to the city metaphorically as Babylon.[6] I Pet 5:13 is, therefore, New Testament indication of the presence of Peter in Rome. Likewise Jn 21:18 is almost certainly a reference within the New Testament to the martyrdom of Peter, probably reflecting the stretching out of the hands in crucifixion.

(475. Beyond the New Testament the references become more specific. The *First Letter of Clement*, written by the head of the church at Rome to the church at Corinth about A.D. 95 or 96, tells of the persecution and martyrdom of Peter and Paul, and groups with them in a like fate a "vast multitude" ($\pi o \lambda \grave{v} \pi \lambda \hat{\eta} \theta o s$) who likewise suffered "among us."[7] Compared with the account by Tacitus[8] of the persecution of the Christians at Rome by Nero, which followed the great fire in A.D. 64, in which he also speaks of the cruel treatment meted out to a "vast multitude" (*multitudo ingens*), this

[2] *Ant.* II, 315 (= II, xv, 1).
[3] I, 46, 3.
[4] xvii, 807.
[5] *Ch. Hist.* II, xv, 2.
[6] Shotwell and Loomis, *The See of Peter*, p.80.
[7] *I Clem.* 5f.   [8] *Annals.* xv, 44.

seems in all probability to indicate that Peter, and also Paul, died at Rome in the time of the persecution by Nero.[9]

⟨ 476.   The great six-day fire, which was followed by Nero's persecution, began according to Tacitus[10] on *XIIII Kal. Sextiles,* i.e., fourteen days before the first of Sextilis (later August) = on the nineteenth day of July (¶141). This was also the anniversary of the burning of Rome by the Senones, and the interval between the two fires, Tacitus says, is capable of resolution into equal numbers of years, of months, and of days. This cryptic definition is to be explained by resolving the four hundred and fifty-four years between the burning of Rome by the Gauls in 390 B.C. and this fire in A.D. 64 into 418 years, 418 months, and 418 days.[11] Therefore it was probably in the summer of A.D. 64 that the martyrdom of Peter, and of Paul, at Rome took place.

⟨ 477.   After this, the tradition increasingly attributes the founding of the church at Rome to Peter and Paul. Actually we know from Paul's Letter to the Romans that the church there was in existence before Paul visited Rome, and it seems likely that its origin was due to causes at work before either Paul or Peter arrived, perhaps to the return of converted "visitors from Rome, both Jews and proselytes," who were present in Jerusalem on the day of Pentecost (Ac 1:10). But Dionysius, bishop of Corinth, about A.D. 170 wrote a letter to the Romans, which Eusebius quotes,[12] and said about Peter and Paul:

> "You have thus by such an admonition bound together the planting of Peter and of Paul at Rome and Corinth. For both of them planted and likewise taught us in our Corinth. And they taught together in like manner in Italy, and suffered martyrdom at the same time."

Irenaeus[13] also speaks of "Peter and Paul . . . preaching at Rome, and laying the foundations of the Church."

⟨ 478.   Tangible evidence of the remembrance at Rome of the martyrdom of Peter and Paul is attested by Gaius of Rome around A.D. 200. According to Eusebius[14] this authority, a presbyter in

[9] Cf. Cullmann, *Peter,* p.109; Klauser, *Die römische Petrustradition,* p.16; Guarducci, *The Tomb of St. Peter,* pp.31, 179.
[10] *Annals.* xv, 41.
[11] Tacitus, *Annals,* ed. John Jackson, LCL IV (1951), p.278 n.1.
[12] *Ch. Hist.* II, 25.   [13] *Against Heresies.* III, i, 5.
[14] *Ch. Hist.* II, xxv.

the Roman church under Zephyrinus (A.D. c.199-217), said that he could show the "trophies" (τρόπαια) of Peter and Paul at the Vatican and on the Ostian Way respectively. These are places where, as excavations have shown, pagan cemeteries existed. The "trophy," presumably meaning burial place and memorial of victory, of Peter has in all probability actually been found under St. Peter's Church in Rome, in the form of a simple niche with columns in the so-called Red Wall, a shrine probably dating around A.D. 160.[15] On the plaster of the Red Wall itself is a graffito dating probably not long after A.D. 160 and probably reading:

ΠΕΤΡ[ΟC]

ΕΝΙ

The ἔνι can be a contraction of ἔνεστι, so that the inscription means, "Peter is within," i.e., "Peter is buried inside here."[16]

〔479.   Tertullian of Carthage (A.D. c.160-c.235), a contemporary of Gaius of Rome, speaks of how blessed the Roman church is, "where Peter endured a passion like his Lord's! where Paul won his crown in a death like John's [i.e., John the Baptist]."[17] Tertullian also mentions "those whom Peter baptized in the Tiber";[18] and says that the church of Rome "states that Clement was ordained by Peter."[19] If the last statement is correct, Linus and Cletus, the predecessors of Clement, must have held office only briefly for Clement also to be ordained by Peter.

〔480.   Origen of Alexandria (A.D. c.185-c.254) is cited by Eusebius[20] as saying that Peter, after preaching in the provinces named in I Pet 1:1, came to Rome and "was crucified head downward, for he had asked that he might suffer in this way," and that Paul, after preaching from Jerusalem to Illyricum (Rom 15:19), "suffered martyrdom in Rome under Nero."

〔481.   Macarius Magnes, probably bishop of Magnesia in Caria or Lydia about A.D. 400, wrote five books of imaginary dialogue between himself and a pagan philosopher, the material which the

---

15 Kirschbaum, *The Tombs of St Peter and St Paul*, pp.63-81.
16 Guarducci, *The Tomb of St. Peter*, pp.131-136.
17 *On Prescription against Heretics*. 36.
18 *On Baptism*. 4.
19 *On Prescription against Heretics*. 32.
20 *Ch. Hist.* III, 1.

latter presents probably being derived largely from Porphyry of Tyre (A.D. 233-c.304). Porphyry was at Rome about the middle of the third century and knew the Christians there. In the dialogue[21] the philosopher tells how Peter escaped from prison under Herod (¶471), and then says, referring to Peter's commission from Jesus to "feed my lambs," that "it is recorded that Peter fed the lambs for several months only before he was crucified." This presumably means several months of activity in Rome before death there. Then the philosopher refers to Paul along with Peter: "This fine fellow was overpowered at Rome and beheaded . . . even as Peter . . . was fastened to the cross and crucified."

¶ 482. Lactantius of Africa, who flourished A.D. c.310, tells how the apostles, including Paul,

> "during twenty-five years, and until the beginning of the reign of the Emperor Nero, . . . occupied themselves in laying the foundations of the Church in every province and city. And while Nero reigned, the Apostle Peter came to Rome, and . . . built up a faithful and steadfast temple unto the Lord. When Nero heard of these things . . . he crucified Peter, and slew Paul."[22]

Here too Peter's work in Rome is represented as relatively short, and all of it takes place under the reign of Nero.

¶ 483. With Eusebius we see plainly that the increasing tendency was to put Peter's arrival in Rome earlier and to make his stay there longer. In the *Church History*[23] Eusebius says that Peter came to Rome during the reign of Claudius (A.D. 41-54). This dating may be intended to harmonize with the description of Peter as contending at Rome with Simon Magus (Ac 8:9ff.), "the author of all heresy,"[24] for according to Justin Martyr[25] Simon came to Rome in the reign of Claudius. The death of Peter and also of Paul is placed in the *Church History*[26] in Rome under Nero, but without giving an exact year. The exact years of Peter's arrival and of the death of the two apostles are available, however, in the *Chronicle* (¶484).

¶ 484. In the *Chronicle* the dating of these events is in relation to the regnal years of the Roman emperors Claudius (A.D. 41-54)

---

[21] *Unigenitus.* III, 22; IV, 4; Shotwell and Loomis, *The See of Peter*, pp.92-93.
[22] *The Deaths of Persecutors.* 2.
[23] II, xiv, 6.   [24] II, xiii, 6.   [25] *First Apology.* 26.   [26] II, xxv, 5.

and Nero (A.D. 54-68) and the Jewish kings Herod Agrippa I (A.D. 37-44) and Herod Agrippa II (A.D. 44-100). Gaius died on Jan 24 and Claudius acceded to the throne on Jan 25, A.D. 41 (Table 42) and that calendar year (A.D. 41) is reckoned as Year 1 of Claudius in the *Chronicle* (Table 145). He died in his fourteenth year of reign, on Oct 12, A.D. 54. Nero was made emperor forthwith on Oct 13 (Table 43), and the short portion of that calendar year remaining is treated in the *Chronicle* as an accession year so that the calendar year A.D. 55 is shown as equivalent to Year 1 of Nero. Thus his fourteenth and last year is A.D. 68 and in that year he died on Jun 9. The regnal years of Herod Agrippa I have already been shown in Table 145 as they appear in the *Chronicle* in parallel with the years of Gaius and Claudius. As for Herod Agrippa II, like his father Agrippa I he too was educated at Rome. When his father died in the spring of A.D. 44 (¶471), Claudius desired to appoint him as successor to his father. But as events transpired, it was only in A.D. 50 that Agrippa received the kingdom in the Lebanon of his uncle, Herod of Chalcis. Then in the thirteenth year of Claudius (A.D. 53), relinquishing Chalcis, he received the former tetrarchy of Philip. Again, after the accession of Nero (A.D. 54), he was given important parts of Galilee and Perea. Nevertheless his reign is reckoned as beginning with his father's death in A.D. 44, and he continued to rule until his own death in A.D. 100.[27] In the *Chronicle* the year 44 is treated as his accession year, and his first regnal year is equated with A.D. 45. With this understanding of the regnal years of the contemporary rulers, we may reproduce a portion of the *Chronicle* in the version of Jerome,[28] to show the dating of events in the life of Peter (Table 146), namely his arrival in Rome in the second year of Claudius (A.D. 42) and his death, together with Paul, in the fourteenth year of Nero (A.D. 68).

¶485.   In the Armenian version of the *Chronicle*,[29] Peter's arrival in Rome is put earlier (Table 147), in the third year of Gaius (A.D. 39), and his death, with Paul, in the thirteenth year of Nero (A.D. 67).

---

27 SHJP I, ii, pp.191-206; Shotwell and Loomis, *The See of Peter*, p.100 n.98.
28 Helm pp.179-185; cf. Shotwell and Loomis, *The See of Peter*, p.116.
29 Karst pp.214-216; cf. Shotwell and Loomis, *The See of Peter*, p.100.

TABLE 146. THE LIFE OF PETER IN THE *Chronicle* OF EUSEBIUS
(JEROME'S VERSION)

Romans		Jews	A.D.
Claudius, thirteen years, eight months, twenty-eight days		Herod Agrippa I, seven years	
Year 1		Year 4	41
Year 2	Peter, the apostle, having first founded the church of Antioch, is sent to Rome, where he preaches the gospel and remains for twenty-five years as bishop of the same city.	Year 5	42
Year 3		Year 6	43
Year 4		Year 7	44
		Herod Agrippa II, twenty-six years (i.e., counting to A.D. 70)	
Year 5		Year 1	45
Year 6		Year 2	46
Year 7		Year 3	47
Year 8		Year 4	48
Year 9		Year 5	49
....		....	
Year 12		Year 8	52
Year 13		Year 9	53
Year 14		Year 10	54
Nero, thirteen years, seven months, twenty-eight days			
Year 1		Year 11	55
Year 2		Year 12	56
....		....	
Year 10		Year 20	64
Year 11		Year 21	65
Year 12		Year 22	66
Year 13		Year 23	67
Year 14	To crown all his other crimes, Nero institutes the first persecution against the Christians, in which Peter and Paul perish gloriously at Rome.	Year 24	68

TABLE 147. THE LIFE OF PETER IN THE *Chronicle* OF EUSEBIUS
(ARMENIAN VERSION)

	Romans	Jews	A.D.
	Gaius, three years and four months	Herod Agrippa I, seven years	
	Year 1	(Accession Year)	37
	Year 2	Year 1	38
Peter the apostle, having first founded the church at Antioch, goes to the city of Rome and there preaches the gospel and abides there as head of the church for twenty years.	Year 3	Year 2	39
	Year 4	Year 3	40
	Claudius, fourteen years and eight months		
	Year 1	Year 4	41
	Year 2	Year 5	42
	Year 3	Year 6	43
	Year 4	Year 7	44
		Herod Agrippa II, twenty-six years	
	Year 5	Year 1	45
	....		
	Year 14	Year 10	54
	Nero, thirteen years and seven months		
	Year 1	Year 11	55
	....		
	Year 10	Year 20	64
	Year 11	Year 21	65
	Year 12	Year 22	66
	Year 13	Year 23	67
			To crown all his other crimes, Nero instituted the first persecution of the Christians, in the course of which the apostles, Peter and Paul, suffered martyrdom at Rome.
	Year 14	Year 24	68

¶486. The arrival of Peter in Rome in the reign of Claudius (as represented in the *Church History* [¶483] and in the *Chronicle* in the version of Jerome [Table 146]) may have been motivated by the report that he contended there with Simon Magus who came in the reign of Claudius (¶483). The even earlier arrival of Peter in Rome in the Armenian version of the *Chronicle* (Table 147) could likewise have been suggested by the fact which Hippolytus[30] seems to imply that Peter was already there when Simon Magus came. Actually Peter could have come to Rome for continuing residence neither in the third year of Caligula and the second year of Agrippa (A.D. 39) (Table 147) nor in the second year of Claudius and the fifth year of Agrippa (A.D. 42) (Table 146), for only in the fourth year of Claudius and the seventh year of Agrippa (A.D. 44) (Table 145 and ¶471) did he escape from his imprisonment under the Jewish king, and even at that point there is no proof that "another place" to which he went was Rome.

¶487. In relation to the date of the martyrdom of Peter and Paul in the *Chronicle* in A.D. 67 (Table 147) or 68 (Table 146), it is to be noted that Eusebius also puts the first general persecution of the Christians at Rome by Nero at the same time. Since according to earlier authorities (¶¶475-476) that persecution came in succession to the great fire, and that was in the summer of the year 64, this later dating of the persecution in 67 or 68 is surely in error. But the placing of the martyrdom of Peter and Paul in the context of the wider persecution confirms our hypothesis that it was at that time (A.D. 64) that the two apostles were put to death, each suffering his particular martyrdom (¶¶474, 479).

¶488. In the *Depositio martyrum* of the *Chronographer of the Year 354* (¶176) this item occurs:

VIII Kal. Martias natale Petri de cathedra

The eighth day before the Kalends (¶141) or first day of March = Feb 22. *Natale* means not just "birthday" but also "memorial day" or "anniversary," and *cathedra* is "chair" or "seat." So in the city calendar of Rome a memorial day was observed on Feb 22 of Peter's entrance upon office.[31]

[30] *The Refutation of All Heresies.* VI, ii, 15.
[31] Lietzmann, *Petrus und Paulus in Rom,* pp.3ff.

【 489.   Also in the same source (¶488) is this item:

III Kal. Iul. Petri in Catacumbas
et Pauli Ostense Tusco et Basso cons.

The third day before the Kalends (¶141) or first day of July = Jun 29. M. Nummius Tuscus and Pomponius Bassus were consuls in A.D. 258.[32] So on Jun 29 there was held a memorial day of Peter *in Catacumbas* and of Paul on the Ostian Way. Catacumbas was the name of a valley on the Via Appia where the Catacomb and Church of Sebastian are found. Third-century graffiti discovered in the excavations here show that both Peter and Paul were honored at this place. The year 258 was the year in which Valerian's brief but violent persecution of the Christians took place. It may be that at that time, for safety, the remains of Peter and Paul, or some portions thereof, were temporarily transferred to this place. Or, even without such a transfer, it could be that at that time, when no liturgical celebration could be held in the pagan cemeteries at the Vatican and on the Ostian Way, there arose at this place a practice of paying devotion to the memory of the two apostles.[33]

【 490.   In a later part of the work of the *Chronographer of the Year 354* (¶176) is a list of bishops of Rome from Peter to Liberius (who was installed as bishop in A.D. 352). This is called the "Liberian Catalogue" (*Catalogus Liberianus*) because it extends to Liberius and must have been compiled in his time (A.D. 352-366), although not necessarily by him.[34] The *Catalogus Liberianus* begins:

> In the reign of Tiberius Caesar our Lord Jesus Christ suffered under the constellation of the Gemini, March 25, and after his ascension blessed Peter instituted the episcopate. From his time we name in due order of succession every one who has been bishop, how many years he was in office and under what emperor.
> Peter, twenty-five years, one month, nine days, was bishop in the time of Tiberius Caesar and of Gaius and of Tiberius Claudius and of Nero, from the consulship of Minucius and Longinus to that of Nero and Verus. He suffered together with Paul, June 29, under the aforesaid consuls in the reign of Nero.

[32] Liebenam, *Fasti Consulares* (KLT 41-43), p.30.
[33] Hertling and Kirschbaum, *The Roman Catacombs and Their Martyrs*, pp.106-120.
[34] Mommsen, *Chronica minora*. 1, p.73; Shotwell and Loomis, *The See of Peter*, p.107; Adolf Harnack, *Geschichte der altchristlichen Literatur bis Eusebius*. 2d ed., II, *Die Chronologie*, 1 (1896 reprinted 1958), p.144.

The consuls, whose names are slightly misspelled in the *Catalogus Liberianus*, are M. Vinicius and L. Cassius Longinus, and Nero and L. Antistius Vetus. The consular date (Table 38) *Vinicio et Longino* indicates A.D. 30; the consular date *Nerone Caesare et Vetere* signifies A.D. 55. As in the *Chronicle* of Eusebius in the version of Jerome (Table 146), Peter serves as bishop for twenty-five years. But here in the *Catalogus Liberianus* he establishes the episcopate immediately after the Ascension and holds the office from A.D. 30 to 55 under the emperors Tiberius, Gaius, Claudius, and Nero. It is not entirely clear whether the twenty-five years are spent in Rome alone or whether they include some prior time, say in Antioch (¶493).

⟨ 491. In the list of consuls which is also given by the *Chronographer of the Year 354* (¶176), the death of Jesus is put under the consulate of the Gemini as usual (¶462), i.e., in A.D. 29; after that Peter and Paul come to Rome in the consulate of Galba and Sulla, i.e., in A.D. 33; and they die under the consuls Nero and Vetus, i.e., in A.D. 55 (Table 38). The notations concerning Peter and Paul are:

> *Galba et Sulla*
> *His cons. Petrus et Paulus ad urbem*
> *venerunt agere episcopatum.*
>
> *Nerone Caesare et Vetere*
> *His cons. passi sunt Petrus et Paulus*
> *III Kal. Iul.*

⟨ 492. In his work *Concerning Illustrious Men*, written at Bethlehem around A.D. 392, Jerome (A.D. c.335-420) appears to use materials on the chronology of Peter and Paul largely derived from Eusebius (¶¶483ff.), for he brings Peter to Rome in the second year of Claudius and places the martyrdom of both Peter and Paul in the fourteenth year of Nero. He writes:

"Simon Peter . . . after his bishopric at Antioch and his preaching to the dispersed of the circumcision who believed, in Pontus, Galatia, Cappadocia, Asia and Bithynia, in the second year of the emperor Claudius, went to Rome to expel Simon Magus and occupied there the sacerdotal seat for twenty-five years until the last year of Nero, that is, the fourteenth. By Nero he was fastened to a cross and crowned with martyrdom, his head downward toward the earth and his feet raised on high, for he maintained that he was unworthy to be crucified in the same manner as his Lord. . . .

He was buried at Rome in the Vatican, near the Via Triumphalis, and is celebrated by the veneration of the whole world."[35]

"So in the fourteenth year of Nero on the same day on which Peter was executed, he [Paul] was beheaded at Rome for the sake of Christ and was buried on the Via Ostiensis, in the thirty-seventh year after the Lord's passion."[36]

Jerome's dates are therefore the same as those of Eusebius (Table 146). Peter comes to Rome in the second year of Claudius = A.D. 42, he serves as bishop for twenty-five years = A.D. 43-67, and he dies there in the fourteenth year of Nero = A.D. 68. If, as one would suppose, Jerome also uses Eusebius' date for the death of Jesus, namely A.D. 31 (Table 82), then the thirty-seventh year thereafter was indeed A.D. 68.

‹[493.   Finally in the *Liber Pontificalis* or "Book of the Popes," compiled in the sixth or seventh century out of earlier materials, the information of the *Catalogus Liberianus* (¶490) is developed into an extended account from which we quote the following:[37]

"Blessed Peter . . . first occupied the seat of the bishop in Anthiocia [Antiochia] for seven years. This Peter entered the city of Rome when Nero was Caesar and there occupied the seat of the bishop for twenty-five years, one month, and eight days.

"He was bishop in the time of Tiberius Caesar and of Gaius and of Tiberius Claudius and of Nero.

"He wrote two epistles which are called catholic, and the gospel of Mark, for Mark was his disciple and son by baptism. . . .

"He ordained two bishops, Linus and Cletus. . . .

"He disputed many times with Simon Magus both before Nero, the emperor, and before the people. . . .

"He consecrated blessed Clement as bishop and committed to him the government of the see and all the church. . . .

"After he had thus disposed affairs he received the crown of martyrdom with Paul in the year 38 after the Lord's passion.

"He was buried also on the Via Aurelia, in the shrine of Apollo, near the place where he was crucified, near the palace of Nero, in the Vatican, near the triumphal district, on June 29."

‹[494.   The foregoing statement (¶493) agrees with the *Catalogus Liberianus* (¶490) in making Peter bishop under Tiberius, Gaius, Claudius, and Nero, and it explicitly gives him seven years as bishop of Antioch prior to twenty-five years as bishop of Rome.

---

[35] *De Viris Illustribus.* I.
[36] *De Viris Illustribus.* V.
[37] Louise R. Loomis, *The Book of the Popes* (*Liber Pontificalis*) (Records of Civilization: Sources and Studies). I, *To the Pontificate of Gregory I.* 1916, pp.4-5.

The death of Peter (and of Paul) is placed in the thirty-eighth year after the Lord's passion. If this is based on the widely accepted date of A.D. 29 for the death of Jesus (¶462) it presumably means A.D. 67. If Peter had been in Rome for twenty-five years at that time he could have come in A.D. 42 if we simply add 42 + 25 = 67 (cf. ¶492, where there are twenty-five years between A.D. 42 and A.D. 68).

¶495. The *Liber Pontificalis* is self-contradictory, however, because it also contains the affirmation in the same passage that "Peter entered the city of Rome when Nero was Caesar." Since Nero became emperor only in A.D. 54 (Table 43), there is evidently preserved here an older remembrance (which is contrary to the tendency [¶483] to put Peter's arrival earlier and earlier) that in fact Peter came to Rome only at a relatively late date and indeed after A.D. 54. In the light of the evidence surveyed it is probable that Peter left Jerusalem after imprisonment under Herod Agrippa I in the spring of A.D. 44 (¶471), came to Rome sometime under Nero (as the *Liber Pontificalis* says) and therefore after A.D. 54, and died there, at the same time as Paul, in the summer of A.D. 64 (¶476).

C. THE LIFE OF PAUL

LITERATURE: Hans Lietzmann, "Ein neuer Fund zur Chronologie des Paulus," in *Zeitschrift für wissenschaftliche Theologie.* 53 (N.F. 18), 1911, pp.345-354; Adolf Deissmann, *Paul, A Study in Social and Religious History.* 2d ed. 1926; L. Hennequin, "Delphes (Inscription de)," in *Dictionnaire de la Bible*, Supplément, II (1934), cols. 355-373; Edmund Groag, *Die römischen Reichsbeamten von Achaia bis auf Diokletian* (Akademie der Wissenschaften in Wien, Schriften der Balkankommission, Antiquarische Abteilung, IX). 1939; E. Groag, *Die Reichsbeamten von Achaia in spätrömischer Zeit* (Dissertationes Pannonicae. Budapest: Institut für Münzkunde und Archaeologie der P. Pázmány-Universität). 1946; Paul Lemerle, *Philippes et la Macedoine orientale a l'époque chretienne et byzantine.* 1945; John Knox, *Chapters in a Life of Paul.* 1950; Henry J. Cadbury, *The Book of Acts in History.* 1955; Jacques Dupont, "Notes sur les Actes des Apôtres, V. Chronologie Paulinienne," in RB 62 (1955), pp.55-59.

¶496. If the attempt is made to deal with the chronology of the life of Paul exclusively or primarily on the basis of such letters as are recognized by the critic to have been written by him, then only a rather broad outline is usually found attainable.[1] If the rele-

[1] Knox, *Chapters in a Life of Paul*, pp.74-88.

vant materials in the book of Acts are taken as they stand, certain problems are raised, particularly in the earlier part, but a relatively detailed chronology, particularly in the later part, can be worked out.[2]

1. GALLIO

¶ 497.   The mention of Gallio as proconsul of Achaia in Ac 18:12 offers the possibility of the establishment of a fixed point in the chronology of Paul's life. The land which the Greeks and Romans called Achaia comprised most of ancient Greece south of Macedonia. This region was taken by the Romans in 146 B.C. When Augustus reorganized the empire in 27 B.C., Achaia was made a senatorial province under a proconsul (ἀνθύπατος) of praetorian rank.[3] Although Tiberius combined Achaia and Macedonia administratively, in A.D. 44 Claudius (A.D. 41-54) again made Achaia a separate province responsible to the senate.[4] In the province of Achaia, Corinth was the seat of administration.

¶ 498.   The standard term of office for a proconsul or governor of a senatorial province was one year, and when Dio[5] says that Claudius allowed some governors to hold office for two years he is clearly describing exceptional cases. Provincial governors tended, it seems, to be slow about leaving Rome for their presumably more frontier-like posts. It was no doubt for this reason that in the consulship of Drusus Iulius f. Caesar and C. Norbanus C. f. Flaccus (Table 38: *Druso Caesare et Flacco* = A.D. 15), Tiberius commanded that provincial governors take their departure by the first day of June,[6] which would presumably allow time for travel and entry upon office by, say, July 1. Claudius in turn, in the next year after his accession (A.D. 42, Table 42), introduced the law that the governors were to set out before the first day of April.[7] But the following year, when he was consul the third time (A.D. 43, Table 42), he reduced the stringency of the requirement slightly by giving notice to the governors "that they must begin their journey before the middle of April."[8] At this time, therefore, office was presumably entered upon in the province in, say, May/Jun, at any rate in the early summer.

[2] Lietzmann in *Zeitschrift für wissenschaftliche Chronologie.* 53 (N.F. 18), 1911, pp.345-354.
[3] Strabo XVII, 840.   [4] Dio LX, 24, 1; Suetonius, *Claudius.* XXV, 3.
[5] LX, 25, 6.   [6] Dio LVII, 14, 5.   [7] Dio LX, 11, 6.   [8] Dio LX, 17, 3.

⟨ 499. L. Junius Gallio Annaeanus was a brother of Seneca, the Roman philosopher, and is mentioned by Tacitus[9] and Dio.[10] At Delphi, across the Gulf of Corinth from Corinth, a stone was found and is preserved in the Delphi Museum which mentions the name of Gallio in his official position with which we are concerned. This record, which was set up in the temple of Apollo, is a copy of a letter from the emperor Claudius (A.D. 41-54) to the city of Delphi. Although the inscription is fragmentary the restorations, at points critical for our concern, seem positive. As emperor the full name of Claudius was Tiberius Claudius Caesar Augustus Germanicus (Table 42), and the inscription begins (Line 1) with this full name:

$$\text{Τιβέρ[ιος Κλαύδιος Κ]αῖσ[αρ Σεβαστ]ὸς Γ[ερμανικός}$$

Line 2 begins with the letters σιας, probably the last letters of δημαρ-χικῆς ἐξουσίας, "of tribunician power" (¶179), referring to the number of times he had been given this honor. Since it corresponds to the normal sequence in which honors were listed, there doubtless came after this the word αὐτοκράτωρ, signifying the "imperial acclamation" (¶180). Then the text preserves the number κϛ = 26, thus meaning that he had received the imperial acclamation for the twenty-sixth time.

⟨ 500. As shown in Table 42, the twenty-sixth acclamation of Claudius as *imperator* (αὐτοκράτωρ) was in the year 52, as was also the twenty-seventh acclamation. Since the Delphi inscription is evidently dated in terms of the twenty-sixth imperial acclamation (¶499), it becomes important to establish even more precisely, if possible, the time signified by this honor. While in the Delphi inscription the number of times Claudius had received the tribunician power is lost in a gap in the text, there is a Carian inscription which puts together the twelfth tribunician power and the twenty-sixth imperial acclamation of Claudius (δημαρχικῆς ἐξουσίας τὸ δωδέκατον . . . αὐτοκράτορα τὸ εἰκοστὸν καὶ ἔκτον).[11] As also shown in Table 42, the tribunician power of Claudius was reckoned from Jan 25, A.D. 41 and renewed annually, therefore his *tribunicia potestate XII* corresponded to Jan 25, A.D. 52, to Jan 24, A.D. 53. Therefore, as the Carian inscription shows, the twenty-sixth imperial acclamation

[9] *Annals.* xv, 73.   [10] LXI, xxxv, 2.
[11] Groag, *Die römischen Reichsbeamten von Achaia bis auf Diokletian*, col. 33 n.123.

must fall within this same period. But on the Aqua Claudia at Rome, an aqueduct dedicated on Aug 1, A.D. 52, an inscription names Claudius as of tribunician power the twelfth time and imperator the twenty-seventh time (*tribunicia potestate XII . . . imperator XXVII*).[12] Therefore within the same twelfth period of tribunician power (= Jan 25, A.D. 52-Jan 24, A.D. 53) and indeed before Aug 1, A.D. 52 (when the honor appears in the Aqua Claudia inscription) he had received his twenty-seventh imperial acclamation. Accordingly the twenty-sixth acclamation (which also fell within the twelfth tribunician power) must have come within the first half of the *tribunicia potestate XII*, i.e., between Jan 25, A.D. 52 and some time before Aug 1, A.D. 52. Since the Delphi inscription of Claudius evidently refers (¶499) to his twenty-sixth imperial acclamation, it is to be dated in the first half (Jan-Jul) of A.D. 52.

¶ 501.   Much of the subject matter of the Delphi inscription is lost in the gaps in the text, but in Lines 5-6 Claudius mentions Gallio as his friend and proconsul. At the end of Line 5 were probably the name Lucius and certainly the first letters of the name Junius. Then Line 6 continues:

['Ἰού-

νιος Γαλλίων ὁ φ[ίλος] μου κα[ὶ ἀνθύ]πατος

[Ju-

nius Gallio my friend and proconsul

The designation of Gallio as "friend" probably refers to the title of honor, *amicus Caesaris* (¶375) given to a person who enjoyed the imperial favor and was charged with an important mission.[13] The designation of Gallio as "proconsul" can only refer, in an inscription of this date, to his proconsulate in Achaia. Since Gallio was thus proconsul of Achaia in the first half of A.D. 52 (the date established above [¶500] for this inscription), he must have entered upon that office in the early summer, say May/Jun (¶498), of the year 51.[14]

---

[12] Deissmann, *Paul*, p.275.

[13] Hennequin in *Dictionnaire de la Bible*, Supplément, II, col. 366; cf. Ethelbert Stauffer, *Jesus and His Story*, p.133.

[14] For this date see Deissmann, *Paul*, p.272; Groag, *Die römischen Reichsbeamten von Achaia bis auf Diokletian*, cols. 32-35; Lemerle, *Philippes et la Macedoine orientale*, pp.18-19. For the arrival of Gallio one year later in the spring of A.D. 52, see Hennequin in *Dictionnaire de la Bible*, Supplément, II, cols. 367-368; Dupont in RB 62 (1955), pp.55-56.

¶ 502.   Ac 18:11-12 states that Paul stayed a year and six months in Corinth and then, "when Gallio was proconsul of Achaia," was attacked by the Jews and brought before the tribunal of the governor. The language seems to suggest that Gallio arrived at that time, and it seems inherently likely that the coming of a new governor, who was inexperienced in that place, would provide a good opportunity for such an attack. It is probable, therefore, that Paul was brought before Gallio (who had arrived perhaps in May/Jun [¶501]) in the early summer of A.D. 51. Since at that time he had been in Corinth a year and six months (Ac 18:11), Paul's original arrival in Corinth may be dated in midwinter A.D. 49/50, say perhaps in January, A.D. 50.

¶ 503.   When he arrived in Corinth Paul "found a Jew named Aquila, a native of Pontus, lately come from Italy with his wife Priscilla, because Claudius had commanded all the Jews to leave Rome" (Ac 18:2). This expulsion of Jews from Rome is presumably part of the same event described by Suetonius, who writes in his life of Claudius:[15] "Since the Jews constantly made disturbances at the instigation of Chrestus (*impulsore Chresto*) he expelled them from Rome." In his *Seven Books of History against the Pagans*, written in A.D. 416-417, Orosius, a contemporary of Augustine and Jerome, says that Claudius expelled the Jews from Rome in the ninth year of his reign, and gives as his sources both Josephus and Suetonius, choosing to quote only the latter.[16] Josephus is presumably the well-known Jewish historian, but this date is not found in extant texts of Josephus. Since Claudius began to reign Jan 25, A.D. 41 (Table 42), it is probable that that calendar year was considered his first regnal year; accordingly his ninth year was the year 49 (Table 146). If Aquila and Priscilla had to leave Rome in A.D. 49 they would indeed be "lately come" when Paul met them in Corinth upon his arrival, by our reckoning in midwinter A.D. 49/50, perhaps in Jan A.D. 50 (¶502).

¶ 504.   If Paul's arrival at Corinth in midwinter A.D. 49/50, perhaps in Jan A.D. 50 (¶¶502, 503), may be accepted as a fixed point then reckoning may be made both backward and forward from this point in terms of other references in Acts and references

---

[15] *Claudius.* 25.
[16] Orosius, *Seven Books of History against the Pagans.* tr. Irving W. Raymond, 1936, p.332; MPL 31, col. 1075.

in the Pauline letters. Reckoning backward we find that immediately before arrival in Corinth Paul had been in Athens apparently briefly (Ac 17:15; 18:1), in Beroea very briefly (Ac 17:14), in Thessalonica three weeks (Ac 17:2), and in Philippi (Ac 16:12ff.). Therefore Paul's work in Philippi was in the autumn or early winter of A.D. 49.[17] In the yet earlier part of this journey, as described in the book of Acts, Paul was in Troas, Bithynia, and Mysia (Ac 16:7-8), in Galatia and Phrygia (Ac 16:6), and in Cilicia and came originally from Syria (Ac 15:41). Such an itinerary must carry the beginning of this journey, commonly known as the "second missionary journey," back to, say, early spring A.D. 49.

¶ 505. This (¶504) would appear to put the conference in Jerusalem which is described in Ac 15 in, say, the winter of A.D. 48/49. The preceding "first missionary journey" narrated in Ac 13-14 could have been in A.D. 47-48 if not earlier. If the conference at Jerusalem was in A.D. 48/49, and if the visit of Paul to Jerusalem at this time is the same visit as that reported in Gal 2:1, then we may reckon that the point fourteen years before that, to which Paul refers in the Galatian letter, was equivalent to A.D. 35/36. If Gal 1:18 "after three years" and Gal 2:1 "after fourteen years" are two separate references each going back to the decisive point of Paul's conversion, then the conversion may be put in A.D. 35/36. If the fourteen years of Gal 2:1 follow upon the three years of Gal 1:18, as seems more probable in view of their sequence in the Galatian letter, then the conversion was probably in A.D. 33/34. The sequence of years on the latter supposition appears in Table 148. This date of A.D. 33/34 for the conversion of Paul is after both the spring of A.D. 30 and the spring of A.D. 33, which are the dates we have considered probable for the death of Jesus (Tables 142, 143, 144). It fits therefore with either date, but more adequate time for intervening events (Ac 1-9) is probably allowed by the earlier alternative which, at least as it is correlated with other data in Table 142, we have preferred anyway. We conclude it to be probable that the death of Jesus was in the spring of A.D. 30 and the conversion of Paul in A.D. 33/34.

¶ 506. Counting forward from the fixed point of Paul's arrival at Corinth in midwinter A.D. 49/50, say perhaps in Jan A.D. 50

[17] Cf. Lemerle, *Philippes et la Macedoine orientale*, pp.18-19.

TABLE 148. FROM THE CONVERSION OF PAUL TO THE CONFERENCE
AT JERUSALEM

A.D.		
33/34	Conversion of Saul (Ac 9)	
34/35		3 years
35/36	Visit to Jerusalem "after three years" (Gal 1:18)	
36/37		
37/38		
38/39		
39/40		
40/41		
41/42		
42/43		
43/44		14 years
44/45		
45/46		
46/47		
47/48		
48/49	Visit to Jerusalem "after fourteen years" (Gal 2:1) and the Jerusalem conference (Ac 15)	

(¶504) and his appearance before Gallio in the early summer of A.D. 51 (¶502), we find that Paul stayed on in Corinth ἡμέρας ἱκανάς (Ac 18:18). In view of the riot we may think that this was hardly the "many days" of the RSV but more probably the "several days" of the Berkeley Version. From there Paul went to Ephesus for a short time (Ac 18:20), and then proceeded by way of Caesarea to Antioch (Ac 18:22). Thus this so-called "second missionary journey" (¶504) came to an end probably in the fall of A.D. 51.

《 507. Ac 18:23 would allow wintering in Antioch and departure on the "third missionary journey" in the spring of A.D. 52. Paul then went through Galatia and Phrygia (Ac 18:23) to Ephesus (Ac 19:1). In Ephesus he spent three months in the synagogue (Ac 19:8), which would be in the summer of A.D. 52; and then two years in the hall of Tyrannus (Ac 19:10), which would extend until the summer of A.D. 54. In accordance with the Jewish principle whereby the part stands for the whole and a part of a year is considered a whole year (¶165), the two years and three months are called "three years" in Ac 20:31. Leaving Ephesus after the riot inspired by Demetrius, Paul went through Macedonia (Ac

20:1) (fall A.D. 54) and came to Greece where he spent three months (Ac 20:3) (midwinter A.D. 54/55). Returning through Macedonia (Ac 20:3) (spring A.D. 55), he sailed from Philippi "after the days of Unleavened Bread" (Ac 20:6). In A.D. 55 Nisan 1 fell on Mar 19 (or if the standard Babylonian intercalation of a second Adar was made, it fell on Apr 17),[18] and Nisan 14 was accordingly on Apr 1 (or Apr 30). The seven days of unleavened bread followed (¶446). Pentecost came fifty days after Passover time (Table 133), and Paul was "hastening to be at Jerusalem, if possible, on the day of Pentecost" (Ac 20:16). His arrival in Jerusalem was presumably, therefore, in May or June, A.D. 55, and with this arrival the "third missionary journey" came to an end.

❲ 508.   In Jerusalem Paul was arrested (Ac 21:33), then transferred to Caesarea (Ac 23:23). By our sequence of events this would be in the summer of A.D. 55. At Caesarea he spoke before Felix the governor who had then been "for many years . . . judge over this nation" (Ac 24:10). When two years had elapsed, Felix was succeeded by Porcius Festus and Paul was still left in prison (Ac 24:27). By our count this would bring us to the summer of A.D. 57.

2. FELIX AND PORCIUS FESTUS

❲ 509.   Felix, called Antonius Felix by Tacitus,[1] and brother of the influential Pallas, was appointed procurator of Palestine by the emperor Claudius (A.D. 41-54). Suetonius[2] says that Claudius was fond of Felix and gave him command of the province of Judea. Josephus says in the *War*[3] that Claudius sent Felix out as procurator of Judea, Samaria, Galilee, and Perea; and in the *Antiquities*[4] tells of the same appointment and immediately afterward mentions the completion by Claudius of his twelfth year of reign. Claudius began to reign Jan 25, A.D. 41 (Table 42), and that calendar year was probably counted as his first regnal year (¶503). Therefore the twelfth year of Claudius was probably A.D. 52 (Table 146), and this was accordingly the year of the appointment of Felix. If Felix began his procuratorship in A.D. 52 Paul could well have said in

---

[18] PDBC p.47.

[1] *Histories.* v, 9.
[2] *Claudius.* 28.
[3] II, 247 (= II, xii, 8).
[4] XX, 137 (= XX, vii, 1).

A.D. 55, no doubt with a desire to make as favorable a comment as possible, that he had been judge over the nation "for many years" (Ac 24:10).

([510.   Upon the death of Claudius, Felix was confirmed in his previous appointment by Nero (A.D. 54-68),[5] and continued to serve under this emperor, as both Josephus[6] and Eusebius[7] attest. Then, still under Nero, in succession to Felix, Porcius Festus was sent out as the next procurator. This is stated by Josephus,[8] but without exact indication of the date of the change. As to when it was, opinions of modern scholars run from A.D. 55[9] to A.D. 59[10] or A.D. 60.[11]

([511.   In the Armenian version of the *Chronicle* of Eusebius the replacement of Felix by Festus is placed in the fourteenth and last year of Claudius (= A.D. 54 [Table 146]), but this can hardly be correct since in the *Church History* Eusebius speaks of Felix as still procurator in the time of Nero (¶510). In Jerome's version of the *Chronicle*, however, the tabulation at this point is as shown in Table 149 (cf. Tables 84, 146).[12]

TABLE 149. The Succession of Porcius Festus to Felix in the *Chronicle* of Eusebius (Jerome's Version)

Romans		Jews	A.D.
Nero, thirteen years, seven months, twenty-eight days		Herod Agrippa II, twenty-six years	
Year 1		Year 11	55
Year 2	Festus succeeds Felix, before whom, with King Agrippa present, the Apostle Paul sets forth the reason for his faith and, being convicted, is sent to Rome.	Year 12	56

[5] Josephus, *War.* II, 252 (= II, xiii, 2).
[6] *Ant.* xx, 160-172 (= xx, viii, 5-6).
[7] *Ch. Hist.* II, xx, 1.
[8] *Ant.* xx, 182 (= xx, viii, 9); *War.* II, 271 (= II, xiv, 1).
[9] Knox, *Chapters in a Life of Paul*, p.66.
[10] Cadbury, *The Book of Acts in History*, p.10.
[11] SHJP I, ii, p.182.
[12] Helm pp.181-182.

If Eusebius reckons Year 2 of Nero as beginning according to the Syro-Macedonian calendar on Oct 1 (¶253), A.D. 56, and if it was during this regnal year (i.e., Oct 1, A.D. 56-Sep 30, A.D. 57) that Festus succeeded Felix, then that succession could very well have fallen close to the time when, by our reckoning, Paul stood before him in the summer of A.D. 57.

⟨ 512. Before Festus Paul appealed to Caesar (Ac 25:11) and Agrippa, who also heard Paul, did not reverse the decision of Festus (Ac 25:12) to send him to Rome (Ac 26:32). By our reckoning departure on the trip to Rome, which became the famous "shipwreck journey," would have been at the end of summer A.D. 57. The voyage went slowly (Ac 27:7) and when they were at Fair Havens on the island of Crete (Ac 27:8) "the fast" (ἡ νηστεία) had already gone by (Ac 27:9). The great fast of the Jewish religious year was the Day of Atonement (¶436), and Josephus[13] uses the same Greek word as in Ac 27:9 evidently meaning the Day of Atonement. The date of the fast was the tenth day of the seventh month = Tishri. In A.D. 57 the first day of Tishri fell on Sep 20,[14] therefore the fast on the tenth day was on Sep 29, A.D. 57. This date was now past.

⟨ 513. In the subsequent storm Paul's ship drifted for fourteen days (Ac 27:27) and was wrecked on Malta (Ac 28:1), presumably in the latter part of October. They stayed there for three months, presumably Nov-Dec-Jan, A.D. 57/58, i.e., the worst part of the winter (Ac 28:11). Then in the early spring, say Feb A.D. 58, they proceeded to Rome. There Paul remained in custody two whole years (Ac 28:30), by our chronology from the spring of A.D. 58 to the spring of A.D. 60.

⟨ 514. After that there was time for the hoped-for trip to Spain (Rom 15:24, 28), which the references of I Clement 5 and the Muratorian Fragment[15] make it probable that he actually made. Then came the time (καιρός) of Paul's departure (II Tim 4:6). For reasons already discussed sufficiently in connection with the death of Peter (¶¶475ff.), the martyrdom of the apostle to the Gentiles, like that of the apostle to the circumcision (Gal 2:7-8), may be put probably in the summer of A.D. 64.

---

[13] *Ant.* XIV, 487 (= XIV, xvi, 4).   [14] PDBC p.47.   [15] FLP p.377 n.4.

❪515. On the basis of the foregoing evidence (¶¶496-514) the chronological outline of the life of Paul appears as follows.

TABLE 150. CHRONOLOGICAL OUTLINE OF THE LIFE OF PAUL

	A.D.
Conversion (¶505)	33/34
First Missionary Journey (¶505)	47-48
Conference at Jerusalem (¶505)	48/49
Second Missionary Journey (¶¶504, 506)	49-51
Third Missionary Journey (¶507)	52-55
Imprisonment in Caesarea (¶508)	55-57
Shipwreck Journey to Rome (¶¶512, 513)	57/58
Imprisonment in Rome (¶513)	58-60
Death (¶514)	64

INDEX OF SCRIPTURAL
REFERENCES

INDEX OF SCRIPTURAL REFERENCES

GENERAL INDEX

All references are to Sections (¶¶) of this book. In addition to this Index consult also the analytical Table of Contents and detailed List of Tables.

Biruni, al-, 104
Bur-Sagale, 159

Caesar, C., ⟨371
Caiaphas, 442, 449
Cambyses, 274, 275, 276, 279, 280, 281, 473
Cassiodorus Senator, 142, 177, 359, 360
Censorinus, 46, 189
Chaeremon, 154
Chronographer of the Year 354, 175, 176, 178, 358, 360, 488, 490, 491
Chrysis, 171
Chrysostom, 404, 405, 406, 407, 408
Claudius, 183, 288, 289, 469, 470, 483, 484, 485, 486, 490, 492, 493, 494, 497, 498, 499, 500, 501, 503, 509, 510, 511
Cleopatra, 183, 251, 284, 289, 337, 339, 343, 344, 351, 354
Cleopatra VII, 152, 153
Clement of Alexandria, 48, 188, 231, 235, 350, 360, 393, 394, 400, 438, 443, 460, 462, 474
Clement of Rome, 475, 479, 493, 514
Cletus, 479, 493
Commodus, 350, 393
Constantine, 255
Coponius, 373
Cornelius Nepos, 225
Consuls, 46, 172-179, 181, 183, 355, 356, 358, 359, 362, 363, 371, 373, 394, 395, 420, 421, 430, 489, 490, 491, 498
Cyril of Alexandria, 218
Cyrus, 240, 241, 242, 244, 274, 275, 276, 277, 278, 280, 334

Damasias, ⟨186
Damasus, Pope, 176
Darius I, 274, 279, 280, 281, 282, 283, 284, 285, 289, 290, 292, 293, 295. 296, 307, 335
Darius Nothus, 284
Darius, son of Arsames, 284
David, 245, 265
Day of Atonement, 12, 90, 92, 93, 406, 436, 512
Dead Sea Scrolls, 82-93
Deborah, 265
Demetrius Poliorcetes, 192
Demogenes, 186
depositio episcoporum, 176, 402, 403
depositio martyrum, 176, 402, 403, 488
Deucalion, 238

Didascalia, 449
Dio Cassius, 25, 179, 180, 363, 420, 430, 497, 499
Diocletian, 47, 217, 218, 254
Diodorus, 191, 192, 240, 262, 275, 473
Dionysius, bishop of Alexandria, 249
Dionysius, bishop of Corinth, 477
Dionysius Exiguus, 218, 219
Dionysius of Halicarnassus, 188, 191, 224, 226

Ebishum, ⟨158
Egyptian calendar, 37-49
Ehud, 265
Eleazar, high priest, 442
Eleazar, rabbi, 164, 169
Eli, 265
Eliakim, 313
Elon, 260, 265
Enoch, 206
Enoch, Book of, 98, 99, 103
Enosh, 206, 236, 244
Epiphanius, 355, 356, 360, 361, 370, 394, 395, 396, 397, 398, 399, 400, 401, 407, 419, 424, 426, 442, 443
Eratosthenes, 188, 224, 226
Essenes, 82, 84
Eusebius, 191, 197, 229, 233, 235, 246-296, 354, 355, 360, 361, 369, 442, 443, 474, 477, 478, 480, 483, 484, 487, 490, 492, 509, 510, 511
Evil-merodach, 329
Ezekiel, 332
Ezra, 332, 336

Fasti Capitolini, ⟨175
Fasti consulares, 141
Feasts, Jewish, 436
Felix, 289, 508, 509-515
Festus, 289, 508, 509-515
Filocalus, 176, 402
Fotheringham, J. K., 382, 455, 458

Gaius (Caligula), ⟨183, 288, 289, 469, 470, 484, 485, 486, 490, 493, 494
Gaius of Rome, 478, 479
Galba, 156
Gallienus, 249, 251
Gallio, 497-508
Gamaliel I, 79
Gamaliel II, 73, 79
Gamaliel the Elder, 73
Gaumata, 280
Gedaliah, 326
Gemino et Gemino, 462, 491